WORLD
WHISKEY

WORLD
WHISKEY

EDITOR-IN-CHIEF

CHARLES MACLEAN

WRITTEN BY

DAVE BROOM, TOM BRUCE-GARDYNE,
IAN BUXTON, CHARLES MACLEAN, PETER MULRYAN,
HANS OFFRINGA, GAVIN D. SMITH

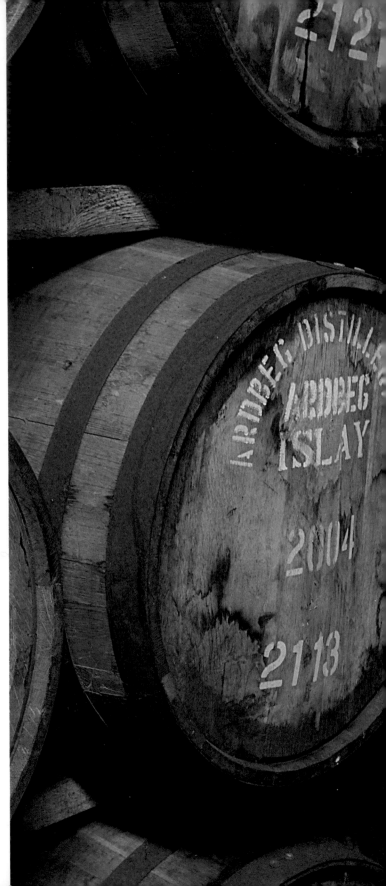

LONDON • NEW YORK
MELBOURNE • MUNICH • DELHI

Produced for Dorling Kindersley by

Thameside Media
www.thamesidemedia.com

Directors Michael Ellis, Rosalyn Ellis
Editors Fay Franklin, Michael Fullalove, Caroline Blake, Zoe Ross
Designers Nora Zimerman, Kate Leonard, Ian Midson
Retoucher Steve Crozier

For **Dorling Kindersley**

Project Editor Danielle Di Michiel
Project Designer Will Hicks
Editorial Assistance Andrew Roff
Senior Jacket Creative Nicola Powling
Managing Editor Dawn Henderson
Managing Art Editor Christine Keilty
Production Editor Ben Marcus
Creative Technical Support Sonia Charbonnier
US Editor Chuck Wills

First American Edition, 2009

Published in the United States by
DK Publishing
375 Hudson Street
New York, New York 10014

10 11 12 10 9 8 7 6 5 4 3

TD428—October 2009

Published in Great Britain by Dorling Kindersley Limited.

A CIP catalog record for this book is available
from the Library of Congress

ISBN 978–0–7566–5443–6

DK books are available at special discounts when purchased in bulk for sales
promotions, premiums, fund-raising, or educational use. For details, contact: DK
Publishing Special Markets, 375 Hudson Street, New York, New York 10014 or
SpecialSales@dk.com.

Color reproduction by Colorscan, Singapore
Printed and bound in Singapore by TWP

Discover more at
www.dk.com

CONTENTS

INTRODUCTION

Global interest in and enthusiasm for whiskey has never been greater. In recent years, many new distilleries have opened in Australia, Europe, Taiwan, and Japan, as well as in Scotland. Most of these are small concerns, designed to meet local demand, but some are major production sites. Several leading malt distilleries have recently expanded capacity—Glenlivet, Macallan, and Glenmorangie to name but three—and in Europe a handful of liqueur distillers are now producing whiskey as well.

What has prompted this expansion and confident investment? Two factors: first the interest in single malts, which continues to grow in every market, and second the anticipated demand from emerging markets in China, India, Russia, and Brazil.

The burgeoning interest in single malts is proved not only by the year-on-year rise in sales, but also the phenomenal enthusiasm for whiskey festivals around the world—from Finland to New Zealand, San Francisco to Moscow. Once a taste for whiskey is developed, the passion for information about this beguiling subject is inexhaustible.

It is important to remember that the whiskey made today cannot be sold as "whiskey" until it has matured for at least two years in the US and at least three years in Scotland—and is often aged for far longer periods. The distiller must, therefore, peer into the future, gauge the likely demand in 5, 10, 15, or 20 years, in various markets, and gear production accordingly.

From time to time they get it wrong, and, to a large extent, the availability today of some very fine old whiskies, both single malts and blended, is a reflection of over-production in the early 1980s. The point remains, though, that the excellence of the spirit will always be recognized. Fashions in drinks may come and go, but, for the discriminating consumer, whiskey goes on forever!

The book you are holding offers a superb catalog of the aforementioned whiskies that are available around the world today. Not only does it cover the output of major and lesser-known whiskey distilleries, but it also includes a wide selection of blended whiskies. The main section of the book—Whiskies Worth the Wait—is broken down into countries. It catalogs in A–Z format first the key whiskey-making nations of Scotland, Ireland, the USA, Canada, and Japan, followed by whiskies from other parts of Europe, South Asia, and Australasia. Secreted within this listing of world whiskies are features on the production processes and the varied types of whiskey made, examinations of particular distilleries to divulge the secrets of their whiskey-making, and tours that will guide you to the whiskey regions of Scotland, Ireland, the USA, and Japan. For no experience adds more to the enjoyment of whiskey than visiting a working distillery, to savor the aromas, appreciate the skill, dedication, and time that goes into making this profound spirit, and, of course, to sample a dram right at its source.

Charles MacLean

Making Whiskey

Whiskey is both a simple product and an endlessly ponderable drink. It is made from just grain, water, and yeast, and yet the spectrum of aromas and tastes that emerge from a mature whiskey can be wondrous and beguiling. How can such basic ingredients produce such an array of flavors? The answer lies in all the small variations in the whiskey-making process: the grain(s) used, how the barley is malted, the shape of the stills, the angle of the lyne arms, the length of maturation, and types of casks used. But to understand those nuances, first you need to be familiar with the basics— the principal stages of whiskey-making.

The first step is choosing the grain. Barley is the most commonly used grain in whiskey-making. It is the sole grain in Scotch malt, and a percentage of malted barley is used in almost all whiskey. Corn, wheat, and rye are the other grains used in whiskey-making. Corn is the principal grain for making bourbon and Tennessee whiskey, and rye grain is the key ingredient in rye whiskey. The term "grain whiskey" refers to whiskey made principally from grains other than barley for primary use in making blended whiskey. The main grains used for making grain whiskey are either corn or wheat. For more on whiskey types, *see pp12–13*.

1 MALTING

Barley goes through a malting process to activate enzymes and maximize its starch content, which is later converted to sugar and then alcohol. If peat is burned while drying the grains, the whiskey will have a smoky flavor. Some distilleries have their own floor maltings *(above)*, but most use independent maltsters. *(See also pp40–41)*

2 MASHING

At the distillery, the malt is milled to produce a coarse flour called grist. The grist is then mixed with hot water in a mashtun *(above)* to extract soluble sugars. The sugar-laden water, known as wort, is piped off for use. Other unmalted grain can be combined with the grist in the mashtun for making non-malt whiskies.

3 FERMENTING

The wort is mixed with yeast and heated in a washback *(above)*. The yeast feeds off the sugars in the wort, so producing alcohol and carbon dioxide. This process, known as fermentation, lasts between 48 and 74 hours, and results in what is effectively a strong and rather tart beer, called wash.

4 DISTILLING

The next stage is for the wash to be distilled. Whether using a column still for continuous distillation or a pot still for batch distillation, the purpose is the same: to extract alcohol spirit from the wash. The essential process is simple: the wash is boiled and, as alcohol boils at a lower temperature than water, the alcohol is driven off the wash as vapor; this vapor is then condensed into liquid. With pot still distillation, the spirit is condensed either in a shell-and-tube condenser *(as above)* or an old-fashioned worm tub *(see p169)*, which produces a heavier, oilier style of spirit. Most whiskey is distilled twice—the first time in a wash still (known as a "beer still" in the US), the second time in a spirit (or "low wines") still. But Irish whiskey is traditionally triple-distilled to create an even purer spirit.

5 THE CUT

A spirit safe *(above)* is used at distilleries using pot still distillation to enable the distillers to assess the spirit. The first and last parts of the "run" during the second distillation are not pure enough for use. Known as the "foreshots" and the "feints," respectively, they will go back for redistillation along with the "low wines" from the first distillation. The desired and usable part of the distillation, however, is the middle section, and this is known as the "middle cut," or just "the cut". This usable spirit, which is called "new make," is drinkable and exhibits some of the characteristics that will be in the final whiskey. However, it will not have achieved any depth of flavor or color yet, and it is not allowed to be called whiskey.

6 FILLING INTO CASKS

The new make will have its strength slightly reduced to about 63 or 64% ABV—the optimum strength to begin maturation. The spirit is then piped from a holding tank into oak casks *(above)*. In the US, the spirit is filled into new, charred barrels; in Scotland, it is filled into used casks.

7 MATURATION

The process that turns raw, clear, new make into the richly hued, complex-tasting drink we know as whiskey is maturation. The length of time for maturation varies, depending on climatic conditions, the size and type of the casks used, and legal requirements—at least three years for Scotch. *(See also pp68–9 and 74–5)*

8 BLENDING

The majority of whiskey sold is blended whiskey—a mix of malt whiskey and grain whiskey. As many as 40 or more whiskies may be combined in a blend, and the art of the blender *(above)* is to marry flavors so that they balance and unify. Blends tend to be tailored to specific tastes and markets. *(See also p79)*

9 BOTTLING

The bottling of whiskey is often carried out at automated plants *(above)*, but sometimes the bottling and labeling is done by hand. Most whiskey is reduced with water to a bottling strength of 40 or 43% ABV, but cask strength bottlings are released at the strength they came out of the cask (in the region of 53–65% ABV).

Whiskey Types

There are several distinct types of whiskey, and the variations depend upon the type and proportion of grains used and the methods employed in making the whiskey. Barley, corn, wheat, and rye are the principal grains, while the variations in methods that lead to different classifications of whiskey include the way of distilling (batch or continuous distillation) and the process and period of maturation. American whiskies are mostly aged in new oak, while Scotch and Irish whiskies employ re-used casks.

GRAIN Distilled in a continuous still, grain whiskey is typically made from wheat or corn (maize), along with unmalted and malted barley. Though mostly used for blending, some is bottled as grain whiskey. (See p165)

MALT Made solely from malted barley in copper pot stills, this is the "original" whisky of the Scottish Highlands. It has also been made in Japan since the 1920s, and is now made in Canada, parts of Asia, and (in small amounts) in almost every European country. "Single malt" is the product of an individual distillery. In Scotland it must be matured for a minimum of three years. (See p28)

BLENDS A mix of malt whisky and grain whiskey, blends typically have a proportion of 40 percent malt to 60 percent grain. More malt is used in deluxe blends, less in standard blends. They account for 92% of all Scotch. (See p79)

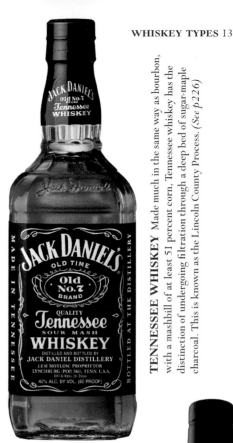

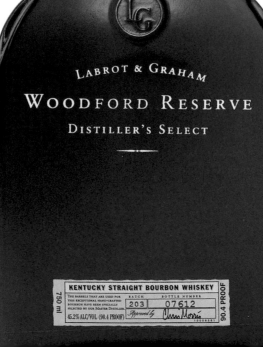

BLENDED MALT While single malt is the product of just one distillery, a blended malt is a mix of malt whiskies from more than one. *(See p174)*

PURE POT STILL WHISKEY Made from a mix of malted and unmalted barley, pure pot still whiskey is unique to Ireland. *(See p193)*

TENNESSEE WHISKEY Made much in the same way as bourbon, with a mashbill of at least 51 percent corn, Tennessee whiskey has the distinction of undergoing filtration through a deep bed of sugar-maple charcoal. This is known as the Lincoln County Process. *(See p226)*

BOURBON For a whiskey to be deemed bourbon, it must contain at least 51 percent corn in the mashbill, the remainder being made up of barley, wheat, or rye. It has to be matured in new, charred white-oak casks for a minimum of two years. *(See p223)*

RYE Although relatively uncommon today, rye is the original American whiskey. It must contain at least 51 percent rye and be matured in new, charred white oak for at least two years. Canada produces a lot of rye whiskey, though the process and classification is different to that of US rye. *(See pp262 & 270)*

All about…
Appreciating Whiskey

Whiskey is one of the world's most versatile drinks, and may be enjoyed in a variety of ways. But when it comes to appreciating fully its flavors and complexity, only a little water should be added. Flavor is a combination of aroma and taste, and to properly appreciate whiskey, you must have a glass that will present the aroma to its best advantage *(see pp158–9)*. The addition of a dash of still water (how much depends on the individual whiskey and personal preferences) disturbs the molecules in the liquid and tends to increase the aroma; by contrast, ice closes it down. Here are some pointers on the best way to appreciate whiskey and some of the key flavors associated with the drink.

Tasting

When tasting whiskey, use a clean glass for each drink, have a small jug of water to use when diluting the spirit slightly, and drink more water between each tasting to cleanse the palate. It's a good idea to keep notes as you go *(see p332)*.

I. Appearance Consider the whiskey's color *(see p75)*. Swirl the spirit in the glass and look at the "legs" that trickle down the inside. If they are slow-running and thick, it indicates good body, while skinny, fast-running legs suggest a thinner texture to the whiskey.

2. Aroma Swirl the liquid and sniff it. Note first the physical effects (if any)—prickle, sharpness, warming, cooling. Then try to put words to the smells. Add a drop of water and repeat.

3. Taste By all means taste the whiskey straight, but its character can best be appreciated once a little water has been added. Note the texture or "mouthfeel"—smooth, oily, waxy, drying, acerbic, and so on. Then consider the balance of the four primary tastes: sweetness, acidity, dryness, saltiness. Does the overall taste remind you of anything? Finally, how long is the finish, and does it leave a pleasant aftertaste?

4. Development After 10 minutes or so, sniff and taste the whiskey again to see if it has changed.

A glass that narrows toward the rim is ideal for appreciating whiskey, as it concentrates the all-important aromas.

Flavors

Whiskey should smell and taste of whiskey, but when we are appreciating it to the full, we go beyond this simple description to isolate and identify what the smells and tastes remind us of. Here are some of the key flavor groups:

CEREAL

As you might expect, this flavor comes from the grain. You can taste it in whiskies such as Knockando (p123), Tullibardine (p178), and McDowell's (p324).
• Cookies • breakfast cereals
• bran • new leather • malt extract
• corn mash

FRUITY

The fresh, fruity flavors develop in the spirit itself while being fermented and distilled. Dried and cooked fruit flavors come from the wood in which the whiskey is matured. Glenmorangie (p102), Yoichi (p296), and Yamazaki (p302) are examples of whiskies that offer different fruity flavors.
• fresh fruit (apples, pears, peaches)
• citrus fruits (oranges, lemons, tangerines)
• tropical fruits (pineapples, lychees, bananas) • dried fruits (raisins, candied peel, figs, prunes, fruitcake) • stewed fruits
• hard candy • solvent (nail-varnish remover)

FLORAL

Scottish Lowland malts are the archetypal floral whiskies. The flavor is well suited to aperitif-style whiskies, such a the younger offerings from Auchentoshan (p30) and Glenkinchie (p99).
• florist's shop • scented flowers (rose, lavender, heather) • grass (clippings, dried grass, flower stems) • artificial perfume (air fresheners, Violets)

SMOKY

Peated malt gives us the smokiest flavored whiskies, as exemplified by Islay malts such as Lagavulin (p128) but also Talisker (p167) and Longrow (p137).
• smoked meat, fish, cheese • charred sticks
• bonfires, burning leaves • peat smoke
• tobacco • soot, coal • tar • creosote

MEDICINAL

The medicinal tang is not a taste for everyone, but those who like it tend to really like it and head for the malts of Islay. Taste it in any Laphroaig (p130), in Benriach's Curiositas (p44), and in Ardbeg's 10-year-old (p24).
• bandages • hospitals • mouthwash • coal tar soap • iodine (sea salt) • antiseptic (Germoline, TCP)

WOODY

The influence of the cask is two-fold. The first flavor influence is in woody notes, as can be found in Balvenie (p36) and Glenrothes (p106).
• New wood (sap, pine, bark, fresh oak)
• scented wood (sandalwood, cedar, cigar boxes) • pencil shavings • sawdust

WOOD EXTRACTIVE

The second influence of the cask comes in the form of vanillins and tannins within the wood. Vanillins are particularly strong in American oak, and all bourbons feature these notes. European oak is richer in tannins, giving spicier and winey influences.

Some of the most clearly discernable flavors in whiskey—from sweet vanillins to fragrant spices such as cinnamon, cloves, and nutmeg—derive from the cask in which the spirit was matured.

Tamdhu (p170) displays the former; Glenfiddich Solera (p90) the latter.
• Vanilla (vanilla pods and essence, ice cream, custard, cake mix, pastry)
• coconut (dried coconut, gorse bushes, suntan oil) • caramel (toffee, fudge, cotton candy) • honey • spicy (nutmeg, clove, cinnamon, ginger) • winey (sherry, prune juice, port, rum)

OILY

The heavier spirits tend to have an oily character, which you'll find in Dalmore (p73) and Jura (p122). It also characterizes pure pot still Irish whiskey, like Redbreast (p213), which use unmalted as well as malted barley.
• butter, fat • cream • crème brûlée
• lubricating oil • grease (roasting pans)
• unscented soap • cheese
• leather polish, furniture polish

SULFURY

Subtle sulfury notes can be found in great whiskies, such as Aberlour a'bunadh (p21) and Macallan (p138).
• rubber • struck matches • yeast
• cooked vegetables

KEY NATIONS

SCOTLAND · IRELAND · USA · CANADA · JAPAN

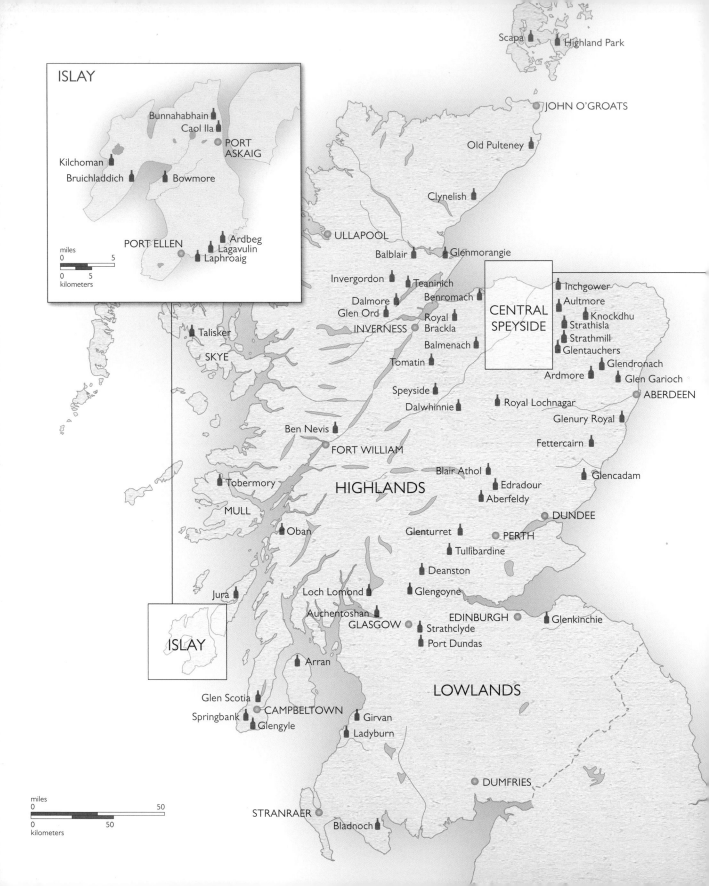

ISLAY

Bunnahabhain
Caol Ila
PORT
ASKAIG
Kilchoman
Bruichladdich
Bowmore
PORT ELLEN
Ardbeg
Lagavulin
Laphroaig

miles
0   5
0   5
kilometers

Scapa
Highland Park

JOHN O'GROATS

Old Pulteney

Clynelish

ULLAPOOL
Balblair
Glenmorangie
Invergordon
Teaninich
Benromach
Dalmore
Glen Ord
Royal
Brackla
INVERNESS
Balmenach
Tomatin
Speyside
Dalwhinnie

CENTRAL
SPEYSIDE
Inchgower
Aultmore
Knockdhu
Strathisla
Strathmill
Glentauchers
Glendronach
Ardmore
Glen Garioch
ABERDEEN
Royal Lochnagar
Glenury Royal
Fettercairn
Glencadam

Talisker
SKYE

Ben Nevis
FORT WILLIAM
HIGHLANDS
Blair Athol
Edradour
Aberfeldy
DUNDEE

Tobermory
MULL
Oban
Glenturret
PERTH
Tullibardine
Deanston
Jura
Loch Lomond
Glengoyne
EDINBURGH
ISLAY
Auchentoshan
GLASGOW
Strathclyde
Port Dundas
Glenkinchie
Arran
LOWLANDS

Glen Scotia
Springbank
CAMPBELTOWN
Glengyle
Girvan
Ladyburn

DUMFRIES

miles
0   50
0   50
kilometers
STRANRAER
Bladnoch

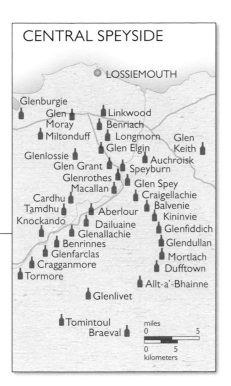

CENTRAL SPEYSIDE

○ LOSSIEMOUTH

Glenburgie
Glen
Moray
Miltonduff
Glenlossie
Glen Grant
Glenrothes
Macallan
Cardhu
Tamdhu
Knockando

Linkwood
Benriach
Longmorn
Glen Elgin
Glen
Keith
Auchroisk
Speyburn
Glen Spey
Craigellachie
Balvenie
Aberlour
Kininvie
Dailuaine
Glenfiddich
Glenallachie
Glendullan
Benrinnes
Glenfarclas
Mortlach
Cragganmore
Dufftown
Tormore
Allt-a'-Bhainne

Glenlivet

Tomintoul
Braeval

miles
0   5

0   5
kilometers

This map shows the location of active distilleries in Scotland, which in most cases have the same names as the Scottish whisky brands. It does not include the names of blended whiskies or independent bottlings that cannot be pinpointed geographically. The Speyside region has about 50 distilleries— the world's greatest concentration of whisky distilleries. Another major whisky region of Scotland is called simply the Highlands, which encompasses a huge area stretching roughly from Loch Lomond up to the north coast of mainland Scotland. Further south is the Lowlands region, which has a sprinkling of distilleries. Whiskies from the Islands region are sometimes called the maritime malts. The island of Islay to the west forms its own whisky region, with a clutch of distilleries that make good use of the island's peat. To the southeast of Islay, Campbeltown had a big whisky industry in the 19th century, though only three distilleries survive today.

SCOTLAND

BRUICHLADDICH—ISLAY

GLENKINCHIE—LOWLANDS

FETTERCAIRN—HIGHLANDS

TALISKER—ISLANDS

GLENLIVET—SPEYSIDE

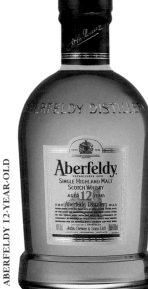

ABERFELDY 12-YEAR-OLD

ABERFELDY 21-YEAR-OLD

ABERLOUR 12-YEAR-OLD SHERRY MATURED

100 PIPERS

Owner: Chivas Brothers

Created in 1965 by Seagram, and named after an old Scots song, 100 Pipers was originally a contender in the "value" sector of the Scotch whisky market, where it was an immediate success. The blend contains Allt-a-Bhainne and Braeval, and probably some Glenlivet and Longmorn as well. Seagrams developed the brand very effectively and it has continued to prosper under the new owners, Chivas Brothers (themselves owned by Pernod Ricard). It is one of the bestselling whiskies in Thailand, a dynamic market for Scotch, and is growing rapidly in many countries, especially Spain, Venezuela, Australia, and India.

100 PIPERS

BLEND 40% ABV

Pale in color. A light and very mixable whisky, with a smooth yet subtly smoky taste.

ABERFELDY

Aberfeldy, Perthshire
www.dewarswow.com

Plenty of malt distilleries claim to be the spiritual home of a particular blend, and celebrate the fact with a plaque on the wall or a large sign by the entrance. In its life-long bond with Dewar's White Label, Aberfeldy takes this a whole lot further: an impressive, fully interactive visitor's center was opened in 2000 and the distillery effectively became the Dewar's World of Whisky. Although visitors get to see the nuts and bolts of malt whisky distilling, the main emphasis is on the art of blending and the role of Tommy Dewar (1864–1930), arguably the greatest whisky baron of them all.

The distillery was built by John Dewar & Sons in 1898 with the express purpose of supplying malts for the company's blends. The site was chosen for its good, consistent

source of water and for the rail link to Perth, where the company was based. It was also a tribute to the original John Dewar, who was born in a bothy nearby and, according to legend, had walked from here to Perth in 1828.

Having spent most of the 20th century as part of DCL (now Diageo), Aberfeldy was bought by Bacardi as part of a billion-pound deal involving five malt distilleries and the gin brand Bombay Sapphire.

ABERFELDY 12-YEAR-OLD

SINGLE MALT: HIGHLANDS 40% ABV

The standard expression has a clean, apple-scented nose with a medium-bodied fruity character in the mouth.

ABERFELDY 21-YEAR-OLD

SINGLE MALT: HIGHLANDS 40% ABV

Launched in 2005, the 21-year-old has greater depth and richness than the 12-year-old, with a sweet, heathery nose and a slight spicy catch on the finish.

ABERLOUR

Aberlour, Banffshire
www.aberlour.com

Although Aberlour is not so well-known in its homeland, it is extremely popular in France, and it can claim to be one of the top ten bestselling malts in the world. As part of the old Campbell Distillers, it has been owned by the French group Pernod Ricard since 1975. Its malt is used in a great number of blends, particularly in Clan Campbell, but up to half the production is bottled as a single malt in a wide range of age statements and finishes.

The village of Aberlour lies a short distance from the Spey, and had only recently been founded when James Gordon and Peter Weir established a distillery on the main street in 1826. It survived for 50 years, but was then gutted by a fire. As a result, a new Aberlour Distillery was built in 1879, a couple of miles upstream, by James

ABERLOUR A'BUNADH

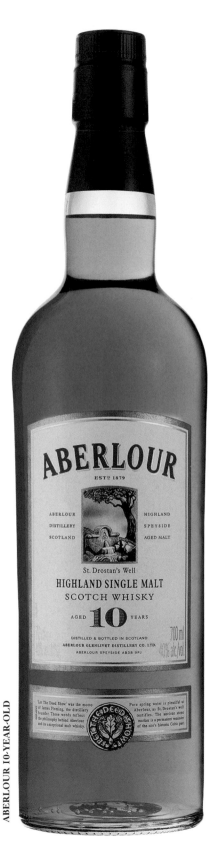

ABERLOUR 10-YEAR-OLD

Fleming, who already owned
Dailuaine *(see p71)*. What you see
today is a classic late-Victorian
distillery, designed by Charles Doig
after another bad fire in 1898.

ABERLOUR 12-YEAR-OLD SHERRY MATURED

SINGLE MALT: SPEYSIDE 40% ABV
With its deep, reddish hue from new
sherry wood, this expression has a
nutty, Christmas-cake character and
a creamy, buttery texture.

ABERLOUR A'BUNADH

SINGLE MALT: SPEYSIDE 60% ABV
A'bunadh (*a-boon-ahh*), "the origin"
in Gaelic, is a cask strength, non chill-
filtered malt matured in Oloroso casks.
It has a sumptuous character of
fruitcake and spice.

ABERLOUR 10-YEAR-OLD

SINGLE MALT: SPEYSIDE 40% ABV
Matured mainly in ex-bourbon casks,
this has a caramel sweetness from the
wood and a gentle nutty, spicy flavor.

ALLT·A·BHAINNE

Glenrinnes, Dufftown, Banffshire

The building of Allt-a-Bhainne in
1975 is a testament to the post-war
success of Chivas Regal. Having
taken the US, Seagram's flagship
Scotch was busy conquering Asia
and Latin America. As sales boomed,
so did demand for the malts needed
for the blend. This primary blend-
supplying role for the distillery has
never changed, nor is it likely to
under its present owner, Pernod
Ricard, which is on a mission to
make its Chivas Regal the world's
number one 12-year-old blend. To
date, there have been very few
independent bottlings of the malt.

ALT-A-BHAINNE CADENHEAD 1980

SINGLE MALT: SPEYSIDE 60.5% ABV
Curiously, this bottling uses an obscure
variant of the spelling of Allt-a-Bhainne
with just one "l". With water, the
sweeter, maltier flavors of this cask-
strength bottling are released.

ANCNOC 1991

ANCNOC 12-YEAR-OLD

ANCNOC 1975

ANCNOC

*Knockdhu Distillery, Knock,
Huntly, Aberdeenshire*
www.ancnoc.com

Named after the nearby "Black
Hill," the springs of which supply
its water, anCnoc is the core
expression of Knockdhu Distillery.

With its solitary pair of stills
and a capacity of just 200,000
gallons (900,000 liters) of spirit
a year, Knockdhu Distillery is no
giant. Yet, from this tiny acorn,
planted in 1893, grew the mighty
oak that is now Diageo. It was the
first—and for years the only—
distillery built by the Distillers
Company (DCL), who preferred
to grow by acquisition. It was not
until 1967 that the company built
its second distillery, Clynelish.

Knockdhu was closed in 1983
and brought back to life six years
later by its new owner, Inver
House, which has been at pains
to preserve the character of the
distillery, keeping the wooden
washbacks and the old stone-built
dunnage warehouses. The traditional
worm tubs for condensing the
spirit have also been retained;
they add a slight sulfury, meaty
character to the new make.

ANCNOC 1991

SINGLE MALT: SPEYSIDE 46% ABV
Vanilla, toffee, and wood on the
nose. Fruity and full-bodied, with
a hint of peatiness.

ANCNOC 12-YEAR-OLD

SINGLE MALT: SPEYSIDE 40% ABV
A relatively full-bodied Speyside
malt, with notes of lemon peel and
heather-honey on the nose, a fairly
luscious mouthfeel, and some length
on the finish.

ANCNOC 1975

SINGLE MALT: SPEYSIDE 50% ABV
Cask strength and non chill-filtered,
this limited release is a big, fulsome
Speyside with rich notes of sherry
wood mixed with cleaner, sweeter
flavors from bourbon casks.

THE DUNDEE

OLD DUNDEE 12-YEAR-OLD

THE ANTIQUARY 12-YEAR-OLD

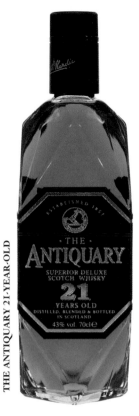

THE ANTIQUARY 21-YEAR-OLD

ANGUS DUNDEE

www.angusdundee.co.uk

With over 50 years' experience in producing, blending, bottling, and distributing top-quality Scotch whiskies and other spirits, Angus Dundee is one of the few remaining truly independent family-owned companies in the Scotch whisky industry. It has two malt distilleries—Tomintoul and Glencadam—but is better known for its blending and broking activities.

The Angus Dundee range includes a standard blend, a 12-year-old deluxe blend, and a top-of-the range 30-year-old blend, which comes in an elegant crystal decanter and is the company's flagship whisky. It's an intensely fruity whisky, with oak spice and dark chocolate on the palate, and a long, caressing finish.

Angus Dundee holds large stocks of both malt and grain whiskies, which supply an extensive international bulk and "bottled-in-Scotland" business. Other company-owned blends include Parkers and Scottish Royal, both found in standard and 12-year-old deluxe expressions, and Big Ben Special Reserve. There is a pronounced family resemblance across the Angus Dundee range, and the recently acquired Glencadam Distillery can be expected to come increasingly to the fore in the blend profile.

THE DUNDEE

BLEND 40% ABV

Hints of orange peel in a malty, medium-weight nose. Traces of smoke and some sweetness. Smooth on the palate.

OLD DUNDEE 12-YEAR-OLD

BLEND 43% ABV

Richer than its younger counterpart, with a longer finish. Orange notes develop into candied-peel. Soft in the mouth, and an elegant palate. There's a sugary tart flavor, but it's not cloying.

THE ANTIQUARY

Owner: Tomatin Distillery
www.antiquary.co.uk

Introduced in 1857 by John and William Hardie, The Antiquary got its name from a novel by Sir Walter Scott. For many years, it was the product of William Sanderson (of VAT 69 fame), but was sold in 1996. Today it is owned by The Tomatin Distillery Company, itself a subsidiary of Takara Shuzo and Okura Ltd of Japan.

Packaged in a decanter-like bottle, The Antiquary was a prized luxury blend in its heyday, but sales gradually ebbed, prompting the sale of the name and the recipe. The current owners offer 12- and 21-year-old expressions, and appear to be making energetic efforts to re-establish the brand. New packaging, reminiscent of the old bottle, has been introduced, and The Antiquary features strongly in Tomatin's marketing. Befitting the blend's deluxe status, The Antiquary has at its heart a very high malt-to-grain ratio, including some of the finest malts from Speyside and Highland distilleries and more than a splash of Tomatin. Islay seems to feature more strongly than previously.

THE ANTIQUARY 12-YEAR-OLD

BLEND 40% ABV

Subtle fruitiness concealing a hint of apples. Outstanding smoothness, depth of flavor, and a long aftertaste. Recent batches may vary somewhat. Other tasters have reported a striking peat influence, new to the blend.

THE ANTIQUARY 21-YEAR-OLD

BLEND 43% ABV

The subtle maltiness with muted peaty notes allows the heather, dandelion, and blackcurrant notes to flourish. A dash of Islay malt creates a truly exceptional dram, as well-balanced as it is rich and smooth. A stand-out blend that deserves to be more widely enjoyed.

ARDBEG 10-YEAR-OLD
SINGLE MALT: ISLAY 46% ABV
This non chill-filtered malt has notes of creosote, tar, and smoked fish on the nose. Any sweetness on the tongue quickly dries to a smoky finish.

ARDBEG BLASDA
SINGLE MALT: ISLAY 40% ABV
The Gaelic name translates as "sweet and delicious," a reference to a much gentler style than usual, made from malt peated at only 8ppm, one-third Ardbeg's usual levels.

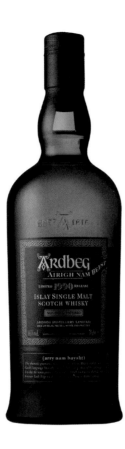

ARDBEG UIGEADAIL

ARDBEG AIRIGH NAM BEIST

ARDBEG ALMOST THERE

ARDBEG RENAISSANCE

ARDBEG

Port Ellen, Islay
www.ardbeg.com

If Islay is the spiritual home of Scotland's pungent, peat-smoked whiskies, then Ardbeg is undoubtedly one of the island's leading disciples. The distillery was first licensed in 1815 in the parish of Kildalton, on Islay's southern coast just beyond Lagavulin and Laphroaig. "Its isolation tends to heighten the romantic sense of its position," wrote the whisky writer Alfred Barnard in the 1880s. Yet, by then, it was fully part of the whisky industry, supplying "pure Islay malt" to the blenders via Buchanan's in Glasgow. Reliance

on the blending market left Ardbeg in a vulnerable position, however, and when "the whisky loch" became full to the brim in the early 1980s, the distillery was moth-balled. Its then owners, Allied Distillers, had decided to mainly concentrate on Laphroaig, which it also owned. The staff, who once numbered 60, were laid off and, despite being cranked back to life at the end of the decade, the distillery had an uncertain future.

In 1997, Ardbeg was rescued by Glenmorangie, who paid a reported £7m and then spent a further £1.4m on upgrading the distillery. At first, the years of non-production caused problems but, as the gaps in the inventory receded, the distillery was finally able to

release a standard 10-year-old bottling. Since then, there has been a raft of new bottlings, which have added to Ardbeg's growing cult status among fans of Islay's smoky malt whiskies.

ARDBEG UIGEADAIL

SINGLE MALT: ISLAY 54.2% ABV
Named after Loch Uigeadail—Ardbeg's water source—this has a deep gold color and a molasses-like sweetness on the nose, with savory, smoky notes following through on the tongue.

ADBEG AIRIGH NAM BEIST

SINGLE MALT: ISLAY 46% ABV
A rich, spicy malt sweetened with vanilla notes from 16 years in bourbon casks. The name, pronounced *arry-nam-bayst*, means "shelter of the beast."

ARDBEG ALMOST THERE

SINGLE MALT: ISLAY 54.1% ABV
Peaty, salty, and citric on the nose; pepper, smoke, and lemon zest on the palate. The finish is long, rumbling, peaty, and warming.

ARDBEG RENAISSANCE

SINGLE MALT: ISLAY 55.9% ABV
Distilled in 1998, the year after Glenmorangie bought the distillery, and bottled in 2008, this heavyweight, peat-soaked whisky follows on from earlier limited-edition bottlings such as Still Young and Almost There.

The stills at Bunnahabhain on Islay have been left to form a patina on their surface—the natural effect of salty sea air interacting with the copper. It emphasizes that these are no-nonsense, working stills, producing very fine spirit.

Malt

The original Scotch whisky—or *uisge beatha* ("water of life" in Gaelic)—from the 15th century or earlier would have been a single malt. That is, a distillation made from barley and the product of just one distillery (or, more likely, pot still on a farm) rather than a blend or vatting of whiskies of different kinds or different provenances. However, it would have been rather different from the malt we know today. It would not have been aged in oak casks but instead drunk almost hot from the still.

The invention of the continuous still in the 19th century created a seismic shift for whisky. It led to the development of blended whisky *(see p79)*, and the international success of blends all but eclipsed the category of single malt whisky, which became virtually unheard of. The resurrection of single malts was led by Glenfiddich in the 1960s, though the real boom in interest has been far more recent. Today you can find single malts from many parts of the world, including pretty much every one of the 90 or so active malt distilleries in Scotland. You can also find bottlings from many of the so-called "silent distilleries"—those that are either mothballed and may one day produce again or have closed entirely (stocks can be eked out for decades after a closure). Even in cases where the distillery has yet to bottle its own malt, the whiskies are usually available somewhere thanks to independent bottlers *(see pp88–9)*, who buy selected casks from distilleries and usually bottle them as single-cask releases.

By law, a single malt can only come from a single distillery, and to protect the category, the Scotch whisky industry has outlawed the use of potentially misleading terms like "pure malt." Today any vatting of malts from different distilleries has to be called a blended malt *(see p174)*.

ARDMORE

Kennethmont, Aberdeenshire
www.ardmorewhisky.com

Ardmore owes its existence to
Teacher's Highland Cream. The
blend was well-established in
Scotland, particularly in Glasgow,
where it was sold through
Teacher's Dram Shops, and sales
were growing abroad. To keep up
with demand, Adam Teacher
decided to build a new distillery in
1898 and found the ideal spot near
Kennethmont, beside the main
Aberdeen-to-Inverness railway.
Famed for producing the smokiest
malt on Speyside, Ardmore released
a 12-year-old in 1999 to celebrate
its centenary. In 2005 the distillery
became part of Fortune Brands.

ARDMORE TRADITIONAL CASK

SINGLE MALT: SPEYSIDE 46% ABV
A smooth, relatively full-bodied malt,
where the sweet American oak flavors
from the cask are balanced by the dry,
earthy character from the peat.

ARRAN

Lochranza, Isle of Arran
www.arranwhisky.com

Arran lies across the water from
Alloway, Robert Burns' birthplace.
This bond with Scotland's national
bard has been kept alive by the Isle
of Arran Distillery, which has
produced a range of blends in his
honor *(see p154)*. It was founded
by Harold Currie in 1993, a time
when the mainstream whisky
industry was closing distilleries as
fast as it could. Arran has survived,
however, and in 2006 released its
first official bottling of a 10-year-
old. Since then there have been
various limited editions and wood
finishes, and in 2008 the first
12-year-old expression was released.
    When the distillery opened in
1993, it marked the return of
distilling on the Isle of Arran after
a hiatus of some 156 years. That's
legal distilling, at least, for there is
thought to have been as many as 50
distilleries quietly going about their

business in an illegal fashion during
much of the 19th century.
    Whatever the case, the rebirth of
legal distilling on Arran was marked
by an impromptu fly-past by two
golden eagles during the opening
ceremony, and a pair of the birds
can often be observed soaring above
the distillery today.
    Arran's whisky-making resources
are somewhat modest—four pine
washbacks and a solitary pair of
stills—but plans for expansion are
already under way. A racked warehouse has recently been added, as
an addition to the original dunnage
warehouse, and a milling machine
has been installed so that the
distillery can now produce its own
grist on site (previously, it had
bought in its malt already ground).
    Arran takes its water from
Loch na Davie, which is located in
the hills above Lochranza on the
north coast of Arran. The island
itself is positioned right in the
Gulf Stream, and the warm waters
and climate system associated with

it are said to be beneficial factors
in speeding up the period of
maturation at Arran.

ARRAN 10-YEAR-OLD

SINGLE MALT: ISLANDS 46% ABV
Bottled without chill-filtering, this
has fresh bread and vanilla aromas,
with citrus notes that carry through
onto the tongue.

ARRAN 12-YEAR-OLD

SINGLE MALT: ISLANDS 46% ABV
This expression has an orange peel and
chocolate sweetness and a rich, creamy
texture thanks to the influence of
sherry wood.

ARRAN FINO SHERRY
WINE CASK

SINGLE MALT: ISLANDS 50% ABV
Vanilla, almonds, and spice. Sweet
on the palate at first, soon becoming
drier and oaky from the sherry
influence, with a nutty finish. Some
tasters detect sea-salt notes.

AUCHENTOSHAN CLASSIC

SINGLE MALT: LOWLANDS 40% ABV

With no age statement, this is a young introduction to the Auchentoshan range, with lots of vanilla sweetness and citrus.

AUCHENTOSHAN 12-YEAR-OLD

SINGLE MALT: LOWLANDS 40% ABV

This expression replaced the old 10-year-old and has a dense, spicy character thanks to the use of sherry casks.

AUCHENTOSHAN

Dalmuir, Clydebank, Glasgow
www.auchentoshan.co.uk

While Glenkinchie sits among the barley fields of East Lothian just south of Edinburgh, Scotland's other main Lowlands distillery lies west of Glasgow by the Erskine Bridge and the Clyde River.

Auchentoshan stands on the site of a monastery that was dissolved in 1560. Whether the monks moved on from the monastic tradition of making beer to distilling spirits is unknown, but if they did, the roots of Auchentoshan whisky would be very old indeed.

There used to be a distillery called Duntocher here, which was first mentioned in 1800. This may have evolved into Auchentoshan, which was licensed in 1823 by a

man called Thorne. With its solitary pair of stills, it produced a modest 50,000 gallons (225,000 liters) a year until it acquired a third still. Ever since, Auchentoshan, with its triple-distilled malt, has been almost unique in Scotland. This being the standard style of Irish whiskey, it soon caught on among the burgeoning Irish community in Glasgow, who arrived seeking work and respite from the potato famine back home.

Having grown up in open countryside, the distillery was gradually swallowed up into a suburb of Clydebank. This area was a key target for the Luftwaffe during World War II and, on 13th and 14th of March, 1941, up to 200,000 bombs fell on the area, badly damaging the distillery.

Since then, Auchentoshan has drawn its cooling water from a pond created in a giant bomb crater. The rest is piped from Loch Katrine in the Highlands.

Auchentoshan joined forces with the Islay distillery Bowmore in 1984, becoming Morrison Bowmore, which is now part of the Japanese Suntory group. In the past decade, the range of single malts has been greatly expanded.

AUCHENTOSHAN 18-YEAR-OLD

SINGLE MALT: LOWLANDS 43% ABV
This is a classic nutty, spicy malt with plenty of age and complexity on the palate and some fruity sherry notes on the nose.

AUCHENTOSHAN 21-YEAR-OLD

SINGLE MALT: LOWLANDS 43% ABV
Despite its age, the oldest standard expression of Auchentoshan is surprisingly crisp and refreshing, with a nutty, honeyed, malty flavor.

AUCHENTOSHAN SELECT

SINGLE MALT: LOWLANDS 40% ABV
Fresh approachable style, with citrus aromas and a malty sweetness on the palate.

AUCHENTOSHAN THREE WOOD

SINGLE MALT: LOWLANDS 43% ABV
This is matured in three different types of cask, and sherry clearly has a big influence on the color and sweet, candied-fruit flavors.

AUCHROISK

Mulben, Banffshire
www.malts.com

This modern distillery lies on the main road between Craigellachie and Keith. The site was bought by IDV in 1970 for £5m, and Auchroisk (which means "ford of the red stream" in Gaelic) was up and running four years later. The principal role of the distillery was to supply malt for the J&B blend, but, after a decade, it was decided to release a distillery bottling as well. This was called the Singleton of Auchroisk. The name was soon abandoned, however, and replaced by a 10-year-old in the Flora & Fauna range and occasional Rare Malt series bottlings.

AUCHROISK FLORA & FAUNA 10-YEAR-OLD

SINGLE MALT: SPEYSIDE 43% ABV
An aromatic Speyside with a wisp of smoke and citrus notes, combined with malty flavors that dry on the finish.

AULTMORE

Keith, Banffshire

Alexander Edward was a seasoned distiller who had helped run Benrinnes with his father before establishing the Craigellachie Distillery with Peter Mackie, the whisky baron and founder of the White Horse blend. In 1895, at the peak of the late-Victorian whisky boom, Edward built a third distillery on the flat farmland between Keith and the sea. It was some distance from the glens but, in good Speyside tradition, he called it the Aultmore-Glenlivet Distillery and promptly doubled its capacity. He also bought Oban and was then in a position to offer the big blenders a choice of Speyside or West Coast malt.

In 1923, Aultmore was sold to John Dewar & Sons. Within three years, it was part of the mighty DCL. Today there is little trace of its Victorian roots, and Aultmore sits wrapped in its concrete cladding like a light industrial unit from the 1970s, when it underwent a major refurbishment.

In 1991 a 12-year-old bottling of Aultmore was released as part of the Flora & Fauna range. A 21-year-old expression was added in 1996. Two years on, the distillery was one of five sold to the Bacardi company.

AULTMORE FLORA & FAUNA 12-YEAR-OLD

SINGLE MALT: SPEYSIDE 40% ABV
The main distillery bottling first appeared in 2004 and is a crisp, herbal, aperitif-style malt with a gentle, perfumed nose and a malty flavor that dries on the finish.

AULTMORE SINGLE MALTS OF SCOTLAND 15-YEAR-OLD

SINGLE MALT: SPEYSIDE 46% ABV
This older expression has a floral, nutty, spicy aroma coupled with a trace of chocolate. It is medium- to full-bodied and quite luscious in texture.

BAILIE NICOL JARVIE

Owner: Glenmorangie

Produced by Glenmorangie, Bailie Nicol Jarvie—or BNJ as it is commonly called in Scotland—is reputed to contain a healthy measure of both Glenmorangie and Glen Moray single malts. In fact, it has one of the highest malt contents of any blended whisky. It is excellent value and has gained something of a cult following, its adherents savoring the idea of being one of the cognoscenti, perhaps, for it is not at all heavily promoted. The label has a satisfying period feel.

BAILIE NICOL JARVIE

BLEND 40% ABV
Smooth, subtle, and full of character, with a delicate balance of sweet Speyside, aromatic Highland, and peaty Islay malt whiskies blended with only the finest grain whisky.

BALBLAIR 89

BALBLAIR 97

BALBLAIR 75

BALBLAIR

Edderton, Tain, Ross-shire
www.balblair.com

While late-18th-century Scotland was awash with distilleries, both legal and illicit, Balblair is one of only a handful that has survived to this day. It was founded by John Ross in 1790 on the Dornoch Firth, north of Inverness, and sourced its water from the Ault Dearg burn, as it still does today. The first recorded sale was for a gallon of whisky on January 25, 1800.

Balblair remained in family hands for over 100 years. It was then taken over by Alexander Cowan, of Balnagowan, who was forced to close the distillery in 1911. It did not reopen until after World War II, when it was bought by Robert Cumming, who sold it on to the Canadian distiller Hiram Walker in 1970. Since 1996, the distillery has been owned by Inver House Distillers, who began with a core range called Elements. This was succeeded by a range of vintage malts in a similar style to The Glenrothes bottlings, right down to the bulbous bottle shape.

BALBLAIR 75

SINGLE MALT: HIGHLANDS 46% ABV
The sherry-matured vintage expression has a distinct rum-raisin character, with notes of butterscotch and some underlying fruit flavors that taper to a long finish.

BALBLAIR 89

SINGLE MALT: HIGHLANDS 43% ABV
Matured mainly in ex-bourbon casks, this has a slightly sweeter nose than the 75, with notes of candy apple, tropical fruits, and vanilla ice cream.

BALBLAIR 97

SINGLE MALT: HIGHLANDS 43% ABV
After 10 years in first-fill bourbon casks, the 97 was released in 2007. It has plenty of clean vanilla aromas and a smooth, mouth-coating texture.

BALLANTINE'S
21-YEAR-OLD

BLEND 43% ABV

The sought-after older expressions of Ballantine's are deep in color, with traces of heather, smoke, licorice, and spice on the nose. The 21-year-old has a complex, balanced palate, with sherry, honey, and floral notes.

BALLANTINE'S
30-YEAR-OLD

BLEND 43% ABV

Ballantine's flagship 30-year-old is one of the world's most prestigious blends. It is characterized by great depth and range, and has a complex mix of vanilla and honey.

BALLANTINE'S FINEST

BALLANTINE'S 12-YEAR-OLD

BALLANTINE'S 17-YEAR-OLD

BALLANTINE'S

www.ballantines.com

Ballantine's is now part of Chivas Brothers, the Scotch whisky arm of Pernod Ricard, the world's number two wines and spirits company after Diageo. The Ballantine's range is arguably the most extensive in the world today, and includes Ballantine's Finest (the standard bottling), as well as Ballantine's 12-year-old, 17-year-old, 21-year-old, and 30-year-old.

Ballantine's was a pioneer in developing aged blends. The flagship 30-year-old was first blended in the late 1920s from special stocks of malt and grain Scotch set aside for many years with the vision of creating a super-

premium product. This remarkable foresight enabled the brand to establish a strong position at the top of the market, which has stood it in good stead despite various changes of ownership.

Relatively hard to find in the UK, Ballantine's Finest has long been popular in Europe, while the older, more premium expressions enjoy huge success in China, Japan, South Korea, and Asian duty-free markets. The range now sells nearly 6.5 million 2-gallon (9-liter) cases a year, making it the world's second biggest Scotch whisky by volume and the top-selling super-premium brand in Asia.

The blend is noted for its complexity, with over 40 different malts and grains being used. The

two Speyside single malts Glenburgie and Miltonduff form the base for the blend, but malts from all parts of Scotland are also employed. For maturation, Ballantine's principally favors the use of ex-bourbon barrels, for the vanilla influences and sweet creamy notes they characteristically bring to the blend.

The Glenburgie Distillery has been completely remodeled and modernized and is today Ballantine's spiritual home. Recently, there has been an emphasis on entering the various Ballantine's expressions into international competitions, and a series of major awards suggests the owners have renewed confidence in the quality of this long-established brand.

BALLANTINE'S FINEST
BLEND 40% ABV

A sweet, soft-textured blend, with the Speyside malts giving chocolate, vanilla, and apple notes.

BALLANTINE'S 12-YEAR-OLD
BLEND 40% ABV

Golden-hued, with a honey sweetness on the nose, and vanilla from the oak. Creamy texture and balanced palate, with floral, honey, and oaky vanilla notes. Some tasters detect a hint of salt.

BALLANTINE'S 17-YEAR-OLD
BLEND 43% ABV

A deep, balanced, and elegant whisky with a hint of wood and vanilla. The body is full and creamy, with a vibrant, honeyed sweetness and hints of oak and peat smoke on the palate.

BALMENACH

*Cromdale, Grantown-on-Spey,
Morayshire*
www.inverhouse.com

In 1824 James McGregor, like
many illicit distillers, decided to
come in from the cold and take out
a license for his farm distillery
near Grantown-on-Spey. It was
owned by the family for 100
years until they sold out to DCL.
Apart from during World War II,
the distillery was in constant
production until 1993, when its
whisky was available as part of the
Flora & Fauna range. In 1997,
Balmenach was sold to Inver House,
who fired up the stills the following
year. A full distillery bottling has
had to wait, owing to a dearth of
inherited stocks.

BALMENACH
GORDON & MACPHAIL 1990

SINGLE MALT: SPEYSIDE 43% ABV
Citrus, grass, and malt on the nose, slight
smoke on the palate. Opens up with water.

BALVENIE

Dufftown, Keith, Banffshire
www.thebalvenie.com

Having spent 16 years as a book-
keeper at Mortlach Distillery in
Dufftown, William Grant finally
took the plunge to go solo in 1886
and set up Glenfiddich. Within six
years he was converting Balvenie
Castle (actually a derelict
Georgian wreck) next door into
another distillery, using second-
hand stills from Lagavulin and
Glen Albyn. His decision to expand
came partly as a result of a request
from an Aberdeen blender who
desperately needed 400 gallons
(1,800 liters) of Glenlivet-style
whisky a week. Glenlivet itself
was closed at the time, after being
damaged by a fire in 1891. People
congratulated Grant on his
romantic idea of turning a "castle"
into a distillery, although one
customer in Liverpool warned
that he was simply adding to the
overproduction in the whisky

industry—a warning that proved
prescient when a slump hit the
trade in the early 20th century.

Despite being physically
overshadowed by Glenfiddich,
Balvenie is no boutique distillery:
it can produce 1.25 million gallons
(5.6 million liters) a year and has
built up an impressive range of
single malts, the first of which was
officially released in 1973. One
early expression came wrapped in
black leatherette with gold
lettering. Recent packaging has
been much more restrained, in
keeping with Balvenie's carefully
crafted image as an artisan
distillery that claims to grow some
of its own barley, in contrast to
Glenfiddich. It has also retained
its floor maltings to satisfy part
of its requirements, and employs a
team of coopers and a coppersmith.
The coopers are kept busy by
repairing and reconditioning the
wide variety of casks employed to
mature the varied expressions of
Balvenie. Indeed, the distillery's

attention to maturation and
different wood finishes rivals
even that of Glenmorangie.

THE BALVENIE
VINTAGE CASK 1976

SINGLE MALT: SPEYSIDE 53.8% ABV
Autumnal wet leaves and damp,
woody aromas. Heavy tannins on
the palate, balanced by fruitiness;
slightly sweet in the finish.

THE BALVENIE SIGNATURE
12-YEAR-OLD

SINGLE MALT: SPEYSIDE 40% ABV
A vatting of three types of cask—
sherry, first-fill bourbon, and refill
bourbon—which give a mix of confected
fruit and vanilla with a syrupy texture.

THE BALVENIE DOUBLEWOOD
12-YEAR-OLD

SINGLE MALT: SPEYSIDE 40% ABV
After a decade in American oak,
Doublewood spends two years in ex-
sherry casks to give it a smooth,
confected, slightly nutty character.

**THE BALVENIE SINGLE
BARREL 15-YEAR-OLD**
SINGLE MALT: SPEYSIDE 47.8% ABV
This 15-year-old is bottled one
cask at a time, so each is subtly
different from the last, although
sharing a sweet woody character
and nutty flavor.

**THE BALVENIE
RUM CASK 17-YEAR-OLD**
SINGLE MALT: SPEYSIDE 43% ABV
A rich, heady nose with notes
of molasses and demerara sugar
leads to ripe bananas and cream
flavors that dry on the finish.

Macallan still has in use 16 traditional dunnage warehouses with earth floors and thick stone walls. The atmosphere is cool and damp year round, and the air is rich with aromas of whisky and oak.

All about...
Malting

Malt is derived from grains of barley. It is the core ingredient of malt whiskey and is vital to almost all whiskies, as a proportion of barley malt is used to produce most types, including grain, rye, and bourbon whiskies. Barley corns are mainly starch. To make alcohol from them, the starch must be converted into sugar and fermented with yeast. Malting prepares the starches in the grain for conversion. It does this by breaking down the tough cell walls and proteins that bind the starch cells, and by activating the enzymes that will later convert the starches into sugar, when the malt is ground into grist and mixed with hot water during "mashing."

FROM BARLEY TO MALT
The malting process starts with raw grains of barley (1). The grains are encouraged to germinate and produce shoots, at which point they are called green malt (2). The green malt is kilned to halt the germination when the starch levels are at their maximum; starch in the resulting malt grain (3) is converted into sugar and then into alcohol through the processes known as mashing and fermentation.

FLOOR MALTINGS
Once the barley has been steeped in water over the course of two days, it will begin to germinate. The traditional method is for the damp barley to be spread out on a cement floor, to a depth of about 2 ft (60 cm). The barley generates heat, so it has to be regularly turned with wooden shovels, to prevent the rootlets from matting.

DRUM MALTINGS These days, most distilleries buy their malt from large industrial maltings. Here, the wet grain is cast into large germination drums *(above)* instead of being laid out on a floor. Cool, humid air is blown through the malt to control the temperature and, every now and again, the drums are turned by motors so the rootlets do not become matted together.

KILNING Once the barley has begun to germinate, its growth must be stopped. This is done by spreading the green malt over a perforated metal floor above a kiln, and blowing hot air through the grain. It is important that the air is not too hot, or vital enzymes in the malt will be damaged. Moisture is reduced to 4.5 percent during kilning, which takes about 30 hours.

I BARLEY The most common form used for Scotch malt is plump "two-row" barley.

2 GREEN MALT The barley is steeped in water to stimulate germination.

3 MALT Once kilned, the grain is more friable and crisp, and rich in starch.

PEAT REEK If a peaty, smoky flavor is desired in the whiskey, peat turfs will be burned during the early hours of kilning. The fragrant peat smoke sticks to the husks of the green malt while it is still damp, so the fires are kept low and cool. *See also pp46–7.*

FROM GRAIN TO GLASS

Once malted, the barley will have shrunk slightly; the grains are not as hard as raw barley, and their moisture content will have reduced from 12 to 4%. When you bite into a malted grain, it has a sweet taste. The malt flavor is often not at all obvious in malt whiskies, but in some, such as Ardmore and Glenfarclas, the taste can be more easily discerned.

BELL'S SPECIAL RESERVE

BELL'S DECANTER

BELL'S ORIGINAL

BELL'S

www.bellswhisky.co.za

"Several fine whiskies blended together please the palates of a greater number of people than one whisky unmixed," wrote the first Arthur Bell, and his confidence in his products led him to appoint a London agent as early as 1863.

Bell's acquired the Blair Athol and Dufftown distilleries in 1933, adding Inchgower three years later. Today the company is owned by Diageo, which has taken a number of steps to consolidate Bell's position. Visitor facilities at the Blair Athol Distillery (the source of the single malt at the heart of the blend) have been enhanced and the blend itself has undergone continuous change and evolution. After 14 years of being sold as an 8-year-old, Bell's has been non-aged since 2008. But, in keeping with the spirit of Arthur Bell himself, great emphasis is laid on the skill of the blenders, and the company insists that, in blind tests they conducted, experienced drinkers prefer the new version.

The famous and very collectable Bell's decanters are limited-edition releases. They were first produced in the 1930s and a decanter decorated with jolly festive imagery *(see above)* has been released each Christmas since 1988. They are also brought out to commemorate historic moments, such as the marriage of Prince Charles and Diana in 1981.

BELL'S ORIGINAL

BLEND 40% ABV

As well as Blair Athol, Dufftown and Inchgower are important components here, along with Glenkinchie and Caol Ila. Medium-bodied blend, with a nutty aroma and a lightly spiced flavor.

BELL'S SPECIAL RESERVE

BLEND 40% ABV

Special Reserve has smoky hints from the Islay malts, tempered with warm pepper and a rich honey complexity.

BEN NEVIS 10-YEAR-OLD

BEN NEVIS SIGNATORY 15-YEAR-OLD

BEN NEVIS SHERRY CASK

BEN NEVIS

Lochy Bridge, Fort William
www.bennevisdistillery.com

It is hard to believe that Scotland's most northerly distillery on the west coast once employed 230 people, when it was owned by the Macdonald family in the 19th century. Not all of them were making whisky, as there were workshops and a sawmill too, as well as a farm with 200 head of cattle that fed on the distillery's rich draff. Sitting by Loch Linnhe on the edge of Fort William, Ben Nevis even had its own small fleet of steamers to ferry the whisky down the loch.

It was founded in 1825 by "Long John" Macdonald, who was the inspiration for the once-popular blend of that name. The brewing company Whitbread briefly owned the distillery during the 1980s, before it left the drinks business to concentrate on hotels. Ben Nevis is currently owned by Nikka.

Despite gaps in its inventory due to periodic closures during the 1970s and 80s, a number of older single malts have been released alongside the various Dew of Ben Nevis blends. Since the mid-1990s the core single malt has been the 10-year-old. It is the only regular distillery bottling, although single cask and wood-finished releases such as the Sherry Cask 2007 (a 14- to 15-year-old whisky) appear occasionally. Various independent bottlings have been released from Duncan Taylor, Douglas Laing, and Signatory, who produced a 15-year-old cask strength, distilled in 1992 and matured in a first-fill sherry butt.

BEN NEVIS 10-YEAR-OLD

SINGLE MALT: HIGHLANDS 46% ABV
A big, mouth-filling West Highlands malt with a sweet smack of oak and an oily texture that finishes dry.

**BENRIACH CURIOSITAS
10-YEAR-OLD**
SINGLE MALT: SPEYSIDE 40% ABV
A bitter-sweet whisky
with a dense peaty flavor.
Beneath the smoke, there are
flavors of tea cookies, cereal,
and some citrus notes.

**BENRIACH
12-YEAR-OLD**
SINGLE MALT: SPEYSIDE 40% ABV
More classically Speyside in
character than the 10-year-
old, with a heathery nose,
creamy vanilla ice cream
flavor, and a hint of honey.

BENRIACH 16-YEAR-OLD

BENRIACH 20-YEAR-OLD

BENRIACH AUTHENTICUS 21-YEAR-OLD

BENRIACH 30-YEAR-OLD

BENRIACH

Longmorn, Elgin, Morayshire
www.benriachdistillery.co.uk

Of all the Speyside distilleries built on the crest of the great speculative wave that ended the chapter on whisky-making in the 19th century, few crashed so badly as BenRiach. It opened in 1897 and, after repossession by the bank two years later, became part of the Longmorn Distilleries Company. It made whisky until 1903 and then shut down for most of the 20th century, although Longmorn, just next door, continued to make use of its floor maltings as well as its warehouses to mature its spirit. Then, in 1965, after a major

refurbishment, its solitary pair of stills was fired up again by its new owners, Glenlivet. It subsequently became part of Seagram, who, having no distillery on Islay, decided to produce a powerful peat-smoked malt at BenRiach in 1983. There were still some stocks of this peated BenRiach left when the distillery's new owners took over in 2004. This led to the Curiositas and Authenticus bottlings—the only commercially available Speyside single malts distilled from peated malted barley.

The new owners were a South African consortium led by Billy Walker, the former head of Burn Stewart Distillers. They paid Chivas Brothers a reported £5.4m.

The deal included around 5,000 casks dating back to 1970. There were no holes in the inventory due to years of non-production and there were plenty of different casks and different levels of peating to play with. This has allowed Billy Walker and his colleagues to dramatically expand the range of BenRiach malts available, although they have quite some way to go if they want to rival Bruichladdich, with its 200-plus releases.

BENRIACH 16-YEAR-OLD

SINGLE MALT: SPEYSIDE 40% ABV
A nutty, spicy Speysider, with a honeyed texture in the mouth and perhaps the faintest wisp of smoke.

BENRIACH 20-YEAR-OLD

SINGLE MALT: SPEYSIDE 40% ABV
The long years in oak have given this expression a dry, woody flavor, with sharp citrus notes and a clean finish.

BENRIACH AUTHENTICUS 21-YEAR-OLD

SINGLE MALT: SPEYSIDE 46% ABV
The 21-year-old big brother to the 10-year-old Curiositas. A mix of peat, oak, raisins, honey, and spices.

BENRIACH 30-YEAR-OLD

SINGLE MALT: SPEYSIDE 50% ABV
A sumptuous, full-bodied malt, full of raisins, candied fruit, dark chocolate, and spice, which linger on the finish.

All about…
Peat

Peat is decayed vegetation, decomposed over thousands of years by water and partially carbonized by chemical changes. The vegetation itself varies from place to place, but usually includes mosses, sedges, heather, and rushes. For peat to develop, the climate must be cool and damp, the drainage poor, and the ground poorly aerated. As it decomposes, the vegetation becomes waterlogged and sinks, piling up and being compressed and carbonized. Once the surface turf is cut away, and a trench (or "bank") dug, the peat is revealed. Once dug out, the peat is laid out on the bank to dry.

PEAT WATER The water on Islay (and in many other places in the Highlands) flows through peat and is the color of tea.

THE PEATING TRADITION After the Little Ice Age, which began around 1300, there were few trees left in the Scottish Highlands, but there were huge tracts of peat bog. Peat was the fuel in the Highlands, and remains so to this day in some places, for domestic fires as well as for drying malt and firing stills.

CUTTING TOOLS All that is needed to "win" peat, as the expression goes, is a peat spade (to cut the turf), a tool called a fal (with a "finger," to cut the peats themselves), and a fork to lift the peats onto the bank where they will dry. A small amount of peat is still dug by hand today, but most is now extracted by machine.

PEAT BOGS Some peat bogs are thought to be as much as 10,000 years old, and they can be up to 30 ft (9 m) deep. Vast swathes of Islay are covered with peat bogs.

PEAT ON THE FIRE
During the kilning of the barley, peat is often burned on the kiln fire. This is best done during the early stages of drying the green malt *(see p41)*, while it is still damp and sticky.

FRAGRANT SMOKE The peat smoke adheres to the husks of the grains, which are laid out on a perforated floor above the kiln. It only sticks while the malt is still damp, so the peat fire must be kept cool and smoldering.

SMOKY FLAVORS The chemicals that impart smoky or medicinal flavors to malt, and the whisky made from it, are called phenols, and are measured in parts per million (ppm). Heavily peated whiskies such as Lagavulin and Laphroaig peat to around 35 ppm phenols, and Ardbeg to around 50 ppm. Peated to an extraordinary 167 ppm phenols, Bruichladdich's limited release Octomore is currently the most heavily peated whisky.

BENROMACH TRADITIONAL

BENROMACH CASK STRENGTH 1981

BENROMACH 25-YEAR-OLD

BENROMACH

Forres, Morayshire
www.benromach.com

With just a single pair of stills and a maximum production of 110,000 gallons (500,000 liters) of pure alcohol a year, Benromach was always something of a pint-sized distillery. It was founded in 1898 and changed hands no fewer than six times in its first 100 years. At one point, it found itself part of National Distillers of America, sharing a stable with bourbon brands such as Old Crow and Old Grand-Dad. Then, like so many dispossessed distilleries, Benromach became part of the giant DCL who, as UDV, mothballed the distillery in 1983, along with many others. This time the stills were ripped out and the warehouses knocked down, and it seemed Benromach would never produce whisky again.

Luckily, it was not just the whisky industry that was in depression, otherwise some wily property developer would doubtless have snapped up the site. Benromach's savior was the famous firm of independent bottlers Gordon & MacPhail of Elgin, who bought the distillery in 1993. A new pair of stills was installed, and the first spirit flowed from it in 1999, when Prince Charles officially opened the new Benromach.

BENROMACH TRADITIONAL

SINGLE MALT: SPEYSIDE 40% ABV

This expression has a clean, light, floral character with a gentle phenolic edge and a trace of caramel.

BENROMACH CASK STRENGTH 1981

SINGLE MALT: SPEYSIDE 54.2% ABV

The nose is quite closed at first, but with water it opens up to reveal ripe orchard fruits and notes of cinnamon and sherry trifle.

BENROMACH 25-YEAR-OLD

SINGLE MALT: SPEYSIDE 43% ABV

The bourbon-cask brother to the sherried Vintage. Mellow, soft in the mouth, with a fruity citrus character.

BENROMACH ORIGINS

SINGLE MALT: SPEYSIDE 50% ABV

Origins is a new series. Batch I Golden Promise is named for the strain of barley used. Maturation is in first- and second-fill sherry casks.

BENROMACH ORGANIC

SINGLE MALT: SPEYSIDE 43% ABV

The first single malt officially certified by the UK's Soil Association has a sweet American oak character with notes of toffee and orange zest.

BENROMACH MADEIRA CASK

SINGLE MALT: SPEYSIDE 45% ABV

Benromach has been experimenting with wood finishing, making use of sweet wine casks, including Tokay, Madeira, and Marsala.

BLACK BOTTLE

BLACK BOTTLE 10-YEAR-OLD

BENRINNES

Aberlour, Banffshire
www.malts.com

The original Benrinnes Distillery was founded in 1826 at Whitehouse Farm on lower Speyside by Peter McKenzie, but was swept away in a flood three years later. In 1834 a new distillery called the Lyne of Ruthrie was built a few miles away and, despite bankruptcies and a bad fire in 1896, it has survived as Benrinnes. What you see today is a modern post-war distillery, which was completely rebuilt in the mid-1950s. It has six stills that operate a partial form of triple distillation, with one wash still paired with two spirit stills.

BENRINNES FLORA & FAUNA 15-YEAR-OLD

SINGLE MALT: SPEYSIDE 43% ABV
The only official distillery bottling is fairly sumptuous, with some smoke and spicy flavors and a creamy mouthfeel.

BLACK BOTTLE

Owner: Burn Stewart Distillers

Black Bottle was created in 1879 by C. D. & G. Grahams, a firm of Aberdeen tea blenders. After surviving various highs and lows over the best part of 90 years, the company was sold to Long John International in 1964. Allied Lyons acquired the brand in 1990 and started investing in it before selling it to Highland Distillers in 1995. When Highland sold Bunnahabhain Distillery to the current owners, Burn Stewart Distillers (itself part of CL WorldBrands Limited, the Trinidadian-owned drinks group) in 2003, the Black Bottle brand was sold along with it. Great efforts have been made by Burn Stewart to invest in the packaging and, more importantly, the blend quality, and many commentators agree that the blend profile now resembles, as nearly as can be determined, that of the 19th-century original. At the time of

writing, the excellent 10-year-old expression is due to be discontinued—a victim of the demand for cheaper blended whisky. Bottles should still be obtainable for the next year or two if you seek them out. This is a quality blend to taste before supplies dry up.

BLACK BOTTLE

BLEND 40% ABV
Black Bottle contains malt from seven Islay distilleries, along with hefty helpings of the company's Deanston malt. The nose is fresh and fruity, with hints of peat, while the palate is full, with a slightly honeyed sweetness followed by a distinctive smoky flavor. The finish is long and warming, with a smoky Islay character.

BLACK BOTTLE 10-YEAR-OLD

BLEND 40% ABV
Like the original blend, the 10-year-old contains malt from seven Islay distilleries, but this expression is richer and more rounded.

BLACK DOG

Owner: Whyte & Mackay

Walter Millard, a Scot trading from Calcutta, was looking for a blended Scotch to sell in India. In 1883, after some research, he appointed Charles Mackinlay & Co. (now part of Whyte & Mackay) to make up the blend. As a keen fisherman, he named it Black Dog after a favorite salmon fly. Black Dog was re-introduced to India in 2006. The following year, United Spirits, the largest distiller in India, bought Whyte & Mackay.

BLACK DOG CENTENARY

BLEND 40% ABV
Sweet malt, light butterscotch, and cream, with light herbal notes on the nose. A firm body, with malt, oak, dark chocolate, and caramel in the mouth.

BLADNOCH 15-YEAR-OLD

BLADNOCH 18-YEAR-OLD

BLACK & WHITE

Owner: Diageo

A fondly regarded brand from the Buchanan's stable, Black & White originally went by the name Buchanan's Special. The story goes that, in the 1890s, James Buchanan supplied his whisky to the House of Commons in a very dark bottle with a white label. Apparently incapable of memorizing the name, British parliamentarians simply called for "Black and White." Buchanan adopted the name and subsequently adorned the label with two dogs—a black Scottish terrier and a white West Highland terrier. Today it is marketed by Diageo in France, Brazil, and Venezuela, where it continues to enjoy a popularity long since lost in its homeland.

BLACK & WHITE

BLEND 40% ABV

A high-class, traditional-style blend. Layered hints of peat, smoke, and oak.

BLADNOCH

Bladnoch, Wigtown, Wigtonshire
www.bladnoch.co.uk

The most southerly distillery in Scotland, Bladnoch has a capacity of just 22,000 gallons (100,000 liters) a year, a figure capped by its previous owners, UDV. This classic doll's house distillery was founded by Thomas and John McClelland in 1817 on the banks of the Bladnoch River and remained in the family's hands until 1911, when it was bought by an Irish company. In 1937 it went bust, and was bought and sold six times over the next few years, spending long periods lying idle in between. Finally, it was taken over by Guinness UDV (now Diageo) in 1985. With the next big whisky slump, its solitary pair of stills went cold once more in 1993, seemingly for good. But just a year later it was bought by Raymond Armstrong from Northern Ireland. The deal brokered was that Bladnoch would

never produce whisky again but, by 2000, Diageo had relented and the distillery is now allowed to produce the equivalent of 250,000 bottles a year. For those with deeper pockets, Bladnoch will also sell you whisky by the cask. After the delay in restarting production, the new bottlings are due in 2009. In the meantime, there are occasional older bottlings and some Bladnoch has been released in Diageo's Flora & Fauna range.

BLADNOCH 15-YEAR-OLD

SINGLE MALT: LOWLANDS 55% ABV

A light, crisp, aperitif-style whisky with a trace of green apples.

BLADNOCH 18-YEAR-OLD

SINGLE MALT: LOWLANDS 55% ABV

This smooth Lowlands malt is bottled at full cask strength without chill-filtration, but is in short supply.

BLAIR ATHOL

Pitlochry, Perthshire
www.malts.com

In 1798 John Stewart and Robert Robertson took out a license for their Aldour Distillery on the edge of Pitlochry. In an area crawling with illicit stills, life was tough for legitimate, tax-paying distilleries, and Aldour soon closed. It was resurrected in 1826 by Alexander Connacher, who re-named it Blair Athol. Within 30 years, some of the malt was being sold to the Perth blender Arthur Bell & Sons, who finally bought the distillery in 1933. Except for the 12-year-old and the occasional rare malt, nearly every drop goes into blends, particularly Bell's.

BLAIR ATHOL FLORA & FAUNA 12-YEAR-OLD

SINGLE MALT: HIGHLANDS 43%

Smooth, well-rounded flavors, with spice and candied fruit, and a trace of smoke on the finish.

BOWMORE LEGEND

SINGLE MALT: ISLAY 40% ABV

Dry and bracing, with
a faint citrus flavor that
develops into a smoky finish.

**BOWMORE
12-YEAR-OLD**

SINGLE MALT: ISLAY 40% ABV

Gently aromatic, with a
mix of citrus fruits and
smoke on the nose, which
carries through to the
tongue, together with
some dark chocolate.

BOWMORE 15-YEAR-OLD   BOWMORE 17-YEAR-OLD   BOWMORE 18-YEAR-OLD   BOWMORE 25-YEAR-OLD

BOWMORE

Bowmore, Isle of Islay
www.bowmore.co.uk

The oldest surviving distillery on Islay was founded in 1779 by John Simpson, who, as a farmer, distiller, builder, quarry-owner, and part-time postmaster, was a man of many parts. Quite how much time he devoted to Bowmore is unclear, but the distillery remained small for years. When it was bought by the Glasgow firm of W. & J. Mutter in 1837, it was producing just 800 gallons (3,640 liters) a year. Within 50 years, annual production had soared to 200,000 gallons (900,000 liters). This was filled into casks and shipped to

Mutter's bonded warehouse beneath Glasgow's Central Station.

After various changes in ownership, including 20 years with DCL, the distillery was bought by another Glasgow-based whisky firm, Stanley P. Morrison. Ever since, it has been the flagship distillery of Morrison Bowmore, now part of the Japanese drinks giant Suntory.

Bowmore stands on the shores of Loch Indaal. With the salty sea breeze blowing right into the warehouses, some of it is bound to seep into the casks. As with most Islay distilleries, the majority of the spirit is tankered off the island to mature on the mainland. The distillery has two pairs of stills,

six Oregon-pine washbacks, and its own floor maltings, which can supply up to 40 per cent of Bowmore's needs. Whether using its own malt, which is peated to around 25 ppm, improves the flavor of Bowmore would be hard to prove, but to see the whole process, from the freshly steeped barley to the peat-fired kiln and its dense blue smoke, certainly makes a visit to the Bowmore Distillery that much more special.

BOWMORE 15-YEAR-OLD
SINGLE MALT: ISLAY 43% ABV
The deep mahogany color comes from two years in Oloroso casks, which also give a raisin-like sweetness to Bowmore's signature note of smoke.

BOWMORE 17-YEAR-OLD
SINGLE MALT: ISLAY 43% ABV
Rich caramel on the nose with a background of peat. Creamy texture, with malt, peat, and fruit interplay on the palate, and a long, warming finish.

BOWMORE 18-YEAR-OLD
SINGLE MALT: ISLAY 43% ABV
A mellow, more autumnal take on the 15-year-old expression, with a waxy, orange-peel flavor mixed with smoke and burned sugar.

BOWMORE 25-YEAR-OLD
SINGLE MALT: ISLAY 43% ABV
The stewed fruit and molasses flavors from the wood subsume the drier, smokier elements of Bowmore, thanks to a heavy sherry influence.

All about...
Pot Stills

To create an acceptable whiskey, the still must be made from copper. The reason for this is that copper purifies the spirit. It acts as a catalyst to extract foul-smelling sulfur compounds and heavy oils, and it assists in creating desirable fragrant and fruity flavors. It follows that the more contact the alcohol vapor has with copper, the purer and lighter the spirit will be. As the vapor rises during the distillation, much of it condenses in the still and trickles back to be boiled up again. This is called "reflux," and leads to greater purity. The amount of reflux depends upon a number of factors. The size and shape of the still is vital, but so is the depth to which it is filled. Typically, this won't exceed two-thirds of the still's capacity; a high fill makes for less reflux. How fast the stills are operated is another factor, with a speedy operation leading to less reflux. The temperature of the distillate is important too—the warmer the spirit, the greater the copper uptake in the condensers. The pitch of the lyne arms connecting the head of the still to the condenser is also crucial, with different angles affecting the purity of the spirit.

SQUAT STILLS These act like a reverse boil-ball and create a similarly complex spirit, without the same level of copper contact as onion stills.

ONION OR PLAIN STILL Large and tall onion-shaped stills afford the greatest copper contact and tend to produce the purest spirit. They are the traditional still shape, and the commonest in Scotch malt distilling.

BOIL-BALL STILL These generally take longer to complete a distillation, because of condensation in the ball. But such condensation does not lead to increased reflux, so these stills tend to make a heavier, more complex spirit.

LAMP GLASS STILL The tight neck of the lamp glass still restricts and slows the upward flow of the spirit vapor. It acts like a reverse boil-ball to create a similarly complex spirit, without the same level of copper contact as onion stills.

ASCENDING LYNE ARMS The more the lyne arm angles upward, the more reflux is created, making for a lighter spirit. The lyne arms here rise up from the stills to connect to a series of shell-and-tube condensers. Shell-and-tube are the most common form of condensers used in the industry today, and allow more contact between the spirit and copper than traditional "worm tub" condensers.

TALL STILLS Tall-necked stills make for increased reflux, whereby part of the spirit vapor condenses on the sides of the still and trickles back down to be re-distilled. The spirit has more contact with copper, therefore, which leads to greater purity and delicacy, but to less "character" than the spirit from squat stills.

DESCENDING LYNE ARM A descending lyne arm encourages the vapor to pass quickly to the condenser, reducing reflux. Where these are found on wash stills, the chance of "carry over" is increased, where liquid rather than vapor makes its way into the condenser, spoiling the spirit.

BRUICHLADDICH

Bruichladdich, Isle of Islay
www.bruichladdich.com

Islay's most westerly distillery stands on the shores of Loch Indaal, across the water from Bowmore. It was built in 1881 by two brothers—Robert William and John Gourlay Harvey, who were also the owners of Dundashill in Glasgow, the largest malt distillery in Scotland at the time. Unlike older distilleries on Islay, it was purpose-built and boasted state-of-the-art cavity walls and its own steam generator.

After a promising start supplying blends with a pungent top dressing of Islay malt, Bruichladdich fell

into disuse from 1929 to 1937, the first of many closures that have dogged the distillery. After repeated sales, it passed in the 1970s to the owners of Whyte & Mackay, who closed it down in 1994, seemingly for good. Then, days before Christmas 2000, it was rescued by a private consortium led by the independent bottler Murray McDavid. The old Victorian decor has been lovingly preserved, and the new owners also proudly claim that no computers are used in the production. The whisky is now bottled on site and even uses barley grown on the island.

From the start, the distiller has been Jim McEwan, who left a long career at Bowmore to join the new

venture in 2001. In recent years Bruichladdich's core range was joined by a heavily peated whisky, called Port Charlotte after a nearby village, and the intensely smoky Octomore, which took its name from an old Islay distillery that closed in 1852.

In 2003 Bruichladdich became the first distillery on Islay to bottle its whiskies on the island. From the heavily sherried Blacker Still and the pink-hued Flirtation, to 3D, Infinity, and The Yellow Submarine, the range of bottlings has been staggering. To date, over 200, many of them in very limited quantities, have been released. While this may cause some frustration among

Bruichladdich's devoted fans, it does allow this solitary distillery to punch way above its weight.

BRUICHLADDICH WAVES

SINGLE MALT: ISLAY 46% ABV
A multi-vintage vatting that offers a moderately peated style of Bruichladdich.

BRUICHLADDICH PEAT

SINGLE MALT: ISLAY 46% ABV
A powerful phenolic whisky with the scent of bonfires, seaweed, and bacon.

BRUICHLADDICH ROCKS

SINGLE MALT: ISLAY 46% ABV
After maturing for an unspecified time in American oak, this brisk, fruity malt is finished in red wine casks.

**BRUICHLADDICH
18-YEAR-OLD**

SINGLE MALT: ISLAY 46% ABV

There have been two
versions of this limited-
release bottling: the first
finished in German sweet-
wine casks, the second
in sweet Jurançon casks
from France.

**BRUICHLADDICH
21-YEAR-OLD**

SINGLE MALT: ISLAY 46% ABV

Aged in Oloroso casks and
suitably deep in color, this is
a pungent, sulfury malt for
those who like their
whiskies well-sherried.

BRAEVAL

Chapeltown of Glenlivet,
Ballindalloch, Banffshire

In the early 1970s, when global sales of blended Scotch were booming, the Braeval Distillery was built to help supply the malt to meet demand. Edgar Bronfmann, heir apparent to the Seagram empire, flew in to cut the turf in 1972 and, within a year, the distillery was in production. A century earlier, such a distillery would have created a whole community, with houses, shops, and perhaps even a school. But today's fully computerized Braeval needs a staff of one. Only independent bottlings of the malt exist. Gordon & MacPhail's goes by the name of Braes of Glenlivet.

**BRAES OF GLENLIVET
GORDON & MACPHAIL 1975**

SINGLE MALT: SPEYSIDE 43% ABV
Floral and vanilla flavors combine to great effect. The finish offers a dry, light touch.

BUCHANAN'S

Owner: Diageo

James Buchanan was one of the most notable whisky barons—the Victorian entrepreneurs who brought Scotch to world attention, amassing personal fortunes along the way. Starting as an agent in 1879, he soon began trading on his own and rapidly saw his whisky adopted in the House of Commons. Today the Buchanan's brand is showing signs of prospering once again under its owners, Diageo. Mainly seen in Venezuela, Mexico, Colombia, and the US, Buchanan's is positioned as a premium-style blend. There are two expressions: a 12-year-old and the Special Reserve at 18 years old.

BUCHANAN'S 12-YEAR-OLD

BLEND 40% ABV
Rich on the nose, with sherry and spice. Thinner on the palate, with bitter, dried-lemon notes. Winey, with a touch of dry wood.

BUNNAHABHAIN

Port Askaig, Islay
www.bunnahabhain.com

Before the distilleries of Islay found fame for the heavily peat-smoked character of their single malts, their market was not the whisky drinker, but the big blending houses. Many of these used Islay malts as a top dressing, to add a smoky intensity to their blends. The trouble was they only required limited quantities, as too much would leave their whiskies unbalanced. With this in mind, Bunnahabhain, the most northerly distillery on the island, used unpeated or lightly peated malt.

It was founded in 1881 on a shingle beach near Port Askaig. Before the distillery was built, a road had to be laid, along with a pier, cottages for the workforce, and a school for their children. The whole venture cost £30,000, yet the business was making a profit of £10,000 by its second year.

The distillery was once part of the Edrington Group. As a consequence, its malt was overshadowed by its stablemates—Macallan and Highland Park. Since 2003, however, it has belonged to Burn Stewart, who are investing heavily in Bunnahabhain's single malts.

The core range consists of the 12-, 18-, and 25-year-old. The first two are the most readily available bottlings. The 25 is boxed in alder wood and has a parchment label to reflect its more rarefied status. Bunnahabhain also produces limited-edition bottlings for the Feis Ile, Islay's annual festival. In 2008, it was a 21-year-old—a vatting of two Spanish oak sherry hogsheads from 1986.

BUNNAHABHAIN 25-YEAR-OLD

SINGLE MALT: ISLAY 43% ABV
A relatively fulsome malt with aromas of polished leather and crème caramel. On the palate there is ripe European oak. The texture is luscious and creamy.

**BUNNAHABHAIN
12-YEAR-OLD**
SINGLE MALT: ISLAY 40% ABV
A clean, refreshing whisky
with a scent of ozone and
sea spray, which gives way
to a nutty malty sweetness
in the mouth.

**BUNNAHABHAIN
18-YEAR-OLD**
SINGLE MALT: ISLAY 43% ABV
With its richer sherry
influence, this has less
of the malty distillery
character than the 12-year-
old. Instead it has a broader
texture and woody flavor.

CAMERON BRIG

Cameronbridge Distillery,
Winygates, Leven, Fife

Greatly misunderstood, little drunk
in their own right, and sadly
misrepresented, grain whiskies are
Scotch's poor relation. Yet, they are
the essential component and base
of all blends and, when found as a
single grain bottling, the source of
much pleasure. Cameron Brig is
made at Diageo's Cameronbridge
distillery in Fife, a massive
complex of giant continuous stills.
The sheer scale of grain whisky
production offends some purists
but, at its best, good grain whisky
is very good indeed. You would not
expect anything less from Diageo in
its only offering in this category,
and Cameron Brig won't disappoint.

CAMERON BRIG 12-YEAR-OLD

SINGLE GRAIN 40% ABV
The nose is clean and grassy, with some
honey. Smooth palate; nutty and firm,
with a hint of bitter coffee in the finish.

CAOL ILA DISTILLERS EDITION 1995

CAOL ILA 12-YEAR-OLD

CAOL ILA

Port Askaig, Islay
www.malts.com

Just as Ardbeg played second fiddle
to Laphroaig when both were
owned by Allied Domecq, the same
was true of Diageo's Caol Ila and
Lagavulin. For years the largest
distillery on Islay—with a
capacity to produce 800,000
gallons (3.6 million liters) of spirits
a year—had a very low profile.
This is beginning to change, as its
owners are now promoting Caol Ila
as a top-quality single malt.

The distillery was built in 1846
by Hector Henderson, who was
forced to sell up six years later to
Norman Buchanan, the owner of
the Jura Distillery across the
water. After just five years, he sold
out to the big Glasgow blender
Bulloch Lade, who reconstructed
Caol Ila on a larger scale in 1879.

In 1972 the distillery was
effectively demolished. When it
reopened two years later, the only

CAOL ILA CASK STRENGTH

CAPERDONICH

Rothes, Morayshire

....

CARDHU 12-YEAR-OLD

CARDHU SPECIAL CASK RESERVE

original building still standing was the warehouse. As demand for Lagavulin began to outstrip supply, Caol Ila's malts were finally given the attention they deserved.

CAOL ILA DISTILLERS EDITION 1995

SINGLE MALT: ISLAY 43% ABV
Sweet, smoky, and malty, with aromatic spices (cinnamon), especially in the lingering finish. The most rounded expression of the core range.

CAOL ILA 12-YEAR-OLD

SINGLE MALT: ISLAY 43% ABV
Balancing the scent of tar and peat is a malty sweetness and some citrus aromas. Oily textured, with flavors of molasses and smoke.

CAOL ILA CASK STRENGTH

SINGLE MALT: ISLAY 55% ABV
Paler in color than other expressions of Caol Ila, the cask-strength version has a strong, assertive character that starts smooth and sweet and dries to a smoky finish.

CAPERDONICH

Rothes, Morayshire

....

Caperdonich was founded in 1897 by James Grant, owner of the distillery next door at Glen Grant. His new venture, Glen Grant No. 2, was designed to expand malt production and was connected by an overhead pipe through which the new-make spirit could be pumped. It closed five years later and remained shut until 1965, when it burst back to life as Caperdonich. It was afterward swallowed up by Seagram and then Chivas (Pernod Ricard).

Apart from a cask-strength 16-year-old in 2005, there are no current distillery bottlings of this Speyside malt, as almost all the production goes into blends for Chivas. But independent bottlings can be found, mostly from very old casks, such as the 1968 bottling from Murray McDavid.

CARDHU

Knockando, Aberlour, Morayshire
www.malts.com

....

Having made whisky on the side for over a decade, John Cumming decided to take out a license for his Cardhu Distillery in 1824. It remained a small farm distillery until his daughter-in-law, Elizabeth Cumming, rebuilt it in the 1880s. Soon after, it was sold to Johnnie Walker and became the spiritual home of the blend. But, at some point in the 1990s, a wrench was thrown into the works. The owners, Diageo, had tried to steer Spain's whisky drinkers on to Johnnie Walker Black Label as an alternative to Chivas Regal, but the Spanish, it seemed, wanted a bottle that had "malt" on the label. Spanish sales of Cardhu 12-year-old grew by 100,000 cases between 1997 and 2002, but supply was becoming a serious issue. Rather than tame demand by putting up the price, Diageo took

the decision to re-christen the whisky as Cardhu Pure Malt, which would allow them to add in other malts. Whether Spanish consumers were bothered is unclear, but the industry certainly was. After much outrage, and even questions in Parliament, Diageo was forced to withdraw the brand in March 2003 and revert to selling Cardhu as a genuine 12-year-old single malt.

CARDHU 12-YEAR-OLD

SINGLE MALT: SPEYSIDE 40% ABV
This heathery, pear-drop-scented malt is on the lighter side of Speyside, with a light to medium body and a malty, slightly nutty flavor that finishes fairly short.

CARDHU SPECIAL CASK RESERVE

SINGLE MALT: SPEYSIDE 40% ABV
This latest bottling has more depth and body than the 12-year-old, with an aroma of peaches and a sweeter, more creamy texture on the tongue.

The Four Ale Bar at the Canny Man's pub in Edinburgh is stocked with several hundred malts as well as numerous objects collected over the course of its nearly 140-year history.

CATTO'S

Owner: Inver House Distillers

James Catto, an Aberdeen-based whisky blender, set up in business in 1861. His whiskies achieved international distribution on the White Star and P&O shipping lines. After the death of his son Robert in World War I, the company passed to the distillers Gilbey's. More recently, it was acquired by Inver House Distillers. Catto's is a deluxe, fully matured, and complex blend. Two versions are available: a non-age standard bottling and a 12-year-old expression with a yellow-gold, straw-like appearance that belies its complexity and warm finish.

CATTO'S

BLEND 40% ABV

The standard Catto blend is aromatic and well-rounded in character, with a smooth, mellow finish.

CHIVAS REGAL 25-YEAR-OLD

CHIVAS REGAL 12-YEAR-OLD

CHIVAS REGAL

Owner: Chivas Brothers

Chivas Regal is one of the top five bestselling blends in the world and among the few truly global brands in terms of distribution. Chivas Brothers was founded in the early 19th century and prospered, due in part to some favorable royal connections. The business is owned today by the French multinational Pernod Ricard.

At the heart of Chivas Regal blends are Speyside single malt whiskies, in particular Strathisla Distillery's rich and full single malt. To safeguard the supply of this critically important ingredient, Chivas Brothers bought the distillery in 1950. It maintains attractive visitor facilities there.

Chivas Regal 18 was launched in 1997 and is a super-premium blend. Strathisla 18-year-old contributes to its memorable, warm finish, but is not available commercially anywhere in the

CHIVAS REGAL 18-YEAR-OLD

world. Chivas Regal 25 represents a further move upmarket, although supplies of it are strictly limited.

CHIVAS REGAL 25-YEAR-OLD

BLEND 40% ABV

The flagship blend, Chivas Regal 25-year-old is classy and rich. A luxury blend for indulgent sipping. Well-mannered, balanced, and stylish.

CHIVAS REGAL 12-YEAR-OLD

BLEND 40% ABV

An aromatic infusion of wild herbs, heather, honey, and orchard fruits. Round and creamy on the palate, with a full, rich taste of honey and ripe apples and notes of vanilla, hazelnut, and butterscotch. Rich and lingering.

CHIVAS REGAL 18-YEAR-OLD

BLEND 40% ABV

An intense dark amber color. Multi-layered aromas of dried fruits, spice, and buttery toffee. Exceptionally rich and smooth, with a velvety, dark chocolate palate, elegant floral notes, and a wisp of sweet mellow smokiness.

CLAN CAMPBELL

Owner: Chivas Brothers

Launched as recently as 1984, Clan Campbell is a million-case-selling brand from Chivas Brothers, the whisky arm of drinks giant Pernod Ricard. It is not available in the UK, but is a leader in the important French market, and may also be found in Italy, Spain, and some Asian countries. Despite its relative youth, its origins are now inextricably entwined with Scottish heritage, thanks to clever marketing and a link to the Duke of Argyll, head of the clan. Indeed, what is claimed to be the oldest whisky-distilling relic in Scotland, a distiller's worm was luckily found on Campbell lands.

CLAN CAMPBELL

BLEND 40% ABV

The malt component of Clan Campbell comes largely from Speyside (Aberlour and Glenallachie especially). A smooth, light whisky with a fruity finish.

CLAN MACGREGOR

Owner: William Grant & Sons

This budget-priced blend is sold largely in North America and from Venezuela to the Middle East to Thailand, but not by and large in its Scottish homeland. Sales approach an impressive 1.5 million cases a year and it is one of the world's fastest-growing whisky brands. Owned by William Grant & Sons, it is primarily a mix of Grant's own malts (Glenfiddich, Balvenie, and Kininvie) and grain whisky from its substantial Girvan operation. The label proudly carries the badge, motto, and personal crest of the 24th clan chief, Sir Malcolm MacGregor of MacGregor.

CLAN MACGREGOR

BLEND 40% ABV

A blend of grain whiskies and some Speyside malt. Light in style, fragrant, with just a little fruitiness.

THE CLAYMORE

Owner: Whyte & Mackay

A claymore is a Highland broadsword. The name was deemed appropriate by DCL (forerunner of drinks giant Diageo) when, in 1977, it attempted to recover some of the market share it had lost when it withdrew Johnnie Walker Red Label from the UK market. Competitively priced, The Claymore was an immediate success. In 1985, the brand was sold to Whyte & Mackay. It continued to sell well for some time, but in recent years has declined and is now principally seen as a low-priced secondary brand. Dalmore is believed to be the main malt whisky in the blend.

THE CLAYMORE

BLEND 40% ABV

The nose is heavy and full, with silky mellow tones. Well-balanced and full-bodied on the palate. Polished finish.

COMPASS BOX OAK CROSS

COMPASS BOX THE PEAT MONSTER

CLUNY

Owner: Whyte & Mackay

Although it is produced by Whyte & Mackay, Cluny is supplied in bulk to Heaven Hill Distilleries, which has bottled the whisky in the US since 1988. Today it is one of America's top-selling domestically bottled blended Scotch whiskies. It contains over 30 malts from all regions of Scotland (Isle of Jura, Dalmore, and Fettercairn single malts among them), along with grain whisky that is almost certainly largely sourced from Whyte & Mackay's Invergordon plant. Cluny is sold primarily on its competitive price. Under Whyte & Mackay's new Indian ownership, it may be a candidate for further international development.

CLUNY

BLEND 40% ABV

Subtle sweet and sour nose, with a slight metallic, bitter tang on the palate.

CLYNELISH

Brora, Sutherland
www.malts.com

A large box-shaped distillery dating from 1967, Clynelish has six stills and a capacity of 750,000 gallons (3.4 million liters). Within its grounds is a much older distillery that ran alongside it until 1983. This was Brora, founded in 1819 by the Marquis of Stafford. Known briefly as Old Clynelish, Brora made a heavily peated malt during the 1970s to ensure a supply of Islay-style malts for blends like Johnnie Walker Black Label. In 1983 Brora closed for good, leaving just Clynelish. There have been various rare malts and independent bottlings from Douglas Laing and Caidenheads among others.

CLYNELISH 14-YEAR-OLD

SINGLE MALT: HIGHLANDS 46% ABV

A mouthfilling malt, quite fruity with a creamy texture, a wisp of smoke, and a firm, dry finish.

COMPASS BOX

www.compassboxwhisky.com

Compass Box is the brainchild of ex-Diageo marketing executive John Glaser. The company was formed in 2000 and describes itself as an "artisanal whisky maker," which may seem disingenuous since it isn't a distiller but a blender, albeit a highly innovative and experimental one. From time to time this brings it into conflict with the industry's establishment. The company's technique of inserting additional oak staves into a barrel to produce Spice Tree led to pressure from the Scotch Whisky Association and the eventual withdrawal of the product. For all this, the company has been highly influential and in its short life has won more than 60 medals and awards. Its limited release "small batch" whiskies sell out quickly.

There are two main ranges: Signature and Limited Release. The former is regularly available and comprises the company's three most popular products: Oak Cross, The Peat Monster, and Asyla. The Limited Release range is indeed very limited: Optimism, for example, was restricted to just 163 bottles.

COMPASS BOX OAK CROSS

BLENDED MALT 43% ABV

Notes of clove and vanilla on the palate accent a sweet maltiness and subtle fruit character.

COMPASS BOX THE PEAT MONSTER

BLENDED MALT: ISLAY / SPEYSIDE 46% ABV

Rich and loaded with flavor: a bacon-fat smokiness, full-blown peat, hints of fruit and spice. A long finish, echoing peat and smoke for several minutes.

COMPASS BOX ASYLA

BLEND 40% ABV

A frequent award-winner. Sweet, delicate, and very smooth on the palate, with flavors of vanilla cream, cereals, and a subtle apple-like character.

ASYLA

MALT & GRAIN
BLENDED SCOTCH WHISKY

Finesse, Softness & Sweetness

on the palate. Our multiple award-winning 'Asyla'
is made from perfectly mature malt and grain
whiskies from hand-picked American oak casks.
·John Glaser, Whiskymaker.

COMPASS BOX
WHISKY COMPANY

40%vol PRODUCT OF SCOTLAND 70cl e
Compass Box Whisky Co. 24 Great King St, Edinburgh, Scotland

CRAGGANMORE

Ballindalloch, Morayshire
www.malts.com

When Diageo launched its Classic
Malts to showcase the great malt
whisky regions of Scotland,
deciding which malts to pick must
have been challenging, especially
on Speyside, where there were so
many distilleries to choose from. But
most agree that the decision to run
with Cragganmore was a good one.

This was a well-conceived
distillery from the start. It was
built in 1869 by John Smith, a
highly experienced distiller who
had been involved in Glenfarclas,
Macallan, and Glenlivet. He had a
reliable source of pure water from
the Craggan burn, which also
provided the distillery with
power. He had nearby access to
peat and barley, and he was close
to Ballindalloch station. By laying
a short stretch of track,
Cragganmore became the first
distillery in Scotland to have its

own railway siding, to bring in
supplies and carry off the freshly
filled casks of whisky. It was a
model that was widely copied on
Speyside, where distilleries sprang
up beside the track like farmsteads
in the American Midwest.

Part of Cragganmore's famed
complexity as a single malt may
come from the unusual flat-topped
stills and the use of worm tubs to
create a heavier spirit.

CRAGGANMORE 12-YEAR-OLD

SINGLE MALT: SPEYSIDE 40% ABV
With its floral, heathery aromas,
Cragganmore smells typically Speyside,
but there is a robust woody complexity
with a trace of smoke on the palate.

CRAGGANMORE DISTILLERS
EDITION 1992

SINGLE MALT: SPEYSIDE 43% ABV
This is double-matured, with the final
part of its maturation being in a port
cask. This results in a cherry and
orange sweetness that dies away into
a lightly smoky finish.

All about…
Casks

"The wood makes the whisky" has long been a saying in Scotland, but it is only over the past 25 years that scientists have discovered why the cask is so important. Oak is the best wood (and incorporated into the legal definition of most whiskies). Most is *Quercus alba* (American white oak), some *Quercus robur* (European oak), and a very small amount of *Quercus mongolica* (Japanese oak). Each type matures its contents slightly differently. The oak cask performs three vital functions: it removes harshness and unwanted flavors (charring plays an important role in this); it adds desirable flavors—vanilla and coconut in the case of American oak, astringency, and dried fruit notes in the case of European oak; and, being semi-porous, it allows the spirit to "breathe" and interact with the surrounding air to oxidize, develop mellowness, increase complexity, and add fruitiness.

INTERACTION WITH WOOD The vast majority of the character of mature whisky develops during its ageing in oak casks, so the types of casks used are vitally important.

CONSTRUCTION OF A CASK
Stave blanks are cut from the tree trunk in a pattern called "quarter-sawing," which cuts across the grain so the staves won't leak.
The blanks are shaped so they fit snugly. Hoops hold them in place while they are heated (traditionally by fire) to bend the wood into the right shape.

AMERICAN BARRELS
By law, to be called bourbon or rye whiskey, the spirit must be matured in new white-oak barrels, which hold 44 gallons (200 liters). Maturation lasts for at least two years. The barrels have a second life in Scotland and other countries where they are exported to be used for maturation. Most Scotch is matured in bourbon casks.

SHERRY BUTTS
Butts and puncheons hold 110 gallons (500 liters) and are usually made from European oak. They are seasoned with sherry for one or two years before being filled with whisky.

MAKING HOGSHEADS The majority of casks used by the whiskey industries of Scotland, Japan, and Ireland began life as American barrels. Having been used to mature American whiskey, the barrels are taken apart and transported in bundles to be "re-made" as hogsheads, which contain around 55 gallons (250 liters) by cannibalizing one barrel in five. A hogshead cask will then be used several times for maturing whiskey.

TOASTING AND CHARRING Burning the inside of the cask causes essential chemical changes within the surface of the wood, without which the spirit will not mature. European oak casks are generally lightly "toasted" to activate the changes; American barrels are more heavily burned, so the surface blisters.

CASK FINISHING This is the process in which whisky is aged in one cask, then re-racked into another for the final year or two of its maturation to add an extra layer of flavors. The "finishing cask" is most often a wine, sherry, or—as in the case of the Glenmorangie Quinta Ruban single malt *(right)*—a port cask.

CRAIGELLACHIE

Craigellachie, Banffshire

Although the name of John Dewar
& Sons is writ large above the
modern, plate-glass still house that
sits on the main road out of
Craigellachie, the distillery was
originally tied to White Horse.
Peter Mackie, the man behind the
famous blend, built Craigellachie
in 1891 in partnership with
Alexander Edward. Of all the
Victorian whisky barons, Mackie
was the most connected to malt
distilling, having served as an
apprentice at Lagavulin, whose
whisky was also part of White
Horse. Since 1998, Craigellachie
has been owned by Bacardi.

CRAIGELLACHIE 14-YEAR-OLD

SINGLE MALT: SPEYSIDE 40% ABV
Rich and aromatic, with a scent of
fruit pie and a touch of smoke. More
delicate on the tongue, and some woody
notes on the finish.

CRAWFORD'S

Owner: Whyte & Mackay / Diageo

Crawford's 3 Star was established
by Leith firm A. & A. Crawford,
and by the time the company joined
the Distillers Company (DCL) in
1944 the blend was a Scottish
favorite. Although its popularity
continued, it was not of strategic
significance to its owners, hence
the decision to license the brand to
Whyte & Mackay in 1986. Whyte
& Mackay are today owned by the
Indian UB Group, so the future of
this venerable label may lie on the
subcontinent. Diageo, successors to
DCL, retain the rights to the name
Crawford's 3 Star Special Reserve
outside the UK. Benrinnes single
malt *(see p50)* has been a long-time
component in the Crawford's blend.

CRAWFORD'S 3 STAR

BLEND 40% ABV
Spirity, fruity, fresh-tasting blend,
with a smack of citrus, a sweet center,
and a dry, slightly sooty finish.

CUTTY SARK ORIGINAL

CUTTY SARK

Owner: Berry Brothers & Rudd

Cutty Sark is blended and bottled in Glasgow by The Edrington Group (proprietors of The Famous Grouse), who supply much of the whisky for the blend. The first very pale-colored whisky in the world, Cutty Sark was created in 1923 for Berry Bros & Rudd Ltd., a well-established London wine and spirit merchants who are still the brand owner. The company was looking to innovate with its whisky and decided to produce an original style. The result was a naturally light-colored blend of quality and character, with a name inspired by the most famous of all the Scottish-built clipper ships.

One of the acclaimed blended whiskies of the world, Cutty Sark uses some 20 single malt whiskies, many from Speyside distilleries such as Glenrothes and Macallan. Maturation and marriage both contribute to the distinguishing qualities of the blend. The wood for the oak casks is carefully chosen to bring out the characteristic flavor and aroma of each whisky in the Cutty Sark blend and to impart color gently during the long maturation. There is a non-age expression and a deluxe range at 12, 15, 18, and 25 years old.

CUTTY SARK ORIGINAL

BLEND 40% ABV

Light and fragrant aroma, with hints of vanilla and oak. Sweet and creamy, with a vanilla note, and a crisp finish.

CUTTY SARK 12-YEAR-OLD

BLEND 43% ABV

Elegant and fruity, with a subtle vanilla sweetness. Here the malts used are between 12 and 15 years old.

CUTTY SARK 18-YEAR-OLD

BLEND 43% ABV

Balance of vanilla sweetness and bitter and spicy notes—lemon peel, wood, and coal smoke. A dry, wood influence on the finish.

DAILUAINE

Carron, Banffshire
www.malts.com

Under the shadow of Benrinnes, a local farmer called William Mackenzie built Dailuaine in 1854. His son Thomas later went into partnership with James Fleming to form Dailuaine-Talisker Distilleries Ltd. In 1889 Dailuaine was rebuilt and became one of the biggest distilleries in Scotland. The architect Charles Doig erected his first pagoda roof here, to draw smoke from the kiln through the malt. The idea caught on at other distilleries. With all but 2 percent of Dailuaine used as fillings, single malt bottlings are relatively rare.

DAILUAINE GORDON & MACPHAIL 1993

SINGLE MALT: SPEYSIDE 43% ABV

Sweet and malty, with spicy notes of licorice and aniseed. Oaky, toasty notes too. Creamier with a little water.

DALLAS DHU

Forres, Morayshire

This late-Victorian distillery, founded in 1898 by the Master Distiller Alexander Edward, was one of many owned by the Distillers Company (DCL) to be shut down in 1983 to await its fate. With just two stills and a waterwheel that had provided the power right up until 1971, Dallas Dhu never fully embraced the 20th century. But, while its stills have never been fired up again, it has lived on as a museum run by Historic Scotland. Thousands of visitors have taken the tour and tried a drop of the malt in a blend called Roderick Dhu.

DALLAS DHU RARE MALTS 21-YEAR-OLD

SINGLE MALT: SPEYSIDE 61.9% ABV

Full-bodied, almost Highland character on the nose, with a trace of smoke and a robust, malty flavor.

CUTTY SARK 12-YEAR-OLD

CUTTY SARK 18-YEAR-OLD

**THE DALMORE
12-YEAR-OLD**

SINGLE MALT: HIGHLANDS
40% ABV

The well-established
12-year-old has moved
upmarket in its packaging
and price. It has a gentle
flavor of candied peel
and vanilla fudge.

**THE DALMORE
15-YEAR-OLD**

SINGLE MALT: HIGHLANDS
40% ABV

This has the characteristic
rich, fruity sherry
influence, but with rather
more spice—cloves,
cinnamon, and ginger.

THE DALMORE GRAN RESERVA   THE DALMORE 40-YEAR-OLD   THE DALMORE 1974   THE DALMORE 1263 KING ALEXANDER III

DALMORE

Alness, Ross-shire
www.thedalmore.com

While the Whyte & Mackay blend has a long association with Glasgow, its heart lies in the Highlands, in Dalmore on the banks of the Cromarty Firth. The distillery became part of Whyte & Mackay in 1960, and The Dalmore is now the company's flagship single malt.

The name Dalmore is a fusion of Norse and Gaelic and means "the big meadowland." Founded in 1839 by Alexander Matheson, the distillery stands facing the Black Isle, where some of Scotland's best barley is grown. With ample supplies of grain, plenty of local peat, and water from the Alness River, the site was well-chosen.

Matheson soon let others run the distillery for him, among them the Mackenzie brothers, who eventually bought Dalmore in 1891. They were actively involved for a century and today their family motto, "*I shine, not burn*", has been adopted by the brand. According to legend, the Mackenzie clan saved King Alexander III from being gored to death by a stag in 1263. In gratitude, the king granted the Mackenzies the right to bear the head of a 12-point stag on their coat of arms. This has become Dalmore's official crest.

For years, the only distillery bottling of Dalmore was a 12-year-old single malt, but in time a 21- and 30-year-old were added, together with Gran Reserva (formerly known as the Cigar Malt) in 2002. That year also saw the sale at auction of a 62-year-old expression for a record-beating £25,877. Since then, the core range has swelled alongside limited-release bottlings. Many of these have played on different cask maturation, a subject that clearly fascinates Whyte & Mackay's Master Blender, Richard Paterson.

THE DALMORE GRAN RESERVA

BLENDED MALT: HIGHLANDS 40% ABV
A blend of Dalmore malts. Subtly smoky, with traces of burned sugar.

THE DALMORE 40-YEAR-OLD

SINGLE MALT: HIGHLANDS 40% ABV
After years in American oak casks, this Dalmore was poured into second-fill Matusalem Oloroso sherry butts and then Amoroso sherry wood.

THE DALMORE 1974

SINGLE MALT: HIGHLANDS 45% ABV
Smooth and full-bodied, with sherry notes, bananas, dark chocolate orange, coffee, and walnuts, and a long finish.

THE DALMORE 1263 KING ALEXANDER III

SINGLE MALT: HIGHLANDS 40% ABV
To make this vatting of different-aged Dalmore malts, Richard Paterson used French wine barrels, sherry butts, port pipes, and bourbon casks.

All about...
Maturation

Whiskey consultant Dr. Jim Swan likens the change in the character of spirit during maturation to the transformation of a caterpillar into a butterfly: the new-make spirit is the caterpillar, the butterfly is the mature whiskey, the cask the chrysalis. The process of ageing in oak wood rounds off, fills out, and mellows the harsh characteristics of the new spirit and develops a huge range of additional aromas and tastes. However, advanced age is not necessarily a good thing: long maturation in an over-active cask can lead to the spirit being dominated by wood-derived flavors. Moreover, a long period in an exhausted cask will not mature the whiskey successfully, for the wood will be unable to transform undesirable and immature characteristics of the spirit.

NEW MAKE Fresh off the still, new make—it cannot be called "whiskey" until it has matured for 3 years (2 years in the US)—is crystal clear, fiery, and estery (acetone). It can be quite fruity and drinkable—some is even bottled—but it offers only the merest indication of how the mature whiskey will taste.

HOGSHEADS American whiskey is mostly matured in new oak, while Scotch is always matured in re-used casks. The most commonly used cask for maturing Scotch is an ex-bourbon cask, which is remade into what is known as a hogshead, or a "hoggie" *(see p69)*.

BUTTS Sherry butts and puncheons are also traditionally used in whisky maturation. They are usually made from European oak—though American oak is used as well—and have previously been used to hold sherry *(see p69)*.

DUNNAGE WAREHOUSE Cool, damp, earth-floored, and with casks racked three-high, dunnage warehouses are the traditional Scottish warehouse. During maturation in such a warehouse, the spirit's strength reduces but its volume stays high.

TIME IN CASK The length of maturation is the single most influential factor in the flavor of the mature whiskey. There is no optimum time—this depends on the history of the cask *(see pp68–9)*. Each is unique, and whiskeys of the same vintage and distillery are nevertheless still discernably distinct from one cask to the next.

RACKED WAREHOUSE Ubiquitous in North America but also common elsewhere (including Scotland), racked warehouses allow for the storage of casks up to 80-high. In the USA, the atmosphere can be warm—even hot—close to the roof, and dry. The volume of liquid in the cask reduces in these conditions, but the strength remains high.

TAKING SAMPLES Samples are drawn with a simple tubular instrument called a valinch. Some distilleries draw samples intermittently to monitor the progress of the spirit's maturation.

THE WHISKEY'S HUE The whiskey draws color from the wood: the more tannic the wood, the deeper the tint. European oak, being more tannic, gives an umbrageous, "polished mahogany" hue, while American oak (less tannic) tints the liquid golden. The more times a cask has been filled, the less color it will impart and the less impact it will have on the spirit it carries.

DEWAR'S 12-YEAR-OLD

DEWAR'S 18-YEAR-OLD

DALWHINNIE

Dalwhinnie, Inverness-shire
www.malts.com

Founded in 1897, Dalwhinnie used
to claim to be the highest distillery
in Scotland, at 1,073 ft (327 m)
above sea level, but it has since
been eclipsed by Braeval. Its other
claim to fame holds good, however:
with a mean annual temperature
of just 43°F (6°C), Dalwhinnie
remains the coldest distillery in
the country. In 1905 it became
Scotland's first American-owned
distillery, bought by the New York
company Cook & Bernheimer, and
the Stars and Stripes were raised
above the owners' warehouse in
Leith. Since 1926 it has been part
of DCL (now Diageo), supplying
blends such as Black & White.

DALWHINNIE 15-YEAR-OLD

SINGLE MALT: HIGHLANDS 43% ABV
Sweet, aromatic, and subtly infused
with smoke, this complex malt is thick
on the tongue.

DEANSTON

Deanston, Perthshire
www.burnstewartdistillers.com

Many distilleries evolved from
illicit stills on the farm, others
from breweries or malt mills, but
only Deanston is a former cotton
mill. It was founded in 1785 by
Richard Arkwright, one of the
great pioneers of the Industrial
Revolution. The conversion to
whisky-making took place in
1965, in a joint venture with
Brodie Hepburn, who also owned
Tuillibardine. Deanston was soon
producing a single malt—Old
Bannockburn was released in 1971.
Having spent most of the 1980s in
mothballs, the distillery was
bought by Burn Stewart, now
part of Trinidad-based CL
Financial, in 1990.

DEANSTON 12-YEAR-OLD

SINGLE MALT: HIGHLANDS 40% ABV
A relatively light-bodied Highland malt,
with a nutty flavor and hints of sherry.

DEWAR'S

www.dewars.com

When it was bought by Bacardi in
1988, the whole Dewar's enterprise
was reinvigorated. The brand was
repackaged, with considerable
investment made throughout the
business, from distilling to
warehousing and bottling. New
products were developed to augment
the standard White Label—one
of the biggest selling Scotch blends
in the US. First of these was a
12-year-old expression, Special
Reserve, followed by the 18-year-
old Founder's Reserve bottling,
and finally an ultra-premium non-
age style known as Signature.

The main single malt in the
Dewar's blends is Aberfeldy
(a visitor's center at the latter
distillery celebrates the firm's long
history), although the group's
other single malts—Aultmore,
Craigellachie, Royal Brackla and,
to a lesser extent, MacDuff
(see p83)—are also used.

Dewar's is not widely available
in the UK, but is a dominant
presence in the US. It is also
important in some European
markets and is developing a
following in Asia. Bacardi has
expanded global distribution
for Dewar's and greatly expanded
its profile through increased
advertising and marketing.
Standards of production have been
kept high, and some would say that
the blend quality has improved,
especially in the new products.

DEWAR'S 12-YEAR-OLD

BLEND 40% ABV
Sweetish and floral. A full and rich
blend, with honey and caramel, and
licorice notes in the long finish.

DEWAR'S 18-YEAR-OLD

BLEND 43% ABV
In the 18-year-old expression, the
Dewar's nose is more delicately
perfumed, with notes of pear and
lemon zest. Soft on the palate, but
drying, with a slightly spicy finish.

DEWAR'S WHITE LABEL
BLEND 40% ABV
Sweet and heathery on the nose. Medium-bodied, fresh, malty, and vaguely spicy, with a clean, slightly dry finish.

DEWAR'S SIGNATURE
BLEND 43% ABV
A limited-edition blend, with a heavy share of old Aberfeldy malt. Silky textured and mellow, with rich fruit and dark honey to the fore.

12-YEAR-OLD

15-YEAR-OLD

DIMPLE

Owner: Diageo

Launched to marked success in 1890, Haig's Dimple brand is today part of the Diageo stable. However, despite its long and distinguished history, it is rarely seen in the UK, and is sold mainly in Korea, Greece, Germany, the US, and Mexico.

John Haig began operations in 1627, when there are records of distilling on the family's farm in Stirlingshire. The family united through marriage with the powerful Stein family, also distillers on a prodigious scale, and eventually founded a large grain distillery at Cameronbridge, which is still in business today.

Dimple has always been a deluxe blend, noted for its distinctive packaging introduced by G. O. Haig in the 1890s. It stood out in particular for the wire net over the bottle, originally applied by hand and intended to prevent the cork popping out in warm climates or during sea transport. It was the first bottle of its type to be registered as a trademark in the United States, although this was done only in 1958.

Shortly after World War I, the British military leader Field Marshal Douglas Haig returned to head the family firm. Years spent dominating the UK followed thanks to strong but simple advertising ("Don't be vague, ask for Haig"). Today there are three expressions—at 12, 15, and 18 years old.

DIMPLE 12-YEAR-OLD

BLEND 40% ABV

Aromas of fudge, with woody notes. Hints of mint, and an initial richness on the palate, with candy apples and caramel; spiciness and dried fruits too.

DIMPLE 15-YEAR-OLD

BLEND 43% ABV

In this blend, there are hints of smoke, chocolate, and cocoa, completed by a long, rich finish.

DUFFTOWN

Dufftown, Keith, Banffshire
www.malts.com

This epicenter of Speyside whisky-making was bound to have a distillery named after it, although it took until 1896, by which point there were already five distilleries in town. Within a year, Dufftown was owned outright by Peter Mackenzie, who also owned Blair Athol. He was soon selling whisky to the blender Arthur Bell & Sons, who eventually bought Dufftown in 1933. Now part of Diageo, Dufftown continues to supply malt for the Bell's blend and, until recently, had produced little in the way of its own single malt.

SINGLETON OF DUFFTOWN

SINGLE MALT: SPEYSIDE 40% ABV

A sweet and eminently drinkable, introductory malt. If this recently launched 12-year-old takes off, there should be plenty available—it comes from one of Diageo's biggest distilleries.

EDRADOUR

Pitlochry, Perthshire
www.edradour.co.uk

With a production of just 6,600 gallons (90,000 liters) of pure alcohol a year, this picturesque distillery would have been one of many farm distilleries in the Perthshire hills when it was founded in 1825. Today it feels much more special, and a world apart from the large-scale malt distilleries of Speyside. It became part of Pernod Ricard in 1975 but, as the French group expanded to become a huge global player in the whisky industry, tiny Edradour began to look increasingly out of place. In 2002 it was finally sold to Andrew Symington, owner of independent bottler Signatory.

EDRADOUR 10-YEAR-OLD

SINGLE MALT: HIGHLANDS 40% ABV

Clean peppermint nose, with a trace of smoke. Richer, nutty flavors and a silky texture on the tongue.

Blends

A blended whisky (usually called simply a "blend") is a mixture of one or more single malts and one or more single grain whiskies. The advent of blending in the mid-19th century proved to be the making of the Scotch whisky industry. Drinkers rapidly adopted the lighter, cheaper, and more palatable blends over the then highly variable and strongly flavored "single whiskies" and Irish whiskey.

Today, more than 90 percent of all Scotch whisky is a blend, with brands such as Johnnie Walker, Chivas Regal, Dewar's, Ballantines, and Cutty Sark dominating world markets. In the UK, The Famous Grouse and Bells vie for top spot. Blending was made possible by the invention of the continuous still by Aeneas Coffey and by legislative changes that permitted blending under bond (that is, before the payment of tax on the alcohol). The growth in the popularity of blends was also greatly assisted by the collapse of France's brandy production, following the phylloxera infestation of European vineyards in the 1880s. As a result, whisky was increasingly drunk instead of brandy.

The first blends were produced in about 1853 by Andrew Usher, an Edinburgh whisky merchant. His Old Vatted Glenlivet is often cited as the first blend, and it achieved rapid popularity. Charles Mackinlay and W. P. Lowrie were also early pioneers, as were many well-known whisky houses in the industry today, such as Johnnie Walker, Dewar's, and Buchanan's.

The master blenders are important figures in the distilling business. They are responsible for the selection of the whiskies for a blend—a process described by Whyte & Mackay's Richard Paterson as "90 percent down to instinct and a 'feel-good' factor".

THE FAMOUS GROUSE 10-YEAR-OLD

THE FAMOUS GROUSE 15-YEAR-OLD

THE FAMOUS GROUSE 18-YEAR-OLD

THE FAMOUS GROUSE 30-YEAR-OLD

THE FAMOUS GROUSE

Owner: Edrington Group
www.thefamousgrouse.com

The bestselling blend in Scotland was created by the Victorian entrepreneur Matthew Gloag in 1896. At first, it was known simply as The Grouse Brand, but it evolved to become The Famous Grouse. The company was passed down through the generations until 1970, when death duties forced the family to sell out to Highland Distillers, today part of the powerful Edrington Group. Sales developed well-ahead of the market over the next 20 years and The Famous Grouse increased its visibility. Today, with sales of nearly 3 million cases a year, it is firmly established in the top ten global brands.

The Edrington Group also owns some of Scotland's finest single malt distilleries—Highland Park, Macallan, and Glenrothes among them. Naturally, there are high proportions of these fine whiskies in The Famous Grouse blend.

Since 2007 there has been a number of interesting initiatives. The Black Grouse was tested in Sweden, but is now available elsewhere. It contains more strongly flavored Islay malt in the blend. Snow Grouse is a grain whisky, sold initially in duty-free outlets. The company recommends it is drunk cold from the freezer, like vodka. A creamy mouth-coating effect results. In addition to its blends, The Famous Grouse also produces a range of blended malts, aged from 10 to 30 years.

THE FAMOUS GROUSE BLENDED MALT RANGE

BLENDED MALTS 43% ABV

Aged at 10-, 12-, 15-, 18-, and 30-years-old, each expression is a blend of malt whiskies from Edrington's distilleries. These are all fruity, spicy whiskies, with vanilla and more tannic, sherry influences increasingly marked through the age range. By the 18-year-old, the fruits are dried and rich and the flavor full, with Macallan and Highland Park malts taking main stage.

THE FAMOUS GROUSE FINEST

BLEND 40% ABV

Oak and sherry on the nose, well balanced with a citrus note. Easygoing, and full of bright Speyside fruit. Clean and medium-dry finish.

THE BLACK GROUSE

BLEND 40% ABV

Cream teas, peaches, apples, and jammy aromas. Soft peat and smoke notes on the palate (more so with water), plus vanilla, pepper, and spices, then a gentle finish.

GOLD RESERVE 12-YEAR-OLD

BLEND 40% ABV

Floral and oaky, with a fruity palate, and spicy taste. Rounded off by a long, medium-dry finish.

THE FAMOUS GROUSE FINEST

THE BLACK GROUSE

THE FAMOUS GROUSE GOLD RESERVE 12-YEAR-OLD

FETTERCAIRN

Fettercairn, Laurencekirk, Kincardineshire

While the northeastern flank of the Grampians is full of distilleries spilling down to the Spey, the southern slopes are now depleted. Fettercairn stands as their sole survivor. The distillery was established in 1824 as a farm distillery on the Fasque Estate, which was soon bought by Sir John Gladstone, father of the Victorian prime minister William Gladstone. It remained in family hands until 1939, since when it has been bought, sold, and mothballed several times. Today Fettercairn is part of Whyte & Mackay, but their main priorities are in the shape of Dalmore and Jura.

FETTERCAIRN 12-YEAR-OLD

SINGLE MALT: HIGHLANDS 40% ABV
A relatively closed nose gives way to a nutty toffee flavor in the mouth, which dries on the finish.

FINDLATER'S

Owner: Whyte & Mackay

The Mortlach single malt distillery on Speyside was established in 1823 by Alexander Findlater. In the 1960s things began to unwind, and Findlater Mackie Todd & Co. passed through a number of owners. First, it was bought by Bulmers, then it was sold to Beechams, followed by a management buy-out, which sold to the John Lewis retail chain. The firm is now the mail-order arm of Waitrose's Wine Department. The rights to the whisky brand were sold to Invergordon Distillers (today Whyte & Mackay), with whom they still rest.

FINDLATER'S FINEST

BLEND 40% ABV
Soft, mellow, and creamy textured, with a richness from the Speyside malts at the heart of the blend.

GIRVAN

Grangestone Industrial Estate, Girvan, Ayrshire

The distillery at Girvan was established in 1964 by William Grant & Sons in response to a perceived threat to their grain-whisky supplies. Today it includes a grain-whisky distilling complex, a gin distillery, and the recently opened Ailsa Bay single malt distillery. Girvan is rarely bottled by the proprietors as a single grain, but limited numbers of third-party bottlings are occasionally seen. Older expressions are generally dominated by the corn component and are greatly softened by age to provide a delicate and refined whisky of some subtlety and delightful complexity.

GIRVAN 1964

SINGLE GRAIN 43% ABV
Sweet vanilla nose and a deliciously creamy mouthfeel. Bittersweet caramel palate, with a note of ripe banana.

GLENALLACHIE

Aberlour, Banffshire

This modern gravity-flow distillery was established by a subsidiary of the giant Scottish & Newcastle Breweries in 1967. The architect was William Delmé-Evans, who had earlier designed and part-owned Tullibardine and Jura. With the capacity to produce 615,000 gallons (2.8 million liters) of pure alcohol a year, there should be plenty available for a single malt. And yet, so far there have only been a few independent bottlings and a 16-year-old cask strength expression from the distillery's current owners, Chivas Brothers (Pernod Ricard).

GLENALLACHIE 16-YEAR-OLD 1990

SINGLE MALT: SPEYSIDE 56.9% ABV
A dark, heavily sherried whisky matured in first-fill Oloroso casks, which can be hard to find.

GLENBURGIE

Glenburgie, Forres, Morayshire

Glenburgie began life as the Kilnflat Distillery in 1829. It was renamed Glenburgie in 1878 and, after various changes in ownership, became part of Canada's Hiram Walker in the 1930s. From then on, the primary role of this distillery was to supply whisky for Ballantine's Finest. Yet, as early as 1958, long before most of Speyside began thinking of single malt, Glenburgie released its own bottling under the name Glencraig. In 2004, its then owners, Allied Distillers, demonstrated their faith in Glenburgie by investing £4.3m. The distillery was completely rebuilt. Only the stills and milling equipment were kept.

GLENBURGIE 15-YEAR-OLD

SINGLE MALT: SPEYSIDE 46% ABV
On the fruitier side of Speyside, with a relatively luscious texture and notes of stewed plums.

GLENCADAM

Brechin, Angus
www.glencadamdistillery.co.uk

With the demise of Lochside in 2005, Glencadam became the only distillery left in Angus. It was founded in 1825 by George Cooper and, despite various changes in ownership, remained in private hands until 1954, when it became part of Hiram Walker and later Allied Distillers. While there was some safety in numbers on Speyside, Glencadam looked increasingly isolated. When it shut down in 2000—a victim of overproduction in the industry—its prospects looked bleak. But it slipped back into independent hands in 2003 when bought by Angus Dundee.

GLENCADAM 10-YEAR-OLD

SINGLE MALT: HIGHLANDS 46% ABV
The nose is fresh and grassy, with citrus notes and a trace of spicy oak. Rounded on the palate, citrusy and crisp. Well-balanced, with a long finish.

GLEN DEVERON

Macduff Distillery, Banff, Aberdeenshire

While the single malt is Glen Deveron (named after the water source—the Deveron River in eastern Speyside), the distillery is called Macduff. It was founded in 1962 by a consortium led by the Duff family. Much of the malt was used in blends, particularly William Lawson, whose owners bought the distillery in 1972. Since then it has changed hands twice, increased its number of stills to five, and now belongs to Bacardi. Various age statements are produced, and, just to confuse matters, there are occasional independent bottlings under the name Macduff.

GLEN DEVERON 10-YEAR-OLD

SINGLE MALT: HIGHLANDS 40% ABV
Although it is described as a "Pure Highland Single Malt" on the bottle's label, in style this is a classic, clean, gentle Speyside whisky.

GLENDRONACH

Forgue, Huntly, Aberdeenshire

This distillery is the spiritual sister to Ardmore, and fellow contributor to the Teacher's blend. Although William Teacher & Sons did not buy Glendronach until 1960, the firm had sourced Glendronach malts for years. After Teacher's was swallowed up by Allied Distillers, Glendronach was picked, in 1991, to be one of the "Caledonian Malts"—the company's belated riposte to UDV's Classic Malts. A decade later, after five years in mothballs, the distillery re-opened. By that time the single malts had become less peaty and were matured in American oak ex-bourbon casks rather than sherry casks.

GLENDRONACH 12-YEAR-OLD

SINGLE MALT: SPEYSIDE 40% ABV
This dense, heavily sherried malt replaced the 15-year-old and is best suited to after-dinner sipping.

The landscape of Islay is low-lying and boggy, with plenty of peaty earth and peaty rivulets. Like much of Scotland's coastal peat, Islay's has a slightly sandy texture and sweet, citrus, and maritime characteristics from the mix of sphagnum moss and bog myrtle that produced it.

GLENFARCLAS 10-YEAR-OLD

GLENFARCLAS 105

GLENFARCLAS 12-YEAR-OLD

GLENFARCLAS 15-YEAR-OLD

GLENFARCLAS 21-YEAR-OLD

GLENFARCLAS 25-YEAR-OLD

GLENFARCLAS 30-YEAR-OLD

GLENFARCLAS

Ballindalloch, Banffshire
www.glenfarclas.co.uk

The oldest family-owned distillery in Scotland has belonged to the Grants since 1865, when John Grant and son George took over the tenancy of Rechlarich farm, near Ballindalloch. The small distillery on site was immediately sublet to John Smith, of Glenlivet. Five years later, when Smith left to set up Cragganmore, it was back with the Grants. It gradually assumed importance in the family business, and went on to become the Glenfarclas-Glenlivet Distillery Company in partnership with the Pattison Brothers of Leith, whose bankruptcy at the end of the 19th century almost dragged the distillery down with it.

Surrounded by 10 large dunnage warehouses, Glenfarclas is no boutique distillery. It boasts a modern mill and six stills. It also claims to be the first malt distillery to have offered a cask strength expression—Glenfarclas 105 was released in 1968. At the time, the industry doubted that single malts, let alone something that was 60 percent alcohol, would catch on.

Recently, Glenfarclas offered 10 vintage expressions, ranging from 1952 to 1989. The house style is a robust, outdoors take on Speyside, with a greater affiliation to sherry butts than bourbon barrels.

GLENFARCLAS 10-YEAR-OLD

SINGLE MALT: SPEYSIDE 40% ABV
This rich, malty whisky with a smoky, aromatic nose is a nod to the Highlands.

GLENFARCLAS 105

SINGLE MALT: SPEYSIDE 60% ABV
A cask strength 10-year-old. Water dampens the fiery edge and brings out a sweet, nutty-spicy character.

GLENFARCLAS 12-YEAR-OLD

SINGLE MALT: SPEYSIDE 43% ABV
A distinct sherry nose, with spicy flavors of cinnamon and stewed fruit.

GLENFARCLAS 15-YEAR-OLD

SINGLE MALT: SPEYSIDE 46% ABV
Described by writer Dave Broom as "George Melly in a glass", for its fruity, over-the-top exuberance. It is intensely perfumed, sherried, and powerful.

GLENFARCLAS 21-YEAR-OLD

SINGLE MALT: SPEYSIDE 43% ABV
A ripe, truffly nose. There is plenty of sherry influence on this earthy, leathery malt.

GLENFARCLAS 25-YEAR-OLD

SINGLE MALT: SPEYSIDE 43% ABV
A fruity, toffee-scented whisky with a smooth, spicy character and a taste of ginger and burned sugar.

GLENFARCLAS 30-YEAR-OLD

SINGLE MALT: SPEYSIDE 43% ABV
The wood is more obvious here: oaky, spicy, and nutty. Slight peatiness in the long finish.

All about…
Independent Bottlers

Whiskey is either bottled by the brand owner (proprietary bottlings) or by other companies, clubs, or individuals—these are known as independent bottlings. The former are subject to rigorous quality controls; the latter may be more variable, although the "indies" mentioned here all have high reputations for the quality of their goods. Proprietors also have huge stocks to draw from, while independents select and buy individual casks from distilleries or brokers, and sometimes have their own casks filled by distillers.

GORDON & MACPHAIL Established in Elgin in 1895, Gordon & MacPhail has been bottling single malts for longer than any other company. The business is still family owned and managed, and still operates from the original shop (see p95). The Connoisseur's Choice range was launched in 1956, and the company currently offers around 300 bottlings.

SIGNATORY Based in Leith, the port of Edinburgh, and founded in 1998 by Andrew and Brian Symington, Signatory lists some 50 single malts from operating, mothballed, and closed distilleries, which they bottle at natural strength and at 43% ABV. Andrew Symington bought Edradour Distillery in 2002.

ADELPHI The original Adelphi Distillery was in Glasgow, and ceased production in 1902. Ninety years later the name was revived by the great-grandson of the last owner, to select and bottle around 50 top-quality single-cask malt whiskies each year.

CONNOISSEURS CHOICE

THESE WHISKIES ARE KNOWN AS THE PREMIER CRU OF SINGLE MALT SCOTCH. THEY ARE ELEGANT, FRUITY MALTS WHICH USUALLY HAVE A DRYING SMOKINESS.

Speyside
Single Malt Scotch Whisky

DISTILLED AT
BALMENACH
DISTILLERY
Proprietors: John Crabbie & Co. Ltd.

DISTILLED
1990

CASK STRENGTH
COLLECTION

HIGHLAND SINGLE MALT SCOTCH WHISKY

BEN NEVIS
1992
AGED 15 YEARS

Distilled on: 03/07/1992
Bottled on: 27/03/2008
Matured in a Sherry Butt
Cask No: 2304
Bottle No: 605 of 738
NATURAL COLOUR

70cl   56.6%vol

Casks individually selected and bottled by
Signatory Vintage Scotch Whisky Co. Ltd Edinburgh EH6 5PY
PRODUCT OF SCOTLAND

ADELPHI
Selection
SINGLE MALT SCOTCH WHISKY

Single Cask

NUMBER ONE

番

DRINKS COMPANY

Distilled at

Hanyu Distillery

Distilled 1990
Bottled 2007
Cask No .... #9511
Number of bottles 374bts
Cask Type... Bourbon hogshead,
finished in Japanese oak

Japanese Single Malt Whisky
www.onedrinks.co.uk

Alc/vol
55.5%

シングルカスクウイスキー

CADENHEAD Established in Aberdeen in 1842, Cadenhead is Scotland's oldest firm of independent bottlers. In 1972, the business was bought by J. & A. Mitchell, owners of Springbank Distillery, and Cadenhead is now based in Campbeltown, with outlets in Edinburgh and London.

CADENHEAD'S

SINGLE MALT SCOTCH WHISKY

from

ALT-A-BHAINNE

DISTILLERY

DISTILLED 1980   CASK NO. 100027

BOTTLED BY WILLIAM CADENHEAD LTD. 18 GOLDEN SQUARE, ABERDEEN

CASK STRENGTH

70cl   Bottle No.   60.5% Vol.

NUMBER ONE DRINKS COMPANY This company was founded in 2006 to select and bottle casks of distinguished Japanese single malt whiskey, and to distribute them throughout Europe via specialist retailers and bars.

MURRAY MCDAVID Mark Reynier, owner since 2000 of Bruichladdich Distillery and formerly a wine merchant in London, founded Murray McDavid in 1995. The firm offers a narrow, highly selective range, with around 25 expressions available at any one time.

MURRAY McDAVID

MISSION

· SELECTION NUMBER TWO ·

UNIQUE BOTTLING OF

CAPERDONICH

1968

AGED IN OAK CASKS FOR 35 YEARS

70CL 0000013   OF 600   46%VOL

DUNCAN TAYLOR The company has been filling its own casks and laying down whisky since the 1960s. When Euan Shand bought the company and its stocks in 2001, he acquired one of the world's largest privately held collections of rare Scotch casks.

www.dtscotch.com

DUNCAN TAYLOR

CASK STRENGTH SINGLE GRAIN
DISTILLED AT

Duncan Taylor & Co.Ltd
Scotland AB54 8JU

PORT DUNDAS

Grain   SCOTCH WHISKY
Produced and bottled in Scotland AB54 8JU

volume	alc/vol
700ml	54.5%
cask no.	
128321	
bottle no.	
98 /461	
date distilled	date bottled
01.1973	12.2007

AGED 34 YEARS

Matured in Oak Casks

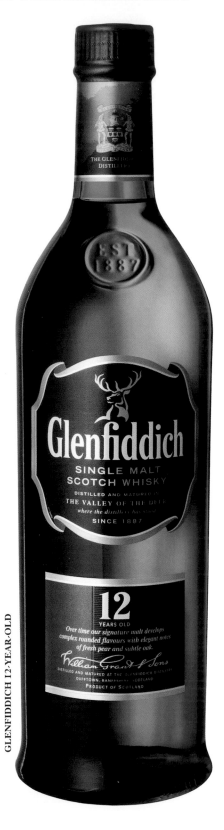

GLENFIDDICH 12-YEAR-OLD

GLENFIDDICH

Dufftown, Keith, Banffshire
www.glenfiddich.com

It was no impulsive decision when William Grant decided to abandon a 16-year career at Mortlach Distillery in 1886 to go it alone. With a wife and nine children to support on a salary of £100 a year, plus the £7 he received as the precentor of the Free Church of Dufftown, he had to scrimp and save until he raised the funds to start Glenfiddich. Using stones from the bed of the Fiddich River, and second-hand stills from neighboring Cardhu, he was able to produce his first spirit on Christmas Day 1887. From these humble beginnings, Glenfiddich has grown into the biggest malt distillery in the world.

In 1899 the distillery almost collapsed when its biggest customer, Pattison Brothers of Leith, went bankrupt. The fact that it survived engendered a spirit of self-reliance in William Grant & Sons. By the time William Grant died in 1923, his firm was already producing its own blends, which were sold as far afield as Australia and Canada. In the same spirit, the company pioneered today's market for single malts in the 1960s. Such whiskies existed, but there was no big brand before Glenfiddich.

To meet demand, Glenfiddich underwent a dramatic expansion in 1974, when 16 new stills were added. Today it has no fewer than 29 stills and a capacity of 2.2 million gallons (10 million liters) of pure alcohol a year. In time this will be matched by Diageo's new

Roseisle Distillery, near Elgin, although the main purpose of this is believed to be supplying malt for the likes of Johnnie Walker. For the moment, Glenfiddich's pole position as the most popular malt whisky in the world looks secure.

The Glenfiddich range includes expressions from a soft 12-year-old up to a luscious, creamy 30-year-old with a trace of ginger.

GLENFIDDICH 12-YEAR-OLD

SINGLE MALT: SPEYSIDE 40% ABV

A gentle aperitif-style whisky with a malty, grassy flavor and a little vanilla sweetness. Quite soft.

GLENFIDDICH 15-YEAR-OLD SOLERA RESERVE

SINGLE MALT: SPEYSIDE 40% ABV

After 15 years in American oak, this is finished off in Spanish casks for an extra-soft layer of fresh fruit and spice.

GLENFIDDICH 18-YEAR-OLD SOLERA RESERVE

SINGLE MALT: SPEYSIDE 40% ABV

A big step up from the 12-year-old, with ripe tropical fruit flavors, a pleasant oaky sweetness, and a trace of sherry.

GLENFIDDICH 21-YEAR-OLD CARIBBEAN RUM CASK

SINGLE MALT: SPEYSIDE 40% ABV

Rich, toffee-flavored malt with flavors of bananas, caramel, spice, and chocolate orange.

GLENFIDDICH 15-YEAR-OLD SOLERA RESERVE

GLENFIDDICH 18-YEAR-OLD SOLERA RESERVE

GLENFIDDICH 21-YEAR-OLD CARIBBEAN RUM CASK

GLEN ELGIN 12-YEAR-OLD

GLEN ELGIN 16-YEAR-OLD

GLEN GARIOCH HIGHLAND TRADITION

GLENDULLAN

Dufftown, Keith, Banffshire
www.malts.com

There were already six distilleries
in Dufftown when the Aberdeen-
based blenders William Williams &
Sons decided to build a seventh.
Work on Glendullan began in 1897,
and within five years its whisky
had secured a royal warrant from
the new king, Edward VII. The
blend has been in almost continual
production ever since, and for years
was a key filling in the deluxe Old
Parr blend. In the 1960s, a modern
distillery was erected next door,
and for the following 20 years the
two sides of Glendullan worked in
tandem. Today, the modern
distillery carries on alone.

GLENDULLAN FLORA & FAUNA
12-YEAR-OLD

SINGLE MALT: SPEYSIDE 43% ABV
A crisp, aperitif-style malt with a
sweeter palate than you would expect.

GLEN ELGIN

Longmorn, Morayshire
www.malts.com

Although Cragganmore's position
as the Speyside among the original
Classic Malts is well-deserved,
Glen Elgin must have been a strong
contender. It has always been
considered a top-rated malt by
blenders, and has long been a key
component of White Horse.

The distillery was founded in
1898 by James Carle and William
Simpson, a former manager of
Glenfarclas, when demand for
Speyside malt from the blenders
was at its peak. It was the last
distillery to be built on Speyside
for 60 years. Within two years,
however, the speculative boom had
turned to bust and the industry
entered a prolonged slump.

During its first three decades,
production at Glen Elgin was
intermittent, as the distillery passed
from one owner to the next. Since
1930, Glen Elgin has been part of

what is now Diageo. In the 1960s
the number of stills was increased
from two to six. The old worm
tubs, which add weight and body
to the new make, were retained.
In 1977 a first distillery bottling
of Glen Elgin was released. The
stills at Glen Elgin were fired up
again in May 1990, only to go cold
five months later.

GLEN ELGIN 12-YEAR-OLD

SINGLE MALT: SPEYSIDE 43% ABV
This is one of the most floral and
perfumed Speyside malts, with a nutty,
honey-blossom aroma and a balanced
flavor that goes from sweet to dry.

GLEN ELGIN 16-YEAR-OLD

SINGLE MALT: SPEYSIDE 58.5% ABV
A recent limited edition, the 16-year-
old is a non chill-filtered, cask-strength
malt with a deep mahogany color and a
ripe, fruitcake flavor from its years in
European oak.

GLEN GARIOCH

Oldmeldrum, Inverurie, Aberdeenshire
www.glengarioch.com

Three centuries old and still going
strong—quite an achievement for
this small Aberdeenshire distillery
on the road between Banff and
Aberdeen. It was founded by
Thomas Simpson in 1798, yet the
first distillery bottling of Glen
Garioch (pronounced *glen geerie*)
as a single malt was not until 1972.
It survived the long years in
between thanks to its popularity
among blenders.

One such was William Sanderson
of Aberdeen, who came across
Glen Garioch when it belonged to
a firm of blenders in Leith. In
1886 he bought a half share in the
distillery, and by 1921 his son,
together with other investors, had
full control of the business. After
numerous changes in ownership
since, and extended periods of
lying idle, Glen Garioch is now
part of Morrison Bowmore, which

GLEN GARIOCH 15-YEAR-OLD

GLEN GARIOCH 21-YEAR-OLD

bottles most, if not all of, the distillery's limited production as a single malt in a range of age statements, from 8 to 21 years old.

GLEN GARIOCH HIGHLAND TRADITION

SINGLE MALT : HIGHLANDS 40% ABV

This duty-free exclusive is a lighter, more grassy style of malt with a slight prickle on the nose and a medium body that finishes dry.

GLEN GARIOCH 15-YEAR-OLD

SINGLE MALT: HIGHLANDS 43% ABV

This has a floral, heathery nose with notes of Lapsang tea. On the palate it has a malty flavor that dries to a spicy finish.

GLEN GARIOCH 21-YEAR-OLD

SINGLE MALT: HIGHLANDS 43% ABV

A smooth, well-rounded malt with a luscious syrupy texture and a mellow, ripe fruit character that shows some influence from sherry casks.

GLENGLASSAUGH

Portsoy, Banffshire
www.glenglassaugh.com

Glenglassaugh was founded by Aberdeenshire entrepreneur James Moir in the 1870s at a cost of £10,000. Although it was also renovated and expanded, it was sold for only £5,000 more 20 years later, when it was bought by the blender Robertson & Baxter, which evolved into the Edrington Group. The distillery has had periodic bursts of production, but has spent much of its life in mothballs. When its stills went cold before the millennium, many feared that Glenglassaugh was doomed. It was rescued by a private consortium, however, and was reopened in November 2008. The 21-year-old is increasingly rare but, since reopening, the distillery has released a 21-year-old—a richly sherried malt, with a hint of vanilla on the nose, and a menthol note on the palate.

Whisky Tour: Speyside

Speyside boasts the greatest concentration of distilleries in the world and thus is a "must see" for all whisky lovers. The concept of the distillery tour was also pioneered here, when William Grant & Sons first opened Glenfiddich to the public in 1969. Its competitors laughed, but soon opened their own centers. Today, Speyside hosts two whisky festivals each year, in May and September, with special events and tastings. Discount bus and taxi travel is available during festival times. Two accommodation options favored by whisky fans are the Highlander Inn in Craigellachie and The Mash Tun in Aberlour.

SCOTLAND

TOUR STATISTICS

DAYS: 3	LENGTH: 90 miles (145 km)		DISTILLERIES: 5
TRAVEL: Car, or bus and taxi		REGION: Banffshire and Moray, Scotland	

DAY 1: GLENFIDDICH, THE BALVENIE

1 Begin at Dufftown's **Glenfiddich**, the ultimate home of whisky tourism. The makers of the world's most popular single malt offer a free tour or, like a number of their competitors, an option with extended tastings at extra cost. You need to pre-book for the extended tour, which lasts for two and a half hours. *(www.glenfiddich.com)*

GLENFIDDICH STILLS

THE BALVENIE

2 After lunch at the Glenfiddich café, you can stroll down the hill to sister distillery **The Balvenie** *(www.thebalvenie. com)*. The three-hour guided tour here, which must also be pre-booked, includes the floor maltings and tastings of exclusive vintages. You can also bottle your own whisky straight from the cask. If time permits after the tour, head to Dufftown's well-stocked Whisky Shop.

FORRES

NAIRN

MILL BUIE

CÀRN NA LÒINE

GRANTOWN-ON-SPEY **7**

NETHY BRIDGE

BOAT OF GARTEN

AVIEMORE

CAIRNGORMS NATIONAL PARK

DAY 2: COOPERAGE, ABERLOUR, THE MACALLAN, CARDHU

3 Start the day at the Speyside **Cooperage**. There you can watch a film about cask-making and see the the coopers at work from a viewing gallery. *(www.speysidecooperage.co.uk)*

4 **Aberlour** Distillery is the next stop and, again, pre-booking is advisable. The tour culminates in a tasting and the chance to bottle your own. *(www.aberlour.com/spiritofaberlour)*

ABERLOUR CASKS

5 Head over the Spey, pausing to admire the Thomas Telford bridge (1812), then take the B9102 to **The Macallan**. Its "Precious Tour" is the one to pre-book for its tutored nosing and tasting of a range of Macallan whiskies. *(www.themacallan.com)*

6 **Cardhu** Distillery is further along the B9102, which you can visit without pre-booking. The malt made here is used in Johnnie Walker blends. *(www.discovering-distilleries.com/cardhu)*

DAY 3: GRANTOWN-ON-SPEY, THE WHISKY CASTLE, THE GLENLIVET, GORDON & MACPHAIL

7 **Grantown-on-Spey** is the gateway to the Cairngorms National Park. It's a handy place to pick up provisions, and has a good little whisky shop on the High Street called the Wee Spey Dram.

8 Head east from Grantown to get to Tomintoul, where **The Whisky Castle** shop has an excellent selection of Scotch malts. *(www.whiskycastle.com)*

9 Pre-register on **The Glenlivet** website as a "Guardian" to gain access to a secret room where you can enjoy some unusual drams. The free tour is a good introduction to the oldest legal distillery in Speyside; better still is its three-day Whisky School. *(www.theglenlivet.com)*

10 The final stop on this tour is a place of pilgrimage for serious whisky fans: the **Gordon & MacPhail** shop in Elgin. Here you'll find all your favorites, some rare bottles, and exceptional value in G&M's own bottlings from their vast stock of whiskies laid down over many years. *(www.gordonandmacphail.com)*

SHOP SIGN

THE WHISKY CASTLE

GORDON & MACPHAIL

Map labels

LOSSIEMOUTH

FINISH

10 GORDON & MACPHAIL

MORAY

THE MACALLAN

CRAIGELLACHIE

5

B9102

6 CARDHU

3 SPEYSIDE COOPERAGE

2 THE BALVENIE

1 GLENFIDDICH

4 ABERLOUR

DUFFTOWN

START

BANFFSHIRE

9 THE GLENLIVET

B9008

CAIRNGORMS NATIONAL PARK

8 THE WHISKY CASTLE

A939

A96

A98

A96

A941

A95

A95

A941

A920

miles
0   5

0   5
kilometers

GLENGOYNE 12-YEAR-OLD CASK STRENGTH

GLENGOYNE 10-YEAR-OLD

GLENGOYNE 17-YEAR-OLD

GLENGOYNE 21-YEAR-OLD

GLENGOYNE

Drumgoyne, Stirlingshire
www.glengoyne.com

The Campsie Fells were once a hotbed of whisky smuggling. Before the Excise Act of 1823, there were at least 18 illicit distillers in this corner of Stirlingshire. Among them was probably George Connell, who finally took out a license for his Burnfoot Distillery in 1833. It went on to become Glenguin and eventually Glengoyne in 1905.

By then the distillery was owned by the blending house of Lang Brothers, who were bought out in the 1960s by Robertson & Baxter, now the Edrington Group. In 2001 it released a novel expression of Glengoyne, involving the first ever use of Scottish oak casks. Two years later, the distillery was sold to the blender and bottler Ian MacLeod & Co. The number of single malts has grown dramatically and includes single cask bottlings alongside the core range.

GLENGOYNE 12-YEAR-OLD CASK STRENGTH

SINGLE MALT: HIGHLANDS 57.2% ABV
Non chill-filtered and bottled at cask strength, this 12-year-old is the purest representation of the distillery. Lightly sweet nose, with notes of heather, pear drops, and marzipan. Malty, cereal palate, seasoned with black pepper.

GLENGOYNE 10-YEAR-OLD

SINGLE MALT: HIGHLANDS 40% ABV
This unpeated whisky has a clean, grassy aroma, with a nutty sweetness that comes through on the palate.

GLENGOYNE 17-YEAR-OLD

SINGLE MALT: HIGHLANDS 43% ABV
A rich, sherried nose with butterscotch and molasses flavors, with some citrus notes.

GLENGOYNE 21-YEAR-OLD

SINGLE MALT: HIGHLANDS 43% ABV
Now matured entirely in first-fill sherry casks, this is a rich, after-dinner malt, with notes of brandy butter, cinnamon, and sweet spice.

The Spey gives its name to Scotland's best-known and most productive whisky region, Speyside. Winter is traditionally the season for whisky-making here.

GLEN GRANT

Rothes, Morayshire
www.glengrant.com

There is something solid and baronial about the Glen Grant Distillery on Speyside. It was the first of the five distilleries in the town of Rothes, built in 1840 from red sandstone, with a pair of pepperpot turrets.

It was founded by James Grant, a lawyer in Elgin, and his brother, John, a grain merchant who is said to have learned about whisky-making from supplying all the illicit distillers in the area.

It was a very good site for a distillery, with the Glen Grant burn supplying water for the mash and to power the machinery. There were plentiful supplies of grain too, from the barley fields of nearby Moray. And, from 1858, when the first train steamed into Rothes, there was also the railway to carry off the filled casks and bring back the empties.

In 1872, James Grant's son took over the business. Known to all as "The Major," permanently clad in tweed and with a bristling walrus mustache, he was very much the quintessential Victorian gent. After dining, he would take guests to a narrow ravine in the garden and unlock a safe secreted in the rock to produce a tray of glasses and a bottle of Glen Grant. For anyone requiring water, they had only to dip their glass into the fast-flowing waters of the nearby stream.

The distillery remained in family hands until 1977 when it was sold to Seagrams. Soon afterward, an Italian visitor persuaded the owners to sell him some cases of Glen Grant 5-year-old, which went on to become Italy's biggest-selling brand of Scotch. Having passed through the hands of Pernod Ricard in 2001–2006, it is now with the Italian Campari group. Though it receives little attention at home, it is one of the top five bestselling malts in the world.

GLEN GRANT SINGLE MALT

SINGLE MALT: SPEYSIDE 40% ABV
Light, spirity, and floral on the nose. Initially dry on the palate, but softer, nut flavors develop. A herby finish rounds off this aperitif-style whisky.

GLEN GRANT 10-YEAR-OLD

SINGLE MALT: SPEYSIDE 40% ABV
A relatively dry nose with the scent of orchard fruit. Light to medium body with a cereal, nutty flavor.

GLEN GRANT 1965

SINGLE MALT: SPEYSIDE 40% ABV
This bottling by Gordon & MacPhail is now hard to find. It has an intense aroma of sherry wood with notes of fig and toffee. The flavor boasts fruitcake and ginger.

GLEN KEITH

Keith, Banffshire

Having bought Strathisla in 1950, Seagram built Glen Keith on the site of an old grain mill seven years later. Both are in Keith and were part of Seagram's whisky arm, Chivas Brothers (now part of Pernod Ricard). Both also shared a simple function—to supply the company's bestselling brands. Glen Keith began life using triple distillation and later pioneered the use of computers in its whisky-making at a time when some distilleries had only recently joined the national power grid.

Glen Keith was mothballed in 2000 and, while independent bottlings are available, its 10-year-old is increasingly hard to find.

GLEN KEITH 10-YEAR-OLD

SINGLE MALT: SPEYSIDE 43% ABV
This relatively rare official bottling is a mix of grassy Speyside aromas and some toffee sweetness on the tongue.

GLENKINCHIE 20-YEAR-OLD

GLENKINCHIE DISTILLERS EDITION 1991

GLENKINCHIE

Pencaitland, Tranent, East Lothian
www.malts.com

Robert Burns described the rolling farmland south of Edinburgh as "the most glorious corn [grain] country I have ever seen", and it was here at Pencaitland that John and George Rate founded Glenkinchie in 1825. It was originally the Milton Distillery and struggled in its early years, spending much of the second half of the 19th century as a saw mill. In 1881 it was rescued by an Edinburgh brewer and a couple of wine merchants, who transformed it into a highly efficient whisky-making machine, with everything from mechanical rakes in the mash tun to its own railway siding. The grain came from the surrounding fields, and the draff was fed to the Aberdeen Angus cattle on site.

In modern times the most important date was probably 1988, when the Glenkinchie 10-Year-Old was picked as one of the original Classic Malts by Diageo. New expressions have recently been added and the 10 has been replaced by a 12-year-old.

GLENKINCHIE 12-YEAR-OLD

SINGLE MALT: LOWLANDS 43% ABV
The nose reveals a sweet, grassy aroma with a faint wisp of smoke. In the mouth it has a firm, cereal flavor and a touch of spice at the end.

GLENKINCHIE 20-YEAR-OLD

SINGLE MALT: LOWLANDS 58.4% ABV
Aged in bourbon casks and then re-racked into brandy barrels, the 20-year-old has a luscious, mouth-coating texture and plenty of spicy, stewed fruit flavors.

GLENKINCHIE DISTILLERS EDITION 1991

SINGLE MALT: LOWLANDS 43% ABV
The malty flavor of tea cookies is well balanced by the drier, oaky flavors from the wood, and these linger to a long, slow finish.

THE GLENLIVET XXV
SINGLE MALT: SPEYSIDE 43% ABV
This 25-year-old is a
sumptuous after-dinner malt
of real complexity, with
flavors of candied orange peel
and raisins and an intense
nutty, spicy character.

**THE GLENLIVET
12-YEAR-OLD**
SINGLE MALT: SPEYSIDE 40% ABV
A citrusy, heathery whisky
with a scent of fresh wood and
soft fruit, a light to medium
body, and a dry, clean finish.

THE GLENLIVET 15-YEAR-OLD

THE GLENLIVET 18-YEAR-OLD

THE GLENLIVET 21-YEAR-OLD

GLENLIVET

Ballindalloch, Banffshire
www.theglenlivet.com

In the early 19th century, before the Excise Act lured so many distillers to come in from the cold and take out a license, Glen Livet was a one-industry glen dedicated to making moonshine after the harvest. It was said that there were at least 200 illicit stills in this small corner of Speyside. Doubtless among them was George Smith, who made whisky on the side at his Upper Drummin farm. In 1824 he established Glenlivet as a licensed distillery there. But breaking ranks with the smuggling fraternity meant that, from then on, Smith had to carry hair-trigger revolvers for his protection.

Smith began supplying Andrew Usher in Edinburgh, who bottled a prototype blend, Old Vatted Glenlivet, in 1853. As blended Scotch took off toward the end of the 19th century, demand for "Glenlivet-style" malts to feed the blends also soared. This encouraged distillers all down the Spey to bolt the magic name "Glenlivet" to their distillery and hope the blenders beat a path to their door.

Glenlivet's current owner—the French giant Pernod Ricard, who bought it from Seagram in 2001, along with Chivas Regal and a host of other whisky brands and distilleries—is determined to restore its good name: although always strong in the US, Glenlivet had been somewhat neglected in other markets.

The core range of malts has been dusted down, expanded, and repackaged, while new expressions such as Nadurra Cask Strength Glenlivet have been launched in duty-free markets. Having created more of a buzz around the distillery, Pernod's whisky division, Chivas Brothers, now seems eager to seize poll position among top-selling malts. In 2008 it announced plans to add a new mash tun, six stills, and eight washbacks. This will boost capacity to 2.2 million gallons (10 million liters) at Glenlivet, the same as Glenfiddich.

THE GLENLIVET FRENCH OAK RESERVE 15-YEAR-OLD

SINGLE MALT: SPEYSIDE 40% ABV
A smoother, richer take on the 12-year-old, with a malty, strawberries-and-cream flavor laced with a little spice.

THE GLENLIVET 18-YEAR-OLD

SINGLE MALT: SPEYSIDE 43% ABV
Far more depth and character than the standard 12-year-old. Honeyed, fragrant, and dries to a long, nutty finish.

THE GLENLIVET ARCHIVE 21-YEAR-OLD

SINGLE MALT: SPEYSIDE 43% ABV
A distinctly smooth and richly fruity whisky. Malty, toasty flavors, an almond sweetness, and a touch of fresh orange. A long, slightly smoky finish.

GLENLOSSIE

Elgin, Morayshire
www.malts.com

Glenlossie was built in 1876 by John Duff, the former manager of Glendronach. For a century it was a single entity, and part of DCL from 1919. Its role was simply to pump out malt whisky for blends. Yet, within the industry, the quality of Glenlossie was appreciated and it was one of only a dozen to be designated "top class." It now shares its site with Mannochmore, a new distillery built in 1971.

Glenlossie has produced a 10-year-old since 1990, although there have been a fair number of independent bottlings from Gordon & MacPhail among others.

GLENLOSSIE FLORA & FAUNA 10-YEAR-OLD

SINGLE MALT: SPEYSIDE 43% ABV
Grassy, heathery, with a smooth, mouth-coating texture and a long spicy finish.

GLENMORANGIE

Tain, Ross-shire
www.glenmorangie.com

The "Glen of Tranquillity," to use the single malt's old slogan, has been bustling with activity since the French luxury goods group LVMH bought Glenmorangie for £300m in 2004. The distillery started life as an old farm distillery, but was taken over and licensed in 1843 by William Matheson, who was already involved with Balblair. It remained a rustic operation for years. In the 1880s Alfred Barnard described Glenmorangie as "the most ancient and primitive we have seen" and "almost in ruins".

Outside investors were brought in just in time and the distillery was rebuilt. For much of the 20th century its key role was to supply malt for blends such as Highland Queen and James Martin's. In the 1970s, though, Glenmorangie started laying down casks for a 10-year-old single malt. In hindsight,

it was the best decision the company ever took—by the late 1990s, this had become the best-selling single malt in Scotland. Glenmorangie's stills are tall and thin, and produce a light, very pure spirit. The real skill of the distillery has been in the way it has combined this elegant spirit with wood—indeed, Glenmorangie has been a pioneer of wood finishes. After endless experiments with increasingly exotic barrels, it became expert in how a particular cask could twist and refocus a mature malt before bottling.

GLENMORANGIE ORIGINAL

SINGLE MALT: HIGHLANDS 40% ABV
This is the ever-popular 10-year-old, dressed up in new packaging. It has honeyed flavors with a hint of almonds.

GLENMORANGIE 18-YEAR-OLD

SINGLE MALT: HIGHLANDS 43% ABV
A rich, well-rounded whisky, with dried fruit notes and a distinctive nuttiness from its finishing in sherry butts.

GLENMORANGIE 25-YEAR-OLD

SINGLE MALT: HIGHLANDS 43% ABV
Packed with flavor, this produces dried fruit, berries, chocolate, and spice. An intense and complex whisky.

GLENMORANGIE NECTAR D'OR

SINGLE MALT: HIGHLANDS 46% ABV
Here, the Glenmorangie honeyed floral character is given a twist of spice and lemon tart from Sauternes casks.

GLENMORANGIE QUINTA RUBAN

SINGLE MALT: HIGHLANDS 46% ABV
The slight reddish-amber tint and Portuguese name are a clue: this malt is finished off in port pipes to give it a fruity, mint-chocolate character.

GLENMORANGIE LASANTA

SINGLE MALT: HIGHLANDS 46% ABV
The facelift and fancy Latin name were not the only changes Glenmorangie made to its finely balanced sherry finish: it is now bottled non chill-filtered.

GLENMORANGIE NECTAR D'OR

GLENMORANGIE QUINTA RUBAN

GLENMORANGIE LASANTA

GLEN MORAY 12-YEAR-OLD

GLEN MORAY CLASSIC

GLEN MORAY 16-YEAR-OLD

GLEN MORAY

Bruceland Road, Elgin
www.glenmoray.com

The trouble with being the little brother of two far more famous siblings is that you are liable to feel unloved at times. Being in the same family as Glenmorangie and Ardbeg must have been tough for the small distillery of Glen Moray. Even its lead role in the premium blend of Bailie Nicol Jarvie went unnoticed. So, when Glenmorangie's parent company, LVMH, announced it was selling Glen Moray to the French group La Martiniquaise, no one was surprised.

Glen Moray began life as a brewery and was converted into a distillery in 1897. It struggled for the first couple of decades, until it was bought by the blenders Macdonald & Muir, who were the owners until 2004, when it was sold to LVMH. Before then, Glen Moray followed the lead of Glenmorangie and released a

range of special wine finishes, including Chenin Blanc and Chardonnay. These have since been abandoned and replaced with three or four core expressions and a raft of limited releases.

GLEN MORAY 12-YEAR-OLD

SINGLE MALT: SPEYSIDE 40% ABV
This is a classic light Speyside malt, with cotton-candy aromas and notes of heather honey. There is a faint taste of dried fruit and orange peel on the tongue.

GLEN MORAY CLASSIC

SINGLE MALT: SPEYSIDE 40% ABV
The distillery also produces this introductory single malt without an age statement. It has a pale straw color and some light grassy notes.

GLEN MORAY 16-YEAR-OLD

SINGLE MALT: SPEYSIDE 40% ABV
Added maturity brings a rich, barley-sugar character to the malt, with aromas of dried fruit, leather, and linseed oil.

Traditional methods persist in the cooperage, and straw remains the best material for creating a watertight seal for the ends of the casks.

THE GLENROTHES 1975

THE GLENROTHES 1978

GLENROTHES

Rothes, Morayshire
www.glenrotheswhisky.com

After Dufftown, Rothes is the second busiest whisky town on Speyside. Not that you would know it, driving through this small town by day: the distilleries are tucked discreetly out of sight, including Glenrothes, which sits quietly in a dip beside the Rothes burn.

The distillery was built in 1878 as a joint venture between James Stuart of Macallan and two local bankers—Robert Dick and Willie Grant. Before building finished, Stuart had pulled out and a banking crisis that year almost scuppered the plans entirely.

After this shaky start, Glenrothes began to build a reputation among blenders for the quality of its malt, and became a key filling in Cutty Sark, which, for a brief period,

was the bestselling Scotch whisky in the US. It was also supplying other blends, and it seemed as if there was never any to spare—until 1987, when the first single malt, a 12-year-old was released. At first, Glenrothes failed to stand out from the crowd: it had entered the 12-year-old stakes late in the day and there was plenty of competition, particularly on Speyside.

This all changed with the launch of the highly acclaimed Glenrothes Vintage malt in 1994. The brand owners, wine merchants Berry Brothers & Rudd, realized that if vintage variation was appreciated by wine-lovers, the same might be true of malt-whisky-lovers. In 2004, Glenrothes Select Reserve was released to provide continuity between vintages.

To date, the oldest vintage released has been the 1972, though the 1975 and 1978 are the only

THE GLENROTHES 1987

THE GLENROTHES 1991

THE GLENROTHES SELECT RESERVE

ones available from the 1970s.
There have also been various
single-cask releases and a
30-year-old.

THE GLENROTHES 1994

SINGLE MALT: SPEYSIDE 43% ABV
A satisfyingly complex malt with
a fruity, toffee-scented bouquet that
leads to a soft citrus flavor and long,
gentle finish.

THE GLENROTHES 1975

SINGLE MALT: SPEYSIDE 43% ABV
Increasingly hard to find, this vintage
offers big, rich flavors—stewed fruits,
toffee, bitter chocolate, and orange
peel. Medium-sweet satisfying finish.

THE GLENROTHES 1978

SINGLE MALT: SPEYSIDE 43% ABV
A very rare expression, released in
2008, with a concentrated plum
pudding and molasses character, a
silky, honeyed texture and great length.

THE GLENROTHES 1987

SINGLE MALT: SPEYSIDE 43% ABV
Fruit, vanilla, and floral notes hit
the nose. The palate is juicy, with
an orange zestiness balancing the
sweetness, and a long, sweetish finish.

THE GLENROTHES 1991

SINGLE MALT: SPEYSIDE 43% ABV
A nose of ripe berry fruits and vanilla,
with some butterscotch and coconut
flavors that last long on the palate.

THE GLENROTHES
SELECT RESERVE

SINGLE MALT: SPEYSIDE 43% ABV
Like non-vintage Champagne, this is
a vatting of different ages to produce
a complex whisky with notes of hard
candy, ripe fruit, vanilla, and spice.
Sweeter on the nose than in the mouth.

GLEN ORD

Muir of Ord, Ross-shire
www.malts.com

Despite its name, Glen Ord is not in a valley, but on the fertile flatlands of the Black Isle, north of Inverness. It was founded in 1838, close to the alleged site of the Ferintosh Distillery, which was established in the 1670s. In 1923 Glen Ord was bought by John Dewar & Sons, shortly before they joined the DCL.

With six stills and a 750,000 gallon (3.4 million liter) production, it has plenty to spare for a single malt. This has been called Ord, Glenordie, and Muir of Ord at various times. Recent bottlings are called The Singleton of Ord, aiming at the US market.

GLEN ORD 12-YEAR-OLD

SINGLE MALT: HIGHLANDS 43% ABV
This citrusy, orange-peel-scented malt has a gentle apple-pie flavor and some spicy ginger notes on the finish.

GLEN SCOTIA

Campbeltown, Argyll
www.lochlomonddistillery.com

Strung-out at the far end of the Mull of Kintyre, Campbeltown's rise and fall as "whiskyopolis" has been well-documented. As has the story of the Springbank Distillery, which managed to pull through and now enjoys cult status. But, it was not the only one, for the much lesser known Glen Scotia also survived. With its single pair of stills, Campbeltown's "other" distillery was founded in the 1830s by the Galbraith family, who retained control for the rest of the century. After various owners followed, it was bought by Glen Catrine (Loch Lomond Distillers) in 1994.

GLEN SCOTIA 12-YEAR-OLD

SINGLE MALT: CAMPBELTOWN 40% ABV
This distillery bottling replaced the 8-year-old and has a spicy aroma with sweeter, richer notes on the palate.

GLEN SPEY

Rothes, Aberlour, Banffshire
www.malts.com

James Stuart was an established distiller with Macallan and the key partner in building the Glenrothes Distillery in 1878, although he quickly pulled out of that venture. A few years later, he decided to convert an oat mill he owned into Glen Spey, on the opposite bank of the Rothes burn from Glenrothes. The project inevitably led to disputes over water rights. In 1887, Glen Spey was sold to the London-based gin distiller Gilbey's, who later merged with Justerini & Brooks. Its J&B blend has contained Glen Spey ever since. The current owners, Diageo, have just one malt bottling in their Flora & Fauna range.

GLEN SPEY FLORA & FAUNA 12-YEAR-OLD

SINGLE MALT: SPEYSIDE 43% ABV
A light, grassy nose and brisk, nutty flavor. Very dry, with a short finish.

GLENTAUCHERS

Mulben, Keith, Banffshire

Many late-Victorian distilleries sprang up in the hope of finding a market among whisky blenders but, in 1897, Glentauchers was built to supply Buchanan's blend, which evolved into the top-selling Black & White. The distillery was a joint venture between James Buchanan and the Glasgow-based blender W. P. Lowrie. They chose an ideal site, right by a main road that connected to the east-coast rail line from Aberdeen to Inverness. Now owned by Pernod Ricard, Glentauchers has the same principal role it always had—supplying malt for blends.

GLENTAUCHERS GORDON & MACPHAIL 1991

SINGLE MALT: SPEYSIDE 43% ABV
This 16-year-old Gordon & MacPhail bottling has a sweet, sherried character, with a subtle smoky flavor.

GLENTURRET 10-YEAR-OLD

GLENTURRET 14-YEAR-OLD SINGLE CASK

GRAND MACNISH ORIGINAL

GRAND MACNISH 12-YEAR-OLD

GLENTURRET

Crieff, Perthshire
www.thefamousgrouse.com

This small Perthshire distillery,
first licensed in 1775, claims to be
the oldest working distillery in
Scotland. It was certainly one of
the first local farm distilleries to go
legal, and this must have made life
tough for the first few decades,
given that most of the competition
would have been untaxed.

Today Glenturret is known as
the spiritual home of The Famous
Grouse *(see p80)*—a fact that is
hard to escape. Even before you
reach the distillery, a grouse road
sign just outside Crieff points the
way while, at the distillery itself,
a 17 ft (5 m) sculpture of the bird
stands in the car park.

Though Glenturret malt may
have gone into the Grouse blend for
years, most visitors would have
been unaware of the fact until fairly
recently. The only animal they
would have been told about was

Towser, the distillery cat, who
won a place in *The Guinness Book
of Records* for killing nearly 30,000
mice between 1963 and 1984.

All changed when Glenturret's
owners, The Edrington Group,
built a modern, interactive visitor
center at the distillery: The
Famous Grouse Experience. More
recently, the Famous Grouse
Whisky School was added offering
a one-day course on malt whisky,
including an in-depth tour of the
distillery and warehouse, where
you can see the various ages of the
Famous Grouse blended malt.

GLENTURRET 10-YEAR-OLD

SINGLE MALT: HIGHLANDS 40%
Replacing the 12-year-old, this floral,
vanilla-scented malt is now the main
Glenturret expression.

GLENTURRET 14-YEAR-OLD

SINGLE MALT: HIGHLANDS 59.7% ABV
This limited-edition, cask-strength
bottling has a molasses-like sweetness
and notes of licorice.

GRAND MACNISH

Owner: Macduff International

The long history of this brand
dates back to Glasgow and 1863,
when the original Robert McNish
(an "a" crept into the brand name
some time later), a grocer and
general merchant, took up blending.
The pioneering family firm was
driven forward by his two sons,
who greatly expanded the business
and developed sales in the whisky
boom of the 1890s.

Things grew harder after World
War I, and the family eventually
sold out to Canadian Industrial
Alcohol (later Corby Distilleries)
in 1927. Further changes of
ownership ensued, but today the
Grand Macnish has returned to
Glasgow in the custody of MacDuff
International, which appears to be
developing an international profile
for the brand and its distinctively
"retro" dimpled bottle.

Two blended expressions are
available: Grand Macnish
Original, which still uses up to
40 whiskies in the blend, as was
Robert McNish's practice, and
a 12-year-old, described by the
company as "more mature, fruity,
and malty" than its younger
sibling. The distinctive bottle
gives Grand Macnish splendid
"on shelf" presence, and the label
is graced by the McNish clan
motto, "*Forti nihil difficile*" ("To
the strong, nothing is difficult").

GRAND MACNISH ORIGINAL

BLEND 40% ABV
Old leather and ripe fruits, giving way
to a brandy-like aroma. Noticeably
sweet on the palate, with strong vanilla
(wood) influences. A sustained and
evolving finish, with some gentle smoke.

GRAND MACNISH 12-YEAR-OLD

BLEND 40% ABV
The extra age shows here in a fuller,
rounder flavor with greater intensity
and a more sustained finish.

GRANT'S ALE CASK RESERVE

BLEND 40% ABV

Grant's has ventured into special wood finishes with great success. This is the only Scotch whisky to be finished in barrels that have previously held beer, and the ale casks give the whisky a uniquely creamy, malty, and honeyed taste.

GRANT'S SHERRY CASK RESERVE

BLEND 40% ABV

Prepared in the same way as the ground-breaking ale cask version, but here the whisky is finished in Spanish Oloroso sherry casks instead, giving it a distinctively warm, rich, and fruity palate.

GRANT'S FAMILY RESERVE

GRANT'S 12-YEAR-OLD

GRANT'S 18-YEAR-OLD

GRANT'S

Owner: William Grant & Sons

This staunchly independent company has prospered on Speyside since 1887, when the original William Grant and family opened the Glenfiddich Distillery. Grant had served a long apprenticeship in rival distilleries and shrewdly applied his knowledge when setting up his own business.

The company remains in private hands and is renowned for its focus on whisky and its determination to pass this down the generations. Today it is famous for Glenfiddich and its sister single malt, Balvenie, but it also produces a third malt, Kininvie, which is reserved for blending. In addition, it built a grain distillery at Girvan in 1963. Chosen for ease of access to North American grain supplies, the site has been expanded massively, and a new single malt distillery, Ailsa Bay, was recently opened there.

This is reserved for blending, the company being determined to maintain close control over their supplies of whisky. And with good reason: Grant's Family Reserve blend broke through the 1 million case barrier as long ago as 1979 and, since then, has continued to grow at an exceptional rate, keeping up with demand from the world's Scotch whisky drinkers. Grant's now sells around 4 million cases of whisky a year and is one of the world's top five Scotch whisky brands, enjoyed in over 180 countries. The fact that the company is privately owned, and therefore not subject to pressures from shareholders, has enabled Grant's blenders to work with a remarkable depth of mature stock, some dating back 40 years or more.

The blended range of whiskies continues to evolve, while still remaining true to the distinctive triangular bottle that marks out the products of this respected firm.

GRANT'S FAMILY RESERVE

BLEND 40% ABV

An unmistakably Speyside nose, with fluting malty notes. A firm mouthfeel, with banana-vanilla sweetness balancing sharper malty notes. Clean, but very complex with a long, smooth finish.

GRANT'S 12-YEAR-OLD

BLEND 40% ABV

A blend of the finest single malt and grain whiskies, matured for at least 12 years in oak casks before being finished in ex-bourbon barrels. A warm and full-bodied Scotch of great richness is the result.

GRANT'S 18-YEAR-OLD

BLEND 40% ABV

Perfectly balanced, with considerable depth of taste. Rich and full-bodied, with fruity notes from the port casks it is finished in.

HAIG

Owner: Diageo

The distinguished name of Haig can trace its whisky-making pedigree back to the 17th century, when distilling began on the family farm. The company developed extensive interests in grain whisky distilling and was an early pioneer of blending. By 1919, however, it was absorbed into the DCL, where it continued to be a powerful force. The company's Dimple brand (*see p 78*) was a highly successful deluxe expression, and Haig was once the bestselling whisky in the UK. But its glory days are far behind it: today, under the control of Diageo, it is found mainly in Greece and the Canary Islands.

HAIG

BLEND 40% ABV

Some sweetness on the nose, with faint smoky notes. Light and delicate, with soft wood notes and some spice on the finish, where a hint of smoke returns.

All about…
Whiskey Cocktails

When it comes to whiskey, cocktails can be a thorny subject, with some traditionalists condemning them as an "adulteration" of the finest of all drinks. They're missing out: the interplay of flavors from the whiskey and its accompanying ingredients can be sublime. What's more, a decent whiskey has the strength and character to maintain its identity in the mix, and delicate layerings of flavors can be achieved. Bartenders today are experimenting with big, characterful malts—even peaty expressions from Islay have their place. Balance of flavors is key, but the results can be astounding. Here are seven using whiskeys from around the globe.

MINT JULEP Roughly tear 12–15 mint leaves and place in a julep glass. Add some crushed ice, 1 oz (30 ml) Buffalo Trace bourbon, 1½ oz (15 ml) sugar syrup, and stir well. Add 5 more torn mint leaves, another 1 oz (30 ml) bourbon, and stir well. Add 5 more torn mint leaves, fill the glass with crushed ice, and stir well. Top with more crushed ice, garnish with a sprig of mint, and serve with two short straws.

PEAT COLLINS Chill a collins glass with ice cubes. Put 2 oz (60 ml) Laphroaig 10-year-old into the mixing glass, add ½ oz (15 ml) freshly squeezed lime juice, ½ oz (15 ml) sugar syrup, a dash of orange bitters, and shake well. Double-strain the Peat Collins into the collins glass, add a couple of dashes of soda water, and stir well. Top with crushed ice and a twist of orange zest.

RYE MANHATTAN Chill a martini glass with crushed ice. Half-fill a mixing glass with ice cubes, add a dash of Angostura bitters, 2 oz (60 ml) Sazerac rye whiskey, and 1 oz (30 ml) Antica Formula sweet red vermouth. Fill with more ice cubes and stir for 20 seconds. Discard the crushed ice from the martini glass and double-strain the Rye Manhattan into it. Garnish with a maraschino cherry.

ROB ILA Chill a coupete glass with crushed ice. Fill the mixing glass with ice cubes, add 2 oz (60 ml) Caol Ila Distillers Edition, ½ oz (15 ml) Muscat de Beaumes de Venise, a dash of orange bitters, ½ oz (15 ml) Drambuie, and stir well for 30 seconds. Discard the ice and double-strain the Rob Ila into it. Run a piece of lemon zest round the rim and garnish with a twist of zest.

ALBANNACH RENAISSANCE Fill a mixing glass with ice cubes, add 1½ oz (45 ml) Ardbeg Renaissance, ½ oz (15 ml) Aperol, ½ oz (15 ml) lime juice, ½ oz (15 ml) sugar syrup, and dashes of orange bitters, and egg white. Cover and shake till frothy. Double-strain into a chilled rocks glass, squeeze in the juice from a small piece of orange zest, and garnish with a twist of orange zest.

BLACK SOUR Put three cardamom seeds in the mixing glass and crush well. Add half a cored Bartlett pear and mash to a pulp. Add 1½ oz (45 ml) Bushmills Black Bush, ½ oz (15 ml) crème de pêche, 2 good dashes of Angostura bitters, 1 oz (30 ml) freshly squeezed lemon juice, 1 oz (30 ml) sugar syrup, a dash of egg white, and shake well. Double-strain into a chilled old-fashioned glass, top with crushed ice, and garnish with fanned Bartlett pear.

YAMAZAKI MARTINI Chill a small martini glass with crushed ice. Fill a mixing glass with ice cubes, add 2 oz (60 ml) Yamazaki 12-year-old, a dash of Angostura bitters, ½ oz (15 ml) orgeat (almond) syrup, ⅓ oz (5 ml) sugar syrup, ½ oz (15 ml) freshly squeezed lime juice, a dash of egg white, and shake well. Discard the ice from the martini glass and double-strain the Yamazaki Martini into it.

**HIGHLAND PARK
12-YEAR-OLD**

SINGLE MALT: ISLANDS 40% ABV
This whisky has been praised
for its all-around quality. There
are soft heather-honey flavors,
some richer spicy notes, and an
enveloping wisp of peat smoke
that leaves the finish quite dry.

**HIGHLAND PARK
15-YEAR-OLD**

SINGLE MALT: ISLANDS 40% ABV
Sweetly aromatic, with ripe
fruits and almond notes. The
fruit is more caramelized on
the palate, which fades to a
dry, smoky finish.

HIGHLAND PARK 16-YEAR-OLD   HIGHLAND PARK 18-YEAR-OLD   HIGHLAND PARK 25-YEAR-OLD   HIGHLAND PARK 30-YEAR-OLD

HIGHLAND PARK

Kirkwall, Orkney
www.highlandpark.co.uk

Unless, and until, a distillery is built on Shetland, Highland Park will remain Scotland's most northerly distillery. Today its far-flung island location is a great asset for the marketing of Highland Park whiskies but, for much of its history, the distance from its core market—the big blenders on the mainland—represented a major challenge for the distillery. It survived, and now produces a Highland malt that is highly regarded. Having invested £18m in the brand so far, its owners have ambitious plans to reach the top ten.

Highland Park was first licensed to David Robertson in 1798 and stands near the island's capital, Kirkwall, on the site of an illicit distillery run by Magnus Eunson, a notorious smuggler. Eunson was finally arrested by John Robertson, an excise officer, who took over the distillery in 1826. In 1895 it was bought by James Grant of Glenlivet, who expanded the number of stills to four. Since 1937 it has been part of Highland Distilleries (now the Edrington Group), which began to invest seriously in single malts from Highland Park in the late 1970s. To this day, a proportion of the barley is malted using the distillery's original floor maltings. The malt is then dried in a kiln, using local peat, which has a slightly sweeter aroma than that from Islay.

The range starts with the 12-year-old and now stretches to a 40-year-old. Since 2005 there has been a number of single Ambassador Cask releases.

HIGHLAND PARK 16-YEAR-OLD

SINGLE MALT: ISLANDS 40% ABV
Sherry, peat, and spice on the nose. Malty flavors come in on the palate; dry and biscuity, with honey sweetness and smokiness. A lingering dry finish.

HIGHLAND PARK 18-YEAR-OLD

SINGLE MALT: ISLANDS 43% ABV
This is a touch sweeter than the 12-year-old, with notes of heather, toffee, and polished leather. The flavor of peat smoke comes through stronger on the finish than on the palate.

HIGHLAND PARK 25-YEAR-OLD

SINGLE MALT: ISLANDS 48.1% ABV
As suggested by its deep amber color, this whisky had plenty of contact with European oak. In fact, half of it was matured in first-fill sherry butts. Despite its age, it has a rich, nutty flavor, with dried fruits and scented smoke.

HIGHLAND PARK 30-YEAR-OLD

SINGLE MALT: ISLANDS 48.1% ABV
The flagship of the range. Caramel sweetness, aromatic spices; dark chocolate, and orange notes. A long, drying, smoky finish, tinged with salt.

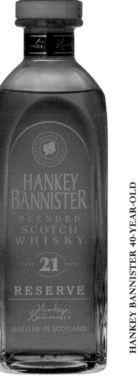

HANKEY BANNISTER 21-YEAR-OLD

HANKEY BANNISTER 40-YEAR-OLD

HAZELBURN

IMPERIAL 15-YEAR-OLD

HANKEY BANNISTER

Owner: Inver House Distillers

Messrs. Hankey and Bannister went into partnership in 1757 and were wine merchants to the great and the good, including the Prince Regent and William IV. Today the company is owned by Inver House Distillers, giving it access to a range of single malts from some of Scotland's distinguished but lesser-known distilleries, such as Balblair, Balmenach, and Knockdhu. Although managed in Scotland, Inver House is owned by Thai Beverage, and key markets for Hankey Bannister include Latin America, Australia, and South America, but it is exported to a total of 47 countries worldwide.

The 12-year-old was awarded a silver medal at the 2007 International Wine and Spirit Competition while, in June 2008, the 40-year-old received the coveted accolade of World's Best Scotch Blended Whisky at the World Whiskies Awards. This rare blend is characterized by the presence of whiskies such as Glen Flagler, Garnheath, and Killyloch, whose distilleries are no more.

The extensive Hankey Bannister range is made up of the original, a 12-year-old, 21-year-old, 40-year-old, and a blended malt.

HANKEY BANNISTER 21-YEAR-OLD

BLEND 43% ABV

A fresh and quite youthful nose. Soft and smooth, creamy toffee, with the vanilla house style coming through. Greater depth on the palate, with malty overtones and a warm finish.

HANKEY BANNISTER 40-YEAR-OLD

BLEND 43.3% ABV

Warm and fragrant aromas of raisin, chocolate, and citrus combine with spicy notes, leading to an exceptionally long-lasting, smooth, full-bodied finish.

HAZELBURN

Well Close, Campbeltown
www.springbankdistillers.com

Springbank Distillery is the great survivor of the Campbeltown whisky boom, which saw a staggering 34 distilleries in town in the 19th century. Today, Springbank is a mini-malt-whisky industry on its own, with three separate distillations under one roof: Springbank itself, the pungently smoky Longrow, and the light, gentle Hazelburn. As well as using no peat in its malt, Hazelburn—which was named after an old, abandoned distillery in Campbeltown—is triple-distilled. The first spirit was produced in 1997 and bottled as an 8-year-old in 2005. The 6,000 bottles released sold out within weeks.

HAZELBURN 8-YEAR-OLD

SINGLE MALT: CAMPBELTOWN 46% ABV

Lowland in style, clean and refreshing, with a subtle, malty flavor.

IMPERIAL

Carron, Morayshire

The year 1897 was an important one for Queen Victoria's subjects: it was her Diamond Jubilee. This was the inspiration for Imperial —a distillery founded by Thomas Mackenzie, to add to Talisker and Dailuaine, which he already owned. Intended as a long-lasting tribute to Queen Victoria, Imperial lasted for just two productive years before it fell silent, brought down by the collapse of Pattison Brothers, the notorious blenders and bottlers in Leith who did much to besmirch the reputation of Scotch whisky at the end of the 19th century.

Under a succession of owners, including DCL, Allied Domecq, and now Chivas Brothers, production has since been sporadic. In fact, the distillery has spent 60 of the past 100 years lying idle. Its longest period of operation was between the mid-1950s and 1985,

IMPERIAL GORDON & MACPHAIL 1991

and its most recent active spell was from 1991 to 1998. Imperial shouldn't be written off quite yet, though, for several distilleries have lain mothballed for 10 or 20 years before being revived, and, most importantly, Imperial's vital distilling equipment is all still intact. With two pairs of stills ready to make 352,000 gallons (1.6 million liters), and demand for Scotch malt high, who knows what Chivas (Pernod Ricard) has in mind for sleepy Imperial?

A 15-year-old official bottling and several independent bottlings of 1990s vintages are available.

IMPERIAL 15-YEAR-OLD

SINGLE MALT: SPEYSIDE 46% ABV

Limey, slightly floury, with pastry-like sweetness. A dry, lightly smoky finish.

IMPERIAL
GORDON & MACPHAIL 1991

SINGLE MALT: SPEYSIDE 43% ABV

Honey and spice, with green apples, earthy notes, and a light smokiness.

INCHGOWER

Buckie, Banffshire
www.malts.com

This is Speyside, but only just—the Inchgower Distillery sits near the mouth of the Spey and the fishing port of Buckie. It was established in 1871 by Alexander Wilson, using equipment from the disused Tochieneal Distillery, which had been founded in 1824 by his father, John Wilson, a short distance down the coast at Cullen. It remained a family business until 1930, when the stills went cold. Six years on, the local town council bought it for just £1,000, selling it on to Arthur Bell & Sons in 1938. Bell's blends swallow up most of the malt.

INCHGOWER FLORA & FAUNA
14-YEAR-OLD

SINGLE MALT: SPEYSIDE 43% ABV

Brisk and fresh, with a floral nose, sweet-and-sour flavor, develping into a very short finish.

INVER HOUSE
GREEN PLAID

Owner: Inver House Distillers

Controlled today by Thai Beverage, Inver House is one of the smaller but more dynamic Scotch whisky companies and, in 2008, was named International Distiller of the Year by *Whisky Magazine*. Its Green Plaid label was originally launched in 1956 in the US, where it remains among the top ten bestselling whiskies. More than 20 malts and grains are used to blend Green Plaid, which is available as a competitively priced non-aged version and as 12- and 21-year-olds. Inver House's Speyburn, anCnoc, Balblair, Old Pulteney, and Balmenach single malts undoubtedly feature strongly in the blend.

INVER HOUSE GREEN PLAID

BLEND 40% ABV

A light, pleasant, undemanding dram, with notes of caramel and vanilla.

INVERGORDON

Cottage Brae, Invergordon, Ross-shire
www.whyteandmackay.com

Located on the shores of the Moray Firth, the Invergordon grain distillery is owned by Whyte & Mackay. It was established in 1961 and expanded in 1963 and 1978. The distillery issued its pioneering official bottling of Invergordon Single Grain as a 10-year-old in 1991, but this was subsequently withdrawn. As a consequence, the only supplies now available are independent bottlings, many of which are very highly regarded by independent tasters.

INVERGORDON
CLAN DENNY 1966

SINGLE GRAIN 49.8% ABV

The independent bottlings of Invergordon are uniformly old (typically 38–42 years), and are characterized by a sweet nose and creamy texture. Expect notes of vanilla and wood, and spices such as cinnamon and nutmeg.

JAMES MARTIN'S 20-YEAR-OLD

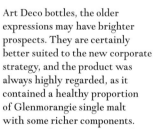

JAMES MARTIN'S 30-YEAR-OLD

J&B JET

ISLAY MIST

Owner: MacDuff International

Created in 1922 for the 21st birthday of the son of the Laird of Islay House, Islay Mist is a highly awarded blend of single malts from the Hebridean island. The strongly flavored Laphroaig is predominant, but is tempered with Speyside and Highland malts. Naturally, Islay Mist is favored by lovers of peat-flavored whiskies, but it also offers an excellent alternative to less characterful blends. It is produced by MacDuff International, and is available in standard, deluxe, 8-year-old, and 17-year-old versions. The latter two use identical blend recipes; the difference is the age.

ISLAY MIST DELUXE

BLEND 40% ABV

A great smoky session whisky that some will find easier to drink than full-on Islay malt. Sweet and complex under all the peat.

JAMES MARTIN'S

Owner: Glenmorangie

This brand exhibits something of a split personality: Martin's VVO (very, very old—a generous description of the blend) remains a low-price contender in parts of the US, where it was once a significant seller; in Portugal, however, the older expressions of Martin's are highly regarded as a prestigious, premium style.

The name relates to the Leith blenders MacDonald Martin Distillers (now Glenmorangie, and thus part of the French luxury goods house LVMH) and dates back to 1878, when the original James Martin set up in business. Given LVMH's influence over Glenmorangie, and its wish to concentrate on prestige products, the future of the VVO style may be in some doubt. It is certainly years since it received any meaningful marketing, trading largely on price. In their stylish

Art Deco bottles, the older expressions may have brighter prospects. They are certainly better suited to the new corporate strategy, and the product was always highly regarded, as it contained a healthy proportion of Glenmorangie single malt with some richer components.

Currently there are 12- and 20-year-old versions of James Martin's. The 30-year-old version appears to have been withdrawn, presumably owing to a shortage of aged stocks—but bottles can still be bought from specialist retailers.

JAMES MARTIN'S 20-YEAR-OLD

BLEND 40% ABV

Citrus on the nose initially, then honey, vanilla, and a rich mead liqueur. With water, hints of coconut and vanilla appear. Very soft on the palate at the start, with cereal (grain) notes to the fore. Complex, lively spice and soft, sweet grain notes. Well-balanced with a soft finish.

J&B

Owner: Diageo

A Diageo brand widely sold in Spain, France, Portugal, Turkey, South Africa, and the US, J&B is one of the world's top-selling blended whiskies. In fact, nearly two bottles are sold every second.

The founding firm dates from 1749. In 1831 it was bought by the entrepreneurial Alfred Brooks, who renamed it Justerini and Brooks. The company began blending in the 1880s, and developed J&B Rare in the 1930s, when the end of Prohibition in the US created a demand for lighter-colored whisky with a more delicate flavor. It was an immediate success, achieving sales in excess of 3 million cases a year by the 1970s.

J&B has long been a favorite with writers and film stars: Truman Capote, Graham Greene, and Bret Easton Ellis have all been connected with the brand. Expressions include J&B Rare, Jet (the leading

J&B ULTIMA

J&B RARE

brand in South Korea), a 15-year-old Reserve sold only in Spain and Portugal, and NOX, a blended malt designed for mixing.

J&B JET

BLEND 40% ABV

A very mellow, smooth whisky, with Speyside malt at its core.

J&B ULTIMA

BLEND 43% ABV

With a blending of whiskies from no fewer than 128 malt and grain distilleries, this is about as rich and complex a blend as its possible to get. Increasingly rare, though, as J&B has discontinued this bottling.

J&B RARE

BLEND 40% ABV

Top-class single malts such as Knockando, Auchroisk, and Glen Spey are at its heart; delicate smokiness suggests an Islay influence. Apple and pear sweetness, vanilla notes and honey hints against a background of restrained peat. A highly distinctive blend.

JOHN BARR

Owner: Whyte & Mackay

Introduced into the UK by DCL to compensate for its withdrawal of Johnnie Walker (the result of a spat with the EU over pricing), John Barr was intended to make up for lost sales. The range echoes Johnnie Walker quite shamelessly, with Red, Black, and Gold being the main variants. Today the brand is owned by Whyte & Mackay and is seen principally in the US, where it competes largely on price. The Whyte & Mackay single malts Jura, Tamnavulin, and Fettercairn appear to play a large part in the blend, along with a good measure of Invergordon grain. Expect to see it in India soon, given Whyte & Mackay's ownership.

JOHN BARR

BLEND 40% ABV

The nose is firm, with luscious, creamy, round tones. Positive and full-flavored, with an almost spicy richness.

JOHNNIE WALKER BLACK LABEL

JOHNNIE WALKER GREEN LABEL

JOHNNIE WALKER GOLD LABEL

JOHNNIE WALKER BLUE LABEL

JOHNNIE WALKER

Owner: Diageo

While the original firm can be traced back to the purchase of a Kilmarnock grocery store in 1820, Walker's did not enter the whisky business in a serious way until the 1860s. Then, with the legalization of blending, John Walker's son and grandson progressively launched and developed their range of whiskies. These were based around the original Walker's Old Highland blend, which was launched in 1865 and is the ancestor of today's Black Label. In 1925 the firm joined DCL and, by 1945, Johnnie

Walker was the world's bestselling brand of Scotch.

Total sales of Johnnie Walker whiskies amount to around 12 million cases a year, and its Red Label is the most successful brand of Scotch whisky in the world. There has been significant growth in Scotch's developing markets (China, Asia, and Russia), where the brand is seen as a symbol of Western affluence and success.

The range comprises Johnnie Walker Red, Black, Gold, Blue, Blue Label King George V, and Green Label. From time to time the firm also releases a number of one-off, limited, or regional expressions, including Swing, Quest, Honour, Excelsior, Old

Harmony, and 1805. In recent years there has been a trend to move the brand upmarket. When Blue Label was launched in 1992 it set new price records for blended whisky. This was followed by the King George V Edition, which cost three times as much as the Blue, and the ultra-exclusive 1805, sold at £1,000 a single glass.

JOHNNIE WALKER BLACK LABEL

BLEND 40% ABV

The flagship, classic blend, recognizable by the smoky kick contributed by Talisker and Diageo's Islay malts, Caol Ila and Lagavulin. Glendullan and Mortlach add some Speyside malt; the grain component is from Cameron Brig.

JOHNNIE WALKER GREEN LABEL

BLENDED MALT 43% ABV

Complex, rich, and powerful. Pepper and oak, fruit aromas, a malty sweetness, and some smoke.

JOHNNIE WALKER GOLD LABEL

BLEND 40% ABV

Honey, fresh fruit, and toffee notes, with smoke in the background. Diageo recommends chilling this in the freezer before serving.

JOHNNIE WALKER BLUE LABEL

BLEND 40% ABV

Smooth and mellow, with traces of spice, honey, and the signature hint of smoke.

**JOHNNIE WALKER
PREMIER**

BLEND 43% ABV

A complex blend of 28
different single malt and
grain whiskies. Rich, with
a subtle oak finish. Sweet
and dark, with dried fruits,
treacle toffee, and chocolate.

**JOHNNIE WALKER
SWING**

BLEND 43% ABV

Notes of sherry wood and
vanilla, with an almost
perfumed sweetness. Fresh,
light, smooth, and intensely
fruity, with traces of oak
and a hint of smoke.

JURA

Isle of Jura, Argyllshire
www.isleofjura.com

When the Indian tycoon Vijay Mallya bought Whyte & Mackay in May 2007, part of the appeal was sentimental: included in the sale was Jura—an island distillery off the northeast tip of Islay, which his father found irresistible. "I remember hearing the name 40 years ago," Mallya told reporters. "It was his favorite whisky and now it's part of Whyte & Mackay. I hope he would be proud."

The original Jura Distillery was licensed in 1831 and later leased to James Ferguson, who rebuilt it in 1875. However, the terms of the lease were so harsh that his family abandoned Jura in 1901, ripping out the equipment as they did so. For the next 20 years the landlord and local laird, Archibald Campbell, pursued them in court, while removing the distillery roof to avoid paying taxes.

In the late 1950s two estate owners on Jura resurrected the distillery in a joint venture with Scottish & Newcastle breweries. They hired the leading distillery architect of his day, William Delmé-Evans, and his design, completed in the early 1960s, still stands today.

The profile of the whisky also changed when the distillery was resurrected. Gone was the strong, phenolic malt of the past, and in came something more Highland in style, with less peat and a more subtle touch. Employing large stills (nearly as tall as those at Glenmorangie) to create a cleaner style of spirit, Jura was able to produce a softer malt whisky— one that would be distinct from those of its peaty neighbors, over on Islay.

Having said that, in recent years Jura has produced an interesting array of limited-edition bottlings, some of which have used various sherry cask finishes and some of which have actually been quite

heavily peated. A whisky called Earth (from the Elements series) was one such bottling.

Jura's core range consists of Superstition and 10-, 16-, 18-, and 21-year-old expressions.

JURA SUPERSTITION
SINGLE MALT: ISLANDS 43% ABV
A mix of heavily peated, young Jura with older whisky, to produce an intensely smoky, smooth-textured malt.

JURA 10-YEAR-OLD
SINGLE MALT: ISLANDS 40% ABV
A lightly peated island malt that seems to have improved in recent years.

JURA 16-YEAR-OLD
SINGLE MALT: ISLANDS 40% ABV
A slightly spicy, cereal nose with a nutty flavor that dries on the finish.

KILCHOMAN

Rockside Farm, Bruichladdich, Islay
www.kilchomandistillery.com

Whisky-making began here in 2005, and this is as quintessential a farm distillery as you'll find. The barley is grown on Rockside Farm, and malting, fermenting, distilling, and maturing all take place on-site; a dam on the farm creates a supply of fresh water. At the time of writing, Kilchoman was yet to bottle its first whisky, but they do sell New Spirit. Matured in bourbon casks for about five months, this isn't technically new make, but then neither is it whisky yet either. It does, though, offer a signpost to the kind of whisky that will one day issue forth from the Kilchoman warehouse.

KILCHOMAN NEW SPIRIT
NEW MAKE SPIRIT 63.5% ABV
A light wave of peat on the nose, but essentially fruity and fresh. There's a butterscotch sweetness too.

KNOCKANDO 12-YEAR-OLD

KNOCKANDO 18-YEAR-OLD

KNOCKANDO 21-YEAR-OLD

KNOCKANDO

Knockando, Morayshire
www.malts.com

Knockando was launched as a single malt in the late 1970s and had some success in Spain, although most of the production went into J&B. The name is an anglicized version of Cnoc-an-Dhu, which is Gaelic for the "dark hillock" that stands close by the distillery, guarding a bend in the Spey.

The distillery was set up by John Thomson in 1898 close to Cardhu, on the old Strathspey railway line, where it had its own station. Although it was one of the first to have electric light, it was only run on a seasonal basis and soon fell victim to the speculative crash that hit the industry at the beginning of the 20th century. Knockando was snapped up by the London gin distillers Gilbey's, who, via a series of acquisitions, became part of what is now Diageo. In 1968, the floor maltings were stopped and the old malt barns converted to host meetings for J&B salesman around the world.

As a single malt, Knockando was originally sold not by age statement, but by vintage in all its markets except the US. It has proved popular in Spain and France.

KNOCKANDO 12-YEAR-OLD

SINGLE MALT: SPEYSIDE 43% ABV
This very gentle, grassy malt has a cereal character and a light, creamy texture.

KNOCKANDO 18-YEAR-OLD

SINGLE MALT: SPEYSIDE 43% ABV
A slightly more fulsome expression of this gentle Speyside malt, with a smooth, mellow texture.

KNOCKANDO 21-YEAR-OLD

SINGLE MALT: SPEYSIDE 43% ABV
Sweet on the nose, with oak and nuts (almonds) on the palate, matched by berry fruits, leading on to a smoky, oaky finish.

Whisky Tour: Islay

"Peat freaks" adore the Islay taste, and tourism to this Hebridean island is booming, particularly during the annual Feis Ile (the Islay Malt and Music Festival) at the end of May. The easiest way to reach Islay is to fly from Glasgow, but you will need to rent a car to get around; the Caledonian MacBrayne ferry from Kennacraig allows you to bring your own vehicle but is a longer journey (four hours). For accommodation, there are converted distillery cottages at Bowmore and Bunnahabhain available to rent, hotels in Bowmore and Port Charlotte, and plenty of B&B and efficiency options too. A four-day itinerary should take in all eight distilleries.

SCOTLAND

TOUR STATISTICS

DAYS: 4	LENGTH: 60 miles (96 km)		DISTILLERIES: 8
TRAVEL: Car, walking		REGION: Islay, Scotland	

DAY 1: CAOL ILA, BUNNAHABHAIN

1 Arriving in Port Askaig by ferry, the logical place to stay is the charming, family-run Port Askaig Hotel on the coast (*www.portaskaig.co.uk*). From there you can walk to **Caol Ila**, a large Diageo distillery that is the most highly productive on the island. (*www.discovering-distilleries. com/caolila*)

2 It's a car trip or hike along the coastal path from Port Askaig to **Bunnahabhain**. This distillery makes the most lightly peated of all Islay whiskies. It is possible to rent one of the distillery cottages and soak up the tranquillity of Bunnahabhain Bay, with its captivating views of Jura. (*www.bunnahabhain.com*)

WASHBACKS AT CAOL ILA

KILCHOMAN **3**

BRUICHLADDICH **4**

BOWMORE **3**

PORT CHARLOTTE

BUNNAHABHAIN DISTILLERY

DAY 2: KILCHOMAN, BRUICHLADDICH

3 Tiny **Kilchoman** is Islay's newest and smallest distillery. It's also a farm with a friendly café. Like other Islay distilleries, it sells special bottlings that may not be available elsewhere. This is a great spot for lunch and the dishes use locally sourced ingredients. Alternatively, in good weather, you can picnic at nearby Machir Bay. (*www.kilchomandistillery.com*)

4 A short drive back over the hill brings you to **Bruichladdich** (*www.bruichladdich.com*), which produces a huge array of whiskies. The distillery is just outside Port Charlotte, where you can learn about illicit whisky production in the Museum of Islay Life (*www.islaymuseum.org*), then enjoy dinner at the Port Charlotte Hotel (*www.portcharlottehotel.co.uk*).

BRUICHLADDICH

DAY 3: LAPHROAIG, LAGAVULIN, ARDBEG

5 Spend today taking in three distilleries and some ancient history. The Kildalton distilleries, as these three are known, are renowned for their strong peaty character, and **Laphroaig** is reputedly Prince Charles's favorite dram. The distillery tour includes the splendidly maintained maltings. (*www.laphroaig.com*)

6 From Laphroaig, take a five-minute stroll to **Lagavulin** to compare these two strongly peated single malts with their assertive flavors. (*www.discovering-distilleries.com/lagavulin*)

7 The last distillery of the day is **Ardbeg** (*www.ardbeg.com*), where lunch at the Old Kiln Café is not to be missed. If you're interested in history, drive a few miles further on the tiny road to Kildalton where there's a very fine 8th-century cross.

MODEL IN LAGAVULIN'S DRAM ROOM

DAY 4: BOWMORE

8 Spend your last morning in the little town of Bowmore, where you can visit the floor maltings, history of distillery exhibition, and visitor center at **Bowmore** Distillery (*www.bowmore.co.uk*). Repair to the Harbour Inn (*www.harbour-inn.com*) for a final lunch of local produce before catching the afternoon ferry from Port Askaig back to the mainland.

BOWMORE WAREHOUSE

BUNNAHABHAIN **2**

CAOL ILA

I

PORT ASKAIG

JURA

Port Askaig – Colonsay ferry

FEOLIN FERRY

START

FINISH

A846

A846

Port Askaig–Kennacraig ferry

Port Ellen–Kennacraig ferry

DGEND

ISLAY

B8016

KILDALTON

7 ARDBEG

5 **6** LAGAVULIN

LAPHROAIG

PORT ELLEN

miles
0   2

0   2
kilometers

LANGS SUPREME

LANGS 12-YEAR-OLD

LABEL 5

Owner: La Martiniquaise

The Label 5 brand is owned by La
Martiniquaise, a French producer
with significant blending and
distilling facilities in Scotland, as
well as interests in rum and other
spirits. Founded in 1934 as a
blending house, the company now
owns Glen Moray single malt and is
building new grain and single malt
facilities at its central Scotland base.

Label 5 is its leading brand,
and sells well over 1 million cases
in the price-competitive "value"
category, mainly in France,
although it is available in more than
50 countries worldwide. A 12-year-
old deluxe version is also available.

LABEL 5 CLASSIC BLACK

BLEND 40% ABV

Delicate, malty, and smoky, with
hints of flowers and fruit. Smooth,
robust, and balanced on the palate,
with subtle oak notes.

LADYBURN

Owner: William Grant & Sons

Now long-since closed, Ladyburn
was a malt distillery within a huge
grain distillery in Girvan on the
Ayrshire coast. Its owners, William
Grant & Sons, moved into grain
whisky in 1964, when DCL
threatened to stop supplying them
with grain spirit for its blends.
Two years later, in 1966, it created
Ladyburn on the site. It only ran
for nine years before being
converted into a vodka distillery in
1975, so single malt bottlings are
very rare. Despite this, official
bottlings, as well as independents,
continue to be eked out of the
remaining stocks, and there are
rumours that the owners kept back
30 casks to release as they choose.

LADYBURN 1973

SINGLE MALT: LOWLANDS 50.4% ABV

A limited-release bottling, with a
mellow, oaky character and delicious
vanilla sweetness.

LANGS

Owner: Ian MacLeod
www.ianmacleod.com

At the heart of this long-established
blend is Glengoyne single malt,
from the distillery just outside
Glasgow. This was bought in 1876
by two local merchants, Alexander
and Gavin Lang. In 1965 the
brand and distillery were sold to
their rivals, Robertson & Baxter,
who invested in the distillery and
developed the brand with some
success. Sales also grew steadily
in Europe and the Far East and,
in 1984, HM The Queen Mother
awarded Langs her royal warrant.

But in 2003, Robertson & Baxter
decided they could take Langs no
further. The sale to Ian MacLeod
marked an important transition
for that business, from blender
and bottler to full-blown distiller.

Since the acquisition, Ian
MacLeod has invested in both the
Glengoyne Distillery, with its
range of alternative visitor

experiences, and in presenting
Langs in new packaging. Today,
the principal Langs products are
Langs Select 12-year-old and Langs
Supreme, both blends noted for
their relatively high malt content.
Langs Select was awarded a gold
medal by *Scottish Field* magazine's
Merchants' Challenge, beating
some very well-known names.

LANGS SUPREME

BLEND 40% ABV

A rich malt aroma on the nose, well-
matured, with just a hint of sherry.
A full-flavored, medium-sweet blend,
with the Glengoyne heart evident.

LANGS SELECT 12-YEAR-OLD

BLEND 40% ABV

Rhubarb and cooking apples on the
nose, with a good helping of vanilla.
Sweet, soft, and delicate. Richer on the
palate, with lots of fruity notes and a
lemon-tart sweetness that build toward
a spicy finish with hints of peat smoke.

Laphroaig *(see p130)* **still uses floor maltings** for some of its malt requirement. These damp grains will be spread out and regularly turned during the germination stage of the malting process.

LAGAVULIN 16-YEAR-OLD

LAGAVULIN 12-YEAR-OLD

LAGAVULIN 21-YEAR-OLD

LAGAVULIN

Port Ellen, Isle of Islay
www.malts.com

Lagavulin is said to have evolved into a distillery from various illicit smuggling botheys in 1817. In 1836 its lease was taken over by Alexander Graham, who sold the island's whiskies through his shop in Glasgow. Peter Mackie, the nephew of Graham's partner, worked for the business and went on to create the famous White Horse blend based on Islay malt. When neighboring Laphroaig refused to supply him, he decided to build Malt Mill Distillery in the grounds of Lagavulin, which he inherited after his uncle's death.

Malt Mill was demolished in the 1960s, but Lagavulin rode on the back of the White Horse until its iconic 16-year-old became a founding member of the "Classic Malts" in 1988.

During the slump in demand for Scotch in the 1980s, Lagavulin was working a two- to three-day week. Sixteen years down the line, the managers were having to juggle the short supply with booming demand. Having been the top-selling Islay malt, low stocks pushed it into third place behind Laphroaig and Bowmore. To try and meet demand, production at Lagavulin was cranked up to a seven-day week, and less and less was made available for blends. It is said that

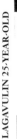

over 85 percent of Lagavulin is now bottled as a single malt. Beyond the core range, recent years have seen two limited-release older expressions, a 25-year-old and a 30-year-old (the oldest ever bottling of Lagavulin). Both are extremely rare, and the 30-year-old in particular is in the territory of collectors only now.

LAGAVULIN 16-YEAR-OLD

SINGLE MALT: ISLAY 43% ABV

The long-time stalwart of the "Classic Malts" has an intensely smoky nose with the scent of seaweed and iodine and a sweetness in the mouth that dries to a peaty finish.

LAGAVULIN 12-YEAR-OLD

SINGLE MALT: ISLAY 56.4% ABV

An initial sweetness gives way to scented smoke and a malty, fruity flavor ahead of the dry, peaty finish.

LAGAVULIN 21-YEAR-OLD

SINGLE MALT: ISLAY 56.5% ABV

Pungent and smoky on one hand, with a sherried, syrupy warmth on the other. The two sides live in harmony.

LAGAVULIN DISTILLERS EDITION

SINGLE MALT: ISLAY 43% ABV

A richer, fuller-flavored take on the 16-year-old, still with plenty of dense smoke and seaweed.

LAPHROAIG 10-YEAR-OLD CASK STRENGTH

LAPHROAIG 18-YEAR-OLD

LAPHROAIG 25-YEAR-OLD

LAPHROAIG 30-YEAR-OLD

LAPHROAIG

Port Ellen, Isle of Islay
www.laphroaig.com

In June 2008, Prince Charles returned to visit the home of his favorite Islay malt after 14 years. This time he came with his wife, Camilla, and did not crash-land on Islay's tiny airstrip, as he had the last time (he made the mistake of landing with a strong tail wind, and the plane came to a halt nose-down in the peat bog).

Laphroaig has always reveled in its pungent smokiness—a mix of hemp, carbolic soap, and bonfire that is about as a far from the creamy, cocktail end of whisky as it is possible to get. Its intense

medicinal character is said to be one reason it was among the few Scotch whiskies allowed into the US during Prohibition—it was accepted as a "medicinal spirit," and could be obtained with a prescription from a doctor.

Laphroaig was founded in 1810 by Alexander and Donald Johnston, although official production did not begin for five years. Living beside the equally famous Lagavulin has not always been easy, and there were the usual fights over water access, but today the feeling is more one of mutual respect.

Laphroaig is one of the very few distilleries to have retained its floor maltings, which supply about a fifth of its needs. The reason may

be more to do with marketing than anything else, but it makes for an interesting distillery visit.

Although Allied Distillers could appear ambivalent about its commitment to Scotch, there were never any doubts about its proud flagship distillery. Just before Allied was bought out in 2005, and Laphroaig became part of Fortune Brands, it released its first Quarter Cask expression: by increasing the proportion of wood to whisky for the final seven months before bottling, the whole process of maturation is speeded up.

At the time of writing, Laphroaig was in the process of replacing the highly regarded 15-year-old with an 18-year-old expression.

LAPHROAIG 10-YEAR-OLD CASK STRENGTH

SINGLE MALT: ISLAY 57.3% ABV
Tar, seaweed, and salt, and some sweet wood too. Iodine and hot peat rumble through a long, dramatic finish.

LAPHROAIG 25-YEAR-OLD

SINGLE MALT: ISLAY 50.9% ABV
A spicy, floral character, with smoke and sea spray taking over only in the finish. Also available in cask strength.

LAPHROAIG 30-YEAR-OLD

SINGLE MALT: ISLAY 43% ABV
This is all but unobtainable now. The late, great whisky writer Michael Jackson described the 30-year-old as "full and creamy" and "beautifully balanced for such a great age".

**LAPHROAIG
QUARTER CASK**

SINGLE MALT: ISLAY 48% ABV

The Quarter Cask is at the heart of Laphroaig's core range. Small casks speed up the maturation process and lead to a sweet, woody taste that succumbs to a triumphal burst of peat smoke.

**LAPHROAIG
10-YEAR-OLD**

SINGLE MALT: ISLAY 40% ABV

The 10-year-old is also very popular. Beneath the dense peat smoke and salty sea spray is a refreshing, youthful malt with a sweet core.

The secrets of… **Laphroaig**

The malt from this great Islay distillery delights in its tough, uncompromising image, and for years it was promoted as a whisky that people would either love or hate.

Laphroaig is one of the smokiest, most pungent malts around, and, as a result, you almost expect the distillery to be perched on a cliff-top, battered by the ocean waves. It is a coastal distillery, but its position is a little more serene, in a quiet bay on the southern shore of the island.

The signature note of Laphroaig is apparent before you step inside. As one of the very few distilleries to have retained its floor maltings, you can see and smell the plumes of peat smoke wafting from the pagoda roof above the kiln. While the maltings provide only some of the malt needed, they do make visiting the distillery particularly interesting. Until 50 years ago, this was how all malt whisky was made.

Other factors that make Laphroaig special include the long years in wood and a unique set of stills. The dominant note remains the same today as it was in the 19th century. Then, when the whisky writer Alfred Barnard asked about the influence of the sea air, he was told it had no effect whatsoever. It was all down to peat.

▲ A SEASIDE LOCATION
It is tempting to relate the maritime character of Laphroaig to the distillery's dramatic position by the sea. Though hard to prove, the whisky does have a distinct taste of seaweed.

▼ SOFT, PEATY WATER
An abundant supply of water is vital for any distillery, yet many believe the character of the water has a minimal effect on the whisky's flavor. Laphroaig's whisky-makers disagree, and say the soft, peaty water from Loch Kilbride is an important factor.

▲ TURNING THE WET BARLEY
Having been steeped in water, the wet barley is spread across a stone floor, about 6 in (15 cm) deep. It is turned regularly with wooden shiels (broad shovels) to prevent the shoots matting together as the barley starts to germinate. After six days this "green" malt is ready for the kilns.

▼ A UNIQUE SET OF STILLS

Laphroaig has three wash stills and four spirit stills in two different sizes, which is very unusual. Another uncommon feature of the stills is the way the lyne arms slope upward rather than downward. This increases reflux during the long, slow distillation.

▼ PEATING BEFORE KILNING

The green malt is spread on a wire mesh suspended 15 ft (5 m) above a kiln, filled with peat. The kiln is fired up, and dense smoke immediately begins to impregnate the grains of malt. Unlike any other Scotch malt distillery, Laphroaig peats the malt first and then dries it afterward. It is maintained that this gives the whisky a much wider range of smoke flavors.

◄ CASKING STRENGTH

The middle cut from the spirit stills comes in at a strength of 68% ABV which is then reduced to 63.5% ABV before filling into casks. This is thought to be the most desirable strength for the maturation process.

LONG YEARS IN WOOD ►

The casks used at Laphroaig are almost entirely from Maker's Mark (see pp246–7), its sister distillery in the USA. Maturation is said to account for a third of the character of the whisky. Recently, the distillery began using quarter casks to increase the ratio of wood to whisky and speed up the process.

THE LAST DROP

www.lastdropdistillers.com

This unusual super-premium blend is the brainchild of three industry veterans—Tom Jago, James Espey, and Peter Fleck. Allegedly, a random discovery of very old whiskies pre-vatted at 12 years of age and then allowed to mature for a further 36 years in sherry casks, The Last Drop would appear to have been something of an accident and cannot be repeated. Included in the blend are whiskies from long-lost distilleries, the youngest reputed to have been distilled in 1960. Savor the tasting notes—at £1,000 or so a bottle and with only 1,347 bottles available, it may be the closest you'll get to tasting it.

THE LAST DROP

BLEND 54.5% ABV

Exceptionally complex nose, with figs, chocolate, and vanilla. An unusual combination of new-mown hay, dried fruit, herbs, and butter cookies.

LAUDER'S

Owner: MacDuff International

Between 1886 and 1893, Lauder's Royal Northern Cream scooped up a total of six gold medals in international competitions—a tribute to the meticulous research and repeated trials undertaken by the original proprietor, Archibald Lauder, a Glasgow publican. The development of the blend is said to have taken him two years. Today Lauder's is once again blended in Glasgow, by MacDuff International, and Lauder's Bar on Sauchiehall Street remains to commemorate Lauder himself. His blend has largely slipped from public view in its homeland, but is imported by Barton Brands of Chicago to the US, where it remains popular among value-conscious consumers.

LAUDER'S

BLEND 40% ABV

A light and fruity blend designed for session drinking and mixing.

LEDAIG

Tobermory Distillery,
Tobermory, Isle of Mull

Tobermory, the capital of Mull and the island's main port, was originally called Ledaig, and this was the name chosen by John Sinclair when he began distilling here in 1798. Quite when the Ledaig Distillery became Tobermory is unclear, as it has had an incredibly interrupted life, spending more time in mothballs than in production. In recent years the distillery adopted a similar approach to Springbank, producing a heavily peated robust West Coast malt called Ledaig and a lightly peated malt called Tobermory. At present there is a 10-year-old Ledaig, first released in 2008, and a 10- and a 15-year-old Tobermory *(see p172).*

LEDAIG 10-YEAR-OLD

SINGLE MALT: ISLANDS 43% ABV

Slightly medicinal, but full of dry, slightly dusty peat smoke.

LINKWOOD

Elgin, Morayshire
www.malts.com

From the outset, Linkwood was a well-conceived, almost self-sufficient distillery. It was named after Linkwood House on the Seafield Estate, where the estate manager, Peter Brown, decided to build a distillery in 1821. It was surrounded by barley fields to supply the grain, and cattle to feed on the spent draff. What you see today dates back to the 1870s, when Brown's son William demolished the original Linkwood and built a new distillery on the same site. It remained in private hands until 1933, when it became part of DCL. As a supplier of a "top dressing" malt used in many blends, Linkwood was highly regarded, and DCL paid a hefty £80,000 for it, around £4.3 million in today's money.

In 1960 the number of stills was tripled to six, with the new stills housed in a separate building.

The two stillrooms are still run in tandem, with the spirit produced in each vatted together prior to bottling. The whisky was part of The Ascot Malt Cellar, a prototype range of malts launched by the company. When UDV (now Diageo) launched its 'Classic Malts' series some years later, Linkwood was dropped from the fold in favor of Cragganmore.

LINKWOOD FLORA & FAUNA 12-YEAR-OLD

SINGLE MALT: SPEYSIDE 43% ABV
This standard expression is on the lighter side of the Speyside style, with a fresh, grassy, green-apple fragrance and faint notes of spice. In the mouth it has a delicate sweet-and-sour flavor and a slow finish.

LINKWOOD RARE MALTS 26-YEAR-OLD

SINGLE MALT: SPEYSIDE 56.1% ABV
Bright and breezy for a 26-year-old. Lightly smoky with caramelized sugar notes. Spicy and warm in the finish.

LOCH FYNE

Owner: Richard Joynson
www.lfw.co.uk

Created by Professor Ronnie Martin, a former production director at United Distillers (now Diageo), Loch Fyne is the exclusive and eponymous house blend of Loch Fyne Whiskies of Inverary. It is blended and bottled under license for this famous Scottish whisky specialist. The label, incidentally, honours the long-lost Highland distillery Glendarroch.

Slightly sweet and smoky, Loch Fyne is an easy-drinking, well-flavored blend, which the proprietors describe as "one to drink and enjoy rather than concentrate on". It has been praised by leading critics and won awards in international competition.

Also available is a full-strength 12-year-old liqueur, which comes in a 23 oz (70 cl) decanter. Created for whisky-lovers on the look-out for a sophisticated and complex

alternative, it can be enjoyed on its own, but is notably successful as a mixer or cocktail ingredient.

In addition to this, Loch Fyne has an ongoing whisky project in the shape of the Living Cask. Inspired by the way whisky was kept and drunk prior to the ubiquity of bottles, this is a cask used simultaneously for maturing and serving. The cask is filled with a vatting of malt whiskies, and tapped halfway down for drawing off bottlings. When about half the contents has been used, it is filled to the top again, so creating an everchanging blended malt, which can be bought in 7 oz (20 cl) sample bottles at cask strength.

LOCH FYNE PREMIUM SCOTCH

BLEND 40% ABV
Apple dumplings on the nose, enlivened by orange and tangerine notes. Subtle, with nutty, oil-related aromas and hints of smoke. The palate is smooth and well-balanced: acidic, salty, sweet, and dry. The finish is surprisingly warming.

LOCH LOMOND

Alexandria, Dumbartonshire
www.lochlomonddistillery.com

Within the confines of the Loch Lomond Distillery, on the southern end of Loch Lomond, all manner of Scotch whiskies are produced, although originally it was just malt. The distillery was built in 1965 as a joint venture between Barton Brands of America and Duncan Thomas. Twenty years later it was bought by Alexander Bulloch and his company, Glen Catrine Bonded Warehouse Ltd. Today, grain whisky is produced alongside the malt. The distillery's stills have rectifying columns that can be adjusted to produce a lighter or heavier spirit.

LOCH LOMOND

SINGLE MALT: HIGHLANDS 40% ABV
With no age statement and a competitive price, this is likely to be a fairly young single malt. It has a light, fresh flavor and no great influence of wood.

LONGMORN 16-YEAR-OLD

LONGMORN CASK STRENGTH 17-YEAR-OLD 1991

LOCHRANZA

Arran Distillers, Lochranza,
Isle of Arran
www.arranwhisky.com

This blended whisky is named after
the picturesque village where the
Isle of Arran Distillery is based.
This was established as recently as
1995 by industry veteran Harold
Currie, but has subsequently
changed hands. Lochranza is a
pleasant, easy-drinking standard
blend. It may well see further
development in future years as a
proportion of the distillery's own
mature stock of single malts can
find its way into the recipe. Arran
Distillers also produce the Robert
Burns blend (*see p154*).

LOCHRANZA

BLEND 40% ABV
The initial impression is of melted toffee,
followed by pears, oak, and hints of
lime. Smooth and sweet, lightly sherried
and oaky, with a medium finish. A dash
of water helps the flavors.

LONG JOHN

Owner: Chivas Brothers

Despite reasonably healthy sales
in France, Scandinavia, and some
Spanish-speaking markets, Long
John appears very much the poor
relation in the Chivas Brothers'
stable, dominated as it is by Chivas
Regal and Ballantine's. The brand
has passed through a number of
owners since it was founded in
the early 19th century by the
eponymous Long John MacDonald.
The Scottish Whisky Association's
Directory of Member's Brands lists
a non-age version as well as a 12-
and 15-year-old.

LONG JOHN 12-YEAR-OLD

BLEND 40% ABV
The blend is said to contain 48
different malts, including Laphroaig
and Highland Park. A deluxe blend,
Long John 12-year-old is a dark,
traditional style of whisky, noted for
its distinctive character.

LONGMORN

Elgin, Morayshire

John Duff was 52 when he went
into partnership with George
Thomson and Charles Shirres
in 1894. Together, they built
Longmorn, in a village of the same
name just south of Elgin. The
distillery occupies the site of an old
chapel (Longmorn means "place of
the holy man" in Gaelic) and, with
its four stills, it was conceived on a
grand scale at a cost of £20,000
(around £2m in today's money).
Yet within five years Duff had
bought out his partners and built
another distillery, Benriach, next
door. While Benriach has often
struggled, Longmorn has been in
almost continuous production since
the start. It seems this classic,
floral Speyside malt was just what
the blenders wanted.

In 1970, Longmorn formed a
small group with Glenlivet and
Glen Grant, which had become
part of Seagram by the end of the

decade. Aside from independent
expressions, a distillery bottling
appeared in Seagram's Heritage
Selection of malts in 1994.

Since 2000, Longmorn has been
owned by Chivas Brothers, the
whisky arm of drinks giant Pernod
Ricard, which has replaced the
existing 15-year-old with one a
year older and clearly aimed at the
super-premium category of malts.

LONGMORN 16-YEAR-OLD

SINGLE MALT: SPEYSIDE 48% ABV
Its cereal aroma is sweetened with
coconut from ageing in bourbon casks.
The mouthfeel is smooth and silky and
dries on the tongue to give a crisp,
slightly austere finish.

LONGMORN CASK STRENGTH
17-YEAR-OLD 1991

SINGLE MALT: SPEYSIDE 49.4% ABV
Richly floral on the nose and palate.
Vanilla and ripe pears combine
beautifully with tantalizing oaky notes.

LONGROW 10-YEAR-OLD

LONGROW 14-YEAR-OLD

LONGROW 7-YEAR-OLD GAJA BAROLO

LONGROW

Springbank Distillery,
Well Close, Campbeltown, Argyll
www.springbankdistillers.com

After being Scotland's most famous whisky town, Campbeltown suffered a swift and brutal demise. As blenders began to source their malt from Speyside, it turned to the US, until Prohibition shut that market down in 1919. From over a dozen distilleries, only Springbank and Glen Scotia were left by 1935.

In 1973, Springbank decided to distil a pungent, heavily smoked whisky alongside its main malt. The new whisky was christened Longrow after a distillery that had once stood next door. It was released as an experiment in 1985 and finally became a regular fixture in 1992.

Today, the core range includes the 10-year-old, its cask strength sibling—the 10-year-old 100 Proof—and the 14-year-old. Various limited-release expressions

have been added, including one finished in old Barolo casks. In 2008, a small amount of Longrow 18-year-old was released, an expression that will come and go depending on stocks.

LONGROW 10-YEAR-OLD

SINGLE MALT: CAMPBELTOWN 46% ABV
This dense, phenolic whisky has plenty of smoky complexity, alongside some sweetness from maturing in a mix of ex-bourbon and sherry casks.

LONGROW 14-YEAR-OLD

SINGLE MALT: CAMPBELTOWN 46% ABV
Coal smoke on the nose and coal dust on the palate may not sound appealing, but to phenol-lovers this is manna. An industrial-tasting mix of hot tar, brine, and coke.

LONGROW 7-YEAR-OLD GAJA BAROLO

SINGLE MALT: CAMPBELTOWN 55.8% ABV
This whiskey spends 18 months in old wine casks, giving a sweet-and-sour edge to the underlying flavors of peat smoke.

THE MACALLAN FINE OAK 10-YEAR-OLD

MACALLAN

Easter Elchies, Craigellachie,
Morayshire
www.themacallan.com

The Macallan stands on the west bank of the Spey, just across the river from Craigellachie and well beyond the bustle of Dufftown and the Speyside whisky trail. The signpost to the distillery is discreet, and visitors tend to come privately, by appointment.

It was first licensed in 1824 as the Elchies Distillery by Alexander Reid, a tenant farmer on Easter Elchies farm. It was a small-scale operation, run as a sideline to the main business of farming. At certain times of year, however, there would have been a good passing trade of cattle drovers on their way to and from the big markets to the south. Being close to a ford through the river, the farm became a good stopping place for them to rest, swap stories, and buy whisky.

Annual production at Macallan was still only 180,000 liters (40,000 gallons) when it was sold to Roderick Kemp in 1892. The distillery was expanded and remained in family control until 1996, when it was bought by Highland Distillers (now part of the Edrington Group), for £180 million. Ironically, Highland had made an unsolicited bid for Macallan back in 1898. Its offer then was a modest £80,000, which was turned down flat.

In the intervening years, the distillery was rebuilt in the 1950s and the number of stills grew to 21. More importantly, The Macallan 10-year-old, launched in 1978, established itself as one of the leading single malts on Speyside.

The distillery had always made a virtue of its use of sherry casks, which were carefully selected and shipped in from Spain. A deep amber color and fruitcake character came to symbolize the whisky. So the launch of the Fine Oak series in 2004, which uses bourbon casks alongside sherry butts, marked a radical departure. It has clearly widened The Macallan's appeal, however. The series starts with an 8-year-old, and progresses through many age variations to a 30-year-old.

THE MACALLAN FINE OAK 10-YEAR-OLD

SINGLE MALT: SPEYSIDE 40% ABV
With less sherry influence than the standard 10-year-old, more of the fresh, brisk, malty distillery character comes through.

THE MACALLAN 10-YEAR-OLD

SINGLE MALT: SPEYSIDE 40% ABV
The signature Macallan, matured in sherry butts. This popular whisky has a dried-fruit, slightly toffee-scented nose and a well-rounded flavor.

THE MACALLAN 25-YEAR-OLD

SINGLE MALT: SPEYSIDE 43% ABV
Spicy citrus notes accompany the ripe dried-fruit character from the sherry casks, which lead to a little wood-smoke on the tongue.

THE MACALLAN 30-YEAR-OLD

SINGLE MALT: SPEYSIDE 43% ABV
A big, post-prandial malt with a sweet, sherried nose and spicy flavors of orange peel, cloves, and dates that linger on the finish.

THE MACALLAN 10-YEAR-OLD

THE MACALLAN 25-YEAR-OLD

THE MACALLAN 30-YEAR-OLD

The secrets of... Macallan

Of everything that goes into making malt whisky, the greatest impact comes from wood, and this is something that Macallan understood and appreciated long before many of its rivals.

Maturation is something that the Speyside distillery has always taken very seriously, and the insistence on expensive sherry butts rather than far cheaper bourbon barrels goes way back. The rich, nutty flavor from the sherry casks remains the signature tune to The Macallan, though The Fine Oak range, launched in 2004, now provides a partly bourbon-matured alternative.

Yet, while maturation may be the biggest single influence on the whisky, the casks can only work their magic on what the distillery provides in terms of new make spirit. The unique character of this is determined by a host of factors—from the choice of barley, to the shape of the stills, to the speed of distillation.

Among the most important choices is selecting the final "cut"—that part of the spirit between the foreshots and the feints that is kept. The Macallan prides itself on one of the finest cuts of any distillery in Scotland: Just 16 percent of what flows from the spirit still is filled into casks.

▲ A FARM DISTILLERY

Long before the distillery was founded in 1824, local farmers were distilling whisky from the barley in surrounding fields. This would have been offered to the drovers who stopped here on their way to market.

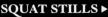

SQUAT STILLS ▶

The five wash stills at the distillery work in tandem with 10 spirit stills—these being the smallest on Speyside. Their unique shape and size helps maximize the contact between the liquid and the copper. This strips out some of the heavier sulfur compounds, leaving the new make spirit clean and fruity.

▲ DOUGLAS FIR WASHBACKS

Macallan has used stainless-steel washbacks for many years, but, as part of a recent expansion, a new set of six Douglas fir washbacks were built, so now fermentation is carried out in both wood and metal.

◄ THE LONG SLEEP

Having been diluted to a strength of 69.8% ABV with water from the estate, the spirit is filled into casks and left to slumber. A quarter of the 140,000 casks are stored in Macallan's 16 traditional dunnage warehouses, which are cool and damp, with earth floors and stone walls. The rest of the casks are kept in five modern racked warehouses that have recently been built on site.

▲ SHERRY AND BOURBON

Although most of the casks in Macallan's warehouses are sherry butts, you can also find puncheons, barrels, and ex-bourbon hogsheads shipped over from Kentucky. The sherry casks are a mixture of European and American oak.

▲ THE FLAVOR PROFILE

The key flavors of The Macallan can be explored in an interactive display at the distillery's visitor center. Traditional Macallan takes a floral, quite fruity Speyside spirit and coats it with a rich layer of spicy sherry flavors. The relatively new Fine Oak range has a fresher, more delicate flavor, with the distillery character more pronounced.

MANNOCHMORE FLORA & FAUNA 12-YEAR-OLD

MANNOCHMORE RARE MALTS 22-YEAR-OLD

MACARTHUR'S

Owner: Inver House Distillers

The MacArthur clan of Argyllshire fought nobly alongside Robert the Bruce in the struggle for Scottish independence and subsequently gave their name to this standard blend. Like so many others, it has its roots in the upsurge of blending from independent merchants in the late-Victorian era and can be traced to the 1870s. Today it is owned by Inver House Distillers, who describe it as having a "light, smooth flavor with toffee and vanilla from cask ageing". MacArthur's is not to be confused with single malts bottled independently under the label James MacArthur.

MACARTHUR'S

BLEND 40% ABV

Fragrant, barley-malt nose with sweet, citrus aftertones. A medium-bodied, uncomplicated whisky, softly aromatic, with a smooth, mellow palate and a fresh, lingering finish.

MAC NA MARA

Owner: The Gaelic Whisky Co.
www.gaelicwhisky.com

Despite its Irish-sounding name, which means "son of the sea" in Gaelic, Mac Na Mara hails from the Isle of Skye whisky company Pràban na Linne (also known as the Gaelic Whisky Co.). A lighter blended whisky with some West Coast character, it was first introduced in 1992 and became popular in France, where the company enjoys its strongest following. A Rum Finish version is also offered from time to time. Unusually for a blended whisky, this is non chill-filtered and aged for a further 12 months in Guyanan rum casks for a sweet finish.

MAC NA MARA

BLEND 40% ABV

A light and essentially undemanding blended whisky with a biscuit-like nose, a citrus tang, and a creamy finish.

MANNOCHMORE

Elgin, Morayshire
www.malts.com

This modern distillery was part of the Haig empire—a separate fiefdom within the Distillers Company Limited. It was built in 1971 as one of a cluster of distilleries between Elgin and Rothes. Nearby are Longmorn and Benriach, while almost next door is Glenlossie, which has operated in tandem with Mannochmore from the start, sharing the same workforce and warehouses.

From conception, Mannochmore's simple role in life was supplying malt for Haig, then the top-selling blend in the UK. Fourteen years later it fell victim to the chronic oversupply in the industry and was mothballed, as the big distillers sought to drain the whisky loch. It was back in production by 1989 and launched its first official malt as part of the Flora & Fauna range three years later.

Mannochmore is famous for launching Loch Dhu in 1996. With its distinctive dark color, it was only produced for four years, but has become something of a cult since, particularly in Denmark. There has been the odd independent bottling, including a cask-strength expression from 1977, released by Signatory, and a youthful 1996 bottling from Duncan Taylor.

MANNOCHMORE FLORA & FAUNA 12-YEAR-OLD

SINGLE MALT: SPEYSIDE 43% ABV

This is very much an aperitif-style malt, with a light, floral nose but, in the mouth, a more luscious, spicy character, with hints of liquorice and vanilla, comes through.

MANNOCHMORE RARE MALTS 22-YEAR-OLD

SINGLE MALT: SPEYSIDE 60.1% ABV

Distilled in 1974, this limited edition exudes fragrant, flowery aromas. Herbaceous and peppery, with a touch of peat in the mix.

MCCLELLAND'S HIGHLAND

MCCLELLAND'S SPEYSIDE

MCCLELLAND'S ISLAY

MCCLELLAND'S LOWLAND

MCCLELLAND'S

Owner: Morrison Bowmore

The range of McClelland's single malts offers a chance to explore Scotland and four of its key whisky-distilling regions. It was first launched in 1986, with a Highland, Lowland, and Islay expression. These proved so successful that a Speyside expression was introduced in 1999. According to the company, each one is carefully selected to reflect the true essence and character of the region in which it is produced.

The brand currently claims to be number four in the US market, where it competes against Glenlivet, Glenfiddich, and The Macallan. It is also distributed to global markets, including Taiwan, Austria, South Africa, Japan, Canada, France, Russia, and the Netherlands. A Speyside 12-year-old was launched in November 2008 and will be joined by Highland, Lowland, and Islay 12-year-olds.

MCCLELLAND'S LOWLAND

SINGLE MALT: LOWLANDS 40% ABV
A richly floral nose with hints of nutmeg, ginger, and citrus fruits. Very clean and delicate on the palate, with floral notes.

MCCLELLAND'S HIGHLAND

SINGLE MALT: HIGHLANDS 40% ABV
Delicate wood notes on the nose, with sweet buttercream and fresh vanilla. Some initial sweetness, giving way to fresh fruit and lime hints.

MCCLELLAND'S SPEYSIDE

SINGLE MALT: SPEYSIDE 40% ABV
Fresh mint, cut pine, hints of dark chocolate, and sweet malt on the nose. Initially sweet, developing nutty flavors and floral hints.

MCCLELLAND'S ISLAY

SINGLE MALT: ISLAY 40% ABV
The nose is unmistakably Islay: wood smoke and cinders, tar, vanilla, and citrus hints. Forceful sea salt, burnt oak, and peat smoke, with vanilla undertones on the palate.

MILTONDUFF 15-YEAR-OLD

MILTONDUFF 1968

MILLBURN

Inverness, Inverness-shire

It was Millburn's misfortune to be located on the outskirts of Inverness on the road to Elgin. When the whisky industry suffered one of its big periodic downturns in the 1980s, the distillery was in the wrong place at the wrong time— not remote enough to simply be mothballed when there was the prospect of redevelopment instead. And so it shut down for good in 1985 and was turned into a steakhouse; today, it's a hotel and restaurant called The Auld Distillery. Limited-edition bottlings are still released intermittently by the owner of its stocks, Diageo.

MILLBURN RARE MALTS 25-YEAR-OLD

SINGLE MALT: SPEYSIDE 61.9% ABV

This Rare Malts bottling is a big, meaty whisky that is dry and chewy in the mouth, with damp wood, smoke, and orange skins.

MILTONDUFF

Miltonduff, Elgin, Morayshire

Illicit whisky-making was widespread in Speyside and not just in remote glens such as Glenlivet. There were allegedly over 50 illicit stills around Elgin, including Miltonduff, which took out a license in 1824. After periodic changes in ownership, it became part of George Ballantine & Son, a division of Hiram Walker, in 1936. In 1964, Miltonduff gained a pair of Lomond stills, to provide different styles of whisky, including the single malt Mosstowie, of which there are still a few independent bottlings around. These are becoming increasingly rare, as the Lomond stills were removed and replaced with traditional pot stills in 1981.

A decade later, Miltonduff was included in a range of malts marketed by its new owner, Allied Distillers. The range, known as "Caledonian Malts," was a belated riposte to the "Classic Malts" of what is now Diageo.

Since 2005, Miltonduff has been owned by the French group Pernod Ricard, which continues to use much of the 1.2 million gallon (5.5 million liter) production to supply malt for its top-selling blend, Ballantine's Finest. An official 15-year-old malt is now available, although a wider range of bottlings exists among the independents, particularly Gordon & MacPhail.

MILTONDUFF 15-YEAR-OLD

SINGLE MALT: SPEYSIDE 46% ABV

This non chill-filtered distillery bottling is hard to find. It has a gentle Speyside character with a honeyed, leathery aroma and a nutty, herbal flavor.

MILTONDUFF GORDON & MACPHAIL 1968

SINGLE MALT: SPEYSIDE 40% ABV

This rare Gordon & MacPhail bottling has a rich sherried character with notes of licorice, menthol, and crystallized ginger.

MONKEY SHOULDER

Owner: William Grant & Sons

The name may seem contrived, but this blended malt from William Grant & Sons refers to a condition known among workers in the maltings—turning the damp grain by hand, they often incurred a repetitive strain injury.

Three metal monkeys decorate the shoulder of the bottle and just three single malts go into the blend—Glenfiddich, Balvenie, and Kininvie. At the launch, great play was made of the whisky's mixability, and you're as likely to encounter it on a cocktail menu as you are in your local liquor store.

MONKEY SHOULDER

BLEND 40% ABV

Banana, honey, pears, and allspice on the nose. Vanilla, nutmeg, citrus hints, and generic fruit on the palate. A dry finish, then a short burst of menthol.

MORTLACH FLORA & FAUNA 16-YEAR-OLD

MORTLACH 21-YEAR-OLD

OBAN 14-YEAR-OLD

OBAN DISTILLERS EDITION 1992

MORTLACH

Dufftown, Keith, Banffshire
www.malts.com

Long before the distillery building
boom on Speyside, James Findlater
became the first licensed distiller
in Dufftown in 1823. By the end of
the century, the town had no fewer
than six distilleries. Mortlach
changed hands at regular intervals,
and was briefly a brewery and
even a temporary home for the
Free Church of Scotland at one
point. In 1897, the number of stills
was doubled to six, making this
one of the largest distilleries in the
Highlands. It became part of DCL
(now Diageo) in 1925, which
used its malt in blends, especially
Johnnie Walker. The first official
bottling as a single malt was not
until 1995, when a 22-year-old
rare malt was released.

The six stills are configured in a
uniquely complex manner, with
a fifth of the spirit being triple-
distilled in an intermediate still

called "Wee Witchie." This process
is intended to add richness and
depth to the spirit, which is then
condensed in traditional worm tubs
outside, to create a more robust
style of whisky.

Mortlach is ever-popular with
blenders, so the amount released
as a single malt is limited to the
standard 16-year-old expression,
the occasional rare malt, and the
odd independent bottling.

MORTLACH FLORA & FAUNA 16-YEAR-OLD

SINGLE MALT: SPEYSIDE 43% ABV
As suggested by the rich amber color,
there is a strong sherry influence at
play, although not enough to unbalance
this beguiling, complex malt with notes
of dark mint-chocolate on the nose.

MORTLACH 21-YEAR-OLD

SINGLE MALT: SPEYSIDE 43% ABV
Caramel and soft fruits on the nose.
The palate is drier, with the sherry
wood influence bringing resinous,
oaky flavors.

OBAN

Oban, Argyll
www.malts.com

Oban Distillery dates back to 1793,
when Oban itself was a tiny West
Coast fishing village. Since then
the town—which is dubbed "The
Gateway to the Isles"—has grown
up around it, choking off any
chance of expansion.

With a capacity of just 150,000
gallons (700,000 liters), Oban was
never the first distillery the big
industry bosses sought to close
during periods of overproduction.
As a consequence, except for a few
years in the 1930s and 1960s,
when the still house was rebuilt, it
has been in continuous production.

Since 1990 Oban has been one
of Diageo's "Classic Malts," albeit
the smallest of them. Given the
success of the range, its owners
may wonder whether it should
have picked a larger distillery.
Today Oban is sold on allocation
in selected markets.

Alongside the official 14-year-old
single malt whisky, older Distillers
Edition malts are released from
time to time.

OBAN 14-YEAR-OLD

SINGLE MALT: HIGHLANDS 43% ABV
The brisk, maritime distillery
character is mellowed by the years in
wood. The influence of sherry adds
a rich, dried-fruit character.

OBAN DISTILLERS EDITION 1992

SINGLE MALT: HIGHLANDS 43% ABV
A 15-year-old malt, aged in different
casks during maturation. Spicy and
oaky flavors dominate from the strong
sherry-wood effect—the result of
finishing in Montilla Fino casks.

All about...
Bottles

It was only in the late 1880s, with the invention of mechanical glass-blowing, that whiskey began to be filled into glass bottles. Prior to this, it was sold in bulk, by the small cask, or the stoneware jar. The advantage of the sealed bottle—until 1913 the seal was always a driven cork, requiring a corkscrew—was that it prevented, or at least discouraged, adulteration. Such bottles as were used for whiskey prior to the 1880s were recycled wine bottles, made from dark glass—clear glass was taxed at 11 times the rate of dark glass.

PETARD In its shape and use of a small, hand-written label, The Glenrothes petard derives its look from a lab sample bottle. The color of the liquid is allowed to shine through, and this design embodies integrity. Introduced in 1994, it quickly became known as the "petard" or "grenade."

EMBOSSED
Heavily embossed bottles speak of luxury and are especially popular in Asia. Crown Royal was introduced to mark the State Visit of Britain's King George VI to Canada in 1939. The bottle is further "enobled" by coming in a purple velvet bag.

STANDARD LIQUOR BOTTLE This shape became the standard bottle for Scotch whisky in the 1890s, although earlier bottles tend to be heavier and of very dark green glass.

CERAMIC Such vessels hark back to the stoneware jars of the late-19th century. Arthur Bell & Sons have been issuing commemorative bell-shaped Christmas decanters annually since 1988. They have become collectors' items, and some are now very valuable.

PINCH George Ogilvy Haig introduced this unusual shape in 1893 for his Dimple brand of Scotch. In the US it was sold as Pinch, and the bottle shape was the first to be patented under US law, in 1958.

SWING Sir Alexander Walker, Johnnie Walker's grandson, created the deluxe blend Swing specifically for luxurious transatlantic liners. The bottle has a rounded base, so it "swings" with the motion of the ship and remains perpendicular!

DISTILLED, BLENDED & BOTTLED IN SCOTLAND JOHN WALKER & SONS

EST? 1820

JOHNNIE WALKER®

Swing

EXCEPTIONALLY SMOOTH
SCOTCH WHISKY

Johnnie Walker

KILMARNOCK 43%vol 70cl KA3 1HD SCOTLAND

SINCE 1887

Grant's
BLENDED SCOTCH WHISKY
THE FAMILY RESERVE
SINCE 1887
PRODUCT OF SCOTLAND

WM GRANT & SONS

TRIANGULAR William Grant & Sons introduced this supremely ergonomic shape for their brand Standfast in the mid-1950s, and adopted it in 1964 for Glenfiddich. The innovative shape was created by the modernist designer Hans Schleger.

WAX-SEALED MAKER'S MARK In the late-19th century, some blenders dipped the neck of the bottle in sealing wax, having driven home the cork. This was common practice with port, and made the bottle "tamper-proof." Marge Samuels, wife of the owner of Maker's Mark, applied it to this brand in the 1950s.

Make
Ma
(S IV)
KENTUCKY STRAIGHT
WHISK
HANDMADE
Distilled, aged and bot
Maker's Mark Distill
Star Hill Farm, Lorett
750ml. 45% alc

GRAND OLD PARR 12-YEAR-OLD

OLD PARR SPRING | OLD PARR SUMMER | OLD PARR WINTER

OLD PARR

Owner: Diageo

"Keep your head cool by temperance and your feet warm by exercise. Rise early, go soon to bed, and if you want to grow fat [prosperous], keep your eyes open and your mouth shut." So said the original "Old Parr," one Thomas Parr, who lived from 1483 to 1635, making him 152 years old when he died. If that seems improbable, his tomb can be inspected in Poets' Corner, Westminster Abbey.

In 1871, Old Parr's name was borrowed by two famous blenders of their day, the Greenlees brothers, for their deluxe whisky. Now under the stewardship of industry giants Diageo, the brand has gone on to success in Japan, Venezuela, Mexico, and Colombia. The square brown bottle appears unchanged in years, and Old Parr whisky has a loyal band of followers who appreciate its distinctive, old-fashioned style.

Old Parr 18-year-old was awarded the title of "World Whisky of the Year" by one popular guide in 2007. By tradition, Cragganmore is the mainstay of the blend.

A few years ago, Old Parr launched a limited-edition series that it called the Four Seasons. Comprising blends of carefully selected casks to obtain four styles of whisky with very different characteristics, the series has become something of a collector's item, with the Autumn expression in particular having become extremely rare.

GRAND OLD PARR 12-YEAR-OLD

BLEND 43% ABV

Pronounced malt, raisin, and orange notes on the nose, with some apple and dried-fruit undertones, and perhaps a hint of peat. Forceful on the palate, with flavors of malt, raisin, burned caramel, and brown sugar.

OLD PULTENEY 12-YEAR-OLD

OLD PULTENEY

Pulteney Distillery, Wick, Caithness
www.oldpulteney.com

Wick, in the far northeast corner of Scotland, is just a short distance from John o' Groats, commonly regarded as Britain's most northerly point. Wick was a tiny village when Sir William Johnstone Pulteney decided to turn it into a major fishing port in the early 1800s. In 1826, with the trade in herring booming, James Henderson built Pulteney in his honor.

The business of fishing, gutting, and packing the herring into barrels was thirsty work, and the town's only distillery thrived. The setting appeared perfect, but dwindled the herring fleet gradually and, in 1922, at the high-water mark of the temperance movement, the town voted to go dry. The distillery closed in 1930 and did not reopen until 1951—by which time the town was no longer a haven of sobriety.

The solitary wash still comes with a giant ball, to increase reflux, and a truncated top, supposedly lopped off to fit the still room. Pulteney's malts are marketed today as "Old Pulteney."

OLD PULTENEY 12-YEAR-OLD

SINGLE MALT: HIGHLANDS 40% ABV
Launched by Inver House in 1997, two years after buying the distillery, this is a brisk, salty, maritime malt with a woody sweetness from aging in bourbon casks.

OLD PULTENEY 17-YEAR-OLD

SINGLE MALT: HIGHLANDS 46% ABV
The non chill-filtered big brother of the 12-year-old is partly matured in sherry wood, to add fruity, butterscotch notes to the flavor, which is long with a medium-full body in the mouth.

OLD PULTENEY 21-YEAR-OLD

SINGLE MALT: HIGHLANDS 46% ABV
The sherry influence comes from the American oak used in the cask. The result is a rich, creamy, honey-scented malt that dries on the finish.

OLD SMUGGLER

Owner: Gruppo Campari

Reputedly, and appropriately, a big favorite during Prohibition, Old Smuggler was first developed by James and George Stodart in 1835. Although the firm is today largely forgotten, history records that it was the first to marry its whisky in sherry butts. The brand is now owned by Gruppo Campari, who acquired it along with its sister blend Braemar and the flagship Glen Grant Distillery from Pernod Ricard in 2006. It continues to hold a significant position in the US and Argentina, where it is the second-bestselling whisky, and is reported to be developing strong sales in Eastern Europe.

OLD SMUGGLER

BLEND 40% ABV

Decent Scotch with no offensive overtones and some smoke hints. Blended for value, and for drinking with a mixer.

PASSPORT

Owner: Chivas Brothers

Passport was developed by Seagram and acquired by Pernod Ricard in 2002. Like many brands that are invisible in the UK, it enjoys conspicuous success elsewhere: Passport's main strongholds are the US, South Korea, Spain, and Brazil, where its fruity taste lends itself to being served on the rocks, in mixed drinks and in cocktails. Packaged in a distinctive retro, rectangular green bottle, Passport is "a unique Scotch whisky, inspired by the revolution of 1960s Britain, with a young and vibrant personality." Such distinguished and famous malts as Glenlivet are found in the blend.

PASSPORT

BLEND 40% ABV

A fruity taste and a deliciously creamy finish. It can be served straight or, more usually, mixed over ice. Medium-bodied, with a soft and mellow finish.

PIG'S NOSE

Owner: Spencerfield Spirits
www.spencerfieldspirit.com

Should you visit one of the UK's many agricultural or county fairs, you may well encounter this whisky being sold from the back of an old horse box. Do not walk away: Pig's Nose has been re-blended by Whyte & Mackay's superstar master blender, Richard Paterson, and launched back on to the market in smart new livery. Brother to the better-known blended malt Sheep Dip *(see p160)*, Pig's Nose is a full-flavored and drinkable blend that more than lives up to the claim that "our Scotch is as soft and smooth as a pig's nose."

PIG'S NOSE

BLEND 40% ABV

The nose is delicate and refined, with soft and sensual floral notes supported by complex fruit flavors. On the palate, there is a forceful array of malty flavors from Scotland's four distilling regions.

PINWINNIE ROYALE

Owner: Inver House Distillers

Pinwinnie Royale stands out from the crowd, its label hinting at an early ecclesiastical manuscript and regal connections, though there is little to support these romantic suppositions. Given its place in the Inver House stable, it would seem likely that Old Pulteney, Speyburn, anCnoc, and Balblair single malts are to be found in the blend, with the emphasis on the lesser-known names. As well as the standard expression, there is a 12-year-old version, which mixes a light Speyside fruitiness with drier background wood notes, and a buttery texture.

PINWHINNIE ROYALE

BLEND 40% ABV

Young, spirity fruitiness on the nose, smooth-textured but spicy in the mouth, with burned, sooty notes in the finish.

POIT DHUBH

Owner: The Gaelic Whisky Co.
www.gaelicwhisky.com

Pràban na Linne (known also as the Gaelic Whisky Co.) was established by Sir Iain Noble in 1976 to create employment in the south of Skye. The business has grown steadily since. Poit Dhubh (pronounced *Potch Ghoo*) is a non chill-filtered blended malt supplied as 8-, 12-, and 21-year-olds. A limited-edition 30-year-old was bottled for the company's 30th anniversary. Poit Dhubh makes much play of the possible bootleg nature of its whisky, stating, "We are unwilling either to confirm or deny that Poit Dhubh comes from an illicit still." This is, of course, complete fantasy.

POIT DHUBH 8-YEAR-OLD

BLENDED MALT 43% ABV
Dried fruits and a light spiciness give a bittersweet character, with dry, woody notes and a trace of peat.

PORT ELLEN

Port Ellen, Isle of Islay

Of all Islay malts, Port Ellen has possibly the largest cult following, owing to its rarity, which has increased every year since the distillery shut down in 1983. It was founded in 1825 by Alexander Kerr Mackay, and remained in family hands until the 1920s, when it became part of DCL (Distillers Company Ltd.). Its misfortune was to be part of the same stable as Laphroaig and Caol Ila: when the downturn came, it was the weakest link. Today it remains active as a maltings plant, supplying Islay's distilleries with most of their malt.

PORT ELLEN DOUGLAS LAING 26-YEAR-OLD

SINGLE MALT: ISLAY 50% ABV
Matured in refill bourbon casks, this bottling has a sweet and fruity nose, with some new leather. Sweetness on the palate, but overwhelmed by peat smoke. A long, tarry finish, with a dab of salt.

PRIME BLUE

Owner: Morrison Bowmore

Prime Blue is a blended malt available largely in Taiwan, where the market has developed in sensational style during the last decade. The color blue is said to convey nobility and royalty, and the brand name was reputedly chosen to reflect sophistication in the whisky's taste. At their peak, sales exceeded 1 million cases a year, although the market for this style in the Far East has declined somewhat in recent years and competition in Taiwan and elsewhere has intensified. Standard, 12-, 17-, and 21-year-old versions are available.

PRIME BLUE

BLENDED MALT 40% ABV
Aromas of vanilla and malted barley are soon followed by light cocoa, and then heathery, floral notes. Initially fruity on the palate, followed by a malty sweetness, and a long finish.

QUEEN ANNE

Owner: Chivas Brothers

A good example of an "orphan brand" that has found its way into the portfolio of a larger company and appears to lack any clear role and purpose. Queen Anne was once a leading name from the distinguished Edinburgh blenders Hill, Thomson & Co. It was first produced in 1884 and blended by one William Shaw. Today it belongs to Chivas Brothers. Like so many once-famous and proud brands, Queen Anne has been left bereft and isolated by consolidation in the Scotch whisky industry, steadfastly clinging on in one or more regions where once it was loved and popular.

QUEEN ANNE

BLEND 40% ABV
Not especially characterful, as the flavors are so tightly integrated that it is difficult to discern individual aromas or tastes. A standard blend for mixing.

Hogsheads are assembled from the broken down staves of bourbon barrels. They are about 20 percent bigger than barrels and, once reassembled, are steam heated to expand the oak and make the joints watertight.

ROBERT BURNS BLEND

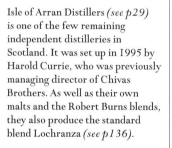

ROBERT BURNS MALT

ROBERT BURNS

Owner: Isle of Arran Distillers
www.arranwhisky.com

With the Scotch whisky industry generally apt to employ Scottish imagery and heritage associations at the drop of a tam-o'-shanter, it is a surprise to find that no one had previously marketed a brand named after Scotland's national bard. Independent distiller Isle of Arran has worked with the World Burns Federation to fill this gap, and now produces an officially endorsed Burns Collection of blended whiskies and malts.

Naturally, the Robert Burns brand contains a significant proportion of Arran single malt, and is claimed by the company to "capture the character of our beautiful island of clear mountain water and soft sea air". Sadly, it seems that the poet never actually visited the Isle of Arran, although he would have been able to see it from his Ayrshire home.

Isle of Arran Distillers *(see p29)* is one of the few remaining independent distilleries in Scotland. It was set up in 1995 by Harold Currie, who was previously managing director of Chivas Brothers. As well as their own malts and the Robert Burns blends, they also produce the standard blend Lochranza *(see p136)*.

ROBERT BURNS SINGLE MALT

BLEND 40% ABV
Hints of oak on the nose give way to sherry, almonds, toffee, and ripe fruits. Plenty of toffee, cake, and dried fruits on the palate, with a light to medium, spicy finish.

ROBERT BURNS MALT

BLEND 40% ABV
A nose of green apples, the acidity tempered by a note of vanilla. Apple and citrus notes on the palate, balanced by vanilla again. An aperitif whisky that is light in style and finish.

ROSEBANK

Camelon, Falkirk

Few distilleries have managed to stay in continuous production. Many closed during the 1980s and '90s when the industry was dealing with oversupply. Whether a distillery survived when demand picked up depended largely on location. Rosebank, near Falkirk, was mothballed in 1993 and has since been redeveloped. Founded in 1840, it was chosen to be part of The Ascot Malt Cellar in 1982. Unfortunately for Rosebank, when this became the "Classic Malts" series, Glenkinchie was picked to represent the Lowlands rather than Rosebank.

ROSEBANK DOUGLAS LAING 16-YEAR-OLD

SINGLE MALT: LOWLANDS 50% ABV
This independent bottling from Douglas Laing is part of its Old Malt Cask collection. Despite its strength and age, it is fresh and citrussy.

ROYAL BRACKLA

Cawdor, Nairn, Nairnshire

Brackla was founded between the River Findhorn and the Murray Firth by Captain William Fraser in 1812. He was soon complaining that, although he was surrounded by whisky-drinkers, he could only sell 100 gallons (450 liters) a year. By way of compensation, he secured the first royal warrant for a distillery in 1835. Whether he would recognize Royal Brackla today seems unlikely: it was fully modernized in the 1970s and 1990s and now belongs to Bacardi, who launched a 10-year-old in 2004.

ROYAL BRACKLA 10-YEAR-OLD

SINGLE MALT: HIGHLANDS 40% ABV
Aside from a limited-edition 25-year-old, this is the only official bottling. It has a grassy, floral nose and some spicy, oily notes on the tongue.

ROYAL LOCHNAGAR SELECTED RESERVE

ROYAL LOCHNAGAR 30-YEAR-OLD

ROYAL LOCHNAGAR 12-YEAR-OLD

ROYAL LOCHNAGAR

Ballater, Aberdeenshire
www.malts.com

This charming distillery sits alone on Deeside as the only whisky-making business in the area. It was founded by John Begg in 1845 as New Lochnagar, to distinguish it from a distillery of the same name that had stood on the other bank, only to be washed away in the great Muckle Spate of 1829. Begg wasted no time in asking his new neighbors at Balmoral—Queen Victoria and Prince Albert—to look around his distillery in 1848. By the end of the year, Lochnagar had become Royal Lochnagar.

Begg prospered until he sold out to John Dewar & Sons in 1916, by which point the malt had become a key component in Vat 69.

With a production of just 90,000 gallons (400,000 liters) from its single pair of stills, it is a fairly pocket-sized distillery and,

being so far from any others, it must have felt vulnerable at times. Yet in recent years its owner, Diageo, has lavished lots of money and attention on Royal Lochnagar. In 2004, a Rare Malts 30-year-old was released from a 1974 distillation. Matured in refill bourbon casks, it was in very short supply and is a real rarity today.

ROYAL LOCHNAGAR 12-YEAR-OLD

SINGLE MALT: HIGHLANDS 40% ABV
A subtle, leathery nose with a flavor that becomes drier and more acidic before a spicy, sandalwood finish.

ROYAL LOCHNAGAR SELECTED RESERVE

SINGLE MALT: HIGHLANDS 43% ABV
Deep, complex malt with a resinous, sweet, woody character and hints of apple pie and burned sugar.

ROYAL SALUTE 21-YEAR OLD

ROYAL SALUTE, THE HUNDRED CASK SELECTION

ROYAL SALUTE 38-YEAR-OLD

ROYAL SALUTE

Owner: Chivas Brothers

Originally produced by Seagram in 1953 to commemorate the coronation of Queen Elizabeth II, Royal Salute claims to be the first super-premium whisky. Today it remains market leader in the over 21 years category.

Historically, Chivas Brothers were noted for their exceptional stocks of rare, aged whiskies, and these formed the basis for the Royal Salute expressions. The company is now controlled by Pernod Ricard, whose blenders, led by the highly respected Colin Scott, have access to single malts from such well-known distilleries as Glenlivet, Aberlour, Strathisla, and Longmorn.

Given the veneration and respect accorded to age by consumers in the Far East, it is no surprise that Royal Salute is particularly successful in Asia, especially in China (where Chivas has invested much effort), Taiwan, Korea, and

Vietnam. Duty-free shops also provide a major source of sales.

The various expressions have won an impressive range of medals, including major awards at the International Wine and Spirit Competition.

ROYAL SALUTE 21-YEAR-OLD
BLEND 40% ABV
Soft, fruity aromas balanced with a delicate floral fragrance and mellow, honeyed sweetness.

ROYAL SALUTE, THE HUNDRED CASK SELECTION
BLEND 40% ABV
Elegant, creamy, and exceptionally smooth, with a mellow, oaky, slightly smoky finish.

ROYAL SALUTE 38-YEAR-OLD
BLEND 40% ABV
Rich notes of cedarwood and almond, with a sherried oakiness. Dried fruits linger with an assertive spiciness. An experience, even for the connoisseur.

SCOTCH BLUE 17-YEAR-OLD

SCOTCH BLUE 21-YEAR-OLD

SCAPA

St. Ola, Orkney
www.scapamalt.com

Founded in 1885 on the "Mainland," as Orcadians call the largest of the Hebridean islands, Scapa kept going more or less continuously until 1994, when it was shut down. Although production resumed three years later, it was only on a seasonal basis, using staff from its neighbor, Highland Park. For years it seemed there was only room for one viable distillery on Orkney—that being Highland Park—but Scapa's rescue came in the form of Allied Domecq, and over £2m was lavished on it in 2004. The company has since been bought by Chivas Brothers.

SCAPA 14-YEAR-OLD

SINGLE MALT: ISLANDS 40% ABV
Compared to the robust, smoky Highland Park, Scapa is softer and a little sweeter. It has a heathery, dried-fruit character with a gentle spiciness.

SCOTCH BLUE

Owner: Lotte Chilsung

The color blue denotes prestige and quality in the Far East, so it is little surprise that Scotch Blue began life in South Korea as a house brand for the Lotte Chilsung conglomerate. The whisky is supplied by Burn Stewart, who, in 2001, signed a 10-year supply deal that has seen sales rise to over 500,000 cases. This caused some concern to rivals Allied Domecq, who took legal action, suggesting that "the color and shape of the Scotch Blue bottle are almost identical to that of 17-year-old Ballantine's". This was not pursued by Ballantine's new owners, Chivas Brothers, and Scotch Blue has continued to grow. Indeed, in 2007 *The Korea Times* reported that "Scotch Blue is no longer limited to the domestic boundaries, but is being exported to Malaysia, Japan, Thailand, and other Asian countries where its popularity is growing".

The line includes Scotch Blue International, New Scotch Blue Special, and Scotch Blue itself, with non-age, 17-, and 21-year-old variations. The product is described by its owners as "customized for local drinkers," and the non-age expressions use a mix of old (21-year-old) and youthful (6-year-old) whiskies, breaking with the notion that premium whiskies have to be at least 12 years old.

SCOTCH BLUE 17-YEAR-OLD

BLEND 40% ABV
Using 17-year-old Burn Stewart whisky (owners of distilleries such as Deanston and Tobermory), this Scotch Blue expression is blended by a Scottish master blender to create a soft-textured, highly aromatic whisky for the Korean palate and market.

SCOTCH BLUE 21-YEAR-OLD

BLEND 40% ABV
Similar in style to the 17-year-old, but with greater age comes a little more depth and complexity of flavors.

SCOTTISH LEADER

Owner: Burn Stewart Distillers

The owner describes Scottish Leader as "An international award-winning blend with a honey rich smooth taste profile. It has a growing presence in a number of world markets". The blend's heart is Deanston single malt, from the Perthshire distillery of the same name. Initially targeted at the value-conscious supermarket buyer, Scottish Leader has recently been repackaged and shows signs of an attempted move somewhat upmarket. The blends are now available in non-aged and 12-year-old expressions.

SCOTTISH LEADER

BLEND 40% ABV
A standard blend in which the flavor characteristics are tightly integrated. Not much to mark it out, but okay for mixing or drinking on the rocks.

All about…
Whiskey Glasses

The traditional whiskey glass is a cut crystal "Old-fashioned" glass. It was invented for drinking brandy and soda (with ice) in the 1840s, and was adopted 30-odd years later for drinking blended Scotch (with soda and ice) or an "Old-fashioned" cocktail, which consists of sugar syrup, Angostura bitters, ice cubes, and bourbon or rye whiskey. Fine for drinking long, it is hopeless for appreciating the aroma and taste of malt whiskey—or indeed of any whisk(e)y worthy of consideration. For this, you need a glass that will present the aroma to the best advantage.

COPITA Also known as a *catavino*—and adopted and adapted from sherry glasses—the copita is the industry standard glass for the organoleptic assessment of whiskey. It has a bowl, so you can swirl the liquid and release its aroma, and the rim narrows, so the aroma is presented to the nose extremely well.

THE RIEDEL "GLAS" Founded in Austria in 1756, and still managed by descendants of the founder, Riedel is the world's leading manufacturer of glasses designed specifically for wines and spirits. Georg Riedel, the current president of the company, created this glass in 1992, but now admits that it was his one failure. Its straight sides do not gather the aroma, although the lip presents the spirit nicely on the palate.

THE GLENCAIRN GLASS The malt whisky industry wanted something more robust than a copita, so Glencairn Crystal in Glasgow came up with a stocky glass, reminiscent of a pot still. It is widely used in the whiskey world.

THE SINGLE MALTS OF SCOTLAND GLASS Developed by The Whiskey Exchange, London, to showcase their range of malts of the same name, this glass is good for both nosing and tasting.

OLD-FASHIONED GLASS Often made of crystal, an Old-fashioned glass is designed for a long drink with lots of ice. Since the liquid will "sweat," coasters should be provided. A smaller version is called a "jigger" and is used as a measure.

THE GLENMORANGIE GLASS This small, elegant glass was first adopted and promoted by Glenmorangie. It is standard practice in the whiskey trade to place a cover on the glass, to hold in the aromas—usually a watch glass is used. Glenmorangie went further with this charming little lid.

QUAICH The Celtic *quaich* ("koo-ayk") is a very ancient drinking vessel. The shape is thought to have evolved from that of a scallop shell. Early examples are wooden, but today they are typically of silver or pewter. The Scotch whisky industry's most exclusive club is The Keepers of the Quaich.

SHEEP DIP

Owner: Spencerfield Spirits
www.spencerfieldspirit.com

Sheep Dip is one of the better blended malts. The brand has been around since the 1970s but, under the ownership of Whyte & Mackay, was largely ignored. In 2005, it was taken on by Alex and Jane Nicol, who aim to rebuild the former glory of so-called "orphan brands." Since then, they've introduced new packaging, appointed a global network of agents and, most important of all, reformulated the whisky under the guidance of master blender Richard Paterson. It seems to be working. The whiskies are aged between 8 and 12 years in quality first-fill wood, producing a great dram.

SHEEP DIP

BLENDED MALT 40% ABV
The nose is delicate and refined. Great finesse on the palate, then a majestic assertion of pure malty flavors.

SOMETHING SPECIAL

Owner: Chivas Brothers

It's quite a name to live up to, but "something special" is a justifiable claim for this premium blend, which is the third bestselling whisky in South America, with sales of over half a million cases. The blend dates back to 1912, when it was created by the directors of Hill Thompson & Co. of Edinburgh. The primary component is drawn from Speyside malts, especially the highly regarded Longmorn, which is at the heart of the blend. A 15-year-old version was launched in 2006. The distinctive bottle is said to have been inspired by an Edinburgh diamond-cutter.

SOMETHING SPECIAL

BLEND 40% ABV
A distinctive blend of dry, fruity, and spicy flavors, with a subtle, smoky, sweetness on the palate.

SPEYBURN

Rothes, Aberlour, Morayshire
www.inverhouse.com

Whether she knew it or not, Queen Victoria's loyal subjects at the newly built Speyburn Distillery near Rothes labored through the night to produce a whisky for her Diamond Jubilee of 1897. It was mid-December and, though the windows were not yet in place and snow was swirling in from outside, the distillery manager ordered the stills to be fired up. Speyburn has retained its Victorian charm and, since 1991, has been owned by Inver House.

SPEYBURN 10-YEAR-OLD

SINGLE MALT: SPEYSIDE 40% ABV
Despite older expressions, including a recently released 25-year-old Solera, the core expression remains the 10-year-old, which has a flavor of vanilla fudge and a sweet, lingering finish.

SPEYSIDE

Glen Tromie, Kingussie, Inverness-shire
www.speysidedistillery.co.uk

With a production of just 130,000 gallons (600,000 liters), the distillery named after Scotland's biggest malt whisky region is no giant. Nor is it all that old. Despite its rustic appearance—only a discreet modern smoke stack belies its youth—Speyside was commissioned in 1962 by the blender and bottler George Christie. Built stone-by-stone, it was not finished until 1987. Among its single malts have been Drumguish (no age-statement) and Speyside 8-, 10-, and 12-year-olds.

SPEYSIDE 12-YEAR-OLD

SINGLE MALT: SPEYSIDE 40% ABV
The flavor of this well-balanced 12-year-old recalls nougat, with a faint smoky edge. It is slightly richer and more full-bodied than you would expect from its restrained nose.

SPRINGBANK 10-YEAR-OLD

SPRINGBANK 100 PROOF

SPRINGBANK 15-YEAR-OLD

SPRINGBANK VINTAGE 1997

SPRINGBANK

Campbeltown, Argyll
www.springbankdistillers.com

Springbank was officially founded in 1823, at a time when there were no fewer than 13 licensed distillers in Campbeltown. Although this end of the Mull of Kintyre stills feels pretty cut off by car, it was always a short hop across the Firth of Clyde to Glasgow by ship. And, as the second city of the empire boomed, distilleries like Springbank were on hand to quench its ever-growing thirst. In the other direction there was the US but, when that went dry during Prohibition, and the big blenders turned ever more to Speyside, Campbeltown's demise was swift.

Yet Springbank survived. Much of this must have been down to its continuity: the distillery was originally owned by the Reid family, who sold out to their in-laws, the Mitchells, in the mid-19th century. The Mitchells are still in charge, and have built up a real cult following for their innovative range of single malts.

SPRINGBANK 10-YEAR-OLD

SINGLE MALT: CAMPBELTOWN 46% ABV
A complex cocktail of flavors, from ripe citrus fruit to peat smoke, vanilla, spice, and a faint underlying salty tang.

SPRINGBANK 100 PROOF

SINGLE MALT: CAMPBELTOWN 57% ABV
A big, full-bodied malt with a dried-fruit and butterscotch flavors, along with traces of spice, nuts, and smoke.

SPRINGBANK 15-YEAR-OLD

SINGLE MALT: CAMPBELTOWN 46% ABV
Sweet toffee and candied peel on the nose give way to more exotic sweet-and-sour flavors in the mouth.

SPRINGBANK VINTAGE 1997

SINGLE MALT: CAMPBELTOWN 54.9% ABV
A complex nose of toffee mixed with smoky, leathery aromas. Drier on the palate, with a meaty, mouth-filling flavor wreathed in smoke.

Standing on the shore of Loch Indaal, Bowmore is Islay's oldest distillery. It was founded in 1779 by a local farmer *(see p53)*, who in its early years complained of having an insufficient supply of barley due to the number of illicit distillers on the island.

STEWARTS CREAM OF THE BARLEY

Owner: Chivas Brothers

First produced around 1831, this old-established brand is today a topseller in Ireland. For many years it enjoyed great popularity in Scotland, too, not least because of its widespread distribution in public house chain of Allied, the owner at the time. Single malt from Glencadam used to be at the heart of the blend. With changes in ownership, Glencadam is now in other hands, but the blend reputedly still contains a healthy proportion of up to 50 different single malts.

STEWARTS CREAM OF THE BARLEY

BLEND 40% ABV
A malty, sweet, soft, and slightly spirity nose. The fruitiness of a young spirit on the palate—raw and a little smoky. Peppery, drying, charred-wood finish.

STRATHCLYDE

Owner: Chivas Brothers

The first grain spirit flowed from Strathclyde in the Gorbals district of Glasgow in 1928. The distillery was constructed by Seager Evans & Co., the owners of Long John blended whisky. Through a series of takeovers, it passed to Allied Domecq, who spent £7m increasing the capacity to 8.6 million gallons (39 million liters) a year. The facility is equipped with two column stills, which manufacture grain whisky, and five that make grain neutral spirit. Strathclyde is considered the most "meaty" of the grain whiskies, especially when young.

Very little Strathclyde is bottled as grain whisky, but a recent Carn Mor bottling made available a 41-year-old single grain from the distillery. Distilled in 1965 and matured in bourbon casks, the whisky was released in a batch of fewer than 300 bottles.

STRATHISLA

Keith, Banffshire
www.maltwhiskydistilleries.com

In 1786, Alexander Milne and George Taylor founded the Milltown Distillery in Keith. The whisky it produced was known as Strathisla and, in 1951, this was adopted as the name for the distillery. Over the years, Strathisla has survived fires, explosions, and bankruptcy, to become the oldest and possibly most handsome distillery in the Highlands, with a high-gabled roof and two pagodas. Bought by Chivas Brothers in 1950, it has been the spiritual home of Chivas Regal ever since.

STRATHISLA 12-YEAR-OLD

SINGLE MALT: SPEYSIDE 43% ABV
A rich, sumptuous nose and a spicy, fruitcake character, thanks to the influence of sherry. It is medium-bodied, with a slight smoky note on the finish.

STRATHMILL

Keith, Banffshire
www.malts.com

With its twin pagoda roof, this handsome late-Victorian distillery was built in 1891 as the Glenisla-Glenlivet Distillery. Four years later it was bought by Gilbey, the London-based gin distiller, and re-christened Strathmill—a reference to the fact that it stood on the site of an old corn mill. A single malt expression was released as early as 1909, but Strathmill's long-term role in life was—and is—to supply malt for blended Scotch, particularly J&B.

STRATHMILL FLORA & FAUNA 12-YEAR-OLD

SINGLE MALT: SPEYSIDE 43% ABV
On the lighter, more delicate side of Speyside, Strathmill has a nutty, malty character with notes of vanilla from the wood. It is quite soft and medium-sweet on the tongue.

Grain Whiskey

Unlike malt whiskey, which is made in pot stills, grain whiskey is made using a continuous still (also known as a Coffey or Patent still). It is distilled from a mixture of malted barley and other unmalted cereals, such as wheat or corn. Barley is malted in the conventional way *(see pp40–41)* and mixed with hot water in a mash tun with the unmalted cereals, which have been cooked under pressure to soften the starch and make it soluble. The resulting sugary liquid (or wort) is then fermented with yeast to produce the wash, ready for distilling.

In the continuous still, the wash passes through two columns fitted with metal plates. Heated wash is pumped into the top of the first column (the analyzer), where it meets steam rising up through the column. As alcohol boils at a lower temperature than water, the alcohol can be extracted as vapor. It is then pumped to the base of the second column (the rectifier). The temperature of the column is highest at the base and coolest at the top, so the higher the vapor rises, the greater its alcohol content. The distiller can draw off the resulting grain whisky at the desired strength from one of the plates, where the vapor condenses. Virtually pure alcohol (about 96% ABV) is collected at the top of the column and water discharged at the base. This kind of still can be operated for several weeks continuously.

Like malt whisky, grain whisky is filled into oak casks and matured in warehouses for many years. It tends to be milder in flavor and aroma than malt, and is predominantly used in blending *(see p79)*. However, a tiny amount is sold as grain whisky. Cameron Brig bottles a single grain 12-year-old *(see p60)* and Compass Box sells a delicately flavored blended grain, called Hedonism.

TALISKER 10-YEAR-OLD

SINGLE MALT: ISLANDS 45.8% ABV

An iconic West Coast malt with a pungent, slightly peaty character that has a peppery catch on the finish.

TALISKER 18-YEAR-OLD

SINGLE MALT: ISLANDS 45.8% ABV

Age has softened the youthful vigor of the 10-year-old, and given it a fine scent of leather and aromatic smoke and a creamy, mouth-filling texture.

TALISKER DISTILLERS EDITION 1996

TALISKER 57° NORTH

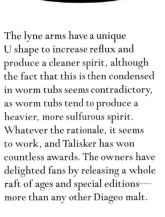

TALISKER 25-YEAR-OLD

TALISKER 30-YEAR-OLD

TALISKER

Carbost, Isle of Skye
www.taliskerwhisky.com

The Scotch Whisky Industry Record of 1823 lists seven licensed distilleries on Skye, of which none has survived. There were doubtless many illicit stills in operation, but these have all long gone, leaving only Talisker, founded in 1830 by Hugh and Kenneth MacAskill, still going strong. Given Skye's size and proximity to the mainland, it seems odd that there is only one distillery there, when Islay has so many.

Talisker struggled through the 19th century, being sold at one point, in 1857, for just £500. Things picked up when Roderick Kemp, an Aberdeen entrepreneur, became a co-partner in 1880. As demand from the blenders increased, small steamers began to call at the distillery to discharge grain and load up with casks.

In 1898, Talisker teamed up with Dailuaine, then the largest distillery in the Highlands. In 1916, the joint venture was taken over by a consortium involving Dewar's, the Distillers Company, and John Walker & Sons. Ever since, Talisker has been a key component in Johnnie Walker Black Label.

Until 1928 Talisker was triple-distilled, like an Irish whiskey, which explains why two-wash stills are paired to one-spirit still.

The lyne arms have a unique U shape to increase reflux and produce a cleaner spirit, although the fact that this is then condensed in worm tubs seems contradictory, as worm tubs tend to produce a heavier, more sulfurous spirit. Whatever the rationale, it seems to work, and Talisker has won countless awards. The owners have delighted fans by releasing a whole raft of ages and special editions—more than any other Diageo malt.

TALISKER DISTILLERS EDITION 1996

SINGLE MALT: ISLANDS 45.8% ABV
With a maturation that ends in Amoroso sherry casks, the Distillers Edition has a peppery, spicy character, softened by a luscious, dried-fruit richness in the mouth.

TALISKER 57° NORTH

SINGLE MALT: ISLANDS 57% ABV
Named in reference to the latitude of the distillery, this is rich, fruity, smoky, peppery, and spicy, with a long finish.

TALISKER 25-YEAR-OLD

SINGLE MALT: ISLANDS 54.2% ABV
A brooding, complex malt, with notes of seaweed and smoke giving way to a leathery, more fruity richness.

TALISKER 30-YEAR-OLD

SINGLE MALT: ISLANDS 49.5% ABV
A highly sophisticated Talisker that's sweet, spicy, fruity, and floral, with understated peat smoke and leather.

The secrets of… Talisker

Distilling whisky on Skye never took off as it did on Islay, possibly because it was always too wet and infertile to grow the barley to kick-start a whisky industry on the island.

In Talisker's case there was also the local minister to contend with and his weekly sermon on the evils of strong drink. In the 1850s his prayers were answered when the distillery was sold for a pittance—half what it cost to build.

From this shaky start, Talisker has risen to cult status among its devotees. Its single malts, with their brooding, pungent character that seems to explode with a peppery catch on the finish, have grown evermore popular and garnered many prestigious awards.

Somehow the physical isolation of Talisker, on the shores of Loch Harport, must play a part in its distinctive taste. Unlike on Speyside, where there were always neighboring distilleries to learn from, Talisker had to work things out for itself. One can imagine early distillers playing with the shape of the lyne arms, adjusting the peating of the barley, the shape of the stills, and the speed of distillation to achieve a desired effect. The result is the Talisker we can taste today, a whisky like no other in Scotland.

▲ SWEET ISOLATION
Though Skye is connected to the mainland by a bridge, Talisker still feels cut off. It sits by the shore of Loch Harport, beneath the blackened, serrated peaks of the Cuillins.

▼ THE WASH STILLS SET-UP
In 1960, Talisker almost burned down when the door to a wash still was left open, and the volatile liquid ignited. They were replaced with stills of exactly the same shape and size. Quite what their unique shape, with their curious U-shaped lyne arms, give to the final character of the whisky is hard to gauge, but the master distiller at the time did not take any chances.

▲ SUGAR LEVELS IN THE WASH
Samples are taken to find the specific gravity of the wash before fermentation. By checking sugar levels before the yeast enzymes have started their work, the distiller can predict the final alcoholic strength of the wash. The other, less scientific, check is simply to sniff the air and make sure it is sweet and malty.

INCREASED REFLUX ▶

Having three spirit stills for just two wash stills is said to be a hangover from the old days, before 1928, when Talisker was triple distilled, like an Irish whiskey. This must have stripped out much of its character. The lyne arms are flat, rather than tilting down, to increase reflux.

▼ OLD-STYLE WORM TUBS

There is no doubt that having traditional, old-style worm tubs to condense the spirit impacts on the character of the new make. Though the famous U-shaped lyne arms will have increased the amount of copper contact, the use of worm tubs works the other way, ensuring a heavier, more sulfurous spirit. It may appear counterintuitive, but it certainly seems to work.

▲ THE DUNNAGE WAREHOUSE

While much Talisker is shipped off the island for maturation on the mainland, some casks are matured on site. The old-fashioned dunnage warehouses have a glorious musty smell of damp earth, wood, and sweet, spirity vapors. How much the scent of sea air and seaweed actually penetrates the casks is hard to say, but Talisker does have an unmistakable maritime character

TAMDHU

TAMDHU 1977

THE TALISMAN

Tomatin Distillery, Inverness-shire
www.tomatin.com

The Talisman is the house blend
from Tomatin Distillery *(see p172)*.
As you might expect, given this,
there is a high proportion of
Tomatin malts in what is a superior
blend. It offers surprises, too:
there are complex and smooth
aromas, with subtle peaty and
savory overtones, and the grain
marries well with the malt. If you
like your blend smooth but with a
bit of bite, this could be the one for
you. Competition judges agree: The
Talisman collected a bronze medal
at the 2007 International Wine &
Spirit Competition.

THE TALISMAN

BLEND 40% ABV
A complex aroma on the nose: fruits and
maltiness with some pleasing grain or
cereal highlights. Honey and vanilla
with hints of apple on the palate. Subtle
peaty notes linger to give a long finish.

TAMDHU

Knockando, Aberlour,
Morayshire
www.edringtongroup.com

For all the misty-eyed romance
about Speyside's early roots as a
region teeming with smugglers and
illicit stills, the railways, which
arrived in the second half of the
19th century, had a far greater
impact. Before the opening of the
Strathspey line in 1863, the region
was simply too cut-off to flourish.
But once the rails were laid,
distilleries began popping up. One
such was Tamdhu, founded in
1896 between Cardhu and
Knockando. In fact, Knockando's
old station is now the reception
center of Tamdhu Distillery.

While it may keep a low profile,
offering just one young distillery
bottling, Tamdhu is a large set-up,
with nine pine washbacks, three
pairs of stills, and a mix of dunnage
and racked warehousing on site.
There's a maltings, too, and part of

Tamdhu's role in the Edrington
Group is to provide some of the
malt for the company's other
distilleries, as well as all the
malt for its own whisky.

As you might expect of a
distillery with only one official
expression, there are several
independent bottlings of Tamdhu
—from Duncan Taylor, Douglas
Laing, Gordon & MacPhail, and
a 29-year-old from the Douglas
Laing Old Malt Cask series,
distilled in 1977.

TAMDHU

SINGLE MALT: SPEYSIDE 40% ABV
Bottled by the distiller to replace the
old 8-year-old, this is a youthful
introduction to Speyside, with no age
statement and a slight peppery edge.

TAMNAVULIN

Ballindalloch, Banffshire

In 1966, Invergordon Distillers,
now part of Whyte & Mackay,
decided to build a big new
distillery in a picturesque corner
of Upper Speyside by the River
Livet. Its six stills could pump
out as much as 880,000 gallons
(4 million liters) of pure alcohol
a year. Yet, in 1995, Tamnavulin
closed down—the owners, it
seemed, had decided to focus their
attention on their other distilleries,
Dalmore and Jura in particular.
The UB Group bought Whyte
& Mackay in 2007, and now
Tamnavulin is back up and running.

TAMNAVULIN 12-YEAR-OLD

SINGLE MALT: SPEYSIDE 40% ABV
A light, aperitif-style malt, with a
dry, cereal character and minty nose.
This standard release of the so-called
"Stillman's Dram" is joined by
occasional older expressions.

TEACHER'S

Owner: Beam Global

This venerable brand can be dated to 1830, when William Teacher opened a grocery shop in Glasgow. Like other whisky entrepreneurs, he soon branched out into the spirits trade. His sons took over, and blending became increasingly important. In 1884 the trademark Teacher's Highland Cream was registered, and this single brand eventually came to dominate the business. The whisky was always forceful in character, built around single malts from Glendronach and Ardmore. Today it continues to prove popular in South America.

TEACHER'S HIGHLAND CREAM

BLEND 40% ABV
Full-flavored, oily, with fudge and caramel notes on the nose, toffee and licorice on the palate. A well-rounded, smooth texture and quite a quick finish that leaves the palate refreshed.

TEANINICH

Alness, Ross-shire
www.malts.com

Distillery visitors to the Highland village of Alness, just north of Inverness, rarely notice Teaninich as they make their way to its more famous neighbor Dalmore. And yet Teaninich has been quietly distilling away with barely a break since 1817, when it was set up by Captain Hugh Munro, who named it after his Highland estate beside the River Alness.

Teaninich, it seems, was run as a hobby until 1852, when it was leased out to Robert Pattison of Leith, whose family firm almost brought down the entire whisky industry when it collapsed in 1899. Despite this, the distillery has been in almost continual production, stopping during World War II and briefly again in the 1980s. By then there were two still rooms working in tandem. These were known as Side A and Side B—not the most

poetic of names, but then no one was interested in marketing Teaninich as a single malt to whisky-drinkers—its role was to supply the spirit for blending.

In 1992, Teaninich's owners, UDV (now Diageo), released a 10-year-old expression. Seven years later it decommissioned Side B. The distillery crushes its malted barley with an Asnong hammer mill, as opposed to the more traditional roller mills. Whether this affects the flavor of the malt is hard to say.

TEANINICH FLORA & FAUNA 10-YEAR-OLD

SINGLE MALT: HIGHLANDS 43% ABV
The only official distillery bottling is polished and grassy, with a predominantly malty flavor.

TEANINICH GORDON & MACPHAIL 1991

SINGLE MALT: HIGHLANDS 46% ABV
A deep amber, fruitcake-flavored malt, with notes of mint, tobacco, cloves, and wood smoke.

TÉ BHEAG

Owner: The Gaelic Whisky Co.
www.gaelicwhisky.com

Although it is blended and bottled elsewhere in Scotland, this is another brand from the Pràban na Linne company on Skye (The Gaelic Whisky Company). Té Bheag (pronounced *Chey Vek*) means "the little lady" and is the name of the boat in the logo. It is also colloquial Gaelic for a "wee dram." The blend is popular in France and has won medals in international competition. Té Bheag is non chill-filtered, and Islay, Island, Highland, and Speyside malts aged from 8–11 years are used in the blend.

TÉ BHEAG

BLEND 40% ABV
The nose is fresh, with a citrus note, good richness, a delicate peatiness, and a touch of cereal. Weighty on the palate, with a good touch of licorice, a toffee-like richness, and some peat.

TOBERMORY

Tobermory, Isle of Mull
www.tobermory.co.uk

If Islay to the south can boast eight working distilleries (at the last count), it seems only fair that Mull should have at least one. And yet the very survival of Tobermory has been something of a miracle, given that it has spent much of its life lying idle.

Tobermory was founded as the Ledaig Distillery by John Sinclair in 1797. For Sinclair, whisky was a sideline to his main business of dealing in kelp and, when he died in 1837, the distillery died with him, remaining shut for the next 40 years. It was bought by the Distillers Company in 1916, but became an early casualty of the Depression and closed in 1930.

Once the place had been gutted, few believed whisky would ever be made here again. Then, in 1972, the site was bought and restored by a consortium that included a

shipping company and the famous sherry house of Domecq. The new Ledaig distillery company soon collapsed but, having installed new stills and other whisky-making equipment, Tobermory's future was finally made secure. Production resumed in 1989 and, in 1993, the distillery was bought by its current owner, Burn Stewart.

TOBERMORY 10-YEAR-OLD

SINGLE MALT: ISLANDS 40% ABV
This fresh, unpeated, maritime malt claims to have a slight smoky character, thanks to the water from Mull's peat lochans. If true, the effect is subtle.

TOBERMORY 15-YEAR-OLD

SINGLE MALT: ISLANDS 46.3% ABV
The nose has rich fruitcake notes and a trace of marmalade, thanks to ageing in sherry casks. The spicy character comes through on the tongue. It is non chill-filtered and cask strength.

TOMATIN

Tomatin, Inverness-shire
www.tomatin.com

With 23 stills and a capacity of 2.6 million gallons (12 million liters) of pure alcohol, Tomatin was the colossus of the malt whisky industry. In 1974, at the time of its expansion, it eclipsed even Glenfiddich, whose capacity remains at 2.2 million gallons (10 million liters).

Tomatin was founded in 1897, and took a while to reach its super-size status. Its two stills were increased to four as recently as 1956; thereafter expansion was rapid until it peaked in the 1970s, just in time for the first big post-war slump. Tomatin struggled on as an independent distillery until 1985, when the liquidators arrived. A year later it was sold to two of its long-standing customers— Takara Shuzo and Okara & Co— thus becoming the first Scottish distillery in Japanese hands.

With 11 fewer stills, production has been cut back to 1.1 million gallons (5 million liters), which still allows plenty of capacity for bottling as a single malt. Tomatin's biggest seller is the standard 12-year-old; the 18- and 25-year-olds form part of the core range, while older expressions and specific vintages are released on a more ad hoc basis.

TOMATIN 25-YEAR-OLD

SINGLE MALT: HIGHLANDS 43% ABV
With its simple packaging, this ripe, zesty malt, full of nuts, and spice is a triumph of substance over style.

TOMATIN 30-YEAR-OLD

SINGLE MALT: HIGHLANDS 49.3% ABV
A voluptuous after-dinner dram with a big, sherried nose and impressive legs.

TOMATIN 12-YEAR-OLD
SINGLE MALT: HIGHLANDS 40% ABV
A mellow, soft-centered
Speyside-style malt, which
replaced the old core 10-year-old
expression back in 2003.

TOMATIN 18-YEAR-OLD
SINGLE MALT: HIGHLANDS 43% ABV
The deep amber hue betrays a
strong sherry influence that
brings out a fruity, cinnamon
flavor in the malt.

Blended Malt

In 1853 Andrew Usher, an Edinburgh-based wine and spirit merchant, launched the world's first modern brand of Scotch whisky—Old Vatted Glenlivet. Assuming there was no grain spirit in the mix, this would now be called a "Blended Malt," defined by the Scotch Whisky Association (SWA) as; "a blend of Single Malt Scotch Whiskies which have been distilled at more than one distillery."

This definition was hammered out when Diageo decided to relaunch the Speyside whisky as a "Pure Malt" in 2002. No longer a "single malt," it meant other malts could be added to Diageo's Cardhu to satisfy surging demand in Spain and perhaps challenge Glenfiddich for poll position among malts. Glenfiddich's owners, William Grant & Sons, were alarmed and led a campaign that provoked the biggest storm in the whisky industry in recent years. There were cries of betrayal, questions in Parliament, and eventually an embarrassing climbdown by Diageo in March 2003.

While Cardhu reverted to being a single malt, the industry had to decide what to call such whiskies in the future. Within the trade they had always been known as vatted malts, though this was thought to have industrial connotations. "Pure malt" sounded better to marketing folk, though it was no longer politically acceptable within the industry. Eventually, having studied Roget's Thesaurus for many months, the committee responsible came up with "blended malt," though many still question whether this will only confuse consumers even more.

TOMINTOUL 10-YEAR-OLD

TOMINTOUL 16-YEAR-OLD

TOMINTOUL PEATY TANG

TOMINTOUL

Kirkmichael, Ballindalloch, Grampian
www.tomintouldistillery.co.uk

Of all the Speyside distilleries that bolted the magic word "Glenlivet" on to their names in the hope of added luster, Tomintoul-Glenlivet has the best case, being a virtual next-door neighbor. Tomintoul stands 1,165 ft (350 m) up, beside the Avon River, the largest tributary of the Spey River. It opened in 1964—a time of great confidence in the industry, with booming sales of blended Scotch, particularly in export markets such as the US. Tomintoul's role in life was simply to supply malt for these blends. This role continues under Angus Dundee, who bought the distillery in 2000, when it was in need of malt for its own blends *(see p23)*. And yet, while single malts account for a small fraction of the 600,000 gallons (3.3 million liters) produced each year, the number of expressions has

increased greatly. Peaty Tang, for example, is a vatting of young un-peated malt and even younger peated malt. The distillery's oldest expression is a 27-year-old—a luscious, almost resinous whisky, which is sweet on the palate, then drying in the finish.

TOMINTOUL 10-YEAR-OLD

SINGLE MALT: SPEYSIDE 40% ABV
First launched in 2002, this delicate, aperitif-style malt has some vanilla from the wood and a light cereal character.

TOMINTOUL 16-YEAR-OLD

SINGLE MALT: SPEYSIDE 40% ABV
The extra years give this expression a more nutty, spicy character, with notes of orange peel on the nose, as well as more depth and a more rounded texture.

TOMINTOUL PEATY TANG

SINGLE MALT: SPEYSIDE 40% ABV
The peaty character of this malt comes through on the nose, though not so much as to set off the smoke alarm or swamp the underlying cereal character.

All about…
Liqueurs

The earliest way of drinking whiskey was probably to mix the spirit with honey, herbs, and fruits. From as early as the late 14th century, and increasingly during the 16th century, recipe books were available for preparing medicines at home, which involved distilled spirits compounded with many varieties of herbs. An alfresco hunting feast enjoyed by James V, King of Scots, in 1531 includes, among many other drinks, *Hippocras aquavitae*—a mix of spirits with sugar and spices, strained through a "Hippocrates sleeve," named after the patron of physicians. By the 18th century, when whiskey drinking was more widespread, it was commonly served as a "toddy" or a "punch," mixed with sugar, lemons, and spices such as cloves and cinnamon—no doubt to cover the variable quality of the whiskey itself.

DRAMBUIE Supposedly made from a recipe gifted by Bonnie Prince Charlie to Captain John McKinnon in 1746, Drambuie began to be made commercially in the 1880s. The recipe is still a family secret, handed down through the female line. It has a honeyed sweetness, a floral heathery note, and a little spiciness.

BAILEYS Launched in 1974, this mix of Irish whiskey and cream is now the bestselling liqueur and the 8th bestselling premium spirit in the world. It is the single most successful spirit to be launched anywhere in the world in the past 30 years. As well as whiskey and cream, there's a touch of vanilla and chocolate in the blend of this silky liqueur.

GLAYVA Created by Ronald Morrison before World War I, and named by his Gaelic-speaking warehouseman (*gle mhath*, pronounced "glay-va", is Gaelic for "very good"). Almond essence and tangerine are discernable in the flavor, and some mildly warming spices. The liqueur makes a good base for fruity cocktails.

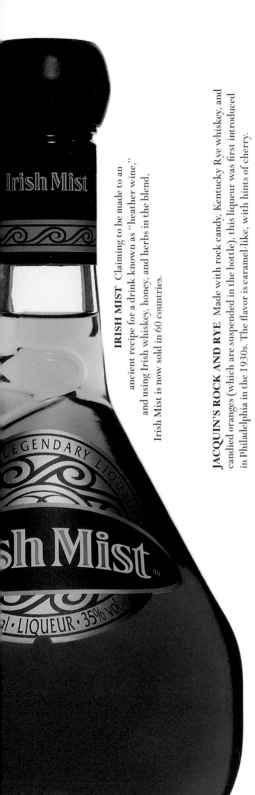

IRISH MIST Claiming to be made to an ancient recipe for a drink known as "heather wine," and using Irish whiskey, honey, and herbs in the blend, Irish Mist is now sold in 60 countries.

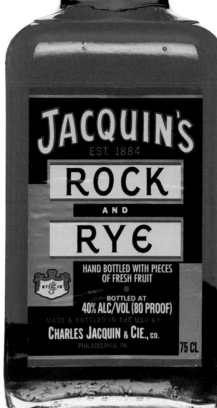

JACQUIN'S ROCK AND RYE Made with rock candy, Kentucky Rye whiskey, and candied oranges (which are suspended in the bottle), this liqueur was first introduced in Philadelphia in the 1930s. The flavor is caramel-like, with hints of cherry.

ORANGERIE Created by John Glaser, the talented and passionate owner of Compass Box, this is an "infusion" of Navalino orange zest, cassia bark, cloves, and blended Scotch. Clean and fresh on the palate, Orangerie is not as sweet as most liqueurs.

SOUTHERN COMFORT This blend of whiskey, sugar, and assorted fruits was invented by New Orleans bar tender Martin Wilkes Heron in 1874. He later patented the drink in Memphis, Tennessee, in 1889. It is produced at various strengths.

SHERRY WOOD FINISH

TULLIBARDINE 1993 SHERRY WOOD FINISH

TULLIBARDINE 1993

TULLIBARDINE 1993 PORT WOOD FINISH

TULLIBARDINE

Blackford, Perthshire
www.tullibardine.com

With its box shape, corrugated roof, and tall metal chimney, Tullibardine is no homely Victorian distillery. It was designed in 1949 by William Delmé-Evans, and survived through various changes in ownership until it was bought by Whyte & Mackay in 1993. The company promptly mothballed the distillery a year later and, as each year passed, the chances of resuscitation appeared to fade.

Then, in 2003 a rescue package was agreed, and Tullibardine was bought by an independent consortium who began distilling again. It soon launched its first official bottling—a 10-year-old—but it will be 2014 before the whisky actually distilled by the new owners sees the light of day. The release is expected to coincide with the Ryder Cup golf tournament at nearby Gleneagles.

In the meantime there has been a raft of releases based on the inventory inherited in 2003, which included some 3,000 casks dating back to 1952.

TULLIBARDINE 1993 SHERRY WOOD FINISH

SINGLE MALT: HIGHLANDS 46% ABV
Eighteen months in Oloroso sherry butts give this malt a deep amber color and a spicy butterscotch flavor that finishes dry.

TULLIBARDINE 1993

SINGLE MALT: HIGHLANDS 40% ABV
This is more akin to a delicate Speyside than a robust Highland malt. It has a light citrus nose with a vanilla sweetness from maturation in bourbon casks.

TULLIBARDINE 1993 PORT WOOD FINISH

SINGLE MALT: HIGHLANDS 46% ABV
The 1993 vintage was given 11 months in a port pipe for added complexity. It has a grapey, woody aroma from the cask and some citrus notes on the palate.

TORMORE

Advie, Grantown-on-Spey, Morayshire

Built on a grand scale in 1958, Tormore symbolizes the whisky industry's self-confidence at a time when global demand for blended Scotch was growing strongly. With its copper-clad roof and giant chimney stack, the distillery towers up beside the A95 in Speyside. It seems no expense was spared by the architect, Sir Albert Richardson, a past president of the Royal Academy. Tormore is now owned by Chivas Brothers (Pernod Ricard), who released an official 12-year-old bottling in 2004.

TORMORE 12-YEAR-OLD

SINGLE MALT: SPEYSIDE 40% ABV

There is a soft malty character to the nose, with notes of melon and grass. In the mouth it has a slight oily texture and a medium-light body that dries on the finish.

USHER'S GREEN STRIPE

Owner: Diageo

One of the foremost names in Scotch whisky, the Edinburgh firm of Usher was a pioneer in the art of blending. In fact, it is recognized for introducing the first modern blend—Old Vatted Glenlivet in 1853. After the firm joined the DCL in 1919, the brand slowly faded away. Today Usher's Green Stripe is among the lowest-priced Scotch available to drinkers in the US, few of whom will either know or care about its distinguished history. But, Usher's whisky remains highly desirable among historians and collectors, owing mostly to the very high standard of its promotional give-away materials.

USHER'S GREEN STRIPE

BLEND 40% ABV

A low-priced blend with a high grain content; well-suited to mixing.

VAT 69

Owner: Diageo

At its peak, VAT 69 was the 10th-bestselling whisky in the world, and references to it crop up in films and books from the 1950s and 60s. It was launched in 1882 and was once the flagship brand of the independent South Queensferry blenders William Sanderson & Co, its name coming from the fact that vat 69 was the finest of 100 possible blends tested. Today its current owner, Diageo, gives precedence to Johnnie Walker and J&B, and it might not be unreasonable to suggest that—despite sales of more than 1 million cases a year in Venezuela, Spain, and Australia— VAT 69's glory days are behind it.

VAT 69

BLEND 40% ABV

A light and well-balanced standard blend with a noticeably sweet impact of vanilla ice cream initially and a pleasantly malty background.

WHITE HORSE

Owner: Diageo

In its heyday, White Horse was one of the world's top ten whiskies, selling more than 2 million cases a year. Its guiding genius was "Restless Peter" Mackie, described in his day as "one-third genius, one-third megalomaniac, and one-third eccentric". He took over the family firm in 1890 and established an enviable reputation as a gifted blender and entrepreneur.

White Horse is still marketed in more than 100 countries. A deluxe 12-year-old version, White Horse Extra Fine, is occasionally seen.

WHITE HORSE

BLEND 40% ABV

Complex and satisfying, White Horse retains the robust flavor of Lagavulin, assisted by renowned Speysiders such as Aultmore. With its long finish, this is a stylish, intriguing blend of crisp grain, clean malt, and earthy peat.

WILLIAM LAWSON'S

Owner: John Dewar & Sons (Bacardi)

Although the brand name of Lawson's dates back to 1849, the "home" distillery today is MacDuff, built in 1960 by a consortium of blenders in northeast Scotland and subsequently sold to Martini.

Lawson's is managed alongside its big brother, Dewar's, and, although dwarfed by it and virtually invisible in the UK, the brand sells well over 1 million cases a year in France, Belgium, Spain, and parts of South America. It is well-known in Europe for its iconoclastic advertising and provocative TV commercials—actress Sharon Stone starred in one recently aired.

Glen Deveron single malt from MacDuff features heavily in the blend. MacDuff employs the highest percentage of sherry wood of any whisky in the Dewar's group, and this contributes to the Lawson house style—a full flavor and rich golden color. In recent years the standard expression, William Lawson's Finest, has been moved into line with other standard blends and is competitive on price while remaining good value for money. The range also comprises the 12-year-old Scottish Gold and two premium styles: an 18-year-old Founder's Reserve and limited quantities of the 21-year-old Private Reserve.

WILLIAM LAWSON'S FINEST

BLEND 40% ABV

The nose is slightly dry, with delicate oak notes. The palate is well-balanced, with hints of a crisp candy-apple flavor. A medium- to full-bodied whisky that punches above its weight.

WILLIAM LAWSON'S SCOTTISH GOLD 12-YEAR-OLD

BLEND 40% ABV

Fuller-flavored than the standard Lawson's expression, suggesting a higher malt content.

WINDSOR

Owner: Diageo

According to its owner Diageo, Windsor is "the largest selling super premium Scotch whisky in the world." As such, the brand has fallen prey to counterfeiting in the highly competitive South Korean market. Drinkers here look for a small, bar-shaped weight that signals the whisky's authencity— once the cap is twisted and opened, the weight is separated and falls into the bottle.

The name Windsor is an overt link to the British royal family, and the packaging strongly confirms the brand's luxury position. Although Windsor was originally developed in a partnership between Seagram and local producer Doosan, Diageo acquired the Seagram interest and launched Windsor 17 as the first super premium whisky in 2000. The Korean market at the time was dominated by 12-year-old premium products. Windsor 17's sweeping popularity posed a strong threat to its competitors, many of whom have since emulated the older style.

Buoyed by the success of Windsor 17, Diageo recently unveiled a 21-year-old variant, aimed at encouraging further trading up to even more premium blends. The company currently supplies Windsor products to China and Japan, and has plans to expand into other Asian countries.

Do not confuse Windsor with its Canadian namesake (*see p279*).

WINDSOR 12-YEAR-OLD

BLEND 40% ABV

Vanilla, wood, and light fresh fruit on the nose. Green apples on the palate, with honey, more vanilla, and spiciness that mellows into a smooth finish.

WINDSOR 17-YEAR-OLD

BLEND 40% ABV

A rich vanilla crème brûlée nose, with fruit and a background layer of malt. Fresh fruit and honey on the palate, with creamy vanilla oak notes.

Quarter casks like these at the Speyside Cooperage accelerate the rate of maturation through increased interaction between the wood and the spririt. Laphroaig uses them to good effect to bottle a relatively young whisky.

**WHYTE & MACKAY
30-YEAR-OLD**
BLEND 40% ABV
The flagship of the Whyte &
Mackay range is a big, rich, oaky
whisky with a deep mahogany
hue. The sherry influence is
strong, with a pepperiness
mellowed by the sweeter flavors.

**WHYTE & MACKAY
OLD LUXURY**
BLEND 40% ABV
A rich bouquet, with malty
notes and a subtle sherry
influence. It all blends smoothly
on the palate. Mellow and silky
textured. Warming finish.

WHYTE & MACKAY SPECIAL

WHYTE & MACKAY THE THIRTEEN

WHYTE & MACKAY SUPREME

WHYTE & MACKAY

www.whyteandmackay.co.uk

The Glasgow-based firm of Whyte & Mackay started blending in the late-19th century. Its flagship Special brand quickly established itself as a Scottish favorite, and remains so to this day among value-conscious consumers. Having been through a bewildering number of owners and a management buy-out in recent years, the company was acquired in May 2007 by the Indian conglomerate UB Group.

One constant through all these changes has been Whyte & Mackay's highly regarded master blender,

Richard Paterson, who joined the firm in 1970 and has received a great number of awards. As well as creating the "new" 40-year-old, Paterson has overseen several aged innovations. The range today includes the Special (which is actually the standard blend) and five expressions aged at 13, 19, 22, 30, and 40 years old. The company defends the unusual age declarations on the grounds that "the extra year gives the whisky a chance to marry for a longer period, giving it a distinct graceful smoothness." A number of own-label customers are also supplied by Whyte & Mackay.

Historically, the company's main market has been the UK, although the older styles, especially the

13-year-old, are popular in Spain, France, and Scandinavia. Sales in India are expected to grow since the launch of the locally bottled Whyte & Mackay range in 2008.

The backbone of the blends emanates from Speyside and the Highlands, although small amounts from Islay, Campbeltown, and the Lowlands are also used. Dalmore and—to a lesser extent—Isle of Jura are the company's flagship single malts, and Dalmore's influence can be clearly felt in the premium blends. Great stress is laid on marrying, the company having long been an adherent to this time-consuming process. All the blends are noticeably smooth and well-balanced.

WHYTE & MACKAY SPECIAL

BLEND 40% ABV

The nose is full, round, and well-balanced. On the palate, honeyed soft fruits in profusion; smooth and rich, with a long finish.

WHYTE & MACKAY
THE THIRTEEN

BLEND 40% ABV

Full, firm, and rich nose, with a slight hint of sherry wood. "Marrying" for a full year before bottling gives great backbone. A well-integrated blend.

WHYTE & MACKAY SUPREME

BLEND 40% ABV

Aged for 22 years, the Supreme is velvet textured, with a soft maltiness and sherry wood notes on nose and palate.

N
W E
S

Bushmills

LONDONDERRY

Northern
Ireland

OMAGH   BELFAST

SLIGO

Cooley

WESTPORT   IRELAND

Kilbeggan
(used by Cooley)   DUBLIN
GALWAY   TULLAMORE

WICKLOW

CARLOW

LIMERICK

CLONMEL

WATERFORD

CORK   Midleton

REDBREAST—MIDLETON

REDBREAST
PURE POT STILL
IRISH WHISKEY
Aged 15 Years
Non Chill Filtered

miles
0   25

0   25
kilometers

TYRCONNEL—COOLEY

POWERS—MIDLETON

Modernday whiskey-making in Ireland centers on just three producers: Bushmills, Midleton, and Cooley. These three are responsible for all of the official brands and bottlings of Irish whiskey, from blends to single malts, to pure pot still whiskeys. Bushmills and Midleton have a long history and are the only distilleries to have survived from Ireland's golden age of whiskey distilling in the 19th century. Other famous whiskey names from the 19th century, such as Jameson and Powers, which used to be made at distilleries in Dublin, were closed as independent operations, but live on as brands from Midleton. The modern Midleton plant, near Cork in the Republic of Ireland, has been in operation since the mid-1970s and produces a wide range of whiskeys. By contrast, the Bushmills Distillery, in Northern Ireland, makes only single malt whiskey—this is mixed with grain whiskey bought in from Midleton for Bushmills blends. The third distillery, Cooley, dates only from 1987, and has revived the Locke's and Tyrconnel names in its whiskey ranges.

IRELAND

LOCKE'S—COOLEY

CONNEMARA—COOLEY

GREEN SPOT—MIDLETON

BUSHMILLS

JAMESON—MIDLETON

BUSHMILLS ORIGINAL

BLEND 40% ABV

A fruity, easy-to-drink, vanilla-infused mouthful. Its clean, clear character makes it very approachable. A lovely entry to the world of Irish whiskey.

BUSHMILLS BLACK BUSH

BLEND 40% ABV

A living legend, Black Bush is the lovable rogue of the family. It is a very classy glassful of honey nut scrumptiousness with an extremely silky mouthfeel. The benchmark for Irish blends.

BUSHMILLS MALT 10-YEAR-OLD

BUSHMILLS MALT 16-YEAR-OLD

BUSHMILLS MALT 21-YEAR-OLD

BUSHMILLS

*2 Distillery Road, Bushmills,
County Antrim
www.bushmills.com*

Old Bushmills has the amazing ability to be all things to all men: a thoroughly modern distillery housed in a beautiful Victorian building; a boutique distillery that nevertheless produces global brands; and a working distillery that welcomes the public.

Bushmills produces only malt whiskey, so the grain used in its blends is made to order in the Midleton Distillery. This is matured on site in one of the 10 working warehouses. Unusually, Old Bushmills doesn't have a

problem selling single malts and blends under the same name: it is a distillery that isn't afraid to push the boundaries. An example of this is the whiskey Bushmills produced to celebrate the 400th anniversary of its original license to distil. Only a company as quixotic as Bushmills would choose a blended whiskey for such an occasion— and one bottled at 46% ABV too. Bushmills 1608 was the result, and at the heart of this limited-edition whiskey was spirit made using crystal malt—the kind of malt mostly found only in breweries. Its effect on the blend was to give it an almost spicy intensity, which was complemented by some fine sherry notes from the Oloroso casks.

BUSHMILLS MALT
10-YEAR-OLD

SINGLE MALT 40% ABV

As you'd expect from a triple-distilled, peat-free whiskey, this charmer appeals to just about everyone. There's a hint of sherry wood, but it is the classy malt that's showcased here—sweet with hints of fudgy chocolate. A classic and very approachable Irish malt.

BUSHMILLS MALT
16-YEAR-OLD

SINGLE MALT 40% ABV

This malt isn't just a straight aging of the classic 10-year-old. Instead, it's a pretty much half-and-half mix of bourbon- and sherry-cask-matured malt, married for a further nine months in port pipes. The three woods bring

their own magic to bear, and produce a riot of dried-fruit flavors cut with almonds and the ever-present honey.

BUSHMILLS MALT
21-YEAR-OLD

SINGLE MALT 40% ABV

This is the rarest of all Bushmills whiskeys—only 900 cases of the 21-year-old malt are produced each year, and then only when stocks of suitably matured whiskey become available. This bottling is made from sherry- and bourbon-matured whiskey, which is then finished for another two years in Madeira drums. As you'd expect after 21 years, the malt is almost chewy, with chocolate notes and a sweetness that has mellowed almost to raisin pastry. Delicious.

The secrets of... Bushmills

Old Bushmills has been around for a very long time. Distilling on this site goes back to 1608 and possibly even further, though the current distillery was built in the Victorian period.

With its twin pagoda roof, the Victorian distillery is a classic of its type. What is really remarkable about Bushmills, though, is that, while production here has expanded time and again, somehow the place has never lost its charm.

Bushmills has survived for this long because it does what it does very well indeed. The equipment may change over time, but the distillery's attention to consistency means that the single malt produced today doesn't taste much different from what was being made here when America was still a colony.

Over the centuries various people and companies have owned this little corner of County Antrim; while they have come and gone, the whiskey has kept on going. In a world of change, this place is truly remarkable.

▲ THE WATER SOURCE
The picturesque lake in front of the distillery nicely frames the buildings. More importantly, however, it is where St. Columb's Rill is pooled. This is the distillery water source, and so this water will one day get turned into whiskey.

▲ REVITALIZED MASH HOUSE
Bushmills' mash house was refitted with a new stainless-steel mashtun and washbacks in 2007. This is part of Diageo's investment in the distillery, with a view to greatly increasing sales of Bushmills over the forthcoming years. The mash house is full of wonderful yeasty and malty aromas; in the stills house, the aromas are more fruity.

◄ CASK SELECTION

Bushmills mostly uses a mix of bourbon and sherry casks for maturation, and the master blender takes regular trips to Spain and Portugal to select casks being seasoned with sherry. Once the new oak has been mellowed by the sherry and has absorbed some of its fruity flavors, it is ready to mature Bushmills whiskey.

▼ WOOD FINISHES

Bushmills was one of the pioneers of exotic wood finishes. The light style of the spirit produced here lends itself nicely to ageing in Port, Madeira, or Oloroso sherry casks. This is best experienced by sampling the 16- and 21-year-old malts. Bushmills 16 is finished in port pipes for the final months of maturation; Bushmills 21 is finished in Madeira casks for about two years.

◄ TRIPLE DISTILLATION

Bushmills has four wash stills and five spirit stills, and uses triple distillation to produce a very light and pure spirit—the traditional Irish way. The distillery produces two kinds of spirit: one is unpeated; the other is given a light peating. The two types of spirit are matured in separate casks, and can be used in combination to produce the final whiskey.

MALTS AND BLENDS ►

Bushmills is highly regarded for the quality of its single malts, but it also pays close attention to the standard of its blends. Grain whiskey from Midleton Distillery is used for Bushmills blends, and, significantly, the malt and grain are "married" in casks for a period so that the flavors fully integrate.

CONNEMARA CASK STRENGTH

CONNEMARA SINGLE CASK 1992

CLONTARF

www.clontarfwhiskey.com

Clontarf has been in the doldrums for a number of years now, and in that time the taste and style have fluctuated wildly. There isn't a distillery in Clontarf; this is simply a brand, so the whiskeys can come from anywhere. This is a problem, as the consumer loves consistency—especially from blended whiskeys. And with Clontarf you never quite know what you are buying.

CLONTARF SINGLE MALT

SINGLE MALT 40% ABV

Sweet and thin with some nice mouthfeel. Cereal notes with hints of honey, but a bit one-dimensional.

CLONTARF CLASSIC BLEND

BLEND 40% ABV

Toffee popcorn comes to mind when tasting this blend, but not in a good way, unfortunately.

COLERAINE

Coleraine Distillery Ltd., Hawthorn Office Park, Stockman's Way, Belfast

Never underestimate the selling power of nostalgia: the sole reason this blend is still produced is because whiskey drinkers are very brand loyal, and the name Coleraine still has resonance some three decades after the distillery fell silent. It once produced a single malt of some repute, then in 1954 it started to make grain whiskey for Bushmills, before it was eventually wound down in the 1970s. The reputation of the distillery was such, however, that customers still look out for the name, and so a brand and blend were created to fill a niche. Though the company's called Coleraine Distillery, the whiskey is produced elsewhere.

COLERAINE

BLEND 40% ABV

Light, sweet, and grainy. Probably best suited to drinking with a mixer.

CONNEMARA

Cooley Distillery, Riverstown, Cooley, County Louth
www.connemarawhiskey.com

Connemara is one of the few whiskeys the Cooley Distillery produces that has no heritage. Names like Millars, Tyrconnell, and Locke's have been around in one form or another for a century or more, but here a totally new brand was created for a totally new whiskey. So what's new? Well, it's a peated malt. Nothing too radical if this were Scotland, but in Ireland it caused quite a stir. In the eyes of the Irish whiskey industry—and many a traditionalist beside—Irish whiskey was a triple-distilled and unpeated drink. Then along came Cooley's John Teeling, who started making Irish whiskey that was double-distilled and peated.

It's not surprising that when Irish Distillers tried to take over Cooley a few years back, IDL boss

Richard Burrows was adamant that brands such as Connemara would have no future. Yet, over the last 15 years, Connemara has gone from being a curiosity to winning gold medals.

As well as the standard single malt, there are 12-year-old, cask strength, and sherry wood finish expressions too. And there have been single cask bottlings, such as the limited-release 1992 Single Cask, which was bottled in 2006.

CONNEMARA CASK STRENGTH

SINGLE MALT 60.7% ABV

This pale straw whiskey isn't colored or chill-filtered. It's as nature, in the shape of master distiller Noel Sweeney, intended. A good splash of water unleashes the nose, which is huge and slightly minty. In the mouth, the beast that had been held in check by the alcohol gets loose and explodes into sparks of dry peat and aromatic timber. The finish is as dry as a Mayo man's throat after climbing Croak Patrick.

CONNEMARA

SINGLE MALT 40% ABV

It would be so wrong to dismiss the Connemara range as "Scotch Light." It's nothing of the sort. Connemara is its own whiskey: it's rural, not coastal, so no iodine or sea spray. Just bog heather, fields of barley, and far off peat reek. At the heart of this sweet whiskey is a smoldering peat fire.

CONNEMARA 12-YEAR-OLD

SINGLE MALT 40% ABV

This is Connemara at its most ethereal: all the elements are here, but somehow they are hard to pin down. It may take two or three samples to get the measure of this fine spirit, in fact. So make sure your chair is comfortable.

KILBEGGAN WHISKEY *(see p199)*

LOCKE'S WHISKEY *(see p204)*

TYRCONNELL WHISKEY *(see p215)*

COOLEY

Riverstown, Cooley, County Louth
www.cooleywhiskey.com

In the 1930s the Irish Government went into the distilling business. It wasn't out to make whiskey; it was simply looking for a way of using up blighted potatoes. Five industrial alcohol factories were built to produce power methylated spirit (PMS), which was then mixed with gasoline to make it go further.

By the 1980s PMS was a thing of the past, and the last of these distilleries on the Cooley Peninsula was being sold for scrap. In 1988 Dr. John Teeling bought the Cooley Distillery unseen: he reckoned the scrap value alone was greater than the £106,000 the government wanted. But Teeling didn't do the sensible thing and sell off the scrap. Instead he opened a distillery.

On July 17, 1992, as the first cask of Cooley whiskey was tapped, Teeling's dream of taking on Irish Distillers had turned into a nightmare: the company was strapped for cash, and Teeling was looking to offload the loss-making distillery. But the only interested buyers were arch-rivals Irish Distillers, who intended to close the place down. Not surprisingly, its offer was blocked by Ireland's Competition Authority, which ruled that any take-over by Irish Distillers would be anti-competitive. By 1994 Teeling was stuck with a distillery that he couldn't sell and neither could afford to run.

How he, Master Distiller Noel Sweeney, and his team turned Cooley around is nothing short of remarkable. They pre-sold whiskey to the American and German markets, and expanded into the retailer own-brand business. Eventually, with the launch of the Tyrconnell single malt and Kilbeggan blend, Cooley started to sell whiskey under its own label. Since then it has added Locke's, Millars *(see p205)*, and Greenore *(see p195)* to its range.

Irish Whiskey

Ireland produces four different styles of whiskey, and it is a unique combination. Pure pot still is the style of whiskey that is as Irish as Leprechauns. You just don't get it anywhere else. Pot still whiskey is made from both malted and unmalted barley in a pot still. It's a full-flavored whiskey, which in the Victorian era accounted for just about all the whiskey made in the country.

Nowadays, it is only produced in Midleton and there are just two expressions of pure pot still currently produced, Redbreast and Green Spot. However it can be found in the make up of the most popular Irish whiskeys, including Jameson, Paddy, and most obviously in Powers Gold Label.

Single malt whiskey is made purely from malted barley. It's a popular style that is produced everywhere from Japan to Scotland. In Ireland it is made by Bushmills and Cooley, and both companies market it at various different ages. Bushmills 10-year-old or The Tyrconnell would be good examples. Most Irish single malts are un-peated, but Connemara bucks the trend, with a classic Irish peated malt.

Produced in a continuous still, grain whiskey is usually made from corn in Ireland. It is lighter in flavor than either malt or pot still whiskey. Midleton and Cooley both make grain whiskey. The former uses grain in Jameson and Paddy for example; Cooley blends its grain— though it also bottles an 8-year-old single grain called Greenore. Irish whiskey brands like Jameson, Powers, Paddy, Black Bush, and Kilbeggan are blends. In Ireland, that means a mixture of grain with either or both pot still and single malt.

CRAOI NA MONA

Cooley Distillery, Riverstown, Cooley, County Louth

Craoi na Mona is Gaelic for "heart of peat." Produced by Cooley, though not one of its own brands, this whiskey can be found in places as diverse as Moscow and London, but so far it hasn't been spotted in Dublin. Given the huge rise in the popularity of Irish whiskey recently, it's not surprising that so many drinks companies are trying to cut themselves a slice of the action. But the market place is very crowded and the amount of whiskey being produced in Ireland is limited. What's left then are too many small companies selling whiskey that's very young indeed.

CRAOI NA MONA

SINGLE MALT 40% ABV

Sweet and young, this is a decidedly immature peated malt.

CRESTED TEN

Midleton Distillery, Midleton, County Cork

Launched in 1963, Crested Ten was Jameson's first venture into distillery bottling. The fact that it came at least a century after the Scots started branding and distillery bottling shows how far behind the times the Irish industry was and how close it came to vanishing entirely. Crested Ten is a whiskey you'll see lurking on a top shelf in many Irish pubs. It's never on an optic, probably because it's no good with mixers. Instead, you'll have to ask for it by name.

CRESTED TEN

BLEND 40% ABV

An old-fashioned Irish whiskey with plenty of pot-still character and its Oloroso maturation in evidence. This is a great big hug of a drink that will reward those brave enough to take it from the top shelf. Have it neat, cut with just a splash of water.

DUNGOURNEY 1964

Midleton Distillery, Midleton, County Cork

No one is quite sure how, but for 30 years some of the last pot still to be produced at the old Midleton Distillery lay undiscovered in the corner of a warehouse at Dungourney. In 1994 the remarkable survivor was bottled and named after the river it had come from some three decades before. Dungourney 1964 is a time machine: one sniff and you are transported back to the days when Jameson, Powers, and Paddy came from competing distilleries.

DUNGOURNEY 1964

IRISH POT STILL WHISKEY 40% ABV

The mushroom edge to the nose gives a hint of age, but the body is still firm. They made whiskey differently back then, which is why this tastes slightly oily, but the tell-tale, almost minty, kick of pure pot still whiskey is still evident.

FECKIN IRISH WHISKEY

www.feckinwhiskey.com

As Irish whiskey sales continue to buck the trend and sail upward, it's not surprising that bright entrepreneurs continue to pour new products onto the market. From its name to the label, this offering is aimed at the younger end of the spectrum, and there's not a tweed jacket in sight. "Feck," by the way, is a very mild and very Irish swear word that was popularized on the British TV show *Father Ted*.

FECKIN IRISH WHISKEY

BLEND 40% ABV

Made using whiskey from the Cooley Distillery, this is light, approachable, and totally inoffensive. It's clearly a young whiskey and lacks much in the way of depth.

GREENORE SINGLE GRAIN 8-YEAR-OLD

GREENORE SINGLE GRAIN 15-YEAR-OLD

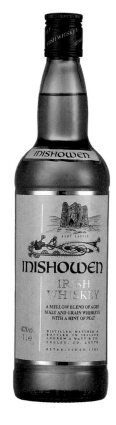

GREENORE SINGLE GRAIN

Cooley Distillery, Riverstown, Cooley, County Louth
www.cooleywhiskey.com

From peated malt to single grain whiskey, Cooley has never been afraid of innovation. In fact, it survived the turbulent early 1990s precisely because it tackled new markets, created niche openings, and launched new products.

Greenore is the only Irish single grain on sale, which is ironic, given that Aeneas Coffey, the man who invented the continuous still, was Irish. Produced in a continuous still rather than in a copper pot still, grain whiskey is lighter in taste and rougher on the back of the throat. For this reason, it is usually kept for blending purposes, where it is mixed with smoother pot still or malt whiskey. Greenore single grain whisky is double-distilled, then matured in bourbon casks for at least eight years.

GREENORE SINGLE GRAIN 8-YEAR-OLD

SINGLE GRAIN 40% ABV

Grain whiskey is the mainstay of most blends. Whether it works on its own or not is totally down to the way it is made. Cooley takes a lot of trouble when producing its grain, and it shows. From the crackle of linseed on the nose to the peppery bite of firm cereal, this is a winner. There is no tell-tale "grain burn" at the end, but rather a sophisticated sprinkle of high-quality grated chocolate.

GREENORE SINGLE GRAIN 15-YEAR-OLD

SINGLE GRAIN 43% ABV

If it's hard to spot that the standard Greenore is a grain whiskey, then it's even more difficult after its spent another seven years in oak. With even more pronounced linseed notes and a minty coolness, there's an almost pot still quality to this classy whiskey.

GREEN SPOT

Midleton Distillery, Midleton, County Cork

In the days before distillers in Ireland spent millions on building brands, they simply used to make the stuff, leaving the filthy job of selling the whiskey to bonders like Mitchell's. This, of course, was a terrible business plan: it allowed the Scots to build global brands, while the Irish were obsessed with an ever-shrinking domestic market. By the time the Irish got back into the race in the 1960s, Irish whiskey had a miserable 1 percent of the global whiskey market. Green Spot is the last bonder's own label. Owned by Mitchell's of Dublin, it's a pure pot still whiskey, made in Midleton.

GREEN SPOT

PURE POT STILL 40% ABV

Greenspot is matured for just six to eight years, but a glass of this is still bracing stuff, with a wonderful lightly sherried finish. One of a kind.

INISHOWEN

Cooley Distillery, Riverstown, Cooley, County Louth
www.cooleywhiskey.com

Inishowen is the kind of concept an accountant would come up with. It's brand economics by numbers. The Scotch industry is worth billions, with blended Scotch making up 90 percent of sales. So if an Irish brand could create a similar product, it would have to be a sure-fire success—wouldn't it? There's nothing much wrong with Inishowen—it is well-made and nicely blended—it's just that it will never be… well, Scotch.

INISHOWEN

BLEND 40% ABV

You won't find any other blended Irish whiskey that has a nose like this: it's both peaty and floral. However, it's the fine grain whiskey and not the malt that gives Inishowen some real charm.

The old Jameson Distillery at Bow Street in Dublin is where the famous Irish whiskey was made until the mid-1970s, when production moved to the new Midleton Distillery. Today it is a visitor center.

THE IRISHMAN SINGLE MALT

THE IRISHMAN CASK STRENGTH

THE IRISHMAN 70

THE IRISHMAN

www.hotirishman.com

Bernard Walsh is the original Hot Irishman. It's not that he looks like Colin Farrell, but rather that he makes what amounts to Irish coffee in a bottle—just add hot water. The Irishman range now includes two new core offerings and a special release.

The single malt uses whiskey from Bushmills, and is a vatting of whiskey matured in bourbon and sherry casks. The second newcomer is the Irishman 70, which is a more innovative concoction. The 70 in the title refers to the percentage of Bushmills malt in the bottle. The remaining 30 percent is pure pot still from Midleton. There is no grain whiskey in this range.

THE IRISHMAN 70

PURE POT STILL/MALT BLEND 40% ABV
The combination of malt and pot still is intriguing, offering a direct hit of dried fruit and rich, almost burned sugar.

THE IRISHMAN SINGLE MALT

SINGLE MALT 40% ABV
Bushmills tends to keep all the best whiskey for itself, which means the Irishman malt has great cereal character but will never be anything outstanding. There is a hint of sherry on the palate, but the malt is slightly premature and could have done with a bit longer in the cask.

THE IRISHMAN CASK STRENGTH

PURE POT STILL/MALT BLEND 56% ABV
A limited-release, cask-strength version of the Irishman 70. The whiskey has a rich, sherried nose. Chocolate notes are in evidence here, alongside rum and raisin, and dark brown sugar. The blend is fresh and vigorous on the palate, with spice and notes of orange zest. The chile-pepper heat creates a lingering finish.

KILBEGGAN

KILBEGGAN 15-YEAR-OLD

KNAPPOGUE CASTLE 1994

KNAPPOGUE CASTLE 1995

KILBEGGAN

The Old Kilbeggan Distillery, Main Street, Kilbeggan, County Westmeath
www.kilbegganwhiskey.com

Kilbeggan has been home to many distilleries, and if you visit the town you can understand why: there's plenty of fresh water (and plenty of rain), and County Westmeath is good barley-growing country. Yet, in the mid-1950s the most famous of the distilleries, John Locke & Sons, fell silent. Although the two remaining Locke family members—sisters Flo and Sweet—had warehouses full of raw ingredients, they had no interest in whiskey-making. With post-war whiskey prices on the rise, they decided to sell the distillery to an international consortium. However, when the deposit of £75,000 never materialized, questions began to be asked. It was rumored that various members of the government were involved in a shady deal to sell the distillery to foreigners. Accusations

of bribery went as high as the Taoiseach, Eamon de Valera, but nothing was ever proven. In the end, the sale fell through, but a year later, the Locke scandal was a factor in the government's subsequent downfall.

Nowadays, Kilbeggan whiskeys are Cooley blends, distilled in County Louth, but the spirits are still matured and bottled on site.

KILBEGGAN

BLEND 40% ABV

This whiskey has improved over the past decade. It is a grainy blend, with strong notes of honey and oatmeal. The end note is a pleasing combination of coffee and dark chocolate. Dollar for dollar, Kilbeggan is one of the best Irish whiskeys that money can buy.

KILBEGGAN 15-YEAR-OLD

BLEND 40% ABV

Age can thin and fracture a whiskey, or it can be its making. The Kilbeggan 15-Year-Old blend is spectacular. Expect the usual Cooley honey and cookie notes, distilled to perfection.

KNAPPOGUE CASTLE

Bushmills Distillery, 2 Distillery Road, County Antrim

After World War II, the owner of Knappogue Castle, near the city of Limerick, took to buying casks of Irish whiskey—particularly from the Tullamore Distillery—which he'd store in a cellar in the family pile. These whiskeys would then be bottled and given away to family and friends over time. The last of these original casks filled with Tullamore whiskey was bottled in 1987, when the spirit was 36 years old.

This particular whiskey is obviously extremely rare now. It is not only its age that makes it rather special, though. It is also that this bottling perfectly captures the flavor of a dying age and a whiskey industry that then looked to be heading the same way. However, fast-forward to the 1990s, and the story begins to

take on a more upbeat air, when the son of the castle's owner, Mark Andrews, decides to follow in his father's footsteps and bottle single vintages of his own, also labelled Knappogue Castle.

The first of these new generation bottlings were created from whiskey produced at Cooley Distillery, but the more recent vintages come from Bushmills.

KNAPPOGUE CASTLE 1995

SINGLE MALT 40% ABV

This whiskey clearly originates from a Bushmills malt, and a seriously classy one to boot. There are strong notes of toasted nuts here, while a juicy, honey sweetness lingers on the palate. However, like many of the independent Bushmills offerings, the whiskey is still a bit too young to display the full potential of its characteristics.

JAMESON

BLEND 40% ABV

This whiskey has a malty smell, which is promising, but the drink itself is a major let-down. The grain is unruly and overwhelms the pot-still, leaving some citrus notes. There is a gently buzz of sherry, but nothing more.

JAMESON GOLD RESERVE

BLEND 43% ABV

This is a viscous, oily, syrupy mouth-coater of a whiskey. Finer, lighter flavors find it hard to fight their way through the fug of sugars. The finish is buzzy and long, in rather the same way as a cough medicine.

JAMESON STANDARD BLEND

JAMESON GOLD RESERVE

JAMESON SPECIAL RESERVE 12-YEAR-OLD

JAMESON LIMITED RESERVE 18-YEAR-OLD

JAMESON RAREST VINTAGE RESERVE

JAMESON

*Midleton Distillery,
Midleton, County Cork
www.jamesonwhiskey.com*

This is the biggest selling Irish whiskey of them all. Jameson is a global brand and can be found in just about every bar in the world. However, if the founder of the company, John Jameson, was around today, he certainly wouldn't recognize the whiskey that now bears his name. The modern standard blend is a 50:50 blend of medium-bodied pot still and grain whiskey. It's a light, approachable spirit that lacks character. Beyond the standard bottling, though, are some

cracking whiskeys. Gold Reserve was originally launched as a premium, duty-free blend, but it is now widely available. Some of the whiskeys used in it are more than 20 years old, but they are cut with younger pot still whiskey, matured in first-fill oak casks. This is the only Irish whiskey to feature virgin wood, and it lends the blend a really sweet, vanilla-like flavor.

Jameson's Special Reserve 12-year-old is a full-bodied whiskey, with plenty of malt from the whiskey and spicy oak after 12 years in Oloroso sherry butts. This whiskey has won several awards and collected Gold at the San Francisco World Spirits Competition in 2007.

Six extra years in the cask doesn't change the flavor profile of the 18-year-old premium offering too much, but what it does do is double the price. The Limited Reserve blend is hand-picked by a Jameson master blender from a limited, but excellent selection of sherry casks.

JAMESON SPECIAL RESERVE 12-YEAR-OLD

BLEND 40% ABV

This world-beating whiskey tweaks the nose firmly with hints of leather and spice. It has an incredible, silky quality, quite unlike the monotone, regular Jameson. Dried fruits wrapped in milk chocolate round off a masterclass in how to make a great whiskey.

JAMESON LIMITED RESERVE 18-YEAR-OLD

BLEND 40% ABV

The pot still here has taken old age well. The body of the whiskey is firm and yielding and the Oloroso wood has to be very fine not to dominate a blend this old. Sweet almond and spiced fudge notes compliment the oiliness of the pot still.

JAMESON RAREST VINTAGE RESERVE

BLEND 40% ABV

An exceptional blending of choice, aged grain, pot still from bourbon wood, and some pot still aged in port pipes. Sweet fruits on the nose, coupled with pot still spice. Rich fruit, oak, and caramel flavors, and a long fruity, spicy finish.

Whiskey Tour: Ireland

In 1887, when the Victorian travel and drinks writer Alfred Barnard visited Ireland, he had 28 different distilleries to visit. Nowadays, the range is markedly more limited, but every bit as enjoyable. Several historic whiskey distilleries have facilities for tourists, and there are other attractions along with the beautiful Irish landscape to further entice the visitor on a whiskey tour of the country.

TOUR STATISTICS		
DAYS: 4	**LENGTH:** 375 miles (600 km)	**DISTILLERIES:** 1 working, 3 converted
TRAVEL: Car, tram, walking	**REGION:** Northern Ireland and Republic of Ireland	

DAY 1: GIANTS CAUSEWAY, BUSHMILLS

1 The North Antrim coast is stunning. Start your journey at the magnificent **Giants Causeway**, a World Heritage Site near the town of Bushmills, where extraordinary hexagonal basalt columns stretch out along the rugged coast.

2 Of all the distilleries in Ireland that are open to the public, **Bushmills** *(www.bushmills.com)* is the only one that is still in production. Enjoy the tour, sample some fine whiskeys, then stroll to the nearby Bushmills Inn *(www.bushmillsinn.com)* for some superb food and a good night's sleep. Rooms in the Mill House are best.

GIANTS CAUSEWAY

DAY 2: COOLEY, OLD JAMESON DISTILLERY

COOLEY DISTILLERY

3 Although **Cooley** Distillery is not open to the public, the hilly Cooley Peninsula and its attractive seaside town of Greenore are worth taking in on the way to Dublin.

4 Avoid the Dublin traffic by taking the LUAS tram from Junction 9 of the M50 to Smithfield in the city center. This is near the **Old Jameson** Distillery, which offers guided tours and the chance to sample Jameson whiskey. *(www.jamesonwhiskey.com)*

FINIS

CORK **7** **8**

THE JAMESON EXPERIENCE

GIANTS CAUSEWAY ①
② BUSHMILLS
START

NORTHERN IRELAND

● BELFAST

③ COOLEY

IRELAND

④ OLD JAMESON

⑤ KILBEGGAN

⑥ TULLAMORE DEW

● WATERFORD

miles
0   25

0   25
kilometers

DAY 3: KILBEGGAN, TULLAMORE DEW

⑤ Take Junction 7 of the M50 and head west out of Dublin to the old Locke's building at **Kilbeggan**. The original distillery fell silent in 1957, but the site has been revived by locals and now houses the Kilbeggan micro-distillery and a whiskey museum with working waterwheel, restaurant, shop, and whiskey bar. Cooley leases warehouses at this site and brings casks of its whiskey here for maturation. *(www.lockesdistillerymuseum.ie)*

KILBEGGAN

TULLAMORE DEW

⑥ The vibrant town of Tullamore is home to the **Tullamore Dew** Heritage Centre. This building used to be a bonded warehouse for storing whiskey casks before they were shipped downstream to Dublin, and is now the setting for an exhibition about traditional whiskey-making. Tullamore Dew whiskey is distilled at Midleton these days, but is, of course, available for tasting at the heritage center. *(www.tullamore-dew.org)*

DAY 4: CORK, THE JAMESON EXPERIENCE AT MIDLETON

⑦ The cross-country trip from Tullamore to Cork traverses the boggy heart of Ireland—a bleak landscape that is strangely beautiful at any time of the year. The city of **Cork** is a food haven, where you can visit the historic English Market to buy a picnic lunch and eat it in nearby Bishop Lucey Park. Alternatively, the Market Café is a great place to try local specialities such as tripe, pigs' feet, and Irish Stew. For a drink, stop at the South County Bar & Café *(www.thesouthcounty.com)*, in Douglas Village, a suburb of Cork. It's a traditional, family-run pub, with its own "whiskey corner" to celebrate Irish whiskey.

POT STILL AT MIDLETON

⑧ **The Jameson Experience** *(www.jamesonwhiskey.com)* is set in the beautifully restored 18th-century distillery at Midleton, and boasts the world's largest pot still, which now stands outside the buildings. For refreshment, try the restaurant at nearby Ballymaloe House, which is overseen by Darina Allen, the doyen of Irish foodies. *(www.ballymaloe.ie)*

KNOCKEEN HILLS 60 PROOF

KNOCKEEN HILLS 70 PROOF

LOCKE'S 8-YEAR-OLD MALT

LOCKE'S BLEND

KNOCKEEN HILLS

www.irish-poteen.com

Poteen (or poitín) is a clear spirit that was traditionally distilled in homemade pot stills throughout Ireland. It was originally made with malted barley or any other available grain, though potatoes were also used. Poteen is synonymous with illegal spirit, and the reason for this can be traced back to the 1660s. This was when the English government in Ireland first started taxing the ancient art of distilling. *Uisce beatha* became the legal, duty-paid whiskey; *uisce poitín* the illegal version. Over the intervening 300 years, its love/hate relationship with the law has been celebrated in story and song. This is a rich folk heritage for drinks companies to draw upon.

In 1997 the government removed their previous objection to the term being used to describe

a white spirit on which duty had been paid. Hackler from Guinness was soon out of the trap and it quickly went the way of Guinness Light. One of the few to survive—and indeed to thrive—is Knockeen Hills. Its spirit is bottled at three strengths: triple-distilled at 60% and 70% ABV, and quadruple-distilled at 90% ABV. It should not be drunk neat.

KNOCKEEN HILLS 60
POTEEN 60% ABV
Clean, fresh, and fruity on the nose. Creamy textured, with tantalizing sweet and juicy fruit notes on the palate. Crisp, mouth-cleansing finish.

KNOCKEEN HILLS 70
POTEEN 70% ABV
Stronger on the nose than the 60. With a large measure of water (almost 50/50), it becomes fruity, with tangerine-skin aromas and a sweet perfumed note. Warming in the mouth, sweet and sour on the palate, with a dry, fruit-tinged finish.

LOCKE'S

Cooley Distillery, Riverstown, Cooley, County Louth
www.cooleywhiskey.com

Locke's Distillery in the town of Kilbeggan is an oasis of calm in the Irish midlands. The ancient stone walls filter what traffic noise there is, while the inner courtyard still echoes to the sound of a blacksmith and the trickle of whiskey-making.

It's hard to believe that, just 25 years ago, this truly remarkable distillery was almost derelict. Since the early 1950s, when the Locke's whiskey business initially folded, the abandoned distillery buildings had been used to house pigs and farm machinery. In the late 1970s, the local community got together and restored the distillery. Shortly after the renovation was completed, fate decided to smile upon Kilbeggan. John Teeling was setting up a new distillery in County Louth and wanted to age his maturing stocks at Locke's.

A deal was done in which Cooley bought the rights to the Locke's brand, leased the buildings and, after decades of dusty silence, whiskey barrels once more trundled into the stone warehouses.

In 2007, to celebrate the distillery's 250th anniversary, a micro-distillery was opened at Locke's. The first of its spirit will come of age in 1010.

LOCKE'S 8-YEAR-OLD MALT
SINGLE MALT 40% ABV
This malt is a vatting of Cooley's unpeated malt, with a top dressing of peated malt. It is not a bad whiskey; but it's just a bit dull. More Daniel O'Donnell than Shane McGowan, as it were.

LOCKE'S BLEND
SINGLE MALT 40% ABV
This is a pleasant enough dram. It would be particularly good in a hot whiskey, where its limited range doesn't have to sing out. Taken neat, Locke's can be a tad monosyllabic, in that it only really has a malty note.

MICHAEL COLLINS SINGLE MALT

MICHAEL COLLINS BLEND

MAGILLIGAN

*Cooley Distillery, Riverstown,
Cooley, County Louth*

This is a confusing whiskey. It may
well say pure pot still on the label,
but you are actually buying a young,
Cooley-produced single malt (though
the Magilligan brand is not part of
Cooley's own stable). The fault lies
with Irish legislature; it has not
legally defined what constitutes
a "pure pot still." At the moment,
any whiskey that is made in a pot
still can be called pot still whiskey.
So, buyers should beware.

Magilligan comes in various
guises, including a limited-edition
1991 vintage bottled at 46% ABV.

MAGILLIGAN

SINGLE MALT 43% ABV

This is a thin young malt, with hints
of greatness, but it has been bottled as
an adolescent. An 8-year-old version
is available, but the regular Magilligan
offering tastes like a vatting of whiskeys
between three and five years old.

MICHAEL COLLINS

www.michaelcollinswhiskey.com

General Michael Collins was one
of the founding fathers of the
modern Irish state. Numerous
movies have been made about his
life, with everyone from Brendan
Gleeson to Liam Neeson playing
"the big fellow," as he was known.
Almost everyone in Ireland knows
just about everything there is to
know about Collins, and yet most
people have never heard of this
whiskey.

The reason for this is that the
whiskey was initially formulated
for the American market by Cooley
Distillery in conjunction with US
importer Sidney Frank. However,
it can now be bought on both sides
of the Atlantic.

Unusually for an Irish whiskey,
the Michael Collins malt is double-
distilled and has a light peating
too. Though released without an
age statement, the malts used have
been aged for between 8 and 12
years. The blend is a mix of the
malt and a younger grain whiskey,
which is subsequently put into
bourbon casks for maturation.

MICHAEL COLLINS
SINGLE MALT

SINGLE MALT 40% ABV

This is like a cream soda for adults—
but in a good way. It is soft and
drinkable, with plenty of biscuity
flavors. Vanilla notes emerge, as a result
of the bourbon casking, with a hint of
light smoke. This is a vatting of peated
and unpeated malt, and a really classy
one at that.

MICHAEL COLLINS BLEND

BLEND 40% ABV

The blend is a lot less impressive than
the malt. It is thin, with the scent
of woody embers at its core, but it
lacks a decent finish.

MILLARS

*Cooley Distillery, Riverstown,
Cooley, County Louth
www.cooleywhiskey.com*

Once upon a time, every single
drop of Irish whiskey was bottled
by bonders. Gilbey's, Mitchell's
or Millars would buy whiskey in
bulk and sell it to their customers,
often straight from the cask.
This method started to die out
during the latter part of the 20th
century, and Adam Millars & Co
in Dublin was one of the only
bonders to survive.

The Millars brand is now owned
by Cooley, and this hard-to-find
whiskey is a grain-heavy blend.

MILLARS SPECIAL RESERVE

BLEND 40% ABV

This is a superb little whiskey. It is
a perky dram, with a real sense of fun.
A peppery character on the nose is
underpinned by a luxurious, spicy
body in the glass.

Bushmills in County Antrim is the only working distillery in Ireland that is open to the public. It is also the world's oldest surviving distillery, dating back to 1608.

MIDLETON VERY RARE

BLEND 40% ABV

The nose is a skillful balancing act; classy oak and bold cereal notes dance on a high wire made of pure beeswax. The body is full and yielding, and the finish breaks on the tongue in waves of silky, walnut whip. You get a classy ball of malt for your money, and so you should. Note that there is a little variation in the whiskey from year to year.

MIDLETON MASTER DISTILLER'S PRIVATE COLLECTION 1973

PURE POT STILL 56% ABV

Even rarer than Midleton Very Rare, this whiskey was distilled in 1973 and is a bottling of pure pot still whiskey from the old Midleton Distillery. It was produced as a 30-year-old in an edition of 800 bottles, and its taste is said to be spicy, fruity, and honeyed, with some dry, sherry nuttiness.

JAMESON *(see p201)*

PADDY *(see p213)*

POWERS *(see p213)*

REDBREAST *(see p213)*

MIDLETON

Midleton, County Cork
www.irishdistillers.ie

Midleton is Ireland's largest distillery. It is home to Jameson, Powers, Paddy, and all of the Irish Distillers' portfolio of whiskeys, as well as their gins, and vodkas. The place looks like an enormous petro-chemical plant, but it can still make some sublime spirits.

The history of distilling on this site goes back as far as 1825, when the Murphy brothers went into the drinks business. One branch of the family started to make a stout, which still bears their name, and the other side of the family went into the whiskey business.

With its proximity to fine fields of barley and a large harbor on its coast, County Cork enjoys a long tradition of distilling. In 1867, five of the local operations joined forces to form Cork Distilleries Company (CDC) and, gradually, all production was centralized at the Midleton plant.

In 1966, CDC, along with Jameson and Powers, were among the founding members of Irish Distillers. As before, all production was eventually moved over to Midleton Distillery. But by 1975, the old Victorian building could no longer cope with the demands of production, and a new state-of-the-art plant was built to the rear of the original Victorian buildings.

The company also produces the only regular bottlings of pure pot still whiskey in the world. Redbreast is available as a 12-year-old version and a limited-edition 15-year-old version—a huge, mouth-filling carnival of sherry and vanilla, aged to perfection. Green Spot is the other pure pot still produced at Midleton. Aged for approximately 8 years, it is a fresher version of this whiskey style, slightly oily with linseed and menthol notes.

Among all the spirits produced at Midleton, there is just one regularly appearing whiskey that carries the actual Midleton moniker. Launched in 1984, Midleton Very Rare is aimed

at the premium market and the price reflects whatever that market can bear. A new vintage is released late every year and, although they vary slightly, the house style is essentially the same. The constituent whiskeys are aged for between 12 and 25 years in seasoned bourbon casks. The spirit in these bottlings was mostly distilled at the new plant, but the oldest vintages were made at the old Midleton Distillery—now beautifully restored to house the Jameson Experience *(see p211)*.

The secrets of… **Midleton**

The town of Midleton is an easy 30-minute drive from Cork city. It's a pleasant market town and on a clear day, with the wind in a certain direction, comes the curious scent of whiskey.

Set back slightly from the main thoroughfare, hugging the bank of the Dungourney River, lie the imposing Victorian buildings of Midleton Distillery. This is the original Cork Distilleries Company (CDC) plant that ceased production in the early 1970s. Nowadays it houses an impressive visitor center, the Jameson Experience.

Behind the old distillery, lies the new one. In 1966 the remaining Irish distilleries—Powers and Jameson in Dublin, and CDC in Cork—came together to form Irish Distillers.

When the two Dublin-based distilleries closed, all production shifted to the new state-of-the-art plant at Midleton. This is now where everything from Jameson whiskey to Cork Dry Gin are produced. You shouldn't be put off by its industrial scale, though, for Midleton has exacting standards and produces fantastic whiskeys, including bottlings of the two remaining Irish pot still whiskeys, Redbreast and Green Spot. It all comes down to the basics: a good water source and local barley.

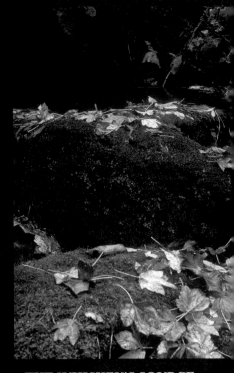

▲ THE WHISKEY'S SOURCE
Dungourney River runs right past the distillery. In fact the river is the reason the factory is sited where it is. The old Midleton distillery was powered by a giant waterwheel *(see bottom right)*. That may have changed, but the new distillery still uses the Dungourney for its whiskey.

◄ LOCAL BARLEY
Midleton uses locally grown barley for its malt. The malt used to produce its great whiskeys is dried by warm air and not with peat smoke, as is common in Scotland. This means that there is nothing to mask the wonderful malty, biscuity taste of fine Irish barley.

THREE MASH PROCESS ▶
The malt (or a mixture of malt and barley if pot still whiskey is being produced) is ground into a coarse flour called grist and dumped into a large tub known as a mashtun, or locally as a kieve. Hot water is added, and the mixture is stirred to help convert the starch in the grain into sugar. At Midleton this process is repeated three times, with the barley water being drained off after each mashing. The final barley water is held and used in the first mashing of the next batch of grist. This ensures a certain continuity between batches.

◀ CHOICE WOOD

Midleton has a very strict wood policy: only the finest American oak barrels are used, while the sherry wood comes from oak butts that are built and seasoned to order in Jerez, Spain. They will be used to mature sherry for one or two years before being brought over to Midleton to age the whiskey. The distillery is currently building new warehousing to cope with its maturing stocks.

◀ BOTTLING

Jameson is the biggest-selling whiskey that Midleton produces, and the vast majority of it is bottled near Dublin. But there is a second line close to Midleton, at the old North Mall Distillery in the heart of Cork. This old distillery no longer produces whiskey, but does at least keep a connection to the industry by bottling some of the output from Midleton.

▼ THE JAMESON EXPERIENCE

The old Midleton Distillery now houses a visitor center, where you can be taken on a tour of the buildings and the grounds, sample some whiskeys, and become an expert on the characteristics of Irish whiskey *(see also p203)*.

▲ PRODUCTION VARIATIONS

There isn't a distillery in the world that can produce the range of whiskeys that comes out of Midleton. Many pure pot still, malt, and grain variations are stored in tanks under the plant. These can then be combined in different quantities and matured in different woods to produce myriad whiskey types and styles.

Without barley, there would be no whiskey; it's as simple as that. Midleton Distillery in County Cork sits among scenic, rolling fields of barley. The distillery makes great use of this local supply.

POWERS GOLD LABEL

POWERS GOLD LABEL 12-YEAR-OLD

PADDY

Midleton Distillery, Midleton,
County Cork
www.irishdistillers.ie

There was a time when Irish whiskey was sold anonymously from casks in pubs. What whiskey a pub stocked was down to the owner and his relationship with the agent for the distillery.

Paddy Flaherty was an agent for the Cork Distillers Company of Midleton in the 1920s and 30s. You knew when he was in town, as he'd buy everyone drinks at the bar, and the whiskey he sold—the CDC's Old Irish Whiskey—became so synonymous with the man himself that it was simply known as Paddy's whiskey.

PADDY

BLEND 40% ABV

This is a malty dram, which is both solid and well matured. It offers a satisfying, spicy, peppery kick.

POWERS

Midleton Distillery, Midleton,
County Cork
www.irishdistillers.ie

For longer than anyone could remember, Jameson and Powers used to stare each other down across the narrow strip of Dublin water they call the Liffey. The Powers family (on Dublin's south side) had been in the business since 1817, and a member of the family sat on the board of Irish Distillers until it was incorporated into the Pernod Ricard group, some 171 years later.

The Powers family had always embraced innovation. They pioneered the production of Irish gin and vodka, and moved into distillery bottling before anyone else in the country. They also invented the miniature, or, as it is known, the "baby Powers."

Incidentally, the picture of the three swallows on the Powers label is an example of typical Dublin wit.

It has long been held that the only way to enjoy a Powers is not to sip it slowly, but to lower the glass in "three swallows."

POWERS GOLD LABEL

BLEND 40% ABV

This whiskey is something really special. Powers Gold Label is an upfront, take-no-prisoners experience. This isn't another bland, global brand; this is a real, solid whiskey. The nose is classically Irish—at once bracing and brittle. At core, this whiskey is pure pot still, cut with just enough good grain. Powers Gold Label is an utterly captivating blend. If this whiskey doesn't make your toes tingle and your heart sing, then you might as well give up now.

POWERS GOLD LABEL 12-YEAR-OLD

BLEND 40% ABV

An older, more layered expression of the same Powers formulation. Spice, honey, crème brûlée, with soft wood tones and sweet, fresh fruits.

REDBREAST

Midleton Distillery, Midleton,
County Cork
www.irishdistillers.ie

Redbreast was the name that wine merchants Gilbey's gave to the Jameson whiskey that they matured and bottled. The bonder trade was finally phased out in 1968, but Redbreast was so popular that it was allowed to continue well into the 1980s. In the 1990s, Irish Distillers bought the brand from Gilbey's and re-launched the drink as a 12-year-old pure pot still, part-matured in sherry wood. There is also a limited-edition 15-year-old version *(see p209).*

REDBREAST 12-YEAR-OLD

PURE POT STILL 40% ABV

This is, without doubt, one of the world's finest whiskeys. Flavors range from ginger to cinnamon, peppermint to linseed, and licorice to camphor. A sherry note sets off an elegant finish.

TULLAMORE DEW

TULLAMORE DEW 10-YEAR-OLD

TULLAMORE DEW 12-YEAR-OLD

TULLAMORE DEW

www.tullamoredew.com

Tullamore is a sizable market town. It is situated pretty much smack-dab in the middle of Ireland. Although Tullamore itself is largely built on bogland, some great barley-producing counties lie nearby that once provided the grain for both this distillery and the operation at Locke's Distillery in nearby Kilbeggan.

In 1901, the worldwide sales of Irish whiskey peaked at 10 million cases, and two years later the Williams family gained control of Tullamore Distillery. In fact, D. E. Williams is the man whose name is still associated with whiskey in Tullamore; as in Tullamore DEW-illiams.

In 1954, the distillery closed and the brand was sold to Powers. It was then absorbed by Irish Distillers, before being sold and

sold, and sold again. Nowadays, the whiskey is all produced to order in Midleton and it sells very well across continental Europe.

TULLAMORE DEW
BLEND 40% ABV
This whiskey is fairly one-dimensional. It has a characteristic bourbon burn, with not much else to recommend it.

**TULLAMORE DEW
10-YEAR-OLD**
BLEND 40% ABV
There's malt, spice, and vanilla on the nose, and a hint of oakiness and spice on the palate. The finish is long and dry, with a citric tang.

**TULLAMORE DEW
12-YEAR-OLD**
BLEND 40% ABV
A considerable step up from the other Tullamore blends, the 12-year-old is reminiscent of a premium Jameson. The precious trinity of pot still, sherry, and oak is very much in evidence.

TYRCONNELL 10-YEAR-OLD PORT CASK

TYRCONNELL 10-YEAR-OLD MADEIRA CASK

TYRCONNELL 10-YEAR-OLD SHERRY CASK

TYRCONNELL SINGLE MALT

TYRCONNELL

*Cooley Distillery, Riverstown,
Cooley, County Louth
www.cooleywhiskey.com*

It would be hard to find anyone who remembers the original Old Tyrconnell whiskey. The distillery that produced it, Andrew A. Watt and Company of Derry City, closed in 1925. In its day, this whiskey (named after a race horse) was very popular in the US, and early film of baseball games at the Yankee Stadium show billboards advertising "Old Tyrconnel."

But the combined effects of civil unrest in Ireland and Prohibition in the US pushed Watt and many other Irish distilleries into the hands of the Scottish United Distillers Company. To protect their core Scotch brands, UDC ruthlessly closed every Irish distillery they bought, bringing the industry across the island to its knees. However, The Tyrconnel was the first brand Cooley's John Teeling

chose to bring back to life when he bottled his first single malt in 1992. Since then, various wood finishes have been tried on the 10-year-old.

TYRCONNELL SINGLE MALT

SINGLE MALT 40% ABV

Cooley's bestselling malt and it's easy to see why. This has the loveliest nose of any Irish whiskey, releasing jasmine, honeysuckle, and malted-milk cookies.

TYRCONNELL PORT CASK

SINGLE MALT 46% ABV

Port changes the nose slightly, spicing things up. The body has aromas of fig pastry and plum pudding.

TYRCONNELL MADEIRA CASK

SINGLE MALT 46% ABV

Madeira and Ireland do each other proud here. Warm hints of cinnamon and mixed spice dance on the palate.

TYRCONNELL SHERRY CASK

SINGLE MALT 46% ABV

The best of the wood finishes—malt and fruity sherry fuse beautifully.

THE WILD GEESE CLASSIC BLEND

THE WILD GEESE RARE IRISH

THE WILD GEESE SINGLE MALT

THE WILD GEESE

www.thewildgeese-irishwhiskey.com

With victory at the Battle of Kinsale, the English crown finally wrestled power from the native Gaelic chieftains, and in 1608 these Irish nobles fled the country. However, this didn't end the conflict in Ireland. The term "Wild Geese" refers to those Irish nobles and soldiers who left to serve in continental European armies from the early 17th century to the dawn of the 20th century. Most of those families remained in Europe. Some, like the Hennessys, started producing cognac. Others, such as the Lynchs, went on to make wine.

The name "Wild Geese" has come down through history to embrace all the men and women who left Ireland in the last 400 years—not just the nobles. The idea of diaspora and immigration has, of course, been a poignant theme in Irish culture and remains so today. Wild Geese raises a glass to this part of Irish history, and they've certainly produced a good whiskey for the job.

THE WILD GEESE CLASSIC BLEND

BLEND 40% ABV

A boiled-sweet nose. The malt doesn't have much impact here, leaving the grain to carry things to the finish.

THE WILD GEESE RARE IRISH

BLEND 43% ABV

A rich and malty blend, with some spiciness and lemon notes in the body. You'll find a little dry oak in the finish.

THE WILD GEESE SINGLE MALT

SINGLE MALT 43% ABV

This whiskey is predominantly malty, with a caramel sweetness. There is also a little oakiness and a hint of spice.

Cooley Distillery matures its whiskey in the old warehouses of the former Locke's Distillery in Kilbeggan. Both the town and the old distillery are honored in two of Cooley's whiskey ranges.

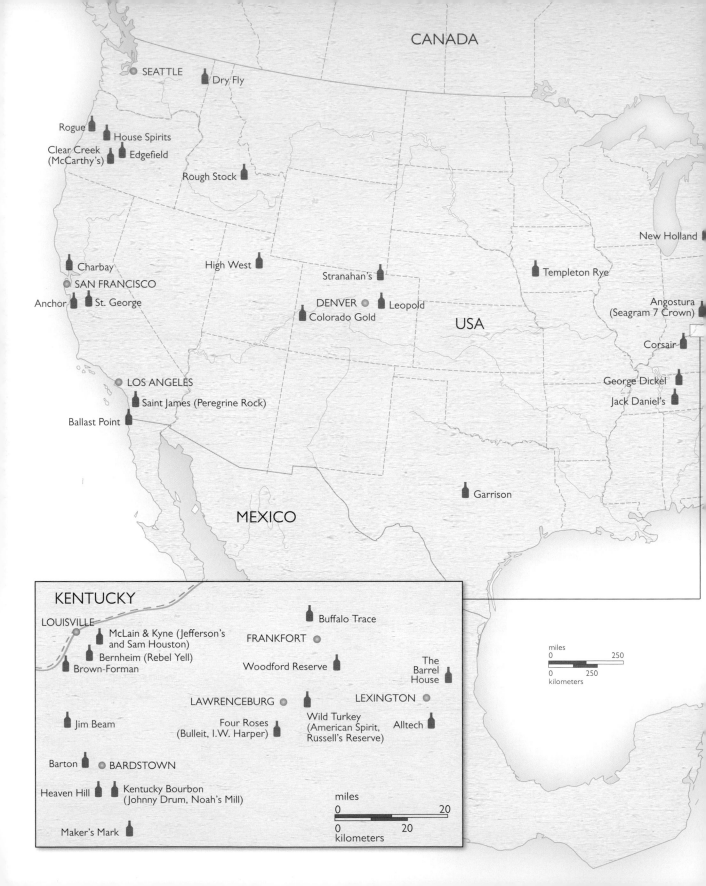

CANADA

SEATTLE
Dry Fly

Rogue
House Spirits
Clear Creek
(McCarthy's)   Edgefield
Rough Stock

New Holland

Charbay   High West
SAN FRANCISCO   Stranahan's
Anchor   St. George   DENVER   Leopold
                                 Colorado Gold

USA

Angostura
(Seagram 7 Crown)

Corsair

Templeton Rye

LOS ANGELES
Saint James (Peregrine Rock)
Ballast Point

George Dickel

Jack Daniel's

MEXICO

Garrison

miles
0   250
0   250
kilometers

KENTUCKY

LOUISVILLE
McLain & Kyne (Jefferson's
and Sam Houston)
Bernheim (Rebel Yell)
Brown-Forman

Buffalo Trace

FRANKFORT

Woodford Reserve

The
Barrel
House

LAWRENCEBURG   LEXINGTON

Jim Beam   Four Roses   Wild Turkey   Alltech
                        (Bulleit, I.W. Harper)   (American Spirit,
                                                  Russell's Reserve)

Barton   BARDSTOWN

Heaven Hill   Kentucky Bourbon
               (Johnny Drum, Noah's Mill)   miles
                                                   0   20
                                                   0   20
Maker's Mark   kilometers

The limestone soil of Kentucky yields rich crops of corn, and it is no coincidence that Kentucky and the surrounding whiskey-producing states of the USA partly overlie the same limestone shelf. Kentucky is the heartland of American whiskey, and is where most of the USA's large-scale commercial distilleries are located, including Jim Beam, Buffalo Trace, Heaven Hill, Barton, and Brown-Forman. To the south, Tennessee has its own legally defined whiskey style and is the home of two other big names in American whiskey: Jack Daniel's and George Dickel. Ownership of these big distilleries and their brand portfolios often changes hands—today the international spirits companies Constellation and Fortune Brands ultimately own many American whiskeys. Besides this core of large-scale distillers, however, is a growing number of micro-distillers, who are often eager to experiment with recipes and production practices, injecting new and dynamic life into the exciting world of American whiskey.

Nashoba Valley
BOSTON
Triple Eight
(The Notch)
Tuthilltown
(Hudson)
NEW YORK

Copper Fox
(Wasmund's)
Mount Vernon
A. Smith Bowman
(Virginia Gentleman)
Belmont Farms (Virginia Lightning)

Piedmont (Catdaddy)

N
W E
S

WILD TURKEY

BUFFALO TRACE

CATDADDY

OLD POTRERO

MELLOW CORN

AMERICAN SPIRIT

Wild Turkey Distillery, US Highway 62 East, Lawrenceburg, Kentucky
www.wildturkeybourbon.com

American Spirit is distilled at the Wild Turkey Distillery *(see p264)* by Austin Nicholls & Co, and was introduced in September 2007. According to Eddie Russell, who developed this expression with his father, Master Distiller Jimmy Russell, the name "American Spirit" seemed to suggest itself.

AMERICAN SPIRIT 15-YEAR-OLD

BOURBON 50% ABV

Richly aromatic and characterful on the nose, silky-smooth in the mouth, with vanilla, brittle toffee, molasses, stewed fruits, spice, and a little mint. The finish is lengthy and spicy, with gentle oak and a final menthol note.

ANCIENT AGE

Buffalo Trace, 1001 Wilkinson Boulevard, Frankfort, Kentucky
www.buffalotrace.com

Ancient Age was, from 1969 to 1999, the name of what is now the Buffalo Trace Distillery *(see p222)*. The brand was introduced in the 1930s shortly after the end of Prohibition, initially being distilled in Canada. After World War II it was reformulated as a straight Kentucky-made bourbon, and went on to become one of the best-known brands produced by its proprietors.

ANCIENT AGE 10-YEAR-OLD

BOURBON 40% ABV

This 10-year-old bourbon is complex and fragrant on the nose, with spices, fudge, oranges, and honey. Medium-bodied and, after a slightly dry opening, the oily palate sweetens with developing vanilla, cocoa, and a lightly charred note.

BAKER'S

Jim Beam Distillery, 149 Happy Hollow Road, Clermont, Kentucky
www.jimbeam.com

Baker's is one of three whiskeys that were introduced in 1992 as Beam's Small Batch Bourbon Collection. It is named for Baker Beam, the former Clermont Master Distiller and grand-nephew of the legendary Jim Beam himself. He is also a cousin of the late Booker Noe, the high-profile distiller who instigated small-batch bourbon distilling. Baker Beam's namesake whiskey is distilled using the standard Jim Beam formula, but is aged for longer and offered at a higher bottling strength.

BAKER'S 7-YEAR-OLD

BOURBON (53.5% ABV)

Baker's is a fruity, toasty expression of the Jim Beam formula: medium-bodied, mellow, and richly flavored, with notes of vanilla and caramel.

BARTON

1 Barton Road, Bardstown, Kentucky
www.bartonbrands.com

Barton Brands Ltd. is a distilling subsidiary of the international Constellation Brands Inc., and is located in Bardstown, Nelson County. Bardstown is in the true heartland of bourbon, and once boasted more than 20 distilleries. Barton's whiskeys are typically youthful, dry, and aromatic.

In addition to the Barton-named brands, the company also owns Kentucky Gentleman *(see p244)*, Kentucky Tavern *(p244)*, Ridgemont *(p254)*, Ten High *(p258)*, and Tom Moore *(p258)*.

VERY OLD BARTON

BOURBON 43% ABV

Six years is comparatively old for a Barton whiskey, hence its name. The nose is rich, syrupy, and spicy, with a prickle of salt. Big-bodied in the mouth, it is fruity and spicy, with spices and ginger in the drying finish.

BASIL HAYDEN'S

Jim Beam Distillery, 149 Happy Hollow Road, Clermont, Kentucky
www.jimbeam.com

Basil Hayden's was one of the three whiskeys that made up Beam's pioneering Small Batch Bourbon Collection, introduced in 1992. Basil Hayden was an early Kentucky settler from Maryland who began making whiskey in the late 18th century near Bardstown, and it is claimed that the recipe for this particular expression dates from that period.

BASIL HAYDEN'S 8-YEAR-OLD

BOURBON 40% ABV
The nose is light, aromatic, and spicy, with flavors of soft rye, wood-polish, spices, pepper, vanilla, and a hint of honey on the comparatively dry palate. The finish is long, with notes of peppery rye.

BERNHEIM

Heaven Hill Distillery, 1701 West Breckinridge Street, Louisville, Kentucky
www.bernheimwheatwhiskey.com

The Bernheim brand takes its name from Heaven Hill's Bernheim Distillery in Louisville, Kentucky, where Heaven Hill whiskeys have been produced since the plant was acquired in 1999. Launched in 2005, Bernheim is the only straight wheat whiskey on the US market.

Heaven Hill father and son Master Distillers Parker and Craig Beam developed the wheat formula with a minimum of 51 percent winter wheat, and the recipe also includes corn and malted barley.

BERNHEIM ORIGINAL

WHEAT WHISKEY 45% ABV
Bernheim exhibits light fruit notes on the spicy nose, with freshly sawn wood, toffee, vanilla, sweetish grain, and a hint of mint on the palate. A long, elegant, honeyed, and spicy finish.

BLANTON'S

Buffalo Trace, 1001 Wilkinson Boulevard, Frankfort, Kentucky
www.buffalotrace.com

Colonel Albert Bacon Blanton worked for no fewer than 55 years at what is now the Buffalo Trace Distillery, starting as office boy in 1897 and graduating to distillery manager in 1912. When he retired in 1955 the distillery was renamed Blanton's in his honor. This single barrel expression was created in 1984 by Master Distiller Elmer T. Lee, who worked with Blanton during the 1950s.

BLANTON'S SINGLE BARREL

BOURBON 46.5% ABV
The nose of Blanton's is soft, with toffee, leather, and a hint of mint. Full-bodied and rounded on the palate, this is a notably sweet bourbon, embracing vanilla, caramel, honey, and spices. The finish is long and creamy, with a hint of late spice.

BOOKER'S

Jim Beam Distillery, 149 Happy Hollow Road, Clermont, Kentucky
www.jimbeam.com

A brand created by the global Jim Beam company, Booker's is named after Jim Beam's grandson, Booker Noe. It is made to the same Jim Beam formula as Baker's, and is still bottled unfiltered and undiluted to maintain its natural barrel flavors.

BOOKER'S KENTUCKY STRAIGHT

BOURBON 60.5–63.5% ABV
Big, fruity, and spicy on the nose, Booker's is sweet and slightly nutty on the palate, with heat and spiciness in the oaky finish. A big, traditional, classy bourbon.

EARLY TIMES *(see p227)*

OLD FORESTER *(see p250)*

BUFFALO TRACE KENTUCKY STRAIGHT BOURBON

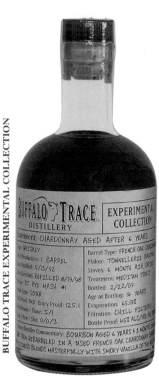

BUFFALO TRACE EXPERIMENTAL COLLECTION

BROWN-FORMAN

850 Dixie Highway,
Louisville, Kentucky
www.brown-forman.com

The Brown-Forman Distillery is situated in the area of Louisville known as "Distillery Row." Half a dozen once operated here, but today only Brown-Forman and Bernheim *(see p221)* survive.

The Brown-Forman Corporation has its origins in a blending and bottling operation established by George Garvin Brown and his half-brother John Thompson Street Brown in 1870. Their practice of selling whiskey in sealed bottles was a major innovation that overcame problems of adulteration, but the Browns were also forward-thinking in acquiring whiskeys from a variety of distillers and blending them to achieve ongoing consistency. Their whiskey brand was originally called Old Forrester (later changed to Forester).

When John Brown left the company he was replaced by accountant George Forman, whose name was added to the company title in 1890.

The firm's Louisville facility was established in 1935 as the Old Kentucky Distillery. Brown-Forman acquired it in 1940 and subsequently rebuilt the plant, renaming it the Early Times Distillery. Brown-Forman's other distillery in Louisville, Old Forester Distillery, closed in 1979, after which production of Old Forester bourbon was moved to the Early Times Distillery.

Today it is simply the Brown-Forman Distillery. Early Times Kentucky Whisky *(see p227)* and Old Forester *(p250)* are now its principal output (Brown-Forman favors the Scottish spelling of "whisky" for some of its output). The Brown-Forman Corporation also owns the Jack Daniel *(p238)* and Woodford Reserve distilleries *(p266)*.

BUFFALO TRACE

Buffalo Trace Distillery, 1001
Wilkinson Boulevard, Frankfort,
Kentucky
www.buffalotrace.com

Formerly known as Ancient Age *(see p220)*, Buffalo Trace is located at a crossing point where, in the past, herds of migrating buffalo forded the Kentucky River. The trail they followed was known as the Great Buffalo Trace.

A distillery was first established here in 1857 by the Blanton family. Later, it was run by "bourbon aristocrat" Edmund Haynes Taylor and the pioneering George T. Stagg, then Albert Bacon Blanton steered and grew the company through flood, Prohibition, and war. He and Stagg have exclusive bourbons named after them *(see pp221 and 233)*.

Buffalo Trace boasts the broadest age-range of whiskey in the USA (from 4 to 23 years) and is the only US distillery using five recipes—a wheat whiskey, a rye whiskey, two

rye bourbons, and a barley. The Buffalo Trace Experimental Collection of cask strength, wine-barrel-aged whiskeys was launched in 2006. It included a "Fire Pot Barrel" for which the barrel was heated to 102°F (39°C) prior to filling, to give a greater "burn" than usual. Subsequent releases in the Experimental Collection have included a 10-year-old Chardonnay, a 14- and a 16-year-old Cabernet Franc, and a 6-year-old Zinfandel.

BUFFALO TRACE KENTUCKY STRAIGHT BOURBON

BOURBON 45% ABV

Aged a minimum of nine years, it has aromas of vanilla, gum, mint, and molasses. Sweet, fruity, and spicy on the palate, with emerging brown sugar and oak. The finish is long, spicy, and fairly dry, with developing vanilla.

Bourbon

Bourbon enjoys a global reputation as the quintessential US whiskey, and boasts a long and colorful heritage. It takes its name from Bourbon County in Kentucky, which in turn was named in honor of the French royal House of Bourbon when the former Western Virginian county of Kentucky was subdivided in the 1780s.

Distilling probably began in the area when settlers of Scottish, Irish, and German origin arrived during the late-18th century. The "invention" of bourbon is often credited to the Baptist minister, entrepreneur, and distiller Elijah Craig, who is said to have pioneered the use of charred casks for maturation at the distillery he founded in 1789. In reality, however, no one person created bourbon, which evolved from the distilling practices of many individuals. It is also a common misconception that bourbon must be distilled in Kentucky. In fact, it can be produced anywhere in the United States where it is legal to distill spirits. However, in practice, some 95 percent of all bourbon is distilled and matured in its "home" state.

The legally binding modern definition of bourbon dates from May 1964, when the US Congress recognized it as a "distinctive product of the United States", and created the Federal Standards of Identity for Bourbon. By law, the whiskey type must be produced from a mash of not less than 51 percent corn grain, and is usually made using between 70 and 90 percent corn, with some barley malt plus rye and/or wheat in the mashbill. It has to be distilled to no more than 80% ABV and casked at 62.5% ABV or less. Legally, bourbon must be matured in new, charred, white-oak barrels for a minimum of two years.

Among the most notable bourbon brands on the market are Jim Beam *(see p242)*, Buffalo Trace *(see p222)*, Maker's Mark *(see p246)*, Wild Turkey *(see p264)*, and Woodford Reserve *(see p266)*.

A misty morning dawns at Buffalo Trace in Frankfort, Kentucky. The distillery's water towers are an iconic landmark in the heartland of Bourbon Country.

BULLEIT

Four Roses Distillery, 1224 Bonds Mill Road, Lawrenceburg, Kentucky
www.bulleitbourbon.com

Bulleit Bourbon originated in the 1830s with tavern-keeper and small-time distiller Augustus Bulleit, but production ceased after his death in 1860. However, the brand was revived, using the original recipe, in 1987 by his great-great-grandson Tom Bulleit. Seagram subsequently took over the label and from there it passed to Diageo. Bulleit Bourbon is now distilled for Diageo by Four Roses Distillery *(see p228)*, and has a high rye content of 29 percent.

BULLEIT BOURBON

BOURBON 40% ABV

Rich, oaky aromas lead into a mellow flavor, focused around vanilla and honey. The medium-length finish features vanilla and a hint of smoke.

CATDADDY

Piedmont Distillers, 203 East Murphy Street, Madison, North Carolina
www.catdaddymoonshine.com

Piedmont is the only licensed distillery in North Carolina, and its Catdaddy Moonshine celebrates the state's great heritage of illicit distilling. In 2005, ex-New Yorker Joe Michalek established Piedmont in Madison. It is the first legal distillery in the Carolinas since before Prohibition. "According to the lore of moonshine, only the best moonshine earns the right to be called the Catdaddy," says Joe Michalek. "True to the history of moonshine, every batch of Catdaddy is born in an authentic copper pot still".

CATDADDY CAROLINA MOONSHINE

CORN WHISKEY 40% ABV

Triple-distilled from corn in small batches, Catdaddy is sweet and spicy, with notes of vanilla and cinnamon.

CHARBAY

Domaine Charbay, 4001 Spring Mountain Road, St. Helena, California
www.charbay.com

The father-and-son partnership of Miles and Marko Karakasevic are 12th and 13th generation wine-makers and distillers. Charbay Double Barrel Hop-Flavored Whiskey is double-distilled in a 1,000-US-gallon (3,750-liter) copper alambic Charentais pot still. It is made using two-row European malted barley, with the addition of hops to the mash for greater aromatic effect. The spirit is put into new American white-oak barrels for maturation.

CHARBAY DOUBLE BARREL

DOUBLE BARREL WHISKEY 64% ABV

The nose also features honey, vanilla, oranges, oak, and spice. This big-bodied whiskey offers citrus, spice, and honey on the palate, moving into a long, hoppy, vanilla, and dried-fruit finish.

EAGLE RARE

Buffalo Trace Distillery, 1001 Wilkinson Boulevard, Frankfort, Kentucky
www.buffalotrace.com

The Eagle Rare brand was introduced in 1975 by Canadian distilling giant Joseph E. Seagram & Sons Inc. In 1989 it was acquired by the Sazerac company of New Orleans. In its present incarnation, Eagle Rare is part of Sazerac's Buffalo Trace Antique Collection, which is updated annually.

EAGLE RARE 2008 EDITION

BOURBON 45% ABV

The latest variant of Eagle Rare is from barrels that were distilled in the spring of 1991, and the nose offers caramel, maple syrup, almonds, and vanilla, while the palate boasts more vanilla, worn leather, summer fruits, dark chocolate, and a hint of mint. There is a delicious, spicy, crème brûlée finish.

Tennessee Whiskey

Whiskey-making in Tennessee dates back at least as far as the 18th century. During the late-19th century there were said to be some 700 stills in operation in the state, but Tennessee went "dry" in 1910 and distilling remained illegal until 1938.

Tennessee whiskeys are essentially bourbon-style spirits that undergo filtration through a thick layer of sugar-maple charcoal before the spirit is casked. The same legal criteria that apply to bourbon, in terms of strength and maturation period *(see p223)*, also apply to Tennessee whiskey, but formal adoption of the classification of Tennessee whiskey as a distinct style can be dated to 1941, when the charcoal filtration process was recognized in a United States tax authority letter to Jack Daniel Distillers. This defining aspect is known as the Lincoln County Process in reference to Lincoln County, Tennessee, where Jack Daniel's was founded.

Jack Daniel's *(see p238)* is undoubtedly the best-known Tennessee whiskey. The distillers like to emphasize that their product has the distinctive classification of Tennessee whiskey—it is not a bourbon, although it has some of the characteristics of bourbon. The difference, according to Jack Daniel's, is that their whiskey is trickled very slowly through 10 feet (3 meters) of hard maple charcoal, right after distillation. The company claims that this extra step in the whiskey-making process provides the special character known only to Tennessee whiskey. The charcoal mellowing process is said to remove some of the congeners and harsh fusel oils that are present in any grain alcohol.

The use of charcoal leaching was actually pioneered in 1825 by Alfred Eaton of Tullahoma, close to where the George Dickel Distillery operates today. Along with Jack Daniel, George Dickel *(see p232)* is the only surviving, licensed, full-scale distillery left in Tennessee.

EARLY TIMES

Brown-Forman Distillery, 850 Dixie Highway, Louisville, Kentucky
www.brown-forman.com

Early Times takes its name from a settlement near Bardstown where it was created in 1860. It cannot be classified as a bourbon because some spirit is put into used barrels, and bourbon legislation dictates that all spirit of that name must be matured in new barrels.

This version of Early Times was introduced in 1981 to compete with the increasingly popular, lighter-bodied Canadian whiskies. The Early Times mashbill is made up of 79 percent corn, 11 percent rye, and 10 percent malted barley.

EARLY TIMES

KENTUCKY WHISKEY 40% ABV
Quite light on the nose, with nuts and spices. The palate offers more of the same, together with honey and butterscotch notes, leading into a medium-length finish.

EDGEFIELD

2126 Southwest Halsey Street, Troutdale, Oregon
www.mcmenamins.com

Operated by the McMenamin's hotel and pub group, Edgefield Distillery is located in a former dry store for root vegetables on the beautiful Edgefield Manor Estate at Troutdale. The distillery has been in production since February 1998 and features a 12-ft (4-m) tall copper and stainless-steel still. According to Mcmenamin's, it resembles a hybrid of a 19th-century diving suit and oversized coffee urn, a design made famous by Holstein of Germany, the world's oldest surviving still manufacturer.

EDGEFIELD HOGSHEAD

OREGON WHISKEY 46% ABV
Hogshead whiskey has banana and malt on the sweet, floral nose, with vanilla and caramel notes on the palate, plus barley, honey, and oak in the medium-length finish.

ELIJAH CRAIG

Heaven Hill Distillery, 1701 West Breckinridge Street, Louisville, Kentucky
www.heaven-hill.com

The Reverend Elijah Craig (1743–1808) was a Baptist minister who is widely viewed as the "father of bourbon," having reputedly invented the concept of using charred barrels to store and mature the spirit he made. There seems to be no hard evidence that he was the first person to make bourbon, but the association between a "man of God" and whiskey was seen as a useful tool in the struggle against the temperance movement.

ELIJAH CRAIG 12-YEAR-OLD

BOURBON 47% ABV
A classic bourbon, with aromas of caramel, vanilla, spice, and honey, plus a bit of mint. Full-bodied, rounded on the mellow palate, with caramel, malt, corn, rye, and a little smoke. Sweet oak, licorice, and vanilla dominate the finish.

ELMER T. LEE

Buffalo Trace Distillery, 1001 Wilkinson Boulevard, Frankfort, Kentucky
www.buffalotrace.com

Elmer T. Lee is a former Master Distiller at Buffalo Trace (*see p222*), having joined what was then the George T. Stagg Distillery in the 1940s. During his time there, the name changed first to the Albert B. Blanton Distillery (1953), then to the Ancient Age Distillery (1962) and finally to the Buffalo Trace Distillery in 2001. Lee is credited with creating the first modern single barrel bourbon in 1984.

ELMER T. LEE SINGLE BARREL

BOURBON 45% ABV
Aged from six to eight years, this expression offers citrus, vanilla, and corn merging on the fragrant nose, with a full and sweet palate, where honey, lingering caramel, and cocoa notes are also evident.

EVAN WILLIAMS

Heaven Hill Distillery, 1701 West
Breckinridge Street, Louisville,
Kentucky
www.heaven-hill.com

The second biggest-selling bourbon after Jim Beam, Evan Williams takes its name from the person considered by many experts to be Kentucky's first distiller.

Evan Williams was born in Wales but emigrated to and settled in Virginia, moving to what would become Kentucky (but was then Fincastle County of Virginia) in around 1780. Subsequently, he set up a small distillery on the Ohio River at the foot of what is now Fifth Street in Louisville.

According to an article in the *Louisville Courier-Journal* for April 29, 1889, Williams was a member of the early Board of Trustees of Louisville, and tradition says he never attended a meeting of the board without bringing a bottle of his whiskey,

and that what he brought was always drunk by the members before the meeting adjourned. He was apparently censured every time for doing so, but still he never left with a full jug.

EVAN WILLIAMS BLACK LABEL
BOURBON 43% ABV

The nose is quite light, yet aromatic, with vanilla and mint notes. The palate is initially sweet, with caramel, malt, and developing leather and spice notes.

EVAN WILLIAMS SINGLE BARREL 1998 VINTAGE
BOURBON 43.3% ABV

This is the world's only vintage-dated single barrel bourbon, selected by Master Distillers Parker and Craig Beam. The latest release, distilled in 1998, offers an aromatic nose of cereal, dried fruit, caramel, and vanilla. The palate comprises maple, molasses, cinnamon, nutmeg, and berry notes. There is a whiff of smoke, plus almonds and honey in the spicy finish.

FOUR ROSES

1224 Bond Mills Road,
Lawrenceburg, Kentucky
www.fourroses.us

Built to a striking Spanish Mission-style design in 1910, Four Roses Distillery near Lawrenceburg takes its name from the brand first trademarked by Georgia-born Paul Jones, Jr., in 1888. Legend has it that the southern belle with whom he was in love wore a corsage of four red roses to signify her acceptance of his marriage proposal, hence the name he gave to his bourbon.

In 2002, after a period of almost 60 years under the ownership of the Seagram organization, when it had become a bestseller in the booming European and Asian market, the Four Roses trademark brand, production, bottling, and warehousing facilities were bought by Tokyo-based Kirin Brewery Company. In addition to its own Four Roses whiskies, the distillery now produces a number of other

well-known brands, including Bulleit Bourbon *(see p225)* and I. W. Harper President's Reserve Bourbon *(see p233)*.

FOUR ROSES SINGLE BARREL
BOURBON (VARIABLE ABV)

Offers a rich, complex nose, comprising malt, fruits, spices, and fudge. Long and mellow in the mouth, with vanilla, oak, and a hint of menthol. The finish is long, spicy, and decidedly mellow.

FOUR ROSES SMALL BATCH
BOURBON 45% ABV

Mild and refined on the nose, with nutmeg and restrained honey. Bold and rich on the well-balanced palate, with spices, fruit, and honey flavors. The finish is long and insinuating, with developing notes of vanilla.

Corn Whiskey

Corn whiskey is distilled from a fermented mash of not less than 80 percent corn at less than 80 percent ABV. It is the one American whiskey that does not have to be aged in new, charred-oak barrels, and no minimum maturation period is specified. It is often sold new and clear and, when maturation does take place, it tends to be for a period of months rather than years.

Corn whiskey was a favorite illicitly distilled, "moonshine" product. The story is told of a well-known early 20th-century North Carolina moonshiner by the name of Quill Rose who, when asked by a judge whether aging would not be beneficial to the liquor, is supposed to have replied, "Your honor has been misinformed. I have kept some for a week one time and I couldn't tell it was a bit better than when it was new and fresh". The growth in production of corn whiskey dates back to the years following the imposition of the first tax on spirits in North America in 1791, and the subsequent Whiskey Rebellion of 1794 by distillers and their supporters, who refused to pay the tax, assaulted excise officers, and marched on Pittsburgh in protest. The rebellion came to an end after 13,000 troops were assembled and marched down the Monongahela River under the command of President George Washington.

After the rebellion had been suppressed, many disgruntled distillers of mainly rye whiskey subsequently moved south and west from Maryland, Pennsylvania, and Virginia into Indiana, Illinois, Kentucky, and Tennessee. As these were great corn-producing states, it was inevitable that this migration led to a growth in whiskeys made from corn rather than rye.

Today, the best-known commercial brands of corn whiskey include Georgia Moon (p233) and Mellow Corn from Heaven Hill (p248), while a number of micro-distillers also produce corn whiskeys.

Whiskey Tour: Kentucky

The state of Kentucky is the bourbon-producing heartland of the USA and home to many of the best-known names in American whiskey. Most of the state's distilleries offer visitor facilities, allowing guests to study the production and maturation of this historic spirit. A tour embracing these distilleries and associated attractions not only provides an opportunity to make a real connection with bourbon and its fascinating heritage, but also offers a great way to experience the beauty of Kentucky and its hospitality.

USA

TOUR STATISTICS

DAYS: 5	LENGTH: 85 miles (137 km)	DISTILLERIES: 8
TRAVEL: Car	REGION: Northern Kentucky, USA	

DAY 1: BUFFALO TRACE, WOODFORD RESERVE

BARRELS AT WOODFORD RESERVE

1 Frankfort, the state capital, has a range of hotels and restaurants, and is the home of **Buffalo Trace**. The distillery has a large visitors' center and offers tours throughout the year. (*www.buffalotrace.com*)

2 **Woodford Reserve** lies near the attractive town of Versailles, in Kentucky's famous "bluegrass" horse-breeding country. Its copper pot stills are the highlight of the distillery tour. (*www.woodfordreserve.com*)

DAY 2: WILD TURKEY, FOUR ROSES

3 Spectacularly situated on a hill above the Kentucky River, **Wild Turkey**'s Boulevard Distillery allows visitors into its production areas at most times of the year. (*www.wildturkeybourbon.com*)

4 **Four Roses** Distillery is a striking structure, built in the style of a Spanish Mission. Tours are available from fall to spring (the distillery is closed throughout the summer). You can also pre-arrange to visit Four Roses' warehouse at Cox's Creek. (*www.fourroses.us*)

LOUISVILLE

ROUTE 71

ROUTE 64

150

KENTUCKY

FINISH

9 **JIM BEAM**

OSCAR GETZ

ROUTE 65

7

BARTON **6**

BARDSTOWN

5

HEAVEN HILL

Loretto Rd

8

MAKER'S MARK

WILD TURKEY EMBLEM

DAY 3: HEAVEN HILL, BARTON, OSCAR GETZ

5 Bardstown is renowned as the "World Capital of Bourbon," and makes an excellent base for visiting the distilleries in the area. Book a room at the Old Talbott Tavern *(www.talbotts. com)*, which is set in a building dating back to the late 1700s and offers a well-stocked bourbon bar. Then head out to the **Heaven Hill** Bourbon Heritage Center, which includes a tour of a bourbon-aging rackhouse and the chance to taste two Heaven Hill whiskeys. *(www.heaven-hill.com)*

HEAVEN HILL, BARDSTOWN

6 **Barton** Brands' Tom Moore Distillery in downtown Bardstown has traditionally maintained a low profile compared to its neighbors. But times are changing, as comprehensive tours of the production areas are now available, together with a state-of-the-art Barton Brands Visitor Center. *(www.bartonbrands.com)*

7 A few blocks from Tom Moore, the **Oscar Getz** Whiskey Museum houses a collection of whiskey artifacts, including rare antique bottles, a moonshine still, advertising art, novelty whiskey containers, and Abraham Lincoln's original liquor license. *(www.whiskeymuseum.com)*

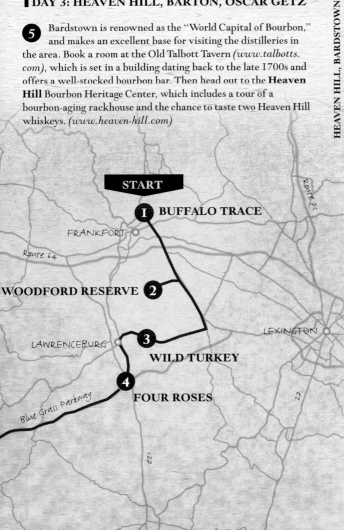

START

1 BUFFALO TRACE

FRANKFORT

Route 64

WOODFORD RESERVE **2**

LAWRENCEBURG

3

WILD TURKEY

4

FOUR ROSES

Blue Grass Parkway

Route 25

LEXINGTON

27

127

DAY 4: MAKER'S MARK

8 The historic **Maker's Mark** Distillery stands on the banks of Hardin's Creek, near Loretto, in Marion County. The distillery grounds are notable as they act as an arboretum, being home to some 275 species of trees and shrubs. Guided tours of the distillery are available daily. *(www.makersmark.com)*

MAKER'S MARK

JIM BEAM'S CLERMONT DISTILLERY

DAY 5: JIM BEAM

9 **Jim Beam**'s Clermont Distillery offers tours of the site grounds, a working rackhouse, and the Hartmann Cooperage Museum. The American Outpost is an on-site visitors' center, with a film about the bourbon-making process at Jim Beam and displays of whiskey memorabilia that take in more than two centuries of bourbon history. *(www.jimbeam.com)*

GEORGE DICKEL NO. 12

GEORGE DICKEL BARREL SELECT

GEORGE DICKEL NO. 8

GEORGE DICKEL

1950 Cascade Hollow Road,
Normandy, Tennessee
www.dickel.com

Along with Jack Daniel's, George
Dickel is the last licensed, full-scale
distillery in the state of Tennessee,
though there were around 700
operating there a century ago.

The distillery uses the spelling
"whisky" because founder George
A. Dickel insisted that the spirit he
made was as smooth as the finest
Scotch. Dickel, who was German
by birth, was a Nashville
merchant before he founded
Cascade Hollow distillery in the
1870s. He used pure water from
the nearby Cascade Springs source.

The year 1910 saw the arrival of
Prohibition in Tennessee, and the
Dickel operation was moved to
Kentucky and subsequently
acquired by Schenley Distilling Co.
In 1958, Schenley decided that
George Dickel should return to its
roots, and a new distillery was

built close to the original Cascade
Hollow location, and using recipes
from Dickel's own notes. Dickel is
now owned by the Diageo group.

GEORGE DICKEL NO. 12

TENNESSEE WHISKEY 45% ABV

The nose is aromatic, with fruit, leather,
butterscotch, and a whiff of charcoal
and vanilla. The palate is rich, with rye,
chocolate, fruit, and vanilla. The finish
offers vanilla toffee and drying oak.

GEORGE DICKEL BARREL
SELECT

TENNESSEE WHISKEY 43% ABV

Aromas of rich corn, honey, nuts, and
caramel lead into a full body with soft
vanilla, spices, and roast nuts. The long,
creamy finish boasts almond and spices.

GEORGE DICKEL NO. 8

TENNESSEE WHISKEY 40% ABV

Sweet on the nose, with chocolate,
cocoa, and vanilla. The palate is quite
sweet and well rounded, with fresh
fruit and vanilla notes. The short finish
features spices and charcoal.

GEORGE T. STAGG

Buffalo Trace Distillery, 1001 Wilkinson Boulevard, Frankfort, Kentucky
www.buffalotrace.com

Part of the Buffalo Trace Antique Collection, George T. Stagg takes its name from the one-time owner of what is now the Buffalo Trace Distillery. In the early 1880s the distillery was owned by Edmund Haynes Taylor, Jr. During tough ecnomic times he obtained a loan from his friend Stagg—who later foreclosed on Taylor, taking over his company in the process.

GEORGE T. STAGG 2008 EDITION

BOURBON 72.4% ABV

Distilled in the spring of 1993, this high-strength whiskey boasts a rich nose of butterscotch, marzipan, sweet oak, and cherries. The palate features corn, coffee beans, leather, spice, and oak, with a long toffee and spice finish.

GEORGIA MOON

Heaven Hill Distillery, 1701 West Breckinridge Street, Louisville, Kentucky
www.heaven-hill.com

Corn whiskey is distilled from a fermented mash of not less than 80 percent corn, and no minimum maturation period is specified. One of the best-known examples is Heaven Hill's Georgia Moon. With a label that promises that the contents be fewer than 30 days old, and available bottled in a mason jar *(pictured on p229)*, Georgia Moon harks back to the old days of moonshining.

GEORGIA MOON

CORN WHISKEY 40% ABV

The nose commences with an initial tang of sour liquor, followed by the smell of sweet corn. The palate suggests cabbage water and plums, along with developing sweeter, candy-corn notes. The finish is short. Drinkers should not expect anything sophisticated.

HANCOCK'S RESERVE

Buffalo Trace Distillery, 1001 Wilkinson Boulevard, Frankfort, Kentucky
www.buffalotrace.com

This whiskey, which is usually created from barrels of spirit aged for around 10 years, takes its name from Hancock Taylor, great-uncle of US president Zachary Taylor, and an early surveyor of Kentucky. He was shot and killed by Native Americans in 1774, and it is said that his deathbed will was one of the first legal documents executed in the region.

HANCOCK'S RESERVE PRESIDENT'S SINGLE BARREL

BOURBON 44.45% ABV

Oily on the nose, with licorice, caramel, and spicy rye. Sweet in the mouth, with malt, fudge, and vanilla notes. Drying in the finish, with oak notes, but the whiskey's residual sweetness remains to the end.

I.W. HARPER

Four Roses Distillery, 1224 Bond Mills Road, Lawrenceburg, Kentucky
www.fourroses.us

The historic and once bestselling I.W. Harper brand was established by Jewish businessman Isaac Wolfe Bernheim (1848–1945), a major figure in the bourbon business at the turn of the 20th century. It was made at the Bernheim Distillery *(see p221)* in Louisville. It is now produced for current owners Diageo by Four Roses Distillery and is one of the leading bourbons in the Japanese market.

I.W. HARPER

BOURBON 43% ABV

A big-bodied bourbon in which pepper combines with mint, oranges, caramel, and quite youthful charring on the nose, while caramel, apples, and oak feature on the elegant palate. The finish is dry and smoky.

Woodford Reserve *(see p266)* may have the smallest distillery in Kentucky, but its triple-distilled bourbons are held in high regard. The distillery is operated by the Brown-Forman Corporation.

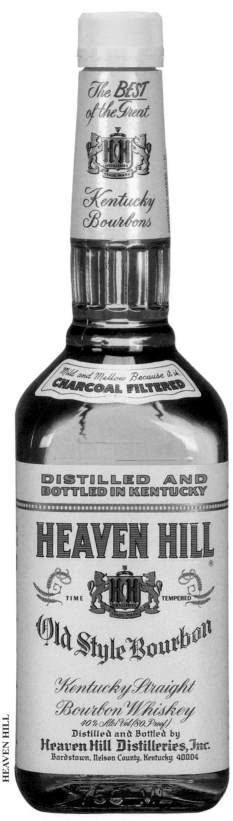

HEAVEN HILL

BERNHEIM ORIGINAL *(see p221)*

PARKER'S HERITAGE *(see p251)*

HEAVEN HILL

1701 West Breckinridge Street,
Louisville, Kentucky
www.heaven-hill.com

Heaven Hill is the USA's largest independent producer of distilled spirits to remain in family ownership, and the last family-owned distillery in Kentucky. A Heaven Hill distillery had been built in 1890, but the present one was established in 1935, soon after the repeal of Prohibition, by five Shapira brothers, who built their distillery just south of Bardstown, and whose descendants control the firm to this day.

On 7 November 1996 the distillery and warehouses were almost completely destroyed by fire, and over 350,000 litres (90,000 US gallons) of maturing spirit was lost. As a result, the company purchased Diageo's technologically advanced Bernheim Distillery in Louisville, and all production was moved to that site.

For most of its existence Heaven Hill has concentrated on its flagship bourbon labels, Evan Williams *(see p228)* and Elijah Craig *(p227)*. Its speciality is older, higher proof bourbons, traditional in character, full-bodied, and complex. As part of its notably diverse portfolio, Heaven Hill also produces Bernheim Original *(see p221)*, Pikesville *(p254)*, Parker's *(p251)*, and Rittenhouse Rye *(p254)*. Additionally, it is the only remaining national producer of corn whiskeys such as Mellow Corn *(see p248)* and Georgia Moon *(p233)*. Heaven Hill is also a major supplier of "own-label" whiskey to other customers.

HEAVEN HILL

BOURBON 40% ABV

An excellent and competitively priced "entry-level" bourbon, with a nose of oranges and corn bread, a sweet, oily mouth-feel, and vanilla and corn featuring on the well-balanced palate.

HENRY MCKENNA

Heaven Hill Distillery, 1701 West Breckinridge Street, Louisville, Kentucky
www.heaven-hill.com

Irish-born Henry McKenna emigrated to Fairfield, Kentucky, where, in 1855, he began to distill a whiskey that soon became very popular. McKenna died in 1893, and, later, Prohibition saw the closure of his distillery. However, McKenna's family reopened the plant after Prohibition was repealed in 1933, and later sold it to Seagram's. The brand was later discontinued, and the name was purchased by Heaven Hill.

HENRY MCKENNA SINGLE BARREL 10-YEAR-OLD

BOURBON 50% ABV
Nose boasts citrus, charcoal, vanilla, and caramel. Contrasts continue to the palate, where spices and charred oak vie pleasingly with mint and honey.

HIRSCH RESERVE

Distribution: Preiss Imports
www.hirschbourbon.com

Hirsch Reserve is a drop of US whiskey history. The spirit itself was distilled in 1974 at Michter's Distillery, the last surviving one in Pennsylvania. Michter's closed in 1988, but one Adolf H. Hirsch had acquired a considerable stock of the spirit some years previously and, after it had been matured for 16 years, it was put into stainless steel tanks to prevent further aging. This whiskey is now available from Preiss Imports but, once gone, is gone forever.

HIRSCH RESERVE

BOURBON 45.8% ABV
Caramel, honey, and rye dominate the complex nose, with a whiff of smoke also coming through. Oily corn, honey, and oak on the rich palate, with rye and more oak in the drying finish.

HUDSON

Tuthilltown Distillery, 14 Gristmill Lane, Gardiner, New York
www.tuthilltown.com

In 1825, New York State had more than 1,000 working distilleries and produced a major share of the nation's whiskey. These days, Tuthilltown is New York's only remaining distillery. Based in a converted granary, the distillery adjoins a gristmill, which dates back to 1788 and is listed on the National Register of Historic Places.

Tuthilltown Distillery was founded in 2001 by Brian Lee and Ralph Erenzo, and is now equipped with a 106-US-gallon (400-liter) pot still that was installed in 2005. Tuthill Spirits produces a quartet of "Hudson" bottlings, including a rich and full-flavored four-grain whiskey and a rich, caramel single malt, which is intended to be an American "re-interpretation"

of traditional Scottish whiskies. The distillery also produces Old Gristmill Authentic American Corn Whiskey.

HUDSON MANHATTAN RYE

RYE WHISKEY 46% ABV
The first whiskey to be distilled in New York State for more than 80 years. Floral notes and a smooth finish on the palate, with a recognizable rye edge.

HUDSON NEW YORK CORN

BOURBON 46% ABV
Made with 100 percent New York State corn, this is the first bourbon ever to be made in New York, and the first pot-distilled whiskey to be produced legally in New York since Prohibition. It is a mildly sweet, smooth spirit with subtle hints of vanilla and caramel.

The secrets of... Jack Daniel's

The story of Jack Daniel's, America's bestselling whiskey, begins with the birth of Jasper "Jack" Newton Daniel in Lincoln County, Tennessee, in 1846.

Legend has it that Jack did not get along with his stepmother and, at the age of just six, left home to live first with an elderly neighbor and his family, and then with local farmer and Lutheran lay preacher Dan Call, of Louse Creek, who also ran a whiskey still. It was one of Call's slaves, Nearest Green, who taught Jack the art of distilling.

Pressure from his congregation eventually forced Call to choose religion over whiskey-making, so young Jack took over the business and, by 1860, the precocious teenager owned the still.

Jack Daniel's Tennessee whiskey has come a long way from those modest beginnings, and enjoys an iconic status as one of the world's highest-profile drink brands. It is distilled in Lynchburg, to which, every year, hundreds of thousands of visitors flock in pilgrimage. However, while they can purchase any number of souvenirs bearing the Jack Daniel's name, they cannot buy the whiskey itself. Lynchburg is situated in Moore County, which is officially "dry."

Despite an image in which the figure of its founder plays a major part, since 1956 Jack Daniel's has belonged to Brown-Forman *(see p222)*, which also owns Kentucky distilleries producing Old Forester *(p250)*, Early Times *(p227)*, and Woodford Reserve *(p266)*.

▲ THE REAL JACK DANIEL

"Mr. Jack" is a flamboyant figure in the history of American whiskey. He was reputedly quite a ladies' man, although he never married, and the brand name Old No. 7 is sometimes said to have referred to the number of his girlfriends.

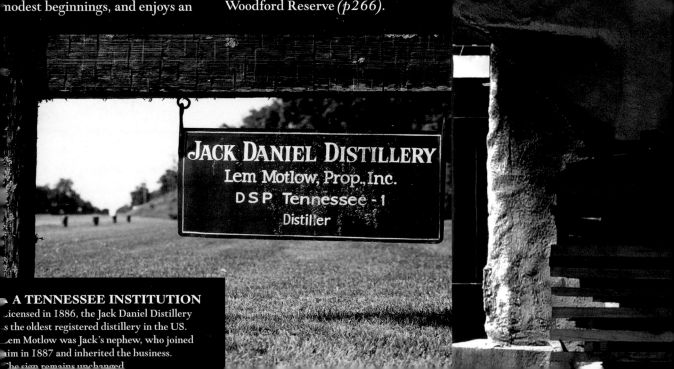

JACK DANIEL DISTILLERY
Lem Motlow, Prop., Inc.
DSP Tennessee - 1
Distiller

▲ A TENNESSEE INSTITUTION

Licensed in 1886, the Jack Daniel Distillery is the oldest registered distillery in the US. Lem Motlow was Jack's nephew, who joined him in 1887 and inherited the business. The sign remains unchanged.

▼ TESTING THE SPIRIT

There is no set schedule to determine when the whiskey is ready, as maturation can vary from barrel to barrel, and by the relative positions of barrels in the warehouses. A panel of experts regularly noses the maturing spirit to decide when it's ready for bottling.

▲ NEW HAND-MADE CASKS

Jack Daniel is the only distillery to craft its own barrels by hand using new white oak. The interiors are then charred to caramelize the wood's natural sugars. As a result, the whiskey matured in these casks is deeply mellow, amber-hued, and aromatic.

◄ THE CHARCOAL ELEMENT

Jack Daniel creates its own charcoal by burning sugar maple wood in the rickyard, to be used in Tennessee whiskey's signature Lincoln County Process. This is a method of mellowing, in which the spirit is filtered slowly through 10 ft (3 m) of charcoal before being matured, resulting in a very smooth whiskey.

▲ MR. JACK'S GRAVE

Jack Daniel died in 1911, having been unfortunate enough to contract blood poisoning after kicking his safe door in frustration when he forgot the combination. He is buried in Lynchburg's cemetery, close to his beloved distillery. The chairs are said to have been placed there for grieving Lynchburg ladies.

JACK DANIEL'S OLD NO. 7

JACK DANIEL'S SINGLE BARREL

GENTLEMAN JACK

JACK DANIEL'S

280 Lynchburg Road,
Lynchburg, Tennessee
www.jackdaniels.com

Jack Daniel's has become an iconic brand worldwide, and is America's bestselling whiskey. Its founder, Jasper Newton "Jack" Daniel reputedly started to make whiskey as a child, and by 1860 was running his own distilling business at the tender age of 14.

Today, the Jack Daniel Distillery at Lynchburg, Tennessee, is owned by the Brown-Forman Corporation *(see p222)* and is a major visitor attraction. Along with its fellow Tennessee distiller George Dickel *(p232)*, Jack Daniel's uses a version of the Lincoln County Process of charcoal mellowing prior to the spirit being put into barrels.

JACK DANIEL'S OLD NO. 7
TENNESSEE WHISKEY 40% ABV
Presents a powerful nose of vanilla, smoke, and licorice. On the palate it

offers oily cough-mixture and molasses, with a final kick of maple syrup and burnt wood lingering in the surprisingly long finish. Not particularly complex, but decidedly muscular and certainly distinctive.

JACK DANIEL'S SINGLE BARREL
TENNESSEE WHISKEY 47% ABV
Introduced in 1997, Single Barrel is charming and smooth on the nose, with notes of peach, vanilla, nuts, and oak. The comparatively dry palate offers depth, richness, and elegance, with oily corn, licorice, malt, and oak. Malt and oak are also highlighted in the lengthy finish, along with a touch of rye spice.

GENTLEMAN JACK
TENNESSEE WHISKEY 40% ABV
After aging for about four years, this is charcoal-mellowed once before barrelling. The result is a nose that is more mellow, muted, and fruity than that of Old No. 7. The palate also yields more fruit, plus notes of caramel, licorice, vanilla, and a whiff of smoke.

Jim Beam *(see overleaf)* is a global company with industrial-scale distilleries, but its American Outpost in Clermont, Kentucky, evokes the older traditions of whiskey.

JIM BEAM BLACK LABEL

JIM BEAM

149 Happy Hollow Road, Clermont, Kentucky
www.jimbeam.com

Jim Beam is the bestselling bourbon brand in the world. Its origins date back to the 18th century, when German-born farmer and miller Jacob Boehm traveled west into Bourbon County, Kentucky, from Virginia, carrying with him his copper pot still. He is reputed to have sold his first barrel of whiskey for cash in 1795, and subsequently moved his distilling operation into Washington County when he inherited land there from his father-in-law.

Jacob had two sons, John and David, and during David Beam's time at the helm, the distillery adopted the name Old Tub. In 1854, his son, also David, moved the venture to Nelson County, where the Clear Springs Distillery was established close to a railroad.

Jim (James Beauregard) Beam himself was Jacob Boehm's great-grandson. He joined the family business at the age of 16, in 1880, and trade prospered in the years before Prohibition forced the closure of Clear Springs.

Jim Beam founded the present Clermont Distillery close to Clear Springs soon after the repeal of Prohibition in 1933, despite being 70 years old at the time. He died in 1947, five years after "Jim Beam" first appeared on the bottle label, and two years after the firm had been sold to Harry Blum of Chicago, previously a partner in the company for several years.

The Beam family connection, however, carries on to this day through Fred Noe, great-grandson of Jim and a seventh-generation Beam family member. Fred's father was Booker Noe, acknowledged as one of the true greats of bourbon distilling, and the man principally responsible for developing "small

batch bourbon." Clermont, near the bourbon capital of Bardstown, remains the principal Jim Beam distillery, but its output is boosted by that of the nearby Boston distillery, which dates from 1953.

In addition to Jim Beam brands, a range of specialist whiskeys is also produced, including Baker's Kentucky *(see p220)*, Booker's Kentucky *(p221)*, Basil Hayden's *(p221)*, Knob Creek *(p245)*, Old Crow *(p249)*, Old Grand-Dad *(p250)*, and Old Taylor *(p251)*. Additionally, Fortune Brands Inc. operates the Maker's Mark Distillery *(p246)* at Loretto.

JIM BEAM BLACK LABEL 8-YEAR-OLD

TENNESSEE WHISKEY 43% ABV
This expression possesses greater depth than White Label, with more complex fruit and vanilla notes, plus licorice and sweet rye.

JIM BEAM WHITE LABEL 4-YEAR-OLD

TENNESSEE WHISKEY 40% ABV
Vanilla and delicate floral notes on the nose. Initially sweet, with restrained vanilla, then drier, oaky notes develop, fading into furniture polish and soft malt in the finish. Once described, with some justification, as "a mellow baritone of a spirit".

JIM BEAM RYE

RYE WHISKEY 40% ABV
Light, perfumed, and aromatic on the nose, with lemon and mint, Jim Beam Rye is oily in the mouth, with soft fruits, honey, and rye on the palate, drying and spicy in the finish.

JIM BEAM CHOICE 5-YEAR-OLD

TENNESSEE WHISKEY 40% ABV
Beam's Choice is charcoal-filtered in the style of Tennessee whiskeys after maturation, and is soft and silky in character, with more caramel notes than other Jim Beam expressions.

JEFFERSON'S

McLain & Kyne Ltd. (Castle Brands), Louisville, Kentucky
www.mclainandkyne.com

The Louisville company of McLain & Kyne Ltd. was formed by Trey Zoeller to carry on the distilling traditions of his ancestors. McLain & Kyne specializes in premium, very small-batch bourbons, most notably Jefferson's and Sam Houston *(see p256).*

JEFFERSON'S SMALL BATCH 8-YEAR-OLD
BOURBON (VARIABLE ABV)
This bourbon has been aged in the heart of metal-clad warehouses to accentuate the extreme temperatures of Kentucky, forcing the bourbon to expand deep into the barrel and extract desirable flavors from the wood. The nose is fresh, with vanilla and ripe peach notes, while the smooth, sweet palate boasts more vanilla, caramel, and berries. The finish is very delicate, with toasted vanilla and cream.

JOHNNY DRUM

Kentucky Bourbon Distillers, 1869 Loretto Road, Bardstown, Kentucky
www.kentuckybourbonwhiskey.com

Johnny Drum is said to have been a Confederate drummer boy during the Civil War, and later a pioneer farmer and distiller in Kentucky. Johnny Drum bourbon was formerly produced in the Willet Distillery near Bardstown, but this closed in the early 1980s when the last of the Willet family members retired. The plant was acquired by Kentucky Bourbon Distillers Ltd., for whom a range of whiskeys is distilled under contract.

JOHNNY DRUM
BOURBON (VARIABLE ABV)
Smooth and elegant on the nose, with vanilla, gentle spices, and smoke. This is a full-bodied bourbon, well-balanced and smooth in the mouth, with vanilla and a hint of smoke. The finish is lingering and sophisticated.

KENTUCKY GENTLEMAN

Barton Distillery, 1 Barton Road, Bardstown, Kentucky
www.bartonbrands.com

Kentucky Gentleman is offered both as a blended whiskey and as a straight bourbon. According to its producers, the blended version is created from a blend of Kentucky straight bourbon whiskey and spirits from the finest grains.

The popular straight expression enjoys a notably loyal following in the southern states, particularly Florida, Alabama, and Virginia.

KENTUCKY GENTLEMAN
BOURBON 40% ABV
Made with a higher percentage of rye than most Barton whiskeys, this offers caramel and sweet oak aromas, and is oily, full-bodied, spicy, and fruity in the mouth. Rye, fruits, vanilla, and cocoa figure in the lingering, flavorful, and comparatively assertive finish.

KENTUCKY TAVERN

Barton Distillery, 1 Barton Road, Bardstown, Kentucky
www.bartonbrands.com

The Kentucky Tavern brand has been established for over a century, and was the leading whiskey produced by the Louisville-based Glenmore Distilleries Company. It was named after a bar and restaurant situated on the east side of Louisville. In 1992, Glenmore was acquired by United Distillers, which has since been amalgamated with Diageo, and the Kentucky Tavern brand was subsequently sold to Barton Brands.

KENTUCKY TAVERN
BOURBON 40% ABV
Assertive and oaky on the nose, with apples and honey. Spices, oak, more apples, and a note of rye contribute to the palate, while the medium-length finish is peppery and oaky.

KESSLER

Jim Beam Distillery, 149 Happy Hollow Road, Clermont, Kentucky www.jimbeam.com

One of the best-known and most highly regarded blended American whiskeys, Kessler traces its origins back to 1888, when it was first blended by one Julius Kessler, who traveled from saloon to saloon across the West, selling his whiskey as he went.

KESSLER
BLEND 40% ABV
Kessler has carried the slogan "Smooth as Silk" for more than half a century, and it certainly lives up to its name. The nose is light and fruity, and the palate sweet, with just enough complexity of licorice and leather to highlight the fact that the bourbon in this blend was aged for a minimum of four years.

KNOB CREEK

Jim Beam Distillery, 149 Happy Hollow Road, Clermont, Kentucky www.jimbeam.com

Knob Creek is the Kentucky town where Abraham Lincoln's father, Thomas, owned a farm and worked at the local distillery. This bourbon is one of three introduced in 1992, when Jim Beam launched its Small Batch Bourbon Collection. It is made to the same high-rye formula as the Jim Beam-distilled Basil Hayden's *(see p221)* and Old Grand-Dad *(p250)* brands.

KNOB CREEK 9-YEAR-OLD
BOURBON 50% ABV
Knob Creek has a nutty nose of sweet, tangy fruit and rye, with malt, spice, and nuts on the fruity palate, drying in the finish with notes of vanilla.

LEOPOLD

4950 Nome Street, Denver, Colorado www.leopoldbros.com

Leopold Bros. is a family owned and operated small-batch distillery based in Denver, Colorado, the home state of brothers Scott and Todd Leopold. Scott takes care of the business side of the company, while Master Distiller Todd Leopold makes liqueurs, vodka, gin, rum, absinthe, and flavored whiskeys in the distillery's 40-gallon (180-liter) copper pot still. The distillery specializes in small-batch blends, so all blends are made using artisan processes and the bottles are subsequently hand-numbered.

Unusual blends include a whiskey made from the juice of Rocky Mountain peaches and another flavored whiskey made in a similar fashion from blackberries. These fruit whiskies are matured in used, charred bourbon barrels, so that the sweetness of the fruit is balanced by the smoothness of a bourbon finish.

GEORGIA PEACH
FLAVORED WHISKEY 30% ABV
Peach juice is blended with small-batch whiskey, and matured in bourbon barrels. The result is a peachy-sweet spirit with oak, vanilla, and raisins.

NEW YORK APPLE
FLAVORED WHISKEY 40% ABV
Blended with apples grown in New York State, this whiskey is racked into used bourbon barrels for additional aging. According to its producers, the barrels add the oak, raisin, and vanilla finish, while the mix of the sweet and tart apples balances perfectly with the charred oak finish.

The secrets of... Maker's Mark

The Maker's Mark Distillery stands on the banks of Hardin's Creek, near Loretto in Marion County, Kentucky. Established in 1805, its modern history dates from 1953.

That was the year Taylor William Samuels, Sr., bought the dilapidated distillery known as Happy Hollow. His great-great-great-grandfather had been a Kentucky whiskey-maker in the 1780s, and Taylor was in possession of the secret family recipe for bourbon. However, one of his first acts on taking over at Happy Hollow was symbolically to burn the recipe, declaring: "Nothing that we need! To craft a truly new and soft-spoken bourbon, we will have to start from scratch."

By this, Samuels meant a more mellow whiskey than was the norm at the time. He achieved this using corn and malted barley, coupled with red winter wheat, rather than the usual rye. He used the spelling "whisky" from the outset, in honor of his Scottish ancestry.

Long acknowledged as one of Kentucky's great bourbons, in 1981 Maker's Mark passed out of family ownership. Since 2005 it has been part of the Fortune Brands group, which includes Jim Beam *(see p242)*.

▲ MASHBILL

The grain recipe, or mashbill, for Maker's Mark comprises 70 percent corn, 16 percent red winter wheat, and 14 percent malted barley, producing a comparatively soft, gentle spirit—the "soft-spoken bourbon" that T. W. Samuels had envisioned from the beginning.

▼ COPPER POT STILLS

The "distiller's beer" is initially distilled in a five-story column still, after which it undergoes a secondary distillation in copper pot stills in order to remove any remaining impurities, leaving a clear 65% ABV spirit.

▲ DISTILLER'S BEER

Yeast is added to the cooked mash in the traditional fermentation tanks or "washbacks" made of rare cypress wood. In these, the action of the yeast on the mash produces what is known as "distiller's beer."

◀ CHARRING THE CASKS

Barrels undergo a "charring" stage, in which their interiors are seared with fire. By law, bourbon must be matured in new, charred white-oak barrels. The layer of char on the wood facilitates the maturation process.

▼ RICK HOUSES

At Maker's Mark, barrels of spirit are stored in three-story warehouses or "rick houses," and are periodically moved around within each warehouse to ensure consistency of maturation.

▲ MONITORING THE CASKS

The new make is put into oak barrels for maturation. A watchful eye is kept on the spirit while it's maturing to ensure that it is bottled at the peak of perfection. As part of this process, each barrel is sampled five times during the maturation period.

◀ DIPPING IN WAX

After being machine-filled, each bottle of Maker's Mark is labeled by hand and then its neck is dipped into hot wax for a few seconds to create the brand's characteristic red wax seal.

▶ CREATING THE SEAL

This was the brainchild of Marge Samuels, wife of T. W. "Bill" Samuels. She collected antique cognac bottles, many of which were sealed with wax. She also designed the "Maker's Mark" symbol itself.

MAKER'S MARK

3350 Burks Springs Road,
Loretto, Kentucky
www.makersmark.com

Maker's Mark Distillery is located
on the banks of Hardin's Creek,
near Loretto. Established in 1805,
it is the USA's oldest working
distillery remaining on its original
site. The Maker's Mark brand was
developed during the 1950s by Bill
Samuels, Jr., and is now owned by
Fortune Brands Inc.

MAKER'S MARK

BOURBON 45% ABV

A subtle, complex, and clean nose, with
vanilla and spice, a delicate floral note
of roses, plus lime and cocoa beans.
Medium in body, it offers a palate of
fresh fruit, spices, eucalyptus, and
ginger cake. The finish features more
spices, fresh oak with a hint of smoke,
and a final flash of peach cheesecake.

MCCARTHY'S

Clear Creek Distillery, 2389 NW
Wilson Street, Portland, Oregon
www.clearcreekdistillery.com

Steve McCarthy established Clear
Creek Distillery more than 20
years ago and has been distilling
whiskey for over a decade. He is
of the opinion that, since it is made
from peat-malted barley brought
in from Scotland, "our whiskey
would be a single malt Scotch if
Oregon were Scotland".

MCCARTHY'S OREGON

SINGLE MALT 40% ABV

McCarthy's is initially matured in
former sherry casks for two or three
years, then for six to twelve months in
barrels made from air-dried Oregon
oak. Kippery and spicy on the nose,
with a hint of sulfur, peat, and vanilla.
It is big-bodied and oily, smoky-sweet
on the meaty palate, and with dry oak,
malt, spice, and salt in the long finish.

MELLOW CORN

Heaven Hill Distillery, 1701 West
Breckinridge Street, Louisville,
Kentucky
www.heaven-hill.com

According to Heaven Hill, "The
forerunner and kissing cousin to
Bourbon, American straight corn
whiskey is defined by the US
Government as having a recipe
or mashbill with a minimum of
81 percent corn, the rest being
malted barley and rye".

Today, Heaven Hill is the sole
remaining national producer of
this classic whiskey style, bottling
Georgia Moon *(see p233)* in
addition to Mellow Corn.

MELLOW CORN

CORN WHISKEY 50% ABV

Wood varnish and vanilla, with floral
and herbal notes on the nose. The
palate is big, oily, and fruity, with
candy apples. More fruit, toffee, and
understated vanilla complete the finish.
Young and boisterous.

NOAH'S MILL

Kentucky Bourbon Distillers Ltd.,
Nelson County, Kentucky
www.kentuckybourbonwhiskey.com

Like Johnny Drum *(see p244)*,
Noah's Mill was once distilled in
the now silent Willet Distillery,
which operated in Bardstown
from 1935 until the early 1980s.
In 1984 the site was bought by
Thompson Willett's Norwegian-
born son-in-law Even Kulsveen,
who runs Kentucky Bourbon
Distillers Ltd. and plans to restore
the old distillery to production.
Noah's Mill is a hand-bottled,
small-batch bourbon, currently
produced under contract.

NOAH'S MILL 15-YEAR-OLD

BOURBON 57.15% ABV

Elegant and well-balanced on the nose,
with caramel, nuts, coffee, dark fruits,
and oak. Noah's Mill has a rich texture
and is notably dry on the palate, with
background notes of soft fruit and
spice. The finish is long and oaky.

THE NOTCH

Triple Eight Distillery, 5&7 Bartlett Farm Road, Nantucket, Massachusetts
www.ciscobrewers.com

Dean and Melissa Long started up their Nantucket Winery in 1981, and added the Cisco Brewery in 1995. Two years later they founded the region's only micro-distillery, Triple Eight. The first single malt whiskey was distilled in 2000 and is called The Notch Whiskey, because it is "not Scotch," though it is produced in the Scottish style. It is matured in former bourbon barrels before being finished in French oak Merlot barrels.

THE NOTCH

SINGLE MALT 44.4% ABV
Sweet aromas of almonds and fruit on the nose, backed by vanilla and toasted oak. Mellow honey and pear notes are present on the palate, which also contains a suggestion of Merlot. The finish is lengthy and herbal.

OLD CHARTER

Buffalo Trace Distillery, 1001 Wilkinson Boulevard, Frankfort, Kentucky
www.buffalotrace.com

The Old Charter brand dates back to 1874, and the name is a direct reference to the Charter Oak tree, where Connecticut's colonial charter was hidden from the English in 1687. The Buffalo Trace Distillery itself dates back to the early 1900s and is listed on the National Register of Historic Places.

OLD CHARTER 8-YEAR-OLD

BOURBON 40% ABV
Initially dry and peppery on the nose, with sweet and buttery aromas following through. Mouth-coating, with fruit, vanilla, old leather, and cloves on the palate. The finish is long and sophisticated.

OLD CROW

Jim Beam Distillery, 149 Happy Hollow Road, Clermont, Kentucky
www.jimbeam.com

Old Crow takes its name from the 19th-century Scottish-born chemist and Kentucky distiller James Christopher Crow. Along with Old Grand-Dad *(see p250)* and Old Taylor *(p251)*, this brand was acquired by Jim Beam *(p242)* from National Distillers in 1987, and the three distilleries associated with these bourbons were closed. All production now takes place at Jim Beam's distilleries in Boston and Clermont.

OLD CROW

BOURBON 40% ABV
Complex on the nose, with malt, rye, and sharp fruit notes combining with gentle spice. The palate follows through with spicy, malty, and citric elements, with citrus and spice notes to the fore.

OLD FITZGERALD

Heaven Hill Distillery, 1701 West Breckinridge Street, Louisville, Kentucky
www.heaven-hill.com

Old Fitzgerald was named by John E. Fitzgerald, who founded a distillery at Frankfort in 1870. The brand moved to its present home of Louisville when the Stitzel brothers, Frederick and Philip, merged their company with that of William LaRue Weller & Sons, and subsequently opened the new Stitzel-Weller distillery at Louisville in 1935.

VERY SPECIAL OLD FITZGERALD 12-YEAR-OLD

BOURBON 45% ABV
A complex and well-balanced bourbon, made with some wheat in the mashbill, rather than rye. The nose is rich, fruity, and leathery, while the palate exhibits sweet and fruity notes balanced by spices and oak. The finish is long and drying, with vanilla fading to oak.

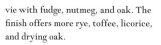

OLD FORESTER

Brown-Forman Distillery, 850 Dixie Highway, Louisville, Kentucky
www.brown-forman.com

The origins of the Old Forester brand date back to 1870, when George Garvin Brown established a distillery in Louisville, Kentucky *(see p222)*. The whiskey initially used the spelling "Forrester," and there are several theories as to the choice of name. Some say it was selected to honor Confederate army officer General Nathan Bedford Forrest, and others that it was inspired by George Garvin Brown's physician Dr. Forrester. It has also been suggested that the name was chosen to appeal to the many timber workers in the area.

OLD FORESTER

BOURBON 43% ABV

Complex, with pronounced floral notes, vanilla, spice, pepper, fruit, chocolate, and menthol on the nose. Full and fruity in the mouth, where rye and peaches vie with fudge, nutmeg, and oak. The finish offers more rye, toffee, licorice, and drying oak.

OLD FORESTER BIRTHDAY BOURBON

BOURBON 47% ABV

Since September 2002 there has been an annual release of vintage Old Forester to commemorate the birthday of George Garvin Brown. The 2007 expression was distilled in the spring of 1994, and consists of fewer than 8,500 bottles. According to Brown-Forman, this vintage strikes a balance between the previous two: 2005 was heavy in cinnamon spice while 2006 had a pronounced mint note.

The 2007 release is sweet on the nose, with cinnamon, caramel, and vanilla, plus a contrasting whiff of mint. The palate is full and complex, with caramel, apples, and vanilla oak, and a lengthy, warm, clean finish.

OLD GRAND-DAD

Jim Beam Distillery, 149 Happy Hollow Road, Clermont, Kentucky
www.jimbeam.com

Old Grand-Dad was established in 1882 by a grandson of distiller Basil Hayden *(see p221)*. The brand and its distillery eventually passed into the hands of American Brands (Now Fortune Brands Inc.) which subsequently closed the distillery. Production now takes place in the Jim Beam Clermont and Boston distilleries.

OLD GRAND-DAD

BOURBON 43–57% ABV

Made with a comparatively high percentage of rye, the nose of Old Grand-dad reveals oranges and peppery spices. Quite heavy-bodied, the taste is full, yet surprisingly smooth, considering the strength. Fruit, nuts, and caramel are foremost on the palate, while the finish is long and oily.

OLD POTRERO

Anchor Distilling Company, 1705 Marisposa Street, San Francisco, California
www.anchorbrewing.com

Fritz Maytag is one of the pioneers of the American "micro-drinks" movement, and has been running San Francisco's historic Anchor Steam Brewery since 1965. In 1994 he added a small distillery to his brewery on San Francisco's Potrero Hill. Here, Maytag aims to "re-create the original whiskey of America", by making small batches of spirits in traditional, open pot stills, using 100 percent rye malt. The distillery produces a variety of blends using near-identical methods.

One of Maytag's illustrious blends is called Hotaling's, commemorating the 1906 San Francisco earthquake and fire, which devastated the city. (One notable survivor of the disaster was A.P. Hotaling & Co.'s Jackson Street whiskey warehouse.)

OLD POTRERO RYE

OLD POTRERO

SINGLE MALT RYE 62.55% ABV

This award-winning, 18th-century-style whiskey is distilled in a small copper pot still from a mash of 100 percent rye malt. It is then aged for one year in new, lightly toasted oak barrels and displays a floral, nutty nose, with vanilla and spice. Oily and smooth on the palate, with mint, honey, chocolate, and pepper in the lengthy finish.

OLD POTRERO RYE

RYE WHISKEY 45% ABV

Aged for three years in new, charred-oak barrels, this 19th-century-style whiskey marks an attempt to recreate the original whiskey of America. It boasts nuts, buttery vanilla, sweet oak, and pepper on the nose. Complex in the mouth, oily, sweet, and spicy, with caramel, oak, and spicy rye notes in the finish.

OLD TAYLOR

Jim Beam Distillery, 149 Happy Hollow Road, Clermont, Kentucky www.jimbeam.com

Old Taylor was introduced by Edmund Haynes Taylor, Jr., who was associated at various times with three distilleries in the Frankfort area of Kentucky, including what is now Buffalo Trace *(see p222)*. He was the man responsible for the Bottled-in-Bond Act of 1897, which guaranteed a whiskey's quality—any bottle bearing an official government seal had to be 100 proof (50% ABV) and at least four years old. Old Taylor was bought by Fortune Brands in 1987.

OLD TAYLOR

BOURBON 40% ABV

Light and orangey on the nose, with a hint of marzipan; sweet, honeyed, and slightly oaky on the palate.

PARKER'S

Heaven Hill Distillery, 1701 West Breckinridge Street, Louisville, Kentucky www.heaven-hill.com

Parker's Heritage Collection is a limited annual series of rare whiskeys that pays tribute to Heaven Hill's sixth-generation Master Distiller Parker Beam.

The first edition is a cask strength 1996 bourbon that was bottled at barrel-proof, the first such barrel-proof bourbon released by the distillers in the USA. The barrels were selected by Parker Beam for their fine nose, robust flavor, and long, smooth finish.

PARKER'S HERITAGE COLLECTION (FIRST EDITION)

BOURBON 61.3% ABV

Honey, vanilla, almonds, leather, and cherries on the nose. The palate displays spicy fruit and caramel, with leather, tobacco, and oak. The finish is long and fruity, with spice and oak.

PEREGRINE ROCK

Saint James Spirits, 5220 Fourth Street, Irwindale, California www.saintjamesspirits.com

Saint James Spirits was founded in 1995 by teacher Jim Busuttil, who learnt the craft of distilling in Germany and Switzerland. He has been making single malt whiskey (note the Scottish spelling) since 1997, and Peregrine Rock is produced from peated Scottish barley in a 40-US-gallon (150-liter) alambic copper pot still and put into bourbon barrels for a minimum period of three years.

PEREGRINE ROCK CALIFORNIA PURE

SINGLE MALT 40% ABV

Floral on the nose, with fresh fruits and a hint of smoke. The palate is delicate and fruity, with a citric twist to it, while sweeter, malty, and new-mown-grass notes develop in the slightly smoky finish.

Fermenting liquid in one of the washbacks at the Jack Daniel Distillery in Tennessee—at this stage of the process the yeast is interacting with the sugars from the wort to create alcohol at a strength of about 8% ABV.

PIKESVILLE

Heaven Hill Distillery, 1701 West Breckinridge Street, Louisville, Kentucky
www.heaven-hill.com

Rye whiskeys fall into two stylistic types, namely the spicy, tangy Pennsylvania style, as exemplified by Rittenhouse, and the Maryland style, which is softer in character. Pikesville is arguably the only example of Maryland rye still being produced today. This whiskey takes its name from Pikesville in Maryland, where it was first distilled during the 1890s and last produced in 1972. A decade later the brand was acquired by Heaven Hill.

PIKESVILLE SUPREME

RYE WHISKEY 40% ABV
The crisp nose presents bubble gum, fruit, and wood varnish, while on the palate there is more bubble gum, spice, oak, and overt vanilla. The finish comprises lingering vanilla and oranges.

REBEL YELL

Luxco, St. Louis, Missouri
www.luxco.com

Made at the Bernheim Distillery in Louisville, Rebel Yell is distilled with a percentage of wheat in its mashbill, instead of rye. Whiskey was first made to the Rebel Yell recipe 1849 and, after enjoying popularity in the southern states for many years, the brand was finally released on an international basis during the 1980s. In addition to the standard bottling, there is also a limited-edition Rebel Reserve expression.

REBEL YELL

BOURBON 40% ABV
A nose of honey, raisins, and butter leads into a big-bodied bourbon, which again features honey and a buttery quality, along with plums and soft leather. The finish is long and spicier than might be expected from the palate.

RIDGEMONT

Barton Distillery, 1 Barton Road, Bardstown, Kentucky
www.bartonbrands.com

The "1792" element of the name pays homage to the year in which Kentucky became a state. When this bourbon was introduced to the market in 2004, it was initially called Ridgewood Reserve but, after litigation between the distillers and Woodford Reserve's owners Brown-Forman, the name was changed.

1792 RIDGEMONT RESERVE

BOURBON 46.85% ABV
This comparatively delicate and complex 8-year-old, small-batch bourbon boasts a soft nose with vanilla, caramel, leather, rye, corn, and spice notes. Oily and initially sweet on the palate, caramel and spicy rye develop along with a suggestion of oak. The finish is oaky, spicy, and quite long, with a hint of lingering caramel.

RITTENHOUSE RYE

Heaven Hill Distillery, 1701 West Breckinridge Street, Louisville, Kentucky
www.heaven-hill.com

Once associated with Pennsylvania, the rye-whiskey making heartland, Rittenhouse Rye now survives in Kentucky, and its mashbill comprises 51 percent rye, 37 percent corn, and 12 percent barley.

Rittenhouse was launched by the Continental Distilling Company of Philadelphia as soon as Prohibition was repealed in 1933, and was later acquired by Heaven Hill, which continued to produce the brand through the lean years when rye whiskey as a style was largely forgotten.

RITTENHOUSE RYE 23-YEAR-OLD

RYE WHISKEY 50% ABV
This limited-release expression of

RITTENHOUSE RYE 100 PROOF

RITTENHOUSE RYE 21-YEAR-OLD

Rittenhouse Rye has been aged for the remarkably lengthy period of 23 years, and inevitably both the nose and palate feature significant amounts of oak and spice, with fruit on the nose and coffee notes in the mouth. The finish is long and dense, with spices and cocoa.

RITTENHOUSE RYE 100 PROOF

RYE WHISKEY 50% ABV

Marshmallow and lemon merge on the notably sweet nose, while the lemon carries over into the mouth, where it is joined by black pepper, licorice, and caramel. The finish features dark chocolate and molasses toffee.

RITTENHOUSE RYE 21-YEAR-OLD

RYE WHISKEY 50% ABV

The nose is notably spicy, with nuts and oranges, while on the palate powerful spices and oak meet lemon and much sweeter notes of lavender and violet. The finish is a long, bitter, rye classic.

ROCK HILL FARMS

Buffalo Trace Distillery, 1001 Wilkinson Boulevard, Frankfort, Kentucky
www.buffalotrace.com

This single cask brand was first introduced to the Buffalo Trace (*see p222*) line-up in 1990, and is named after the home farm of the Blanton family. It was Colonel Benjamin Blanton who first made whiskey on the site of what is now Buffalo Trace Distillery, just after the Civil War. The Rock Hill mansion itself survives within the Buffalo Trace complex.

ROCK HILL FARMS

BOURBON 50% ABV

Oak, raisins, and fruity rye on the nose, with a hint of mint. Medium- to full-bodied, bittersweet on the palate, with rye fruitiness, fudge, oak, and a long, sweet, rye finish with a suggestion of licorice.

ROGUE SPIRITS

Rogue Brewery, 1339 NW Flanders, Portland, Oregon
www.rogue.com

Dead Guy Ale was created in the early 1990s to celebrate the Mayan Day of the Dead (November 1, or All Souls' Day) and, in 2008, the Oregon-based producers launched their Dead Guy Whiskey. It is distilled using the same four malts used in the creation of Dead Guy Ale, and fermented wort from the brewery is taken to the nearby Rogue House of Spirits, where it is double-distilled in a 150-US-gallon (570-liter) copper pot still. A brief maturation period follows, using charred American white-oak casks.

DEAD GUY

BLENDED MALT 40% ABV

Youthful on the nose, with notes of corn, wheat, and fresh, juicy orange. The palate is medium-dry, fruity, and lively. Pepper and cinnamon feature in the finish.

RUSSELL'S RESERVE

Wild Turkey Distillery, US Highway 62 East, Lawrenceburg, Kentucky
www.wildturkeybourbon.com

Austin Nichols' Master Distiller Jimmy Russell and his son Eddie, of Wild Turkey *(see p264)* fame, developed this small-batch rye whiskey, launched in 2007.

Jimmy is one of the great characters of the bourbon world, and now serves as a leading international ambassador for the bourbon industry. James C. Russell, to give him his full name, has been distilling whiskey since the 1950s and both his father and grandfather were also distillers. So, it was no great surprise when his son Eddie joined the company in 1980.

According to Jimmy Russell, "rye whiskey is its own animal and rye fans are a special breed". His son, Eddie Russell, adds that "we knew the whiskey

we wanted, but had never tasted it before. This one really makes the grade—deep character and taste and, at six years, aged to perfection".

RUSSELL'S RESERVE RYE

RYE WHISKEY 45% ABV

Fruity, with fresh oak and almonds on the nose. Full-bodied and robust, yet smooth. Almonds, pepper, and rye dominate the palate, while the finish is long, dry, and characteristically bitter.

RUSSELL'S RESERVE 10-YEAR-OLD

BOURBON 45% ABV

The stable-mate to Russell's Reserve Rye, this bourbon boasts a nose of pine, vanilla, soft leather, and caramel. The palate features more vanilla, along with toffee, almond, honey, coconut, and the appearance of a slightly unusual note of chiles that continues through the lengthy, spicy finish.

SAM HOUSTON

McLain & Kyne Ltd. (Castle Brands), Louisville, Kentucky
www.mclainandkyne.com

McLain & Kyne Ltd. is best known for what it terms "very small batch bourbons", and the firm blends whiskey from as few as eight to 12 barrels of varying ages for their Jefferson's *(see p244)* and Sam Houston bourbon brands.

Sam Houston was introduced in 1999 and is named after the colorful 19th-century soldier, statesman, and politician Samuel Houston, who became the first president of the Republic of Texas.

SAM HOUSTON SMALL BATCH 10-YEAR-OLD

BOURBON (VARIABLE ABV)

The nose offers delicate aromas of red berries, oak, and rye bread, while the rich, tangy palate boasts resin, nutmeg, rye bread, leather, and gentle spice. Long, sweet, and textured in the finish.

SAZERAC RYE

Buffalo Trace Distillery, 1001 Wilkinson Boulevard, Frankfort, Kentucky
www.buffalotrace.com

Sazerac Rye is part of the annually updated Buffalo Trace Antique Collection *(see p222)* and, having been aged for 18 years, is the oldest rye whiskey currently available. According to Buffalo Trace, the 18-year-old 2008 release is comprised of whiskey that has been aging in its warehouse on the first floor, which enables the barrels to age slowly and gracefully.

SAZERAC RYE 18-YEAR-OLD

RYE WHISKEY 45% ABV
Rich on the nose, with maple syrup and a hint of menthol, this expression is oily on the palate, fresh, and lively, with fruit, pepper, and pleasing oak notes. The finish boasts lingering pepper, with returning fruit and a final flavor of molasses.

SEAGRAM'S 7 CROWN

Angostura Distillery, Lawrenceburg, Indiana

One of the best known and most characterful blended American whiskeys, Seagram's 7 Crown has survived the break-up of the Seagram distilling empire and is now produced by Caribbean-based Angostura (of Angosturas Bitters fame). This relative newcomer to the US distilling arena has acquired the former Seagram distillery at Lawrenceburg, where 7 Crown is made, along with the long-shuttered Charles Medley Distillery in Owensboro Kentucky. The Lawrenceburg distillery is the largest spirits facility in the USA in terms of production capacity.

SEAGRAM'S 7 CROWN

BLEND 40% ABV
This possesses a delicate nose with a hint of spicy rye, and is clean and well structured on the spicy palate.

ST. GEORGE

St. George Spirits, 2601 Monarch Street, Alameda, California
www.stgeorgespirits.com

St. George Spirits was established by Jörg Rupf in 1982, and the distillery operates two Holstein copper pot stills. A percentage of heavily roasted barley is used, some of which is smoked over alder and beech wood. Most of the single malt whiskey is put into former bourbon barrels and matured for between three and five years, with a proportion matured in French oak and former port casks.

ST. GEORGE

SINGLE MALT 43% ABV
The nose offers fresh, floral notes, with fruit, nuts, coffee, and vanilla. It is quite delicate on the palate, sweet, nutty, and fruity, with a hint of menthol and cocoa. Vanilla and chocolate notes in the finish, along with gentle smoke.

STRANAHAN'S

Stranahan's Colorado Whiskey, 2405 Blake Street, Denver, Colorado
www.stranahans.com

Jess Graber and George Stranahan established the Denver distillery, the first licensed distillery in Colorado, in March 2004. Whiskey is produced using a four-barley fermented wash produced by the neighboring Flying Dog Brewery. The distillation takes place in a Vendome still, and the spirit is put into new, charred American-oak barrels. It is aged for a minimum of two years, and each bottled batch composed of the contents of between two and six barrels.

STRANAHAN'S COLORADO WHISKEY

COLORADO WHISKEY 47% ABV
The nose is very bourbon-like, with notes of caramel, licorice, spice, and oak. The palate is slightly oily, big, and sweet, with honey and spices. The fairly short finish is quite oaky.

TEMPLETON RYE

East 3rd Street, Templeton, Iowa
www.templetonrye.com

Scott Bush's Templeton Rye whiskey came onto the market in 2006. It is distilled in a 300-US-gallon (1,150-liter) copper pot still before being aged in new, charred-oak barrels.

Bush boasts that his rye is made to a Prohibition-era recipe. During the years of the Great Depression a group of farmers in the Templeton area started to distil a rye whiskey illicitly in order to boost their faltering agricultural incomes. Soon, "Templeton Rye" achieved a widespread reputation as a high quality spirit.

TEMPLETON RYE SMALL BATCH

RYE WHISKEY 40% ABV
Bright, crisp, and mildly sweet on the palate. The finish is smooth, long, and warming.

TEN HIGH

Barton Distillery, ß1 Barton Road, Bardstown, Kentucky
www.bartonbrands.com

Ten High, a long-established name, was first created in 1879 and is now a Barton-owned brand. It is a sour mash, which means that it is made with a small quantity of an old batch of mash containing a certain strain of live yeast, which ensures a consistent taste—similar to the process of making sourdough bread. The whiskey is matured in white-oak barrels. The name Ten High comes from a term used in playing poker.

TEN HIGH KENTUCKY

BOURBON 40% ABV
Grainy and slightly oaky on the nose, Ten High is notably malty on the palate, almost like a young malt Scotch, and has notes of vanilla and caramel. The finish is quite short and drying.

THOMAS H. HANDY SAZERAC

Buffalo Trace Distillery, 1001 Wilkinson Boulevard, Frankfort, Kentucky
www.buffalotrace.com

Thomas H. Handy Sazerac is the newest addition to the Buffalo Trace Antique Collection. It is an uncut and unfiltered straight rye whiskey, named after the New Orleans bartender who first used rye whiskey to make the Sazerac Cocktail. According to the distillers, the barrels are aged six years and five months on the fifth floor of Warehouse M—"it's very flavorful and will remind drinkers of Christmas cake".

THOMAS H. HANDY SAZERAC 2008 EDITION

RYE WHISKEY 63.8% ABV
Summer fruits and pepper notes on the nose. The palate is a blend of soft vanilla and peppery rye; the finish is long, with oily, spicy oak.

TOM MOORE

Barton Distillery, 1 Barton Road, Bardstown, Kentucky
www.bartonbrands.com

This Barton Kentucky straight bourbon brand takes its name from the Tom Moore Distillery, which was established in 1889 by Tom Moore and Ben Mattingly, just a stone's throw from the present Barton Distillery.

The plant was closed during Prohibition but reopened in 1934 and, a decade later, was acquired by the Oscar Getz family, who subsequently established the Barton Distilling Company.

TOM MOORE

BOURBON 50% ABV
Distinct notes of rye and herbs on the nose, along with vanilla, oak, and cooked berries. Medium-bodied, the palate is a blend of sugary sweetness and spicy rye bitterness. Toffee and ginger dominate the finish.

US Micro-distilling

The USA is currently undergoing a boom in small-scale or "micro" distilling, mirroring the country's earlier rapid growth of micro-brewing operations. Whiskey micro-distilling is a notably vibrant area of the market, where experimentation and innovation with different grains and production techniques are the norm. Distillers often operate outside the legally-defined boundaries of bourbon, rye, or corn whiskeys.

A micro-distillery is defined as one manufacturing fewer than 500 barrels of spirits per year. One of the early pioneers of the movement was San Francisco craft brewer Fritz Maytag, who set up the Anchor Distilling Company *(see p250)* in 1994. In Kentucky, three new ventures are in production. Alltech (alltech.com) is making Pearse Lyons Reserve, Kentucky's first malt whiskey. This is distilled using a pair of copper pot stills, and the initial batch of matured spirits should be available in 2010. Also in Lexington, The Barrel House (barrelhousedistillery.com) started distilling Woodshed Whiskey and Barrel House Bourbon in 2009. Over in Bowling Green, Corsair Artisan Distillery (corsairartisan.com) also opened in 2009 and is distilling Wry Moon Unaged Rye Whiskey in a pair of copper pot stills, and laying down rye and bourbon spirit for maturation.

In Virginia, Mount Vernon Distillery (mountvernon.org) is a working recreation of the whiskey-making facility established by President George Washington in 1797. Its 18th-century-style stills were installed in reconstructed buildings in 2006. It functions as a distilling museum as well as a micro-distillery. Other new micro-distilleries include Ballast Point in San Diego (ballastpointspirits.com), Colorado Gold in Colorado (coloradogolddistillery.com), Washington's Dry Fly (dryflydistilling.com), Garrison in Texas (garrisonbros.com), High West in Utah (highwestdistillery.com), House Spirits in Oregon (medoyeff.com), Nashoba Valley in Massachusetts (nashobawinery.com), New Holland in Michigan (newhollandbrew.com), and Rough Stock in Montana (montanawhiskey.com).

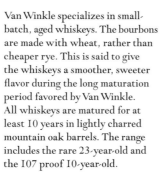

VAN WINKLE

2843 Brownsboro Road
Louisville, Kentucky
www.oldripvanwinke.com

Buffalo Trace *(see p222)* has been in partnership with Julian Van Winkle since 2002, making and distributing his whiskeys. The current expressions were produced at a number of distilleries, and matured at the Van Winkle's now silent Old Hoffman Distillery.

Julian is a grandson of legendary Julian P. "Pappy" Van Winkle Snr, who started working as a salesman for W. L. Weller & Sons in Louisville in 1893 at the age of 18 and went on to become famous for his Old Fitzgerald bourbon.

Van Winkle specializes in small-batch, aged whiskeys. The bourbons are made with wheat, rather than cheaper rye. This is said to give the whiskeys a smoother, sweeter flavor during the long maturation period favored by Van Winkle. All whiskeys are matured for at least 10 years in lightly charred mountain oak barrels. The range includes the rare 23-year-old and the 107 proof 10-year-old.

OLD RIP VAN WINKLE 10-YEAR-OLD
BOURBON 45% ABV
Caramel and molasses on the big nose, then honey and rich, spicy fruit on the profound, mellow palate. The finish is long, with coffee and licorice notes.

PAPPY VAN WINKLE'S FAMILY RESERVE 15-YEAR-OLD
BOURBON 53.5% ABV
A sweet caramel and vanilla nose, with charcoal and oak. Full-bodied, round, and smooth in the mouth, with a long and complex finish of spicy orange, toffee, vanilla, and oak.

PAPPY VAN WINKLE'S FAMILY RESERVE 20-YEAR-OLD
BOURBON 45.2% ABV
Old for a bourbon, this has stood the test of time. Sweet vanilla and caramel nose, plus raisins, apples, and oak. Rich and buttery in the mouth, with molasses and a hint of char. The finish is long and complex, with a touch of oak charring.

VAN WINKLE SPECIAL RESERVE 12-YEAR-OLD
BOURBON 45.2% ABV
Caramel, vanilla, honey, and oak on the nose. A sweet, full-bodied palate exudes caramel, vanilla, and wheat. The finish is long, well-balanced, and elegant.

VAN WINKLE FAMILY RESERVE RYE 13-YEAR-OLD
RYE WHISKEY 47.8% ABV
An almost uniquely aged rye. Powerful nose of fruit and spice. Vanilla, spice, pepper, and cocoa in the mouth. A long finish pairs caramel with black coffee.

American Rye

The heritage of rye whiskey in North America probably dates back to the 1600s. Its development owes much to Irish and Scottish settlers, who found rye less difficult than barley to grow there. The Irish were already familiar with the use of rye in whiskey making.

Rye whiskey was particularly associated with the states of Pennsylvania and Maryland, with each making a distinctive style of the spirit; however, most rye is now distilled in Kentucky. Although rye whiskey was at one time much more widely consumed in the US than bourbon, it never fully recovered from Prohibition. Its distinctive, peppery, and slightly bitter character probably worked against it as drinkers developed a taste for blander spirits. However, there has been a slow revival in rye's fortunes, with a number of US micro-distilleries *(see p259)* producing small quantities of rye for appreciative connoisseurs. For example, in 1996, the pioneering Fritz Maytag of San Francisco's Anchor Brewery began distilling Old Potrero *(see p251)* from 100 percent malted rye. Moreover, the recreated Mount Vernon Distillery in Virginia *(see p259)* now distills rye whiskey to a recipe developed by Scottish-born farm manager, James Anderson.

By law, rye whiskey has to be made from a mash of no less than 51 percent rye, with the other ingredients usually being corn and malted barley. It has to be distilled to no more than 80% ABV and casked at 62.5% ABV or less. As with bourbon, virgin charred-oak barrels are used for maturation and the minimum maturation period is two years. Leading brands of rye whiskey include Pikesville *(see p254)*, Rittenhouse *(see 254)*, and Sazerac *(see p257)*. Jim Beam *(see p242)* and Wild Turkey *(see p265)* also produce expressions of rye.

VIRGINIA GENTLEMAN

A. Smith Bowman Distillery, Bowman
Drive, Fredericksburg, Virginia
www.asmithbowman.com

The only full-scale distillery in a
state that once made more whiskey
than Kentucky, and founded by
Abram Smith Bowman in 1935, it
was acquired in 2003 by Sazerac,
which also owns Buffalo Trace (see
p222). Virginia Gentleman's first
run is fermented and distilled at
Buffalo Trace before a second, slow
run through a copper pot doubler
still on the Smith Bowman site,
where it is also matured in charred
white-oak barrels. A higher corn
percentage than many bourbons
gives it a greater sweetness.

VIRGINIA GENTLEMAN
BOURBON 45% ABV
A light, sweet, toasted nut aroma, and
spicy rye, sweet corn, honey, caramel,
and cocoa on the palate. A complex
finish, with rye, malt, and vanilla.

VIRGINIA LIGHTNING

Belmost Farms of Virginia, 13490
Cedar Run Road, Culpeper, Virginia
www.virginiamoonshine.com

For Virginia Lightning, distiller
Chuck Miller uses an original,
secret family recipe, a blend of
corn, wheat, and barley that is
mashed and fermented in copper
fermentation tanks. Distillation
takes place in a 1930s, 2,000-US-
gallon (7,600-liter) copper still.
Finally, it is passed through a
doubler still to increase strength
and remove impurities. It is then
bottled unaged. Its assertive sister
spirit, Kopper Kettle, is charcoal-
filtered; oak and apple-wood chips
are used to boost maturation before
it is barrel-aged for two years.

VIRGINIA LIGHTNING
CORN WHISKEY 50% ABV
Corn and alcohol on the nose, smooth
and sugary on the palate, with oily
corn, plus a powerful kick in the finish.

WASMUND'S

Copper Fox Distillery, 9 River Lane,
Sperryville, Virginia
www.copperfox.biz

In spring 2003, Rick Wasmund
purchased an existing Virginia
distillery to launch Copper Fox
Whiskey, and in 2005 the
operation moved to its present,
newly built site at Sperryville.

Wasmund malts barley in the
traditional Scottish manner and
then dries it using apple, cherry,
and oak wood. It is distilled in a
double pot still in single barrel
batches and matured using an
original "chip and barrel" aging
process, which dramatically speeds
up maturation.

WASMUND'S
SINGLE MALT WHISKEY 48% ABV
Honey, vanilla, watermelon, and
leather on the nose, and a well-
balanced blend of sweet and dry flavors
on the palate, with nuts, smoke, spices,
and vanilla.

W. L. WELLER

Buffalo Trace Distillery, 1001
Wilkinson Boulevard, Frankfort,
Kentucky
www.buffalotrace.com

Distilled by Buffalo Trace, W. L.
Weller is made with wheat as the
secondary grain, for an extra
smooth taste.

William Larue Weller was
a prominent 19th-century
Kentucky distiller, whose company
ultimately merged with that of
the Stitzel brothers in 1935. A
new Stitzel-Weller Distillery
was subsequently constructed
in Louisville.

W. L. WELLER SPECIAL RESERVE
BOURBON 45% ABV
Fresh fruit, honey, vanilla, and toffee
characterize the nose, while the palate
has lots of flavor, featuring ripe corn
and spicy oak. The medium-length
finish displays sweet, cereal notes and
pleasing oak.

WILD TURKEY 80 PROOF

WILD TURKEY KENTUCKY SPIRIT

WILD TURKEY

Wild Turkey Distillery, US Highway 62 East, Lawrenceburg, Kentucky
www.wildturkeybourbon.com

Wild Turkey's Distillery is situated on Wild Turkey Hill, above the Kentucky River, near Lawrenceburg, in Anderson County. Wild Turkey has been owned by the Pernod Ricard Group since 1980, when the French drinks giant took over the New-York-based Austin Nichols Distilling Co. The distillery was first established in 1905 by the three Ripy brothers, whose family had been making whiskey in the nearby distilling center of Tyrone since the year 1869.

The Wild Turkey brand was conceived in 1940, when Austin Nichols' president, Thomas McCarthy, chose a quantity of 101 proof straight bourbon from his company stocks to take along on a wild turkey shoot. Today, Wild Turkey is distilled under the watchful eyes of legendary Master Distiller Jimmy Russell and his son Eddie (the latter is the fourth-generation Russell to work at the distillery, and has more than 25 years' experience). The Russells have also created some other highly regarded brands, including Russell's Reserve *(see p256)* and American Spirit *(see p220)*.

WILD TURKEY 80 PROOF
BOURBON 40% ABV

Wild Turkey "80" was introduced to the range in 1974 and, according to Jimmy Russell, this expression is ideal served on the rocks, and equally perfect for those who enjoy their bourbon with a mixer. The soft, sweet nose hints at corn, while on the palate this is a very traditional whiskey, nicely balancing caramel and vanilla flavors.

WILD TURKEY 101 PROOF

WILD TURKEY RARE BREED

WILD TURKEY KENTUCKY STRAIGHT RYE

WILD TURKEY KENTUCKY SPIRIT

BOURBON 50.5% ABV

A single barrel whiskey, each one personally selected by Jimmy Russell to be fuller-bodied than normal. A fresh, attractive nose, with oranges and notes of rye. Complex on the palate, with almonds, honey, toffee, more oranges, and a hint of leather. The finish is long and sweet, gradually darkening and becoming more syrupy.

WILD TURKEY 101 PROOF

BOURBON 50.5% ABV

Jimmy Russell maintains that 50.5% (101 proof) is the optimum bottling strength for Wild Turkey. This has a remarkably soft yet rich aroma for such a high-proof whiskey, due in part to its eight years of maturation. Caramel, vanilla, soft fruits, and a touch of spice on the nose, full-bodied, rich, and robust in the mouth, with more vanilla, fresh fruit, and spice, plus brown sugar and honey. Notes of oak develop in the long, and powerful, yet smooth finish.

WILD TURKEY RARE BREED

BOURBON (VARIABLE ABV)

Launched in 1991, this brand is composed of whiskeys aged from 6 to 12 years. Aroma and flavor are notably smooth for a bourbon with such a high alcohol content. A complex, initially assertive nose, with nuts, oranges, spices, and floral notes. Honey, oranges, vanilla, tobacco, mint, and molasses make for an equally complex palate. A long, nutty finish, with spicy, peppery rye.

WILD TURKEY KENTUCKY STRAIGHT RYE

RYE WHISKEY 50.5% ABV

This straight rye has a pleasingly firm nose, crammed with fruit. The body is full and rich, and the well-balanced palate offers intense spices and ripe fruit. A profoundly spicy, nutty, finish.

WOODFORD RESERVE

7855 McCracken Pike,
Versailles, Kentucky
www.woodfordreserve.com

Woodford Reserve is the smallest distillery operating in Kentucky, and it is unique among bourbon distilleries because it uses a triple distillation method and three copper pot stills.

Woodford Reserve is operated by the Louisville-based Brown-Forman Distiller Corporation, which also owns Jack Daniel's *(see p238)*, but the distillery's origins can be traced back as far as 1797. Brown-Forman only began to distil there in 1996, when it was known as the Labrot & Graham Distillery. The company subsequently spent $10.5 million restoring the plant, and in 2003 the present Woodford Reserve name was adopted for both the distillery and its whiskey.

In 2005, the first bottling in the Master's Collection range was released under the Four Grain Bourbon name, and two years later, a Sonoma-Cutrer Finish was added to the line-up. The Master's Collection 1838 Sweet Mash was released in 2008 to commemorate the year the present Woodford Reserve Distillery was constructed, and to also celebrate the historic "sweet mash" method of bourbon production.

WOODFORD RESERVE DISTILLER'S SELECT

BOURBON 45.2% ABV

Distiller's Select is elegant yet robust on the nose, perfumed, with milk chocolate raisins, dried fruit, burned sugar, ginger, and a touch of saddle soap. Equally complex on the palate, Distiller's Select is fragrant and fruity, with raspberries, camomile, and ginger. The finish displays lingering vanilla notes as well as peppery oak.

MASTER'S COLLECTION FOUR GRAIN

BOURBON 46.2% ABV

Spicy apple pie, vanilla, caramel, and mint on the nose, while the rounded and complex palate features more vanilla and caramel, along with orange, nuts, and oak. The lengthy finish exhibits pine and spicy oak. The four grains used are corn, malted barley, rye, and wheat.

MASTER'S COLLECTION SONOMA-CUTRER FINISH

BOURBON 43.2% ABV

The first and only bourbon in the world to be finished in California Chardonnay barrels, after an initial maturation period in new, charred casks. Fruity and sweet on the nose and palate, with the influence of the wine casks very apparent. Butterscotch and almonds are also discernible on the nose, while in the mouth baked apples, peaches, and toffee feature. The finish is medium to long, with furniture polish and fruity oak.

MASTER'S COLLECTION 1838 SWEET MASH

BOURBON 43.2% ABV

Maple syrup and spicy fruit on the nose, along with cinnamon and nutmeg. The rich palate features more maple syrup and rich fruit, with a hint of rye and mint. The finish is lengthy, with notes of soft apples.

LABROT & GRAHAM

WOODFORD RESERVE

DISTILLER'S SELECT

KENTUCKY STRAIGHT BOURBON WHISKEY

THE BARRELS THAT ARE USED FOR THIS EXCEPTIONAL HAND-CRAFTED BOURBON HAVE BEEN SPECIALLY SELECTED BY OUR MASTER DISTILLER.

BATCH 203   BOTTLE NUMBER 07612

45.2% ALC/VOL (90.4 PROOF)

Approved by

750 ml   90.4 PROOF

MASTER'S COLLECTION FOUR GRAIN

MASTER'S COLLECTION SONOMA-CUTRER FINISH

MASTER'S COLLECTION 1838 SWEET MASH

NORTHWEST
TERRITORIES

HUDSON
BAY

BRITISH
COLUMBIA

ALBERTA

MANITOBA

SASKATCHEWAN

ONTARIO

EDMONTON

Alberta

CALGARY

Highwood

Crown Royal

VANCOUVER

REGINA

Black Velvet

WINNIPEG

USA

OTTAWA

Canadian Mist

TORONTO

Hiram Walker
(Canadian Club)

Kittling
Ridge

miles
0   100
0   100
kilometers

N
W   E
S

FORTY CREEK

GLEN BRETON

CROWN ROYAL

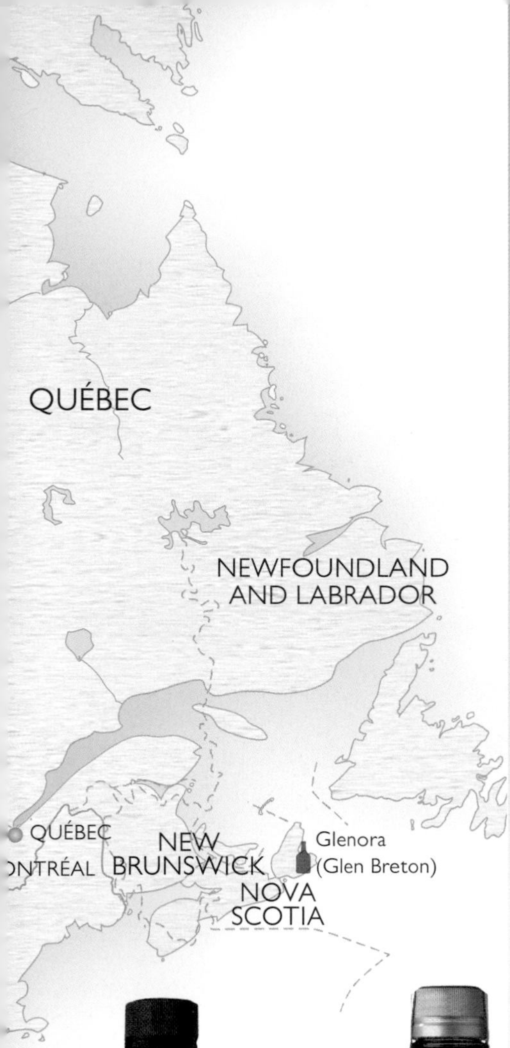

QUÉBEC

NEWFOUNDLAND
AND LABRADOR

QUÉBEC

MONTRÉAL   NEW
           BRUNSWICK
              NOVA
              SCOTIA

Glenora
(Glen Breton)

The golden age of Canadian whiskey was from late 19th to mid-20th centuries, with whiskey makers such as Hiram Walker, creator of Canadian Club, and Sam Bronfman at Seagram forming vast commercial empires. These two dominated much of the world market. From this high point, however, Canadian whiskey experienced a marked decline in the second half of the 20th century, and it now operates on a far more modest scale. Where once 200 distilleries produced rivers of whiskey to serve a seemingly insatiable American market, now Canada has fewer than a dozen distilleries, most of which are owned by US bourbon companies or international spirits producers. Seagram's—a name so closely associated with Canada—is still the brand name for a handful of whiskies, but the Seagram's empire itself is gone. It remains to be seen if the remaining producers can take their nation's whiskey industry back to being a major player on the world stage.

ALBERTA

WISER'S

SEAGRAM'S VO

CANADIAN CLUB

CANADIAN MIST

Canadian Whiskey

All Canadian whiskey is blended, apart from Glen Breton, a single malt (*see p277*). Production is in column stills, but each distillery produces a range of styles, and each blend will use between 15 and 50 different whiskies. As in Scotland, the spirit must be matured for at least 3 years, although much is aged 6 to 8 years. The base spirit is light and relatively neutral in character, distilled from rye, barley, wheat, or corn. Unlike in the US, there is no constraint upon the mashbill. A proportion of rye or malted rye spirit, which adds spice to the blend and body, is added to the mix, and this provides Canadian whiskey with its chief characteristics. It is often described as rye whiskey, but Canadian whiskey is of a different style than American rye whiskey.

Early immigrants to Canada found a country blessed with the necessities for whiskey making. By 1840, there were about 200 distillers in the country. Commercial distilleries usually began as offshoots of grain mills—among them were Hiram Walker, Joseph Seagram, J. P. Wiser, and Gooderham & Worts. Their business was not easy because of a Puritan ethic that constrained the sale of alcohol. Today, liquor stores are run by the state, except in Alberta. Ironically, it was the imposition of Prohibition in the USA, between 1920 and 1933, that provided Canadian whiskey with the impetus it needed. The major players—Seagram, Schenley, and Hiram Walker—realized that they could build an export market for the future.

Today, America consumes more Canadian whiskey than any other spirit, including American whiskey. Indeed, a great deal of Canadian whiskey is blended specifically for the US market, having a light and smooth style, the former coming from a very pure base spirit, and the latter from other elements in the blend.

ALBERTA

1521 34th Avenue Southeast,
Calgary, Alberta

Alberta Distillery was founded in
Calgary in 1946 to take advantage
of the immense prairies of the
Canadian west and the fine water
cascading down from the Rocky
Mountains. It has capacity to
produce over 5 million gallons
(20 million liters) per annum in its
beer, column, and pot stills, and
since 1987 has been owned by
Jim Beam. As well as the Alberta
labels, other brands from this
distillery include Tangle Ridge
and Windsor Canadian *(see p279).*

Rye is at the heart of many
Canadian whiskies, and is
predominant in all the whiskies
that come from Alberta. The bulk
of the distillery's blends are made
up of a base spirit made with rye
rather than corn. This is first
distilled in a beer still, then in a
continuous rectifier. A separate
rye spirit is also made up. This is

distilled once only, leaving oils and
congeners in the spirit to make it
heavy, oily, and rich in flavor.
The two spirits are then blended
together. Maturation takes place
in first-fill bourbon casks, or even
in new white-oak casks.

ALBERTA SPRINGS
10-YEAR-OLD
CANADIAN RYE 40% ABV
A sweet aroma, with rye bread and
black pepper. The taste is very sweet,
even somewhat cloying, becoming
charred and caramelized.

ALBERTA PREMIUM
CANADIAN RYE 40% ABV
Described as "Special Mild Canadian
Rye Whiskey." The aroma presents
vanilla toffee, a hint of spice, light
citric notes, and fruitiness. The taste
is sweet above all, with stewed apples,
plums, and marzipan.

BLACK VELVET

2925 9th Avenue North,
Lethbridge, Alberta
www.blackvelvetwhiskey.com

Black Velvet is the third bestselling
Canadian Whiskey in the US. It
was created by Gilbey Canada
in the 1950s as Black Label, and
made at the Old Palliser Distillery
in Toronto. It was so successful
that, in 1973, the Black Velvet
Distillery was established at
Lethbridge, in the shadow of the
Rockies, only a couple of hours
drive from the US border. In 1999,
both Black Velvet and Palliser were
sold to Barton Brands, now a
division of Constellation Brands.

BLACK VELVET RESERVE
BLEND 40% ABV
A light and mellow nose with vanilla
notes. The palate is mild and sweet,
with butterscotch, a faint citrus note,
and light spiciness. Velvet-smooth
texture, but the flavor lacks depth.

CANADIAN MIST

202 MacDonald Road,
Collingwood, Ontario
www.canadianmist.com

Launched in 1965, this whiskey
now sells 3 million cases a year
in the US. Its distillery is odd in
several ways: the equipment is
all stainless steel; it is the only
Canadian distillery to use a mashbill of corn and malted barley; and
it imports its rye spirit from sister
distillery Early Times *(see p227)*
in Kentucky. Almost all the spirit is
tankered to Kentucky for blending.
In addition to the popular
Canadian Mist brand, the 1185
Special Reserve is also available.

CANADIAN MIST
BLEND 40% ABV
Lightly fruity on the nose, with vanilla
and caramel notes. Mild, sweet flavor
with traces of vanilla toffee.

CANADIAN CLUB RESERVE

CANADIAN CLUB 6-YEAR-OLD

CANADIAN CLUB PREMIUM

CANADIAN CLUB

Hiram Walker Distillery, Riverside Drive East, Walkerville, Ontario
www.canadianclubwhiskey.com

Canadian Club is the oldest and most influential whiskey brand in Canada. Created by businessman Hiram Walker in 1884, it was named simply "Club" and aimed at discerning members of gentlemen's clubs. Unusually, in an era when most whiskies were sold in bulk, it was supplied in bottles, and thus could not be adulterated by the retailer, a practice soon adopted by other Canadian and American distillers. The company has had numerous Royal Warrants, from Queen Victoria to Elizabeth II.

A less lofty customer, Al Capone, smuggled thousands of cases across the border during Prohibition.

In 1927 Hiram Walker & Sons was bought by Harry Hatch, who owned the Gooderham & Worts Distillery in Toronto. The merged company was the largest distiller in the world. Entrepreneur Hatch made a fortune during Prohibition. In 1935, he took a controlling interest in H. Corby (see p279). Then, in 1937, he bought Ballantine's (p35) and a clutch of malt whiskey distillers, and built the Strathclyde grain distillery. Allied Distillers acquired the company in 1987.

The Canadian Club brands were sold to Fortune Brands, the owner of Jim Beam (see p242), in 2005.

CANADIAN CLUB CLASSIC

CANADIAN CLUB 20-YEAR-OLD

CANADIAN CLUB SHERRY CASK

Canadian Club is always "blended at birth"—that is, the component whiskies are mixed prior to a maturation of at least five years. The standard is a 6-year-old; older versions, such as the 20-year-old, are sometimes released onto the domestic and export markets.

CANADIAN CLUB RESERVE

BLEND 40% ABV

Blended at birth, then aged in small oak barrels to give a richer flavor.

CANADIAN CLUB 6-YEAR-OLD 100 PROOF

BLEND 50% ABV

The higher strength allows the signature flavors to come through better with a mixer.

CANADIAN CLUB PREMIUM

BLEND 40% ABV

Creamy and cereal-like; rather spirity. Drier than most Canadian whiskies, with light smokiness and nuttiness.

CANADIAN CLUB CLASSIC

BLEND 40% ABV

Nose of tropical fruits, oak, and honey, with some toffee. Very smooth palate and a very sweet taste with a banana aftertaste.

CANADIAN CLUB SHERRY CASK

BLEND 41.3% ABV

Matured in white oak barrels for at least 8 years then re-racked into ex-sherry casks for a further period, which adds a tannic dimension to the whiskey.

Canada's huge grain silos, standing starkly against the sky, are an icon of the country's landscape and agricultural heritage, including its whiskey distilling industry.

SPECIAL RESERVE

CROWN ROYAL

CROWN ROYAL CASK NO. 16

CROWN ROYAL

Distillery Road, Gimli, Manitoba
www.crownroyal.ca

Crown Royal was created by Sam Bronfman, President of Seagram *(see p278)*, to mark the state visit to Canada of King George VI and Queen Elizabeth in 1939, with its "crown-shaped" bottle and purple velvet bag. Although it was only available in Canada until 1964, it is now one of the best-selling Canadian whiskies in the US.

Since 1992, it has been produced at the Gimli Distillery on Lake Winnipeg. Before that, it was made at the Waterloo Distillery, founded in 1857 and then owned by Joseph Emm Seagram in 1833. It was then sold to the Distillers Corporation in 1928. The driving force behind this company was Sam Bronfman, or "Mr. Sam", a man of energy, daring, ruthlessness, and passion. With the help of his brothers, he built Seagram into the largest liquor company in the world.

Prohibition was their big break, though Sam tended to draw a veil over this period in later life. "We shipped a lot of goods. Of course, we knew where it went, but we had no legal proof. I never went to the other side of the border to count the empty Seagram bottles".

In 2001 the company shed its alcohol interests—Gimli Distillery and Crown Royal went to Diageo.

CROWN ROYAL CASK NO. 16
BLEND 40% ABV
Blended from over 50 whiskies, aged at least 12 years, and finished in oak cognac barrels. Fruit, rye, and cereal on the nose, with brandy in the finish.

SPECIAL RESERVE
BLEND 40% ABV
A big, rich, rounded nose, with fruity (apple, guava, coconut) and floral notes.

CROWN ROYAL
BLEND 40% ABV
Rich, robust, and balanced. Vanilla, oak, and fruit in the mouthfeel and taste.

FORTY CREEK

Kittling Ridge Distillery,
Grimsby, Ontario
www.fortycreekwhiskey.com

Kittling Ridge was named 2008
Canadian Distillery of the Year by
Whiskey magazine. Unusually, it
uses pot stills as well as column
stills, and a mashbill mix of rye,
barley, and corn. Built in 1970, it
is part of a winery and was
originally designed to make *eau de
vie*. John Hall, its owner since
1992, brings the skills of a
winemaker to distilling: "I am not
so bound by tradition as inspired by
it". Whiskey critic Michael Jackson
called Forty Creek "the most
revolutionary whiskey in Canada".

BARREL SELECT

BLEND 40% ABV
A complex, fragrant nose, with soft
fruit, honeysuckle, vanilla, and spice.
A similar palate, with traces of nuts
and leather, and a smooth finish with
lingering fruit and vanilla.

GLEN BRETON

Glenora Distillery, Route 19,
Glenville, Cape Breton, Nova Scotia
www.glenoradistillery.com

This is North America's only malt
whiskey distillery. Cape Breton
Island has a strong Scottish
heritage, but the Scotch Whisky
Association has criticized the name
for sounding too much like a Scotch.

Production began in June 1990,
halting within weeks due to lack
of funds. The distillery was later
bought by Lauchie MacLean, who
has re-distilled earlier, inconsistent
spirit, and bottles at 8 or 9 years.

Glenora has its own maltings and
uses Scottish barley that is given a
light peating. The two stills it uses
are made by Forsyths of Rothes.

GLEN BRETON RARE

SINGLE MALT 43% ABV
Butterscotch, heather, ground ginger,
and honey nose. Light to medium body,
with a creamy mouthfeel and notes of
wood, almonds, caramel, and peat.

HIGHWOOD

114 10th Avenue Southeast,
High River, Alberta
www.highwood-distillers.com

Unusually for Canada, Highwood,
founded in 1974, is independently
owned. It makes a range of spirits
and is the only distillery in Canada
using just wheat in its column stills
as the base spirit for its blends. In
2005, it bought the Potter's and
Cascadia distilleries. Potter's is a
separate brand from Highwood.
It is mixed with sherry, and this
flavor adds another dimension.

HIGHWOOD

CANADIAN RYE 40% ABV
A blend of wheat and rye spirits. The
oaky, vanilla-scented nose has traces of
rye spice, orange blossom, and honey.
The palate balances sweetness with
oak tannins and nuts.

HIRSCH

Distribution: Preiss Imports Inc,
San Diego, USA

This whiskey is no longer being
made, but is still available via a
US distributor. Although Canadian
whiskey is often referred to as
"rye," only a few brands contain
more than 50 percent rye spirit,
which is what makes it a true
rye whiskey. Hirsch is one, and
connoisseurs claim it rivals the best
Kentucky ryes. The whiskies are
bottled in small batches, made in
column stills, aged in ex-bourbon
barrels, selected by Preiss Imports,
and bottled by Glenora Distillers,
Nova Scotia *(see Glen Breton)*.

HIRSCH SELECTION
8-YEAR-OLD

CANADIAN RYE 43% ABV
Solvent and pine essence, then sweet
maple sap on the nose. The taste is
sweet, with caramel, dry coconut, and
oak-wood; full-bodied. A bittersweet
finish with a few earthy notes.

SEAGRAM'S VO

SEAGRAM'S 83

SEAGRAM'S FIVE STAR

SEAGRAM'S

Diageo Canada, West Mall,
Etobicoke, Ontario
www.diageo.com

Joseph Emm Seagram's family
emigrated to Canada from Wiltshire,
England, in 1837. In 1864, he was
appointed manager of a flour mill
at Waterloo, Ontario, where he
became interested in distilling as
a way of using surplus grains.
By 1869, he was a partner in the
company, and, in 1883, by which
time distilling was the core
business, he was the sole owner.
The brand 83 commemorates this.
The VO brand stands for 'Very
Own" and was once the best-selling
Canadian whiskey in the world. It
was also Sam Bronfman's favorite
tipple (*see p276*).

Joseph Seagram's sons sold the
company to Bronfman's Distillers
Corporation Ltd., which used
Seagram's stocks of old whiskey
to good advantage once Prohibition
was repealed in 1933. After

further changes of ownership,
the Seagram's portfolio, which
includes other spirits and wines,
was bought out in 2001 by a
partnership between Diageo
and Pernod Ricard. Diageo now
controls the Canadian Seagram's
labels, as well as Seagram's 7
Crown (*see p257*), which is
marketed as an American whiskey.

SEAGRAM'S VO

BLEND 40% ABV

The nose presents pear drops, caramel,
and some rye spice, along with butter.
Light-bodied, sweet, and lightly spicy,
with a slightly acerbic mouthfeel.

SEAGRAM'S 83

BLEND 40% ABV

At one time, this was even more
popular than VO. Now it is a standard
Canadian: smooth and easy to drink.

SEAGRAM'S FIVE STAR

CANADIAN RYE 40% ABV

A perfectly acceptable budget whiskey
of good mixing quality.

TANGLE RIDGE

Alberta Distillery, 1521 34th Avenue Southeast, Calgary, Alberta

This whiskey from the Alberta Distillery *(see p271)* is sweeter than its stablemates, although, like the other Alberta whiskies, it is made exclusively from rye. Introduced in 1996, it is one of the new school of premium Canadian whiskies: aged 10 years in oak, it is then "dumped" and small amounts of vanilla and sherry are added. The spirit is then re-casked for a time to allow the flavors to marry.

Its name comes from a limestone wall in the Canadian Rockies that was discovered by distinguished explorer, artist, and writer Mary Schaffer (1861–1939).

TANGLE RIDGE DOUBLE CASK

CANADIAN RYE 40% ABV
Butterscotch and burned caramel on the nose, velvet-smooth mouthfeel, and a very sweet taste, with a hint of sherry. Lacks complexity, however.

WINDSOR CANADIAN

Alberta Distillery, 1521 34th Avenue Southeast, Calgary, Alberta

One might think that this comes from the Hiram Walker Distillery at Windsor, Ontario; actually, it is made at the Alberta Distillery *(see p271)*. The name is no doubt meant to recall the British Royal Family, but it should not be confused with the Scotch Windsor *(see p180)*. Like other whiskies made at Alberta, Windsor Canadian is exclusively rye-based.

WINDSOR CANADIAN

BLENDED CANADIAN RYE 40% ABV
Honey, peaches, pine nuts, and cloves on the nose. A medium body and a sweet taste, with cereal and wood notes. An unassuming whiskey; great value for money.

WISER'S

Hiram Walker Distillery, Riverside Drive East, Walkerville, Ontario
www.wisers.ca

John Philip Wiser may well have been the first distiller to use the term "Canadian Whiskey" on his label, at the Chicago World's Fair in 1893. He was the son of Dutch immigrants and, in 1864, he took over a distillery on the banks of the St. Lawrence River at Prescott, Ontario, from a business partner. By the early 1900s, it was the third largest distillery in Canada, and its whiskies were being exported to China and the Philippines, as well as the US.

Not long after the death of J. P. Wiser in 1917, the company decided to form a merger with the H. Corby Distillery Company, which was founded by Henry Corby in 1859 at Corbyville in Ontario. Production of Wiser's brands was moved to here in 1932. Three years later, Hiram Walker,

Gooderham & Worts acquired 51 percent of the company. In 1969, Hiram Walker was bought by Allied Lyons. Corby Distillery was closed in 1989, and production of the Corby/Wiser whiskies moved to the Hiram Walker Distillery at Walkerville, which is now owned by Pernod Ricard, as are the brands. Today Wiser's are the fifth best-selling Canadian whiskies in Canada.

WISER'S DELUXE

BLEND 40% ABV
A fruity and spicy nose, with cereal and linseed oil, vanilla, and toffee.

WISER'S SMALL BATCH

BLEND 43.4% ABV
A recent addition to Wiser's range, Small Batch is a full-flavored Canadian whiskey, with vanilla, oak, and butterscotch on the nose and in the taste. The slightly higher strength makes for more flavor and texture.

SUNTORY YAMAZAKI

KIRIN KARUIZAWA

NIKKA PURE MALT

HOKKAIDO

Nikka Yoichi

SAPPORO

AOMORI

Nikka Miyagikyo

SENDAI

HONSHU

Kirin Karuizawa

Suntory Hakushu

Chichibu

TOKYO

Kirin Gotemba

KYOTO

OSAKA

Suntory Yamazaki

HIROSHIMA

SHIKOKU

FUKUOKA

KYUSHU

NAGASAKI

miles
0   100
0   100
kilometers

NIKKA YOICHI

HANYU

Suntory is Japan's biggest whiskey producer and has two large whiskey distilleries at Yamazaki and Hakushu. Its main competitor, Nikka, has two distilleries at Yoichi and Miyagikyo. The drinks company Kirin has whiskey facilities at Karuizawa and Gotemba. The only other whiskey distillery currently operating in Japan is a new one at Chichibu, which started production in 2007. Other Japanese distilleries abandoned whiskey-making after the Asian financial crisis of 1997, either closing down or shifting their focus to making *shochu*, the traditional Japanese potato spirit. Nikka's Yoichi Distillery is situated on Hokkaido, Japan's northernmost island, where the climate is similar to that in Scotland. The others are located on Honshu island in central Japan. Unlike distilleries in Scotland and other parts of the whiskey-making world, Japanese distillers do not trade whiskies with each other for making blends. Instead, they each produce a range of whiskies to make up their own blends.

JAPAN

SUNTORY HIBIKI

SUNTORY HAKUSHU

NIKKA TAKETSURU

NIKKA MIYAGIKYO

KIRIN FUJI-GOTEMBA

ICHIRO'S MALT—ACE OF DIAMONDS

CHICHIBU

*Distribution: Number One Drinks,
Netherconesford, King Street,
Norwich, UK*
www.one-drinks.com

The newest Japanese distillery was
founded in 2007 by Ichiro Akuto,
previously of Hanyu (*see Hanyu*).
A small plant, it features what
might be the only Japanese oak
washbacks in the world. Aging
takes place in a mix of Japanese
oak, ex-bourbon, ex-sherry, and a
few ex-cognac casks. Two styles are
being tested: one for early maturation;
the other for long-term aging.
There are plans to malt (or at least
kiln) with Japanese peat.

CHICHIBU NEWBORN

NEW MAKE 62.5% ABV
This cannot legally be called whiskey,
but gives an idea of the quality to come.
Warming, with the typical unripe fruit
character of new makes, along with
some green pear and jasmine. The palate
is clean with good balancing sweetness.

GOLDEN HORSE

Toa Shuzo, Chichibu
www.toashuzo.com

The Golden Horse brand is still
owned by Toa Shuzo, the firm
which used to own the Hanyu
distillery (*see Hanyu*), and the
whiskies are drawn from its last
remaining stocks. There are
bottlings at 8, 10, and 12 years.
They are rarely seen on the export
markets and at the time of writing
it is unclear what will happen
to the Golden Horse brand once
the Toa Shuzo stocks have
disappeared.

GOLDEN HORSE 8-YEAR-OLD

SINGLE MALT 40% ABV
A quite vibrant nose with light malt
extract notes and some oak. There's
a basic sweetness to this lightly
perfumed malt, which has just a wisp
of smoke on the finish, but a nagging
acidic touch in some bottlings.

HANYU

*Distribution: Number One Drinks,
Netherconesford, King Street,
Norwich, UK*
www.one-drinks.com

The Hanyu distillery was built by
the Akuto family in the 1940s for
producing *shochu*. Full production
of whiskey began in 1980, and
Hanyu enjoyed success until the
financial crisis of 1996 triggered
the end of the whiskey boom in
Japan. The distillery had to close in
2000. When the firm was bought
out in 2003, Ichiro Akuto (*see Ichiro's
Malt*) was given a few months to
buy back as much stock as he could
before the distillery was demolished.

HANYU 1988 CASK 9501

SINGLE MALT 55.6% ABV
Vibrant and intense, with vanilla, some
citrus, and a delicate cocoa-butter
character. The Japanese oak adds a
bittersweet edge. On the palate there's
a rich depth. The finish shows smoke.

ICHIRO'S MALT

*Distribution: Number One Drinks,
Netherconesford, King Street,
Norwich, UK*
www.one-drinks.com

Ichiro's Malt is a range of
bottlings from Ichiro Akuto, who
was the former president of Hanyu
(*see Hanyu*), and the grandson of
Hanyu's founder, Isouji Akuto.
The whiskies are drawn from the
400 casks of Hanyu single malt
that Akuto managed to obtain
after the Hanyu distillery was
closed down.

As a young man, Ichiro Akuto
had worked as a brand manager
at Suntory and developed a strong
feel for marketing. The bulk of
Hanyu's remaining stock is being
released by Akuto in a series of
53 whiskies named after playing
cards. This Card Series, as it is
known, is memorable not only
for its distinctive branding but
also for the high quality of many
of its expressions.

ICHIRO'S MALT—ACE OF SPADES

ICHIRO'S MALT—KING OF DIAMONDS

ICHIRO'S MALT—FIVE OF SPADES

With distillation dates ranging from 1985 to 2000, the Card Series will be eked out until Akuto's new Chichibu single malt is fully established *(see Chichibu)*.

Some of the Card Series has been give a secondary maturation in other types of barrel—Japanese oak, cognac, and sherry among them. Other old Hanyu casks were re-racked into either new wood or American oak. Some are still untouched.

All of the Card Series bottlings are extremely limited, but some are available in export markets. The Number One Drinks Company is the main overseas distributor.

ACE OF DIAMONDS, DISTILLED 1986, BOTTLED 2008

SINGLE MALT 56.4% ABV

Mature nose, with Seville orange, furniture polish, rose, pipe tobacco, and when diluted, sloe and Moscatel. Spicy and chocolatey on the tongue.

ACE OF SPADES, DISTILLED 1985, BOTTLED 2006

SINGLE MALT 55% ABV

The Ace of Spades—sometimes called the Motorhead malt, after the band best known for singing *Ace of Spades*—is one of the oldest in the Card Series. Bold, rich, and fat with masses of raisin, some tarry notes, and molasses. The palate is chewy and toffee-like, with some prune and a savory finish.

KING OF DIAMONDS, DISTILLED 1988, BOTTLED 2006

SINGLE MALT 56% ABV

Complex and nutty, with some dry burlap notes, sandalwood, citrus, pineapple, and pine. Spicy yet floral on the palate with subtle smoke. One of the most highly complex of the Card Series.

FIVE OF SPADES, DISTILLED 2000, BOTTLED 2008

SINGLE MALT 60.5% ABV.

A sweet nose of sandalwood, light raisin, mint, dark chocolate, and some smoke. Water brings out baked muffins, an incense-like note, and white pepper.

GOTEMBA FUJISANROKU 18-YEAR-OLD

FUJI GOTEMBA 15-YEAR-OLD

FUJI GOTEMBA 18-YEAR-OLD

KIRIN GOTEMBA

Shibanta 970, Gotembashi, Shizuoka
www.kirin.co.jp

Spectacularly situated in the cool foothills of Mount Fuji, 2,000 ft (620 m) above sea level, Kirin's Gotemba distillery was built in 1973 as part of a joint venture with the former Canadian giant Seagram *(see p278)*. It contains both a grain-whiskey distillery and a malt plant. Its output is much in line with the light flavors typical of Seagram's house style. In the 1970s this was also the style preferred by the Japanese consumer and was intended to partner Japanese cuisine. That said, the distillery had to supply all the needs of Kirin's blends, so it made three different grain whiskies and three styles of malt, including peated.

Gotemba Distillery is open to the public, but is currently not in production. Its whiskies are available through specialist retailers in Japan and some overseas outlets.

GOTEMBA FUJISANROKU 18-YEAR-OLD

SINGLE MALT 40% ABV

Gotemba's new 18-year-old bottling, Fujisanroku is more floral and restrained than the "old" Fuji Gotemba 18-year-old, with less of the oakiness. Some peach, lily, and a zesty grapefruit note. The honey found in the grain reappears here.

FUJI GOTEMBA 15-YEAR-OLD

SINGLE GRAIN 40% ABV

A very sweet and concentrated nose, almost liqueur-like in its syrupy, honeyed unctuousness. There are touches of sesame, coconut (from oak), and orange zest. The palate is soft and gentle with a melting butter quality. The finish balances oak and sweetness.

FUJI GOTEMBA 18-YEAR-OLD

SINGLE MALT 40% ABV

A light, sweet, and slightly biscuity start shifts into light leather, suggestive of some age. The spirit underneath is sweet and estery, with pear and apple. On the palate there are nuts and a little grip of oak.

Japanese Whiskey

The Japanese whiskey industry was founded in the 1920s with a partnership between Shinjiro Torii, the owner of a firm importing Scotch, and Masataka Taketsuru, a distiller who had studied whiskey-making in Scotland. Torii built Yamazaki *(see p300)*, Japan's first malt distillery, and employed Taketsuru as his distiller. Torii's company grew to become the drinks giant Suntory. In 1934, Taketsuru founded his own distillery at Yoichi; his company became Suntory's great rival, Nikka.

While Taketsuru preferred a heavier, more Scottish, peaty style that he could develop on Japan's northern island, Hokkaido, Torii continued to develop a light style of whiskey in the mild climate of central Japan. These rivals were joined by a handful of other distilleries starting in the 1950s. Like Scotch, the initial success of the Japanese industry was built on blended varieties. By the 1980s, the biggest-selling single whiskey brand in the world was Suntory Royal, which was selling more than 15 million cases in its home market. Also like Scotch, the Japanese whiskey industry's recent surge has come through the burgeoning interest in single malt and a discovery by whiskey lovers around the world of the Japanese purity of flavor.

The Japanese art of distilling is based on an in-depth, quality-driven, scientific knowledge of production. The minutiae of whiskey-making—water, barley, yeast types, mashing, fermentation, distillation, and maturation in different oaks—has been investigated by the Japanese in depth. This allows firms to produce a wide range of different flavors of single malt from a single distillery, which, in turn, takes Japanese single malt away from the Scotch model. Most Japanese single malts today are blends of different flavored malts from the same distillery.

Like other whiskey bars in Japan, The Crane in Tokyo has a distinctly Scottish feel, though a Japanese barman is more likely to wear a bow tie and hand cut ice than his Scottish counterpart. Japanese whiskies are also based on Scotch models, but have their own character.

KARUIZAWA 1986

KARUIZAWA1995: NOH SERIES

KARUIZAWA 1971

KIRIN KARUIZAWA

Maseguchi 1795–2, Oaza, Miyotamachi, Kitasakugun, Nagano
www.kirin.co.jp

Originally a winery, Kirin's second distillery was converted to whiskey-production in the 1950s. Unusually for most Japanese distilleries, it makes only one style of whiskey. While the majority of Japan's malts tend to be light and delicate, Karuizawa has always specialized in a robust, big-hitting, and smoky style. It retains techniques that are rare now even in Scotland: the heaviness of the Golden Promise strain of barley used is accentuated by the small stills, while maturation in ex-sherry casks adds a dried-fruit character.

The distillery is open to the public, but is currently not in production. Official releases are hard to find, although there are many single-cask bottlings by independents.

KARUIZAWA 1986: CASK NO. 7387, BOTTLED 2008

SINGLE MALT 60.7% ABV

Incense on the nose along with wax, crystallized fruits, dried fig, porcini, cassia, tamarind paste, smoke, and spice. The palate needs water to bring forth dried fruits, rosewood, and coffee.

KARUIZAWA 1995: NOH SERIES, BOTTLED 2008

SINGLE MALT 63% ABV

The nose is hugely resinous, mixing tiger balm, geranium, boot polish, prune, and heavily oiled woods. There's also mint chocolate with water. The palate is lightly astringent and needs a drop of water to release the tannic grip. An exotic and floral whiskey.

KARUIZAWA 1971: CASK NO. 6878, BOTTLED 2008

SINGLE MALT 64.1% ABV

Beeswax and sandalwood becoming fragrant with tea, molasses, and smoke. The palate is resinous with walnut, long pepper, and Bolivar cigar.

NIKKA SINGLE COFFEY MALT

NIKKA ALL MALT

NIKKA WHISKEY FROM THE BARREL

NIKKA—GRAIN & BLENDS

Nikka 1, Aobaku, Sendaishi, Miyagiken; Kurokawacho 7–6, Yoichimachi, Yoichigun, Hokkaido
www.nikka.com

Japan's second-largest distillery company was founded in 1933 by Masataka Taketsuru. This charismatic distiller had learned the art of whiskey-making in Scotland—at Longmorn in Speyside and Hazelburn in Campbeltown. Back in Japan, he initially worked with Shinjiro Torii, helping to establish Yamazaki distillery *(see p300),* which is now owned by Suntory. He then went to Hokkaido island in Japan, where conditions were closer to those in Scotland, and founded Yoichi distillery.

Taketsuru's company, Nikka, now part of Asahi Breweries, and operates two malt distilleries at Yoichi and Miyagikyo. It also has grain plants and an ever-growing portfolio of styles, including blends and single malts. Like its domestic rivals, it produces all the whiskies for its in-house blends.

In recent years, Nikka has been focusing on the export market. Although its blends are available overseas, the thrust of its commercial push has been through its single-malt range branded as Nikka Miyagikyo *(see p292)* and Nikka Yoichi *(p296).* Its blends include the Pure Malt Series *(opposite)* and Nikka Taketsuru Pure Malt range *(p293).*

NIKKA SINGLE COFFEY MALT

MALTED BARLEY MASH 55% ABV
This unusual, if not unique, whiskey is made by distilling a 100 percent malted barley mash in a Coffey still. As a result, no one is sure if it is a malt or a grain. The nose is gentle, sweet, and rounded, with notes of banana, honey, coconut, persimmon, and dry grass. On the palate it is chewy and sweet, with hints of nutmeg, cinnamon, peach, and vanilla.

NIKKA PURE MALT RED

NIKKA PURE MALT WHITE

NIKKA PURE MALT BLACK

NIKKA ALL MALT

BLENDED MALT 40% ABV

A blend of pot still malt and 100 percent malt from a Coffey still. An intriguing mix of sweet and dry oak on the nose alongside some banana. The palate is soft and unctuous.

NIKKA WHISKEY FROM THE BARREL

BLEND 51.4% ABV

Nikka's award-winning blend of malts and grain is given further aging in first-fill bourbon casks. The nose is upfront, and slightly floral, with good intensity, peachiness, and a lift akin to rosemary oil and pine sap. The palate is lightly sweet, with some vanilla, a hint of cherry, and plenty of spiciness on the finish. This is a top blend.

NIKKA PURE MALT SERIES

This trio of "pure" (blended) malts are drawn from the wide range of different styles made at Nikka's two malt distilleries, Yoichi and Miyagikyo:

NIKKA PURE MALT RED

BLENDED MALT 43% ABV

Red is light and fragrant, with faint hints of pineapple, fresh apple, pear, and a gentle almond-like oakiness. This delicacy continues on the palate, along with a light citric finish.

NIKKA PURE MALT WHITE

BLENDED MALT 43% ABV

The smokiest member of the trio, with plenty of salt spray, fragrant dried lavender, and soot on the nose, and the same herbal, oily note as From The Barrel. The palate is rich and soapy.

NIKKA PURE MALT BLACK

BLENDED MALT 43% ABV

Rich and sweet, with lots of black fruits, dark chocolate, and a little polished oak. More substantial than the Red, with an extra layer of smokiness and greater depth and power on the palate. Peppery on the finish.

Whiskey Tour: Japan

Tokyo is a good starting point for the whiskey lover. The city has
myriad whiskey bars and excellent train connections to the
distilleries at Chichibu, Karuizawa, Hakushu, and Gotemba.
Further afield, Suntory's flagship distillery, Yamazaki, is also
accessible by train, and can be easily combined with a visit to Kyoto
or Osaka.

JAPAN

TOUR STATISTICS

DAYS: 8	LENGTH: 300 miles (480 km)	DISTILLERIES: 5
TRAVEL: Shinkansen (bullet trains), local trains		REGION: Central Honshu, Japan

THE STILLROOM AT CHICHIBU

DAY 1: CHICHIBU DISTILLERY

1 **Chichibu**, Japan's newest distillery,
started by Ichiro Akuto, has no visitor
facilities yet, but whiskey enthusiasts can
arrange a personal tour by contacting the
distillery in advance. Chichibu city is 90
minutes by train from Tokyo's Ikebukuro
station. A taxi can be taken from the station
to the distillery, which is outside the city.
(+81 (0)494 62 4601)

DAYS 2–3: KIRIN'S KARUIZAWA DISTILLERY

2 The Kirin Distillery at **Karuizawa** is a
small whiskey-making plant. It is open
to visitors and incorporates an art gallery.
Karuizawa is a spa town that is 65–80
minutes by the Nagano Shinkansen
from Tokyo Station, or by local
train connections from Chichibu
(3–5 hours). There are numerous
spa resort hotels near to the
distillery for those wishing
to make an extended break.
(+81 (0) 267 32 2006)

MATSUE

Chugoku Expy

YAMAZAKI **5**

KYOTO

Chugoku Expy

KOBE

OSAKA

FINISH

OKAYAMA

Sanyo Expy

HIROSHIMA

FUKUOKA

Shinjiro Torii is revered in
Japan as the founder of
Suntory, which operates
the Yamazaki and Hakushu
distilleries on this tour.

DAY 4: SUNTORY'S HAKUSHU DISTILLERY

3 Situated in the southern Japanese Alps, the Suntory Distillery at **Hakushu** is surrounded by a lovely nature reserve. The nearest station is Kobuchizawa, which is accessible by slow trains from Karuizawa, or 2 hours 30 minutes by express train (JR Chou Line) from Tokyo's Shinjuku Station. After exploring the distillery and museum you can try some of the hiking trails that run through the forest. It is then best to return to Tokyo to get a fast train connection to Gotemba.
(+81 (0) 551 35 2211)

HAKUSHU DISTILLERY

DAYS 5–6: KIRIN'S GOTEMBA DISTILLERY

4 The town of **Gotemba** is the start of one of the main routes up Mount Fuji. It is also home to Kirin's Gotemba Distillery. Many visitors come to visit both. They start climbing Fuji in the afternoon to reach the 8th or 9th stage by nightfall, where there are huts for pilgrims. The summit of Fuji is reached at dawn. After descending, it is possible to get a bus back to Gotemba to visit the distillery. Although not the prettiest of distilleries, this has good facilities for visitors and a spectacular view of Fuji from its rooftop terrace. The train from Tokyo's Shinjuku Station takes about 1 hour 40 minutes.
(+81 (0) 550 89 4909)

MOUNT FUJI AND TRAIN

DAYS 7–8: SUNTORY'S YAMAZAKI DISTILLERY

YAMAZAKI DISTILLERY

5 It is best to take the bullet train to either Kyoto or Osaka to make a base for visiting the Suntory Distillery **Yamazaki**, the company's original and flagship whiskey-making plant. Local trains from either city stop at J. R. Yamazaki station. The distillery is a 10-minute walk from the station. There are extensive visitor facilities, including an impressive tasting bar with exclusive bottlings. The distillery offers well-heeled clients a chance to buy a cask through its Owner's Cask scheme. There is also a traditional Shinto shrine to visit.
(+81 (0) 75 961 1234; www.theyamazaki.jp/en/distillery)

Map

SENDAI

FUKUSHIMA

NIIGATA

Banetsu Expy

Tohoku Expy

Joetsu Expy

Kanetsu Expy

START

NAGANO

Nagano Shinkansen Line

2

KARUIZAWA

1

CHICHIBU

3

HAKUSHU

JR Chou Line

TOKYO

JR Asagiri Line

HONSHU

GOTEMBA

4

NAGOYA

Tokaido Shinkansen Line

miles
0   30

0   30
kilometers

NIKKA MIYAGIKYO 10-YEAR-OLD

NIKKA MIYAGIKYO 12-YEAR-OLD

NIKKA MIYAGIKYO 15-YEAR-OLD

NIKKA MIYAGIKYO

Nikka 1, Aobaku, Sendaishi, Miyagiken
www.nikka.com

Also known as Sendai after its nearest main town, Nikka's Miyagikyo was the second distillery built by Nikka founder, Masataka Taketsuru. Today, it has a malt distillery with eight stills, a grain plant with two different set-ups, and extensive warehousing. Like most Japanese distilleries, it makes a wide range of spirit styles. The predominant one—which is most common in the single-malt bottlings—is lightly fragrant and softly fruity. But there are some peaty examples, too. The distillery is open to the public, and is home to Nikka's Coffey Grain Whiskey.

A new release is a Miyagikyo without an age statement, which is made to be drunk *mizuwari*-style (with water). The nose is floral and light, and the palate shows a touch of golden raisins.

NIKKA MIYAGIKYO 10-YEAR-OLD
SINGLE MALT 45% ABV
Typical of the main distillery character, this has an attractive floral lift: lilies, hot gorse, lilac, with a touch of anise in the background. The palate shows balanced, crisp oak, some butterscotch notes, and a pine-like finish.

NIKKA MIYAGIKYO 12-YEAR-OLD
SINGLE MALT 45% ABV
The extra two years fill out the nose with flowers, giving way to soft tropical fruits, such as mango and persimmon, as well as richer vanilla pod character. Good structure with a wisp of smoke.

NIKKA MIYAGIKYO 15-YEAR-OLD
SINGLE MALT 45% ABV
Bigger, with raisiny ex-sherry cask notes alongside the toffee and super-fruits. The gentle distillery character is in evidence, along with a hint of the fresh floral nature of youth. The richest of the expressions.

NIKKA TAKETSURU 17-YEAR-OLD

NIKKA TAKETSURU 12-YEAR-OLD

NIKKA TAKETSURU 21-YEAR-OLD

NIKKA TAKETSURU

Nikka 1, Aobaku, Sendaishi, Miyagiken; Kurokawacho 7–6, Yoichimachi, Yoichigun, Hokkaido
www.nikka.com

This small range of blended (vatted) malts is named after the founder of Nikka, Masataka Taketsuru. Like the Pure Malt range, it is made up of component whiskies from the firm's two sites although, given the range of malts produced at each of them, it would be difficult to guess which element came from which distillery.

NIKKA TAKETSURU 17-YEAR-OLD

BLENDED MALT 43% ABV

The biggest-selling expression in the range, the 17-year-old has all the complexity you would expect from mature stock. There's more obvious smoke at work than in the 12-year-old: some cigar-box aromas, varnish, and light leather. When diluted, a fresh

tropical-fruit character comes out. This is what leads on the palate, before the peat smoke begins to assert itself. A clean, precise, and complex whiskey.

NIKKA TAKETSURU 12-YEAR-OLD

BLENDED MALT 40% ABV

A relatively light nose, with touches of honey, cut flowers, and gentle orchard fruits. Clean, with aromas derived from ex-bourbon casks. The palate is an interesting and successful balance between some very concentrated sweet spirit and clean nutty oak with baked apples and almond.

NIKKA TAKETSURU 21-YEAR-OLD

BLENDED MALT 43% ABV

With this multi-award winner, the smoke is immediate while the spirit behind is thicker, richer, and darker: ripe berries, cake mix, oak, and a touch of mushroom or truffle indicative of age. Fruit syrups, figs, prune, smoke, and multi-layered, complex whiskey.

Nikka's Miyagikyo Distillery is set among the mountains and cherry orchards of Miyagi Prefecture to the northeast of Tokyo. Company legend has it that master distiller Masataka Taketsuru came here in the 1960s, tasted the water, and pronounced it good.

NIKKA YOICHI 10-YEAR-OLD

NIKKA YOICHI 12-YEAR-OLD

NIKKA YOICHI 20-YEAR-OLD

NIKKA YOICHI

Kurokawacho 7–6, Yoichimachi,
Yoichigun, Hokkaido
www.nikka.com

Although Yoichi's malts are most definitely Japanese, they do have close resemblances to their cousins in Scotland—the whiskies of Islay and Campbeltown in particular. A wide range of styles is made, but Yoichi is famous for its complex, robust, oily, and smoky malts.

The most youthful Yoichi, without an age statement, is intended as an introduction to the distillery and should be drunk *mizuwari*-style (with water) or *sodawari* (with soda). It is crisp and clean with light smoke, a hay-like note, and a sweet spot in the middle of the palate.

NIKKA YOICHI 10-YEAR-OLD

SINGLE MALT 45% ABV

There's a hint of maltiness in here, unusual for a Japanese single malt. Salt spray and light smoke on the nose initially, with some caramelized fruit notes. Yoichi's oiliness coats the tongue while the smoke changes from fragrant to sooty with dried flowers toward the finish.

NIKKA YOICHI 12-YEAR-OLD

SINGLE MALT 45% ABV

The understated qualities have been banished here. This is classic Yoichi— big, deep, robust, and complex. The peatiness adds an earthy character to the coal-like sootiness. Poached pear and baked peach give a balancing sweetness, offset by smoke, licorice, and heather.

NIKKA YOICHI 20-YEAR-OLD

SINGLE MALT 52% ABV

A huge, uncompromising nose, where the oiliness apparent in all the expressions is now to the fore. Deck oil or gun oil, seashores, kippers, and the funky notes of great maturity—leather, cedar, yew, and leaf-mold. Clean turmeric and coriander spiciness. The palate is massive, with decent mouthwatering acidity balancing the dry oak and smoke. Still fresh on the finish.

Nikka's Yoichi Distillery on Hokkaido island was founded by Masataka Taketsuru in 1933; the first Yoichi whiskies were being sold by 1940.

SUNTORY HAKUSHU 12-YEAR-OLD

SUNTORY HAKUSHU 10-YEAR-OLD

SUNTORY HAKUSHU 18-YEAR-OLD

SUNTORY HAKUSHU

*Torihara 2913–1, Hakushucho,
Komagun, Yamanashi
www.suntory.co.jp*

Located in a forest high in the Japanese Alps, Hakushu was once the largest malt distillery in the world, with two huge stillhouses producing a vast array of different makes for the Suntory blenders. These days, only one of the stillhouses is operational, but the ethos of variety is still adhered to. Nowhere else offers such an array of shapes and sizes of pot stills. The Suntory bottlings of Hakushu as a single malt seem to echo the location, being light, gentle, and fresh, though there are also smoky and heavy versions.

SUNTORY HAKUSHU 12-YEAR-OLD

SINGLE MALT 43.5% ABV
The bestselling Hakushu, the 12-year-old's nose is very cool, with cut grass and a growing mintiness. There's a hint of linseed oil, suggestive of youth. The palate is sweet but quite slow, with that minty, grassy character being given a little depth by apricot fruitiness and extra fragrance by a camomile note.

SUNTORY HAKUSHU 10-YEAR-OLD

SINGLE MALT 43% ABV
Light in character with a slight floral note, an almost pine-like aroma, and just a hint of smoke.

SUNTORY HAKUSHU 18-YEAR-OLD

SINGLE MALT 43% ABV
Balanced and slightly restrained. Once again a vegetal note, this time more like a tropical rain forest. There's also plum, mango, hay, and fresh ginger. Good acidity and toasty oaky finish. There's a general fresh acidity, cut with a generous delicate sweetness. The palate is direct and shows more toasty oak.

SUNTORY HIBIKI

*Torihara 2913–1, Hakushucho,
Komagun, Yamanashi
www.suntory.co.jp*

Japan's most powerful distiller was founded in 1923 by Shinjiro Torii. Its fortunes were built on blended whiskies based on malts from its two distilleries: Yamazaki and Hakushu. Although there is a move toward single malts globally, Suntory's blends, such as the Hibiki range, are still regarded as very important.

The Hibiki 12-year-old is the most recent member of the stable. It has a nose akin to plum, pineapple, lemon, then fudge and fresh, sappy oak. It is sweet and thick on the tongue with a menthol-like finish.

SUNTORY HIBIKI 17-YEAR-OLD
BLENDED MALT 43% ABV

This, the original Hibiki, has a soft, generous nose featuring super-ripe fruits, light peatiness, a hint of heavy florals (jasmine), and citrus. On the palate, there's caramel, black cherry, vanilla, rosehip, and light oak structure.

SUNTORY HIBIKI 21-YEAR-OLD
BLENDED MALT 43% ABV

Deep and sensual, with the density and musty nature of great aged whiskey. Black butter, sandalwood, and an intriguing green herbal thread. Perfumed and hinting at light smoke. The palate is thick and ripe with plenty of flowers and dried fruits. Sweet and long on the tongue.

SUNTORY HIBIKI 30-YEAR-OLD
BLENDED MALT 43% ABV

This multi-award winner (it won Best Blend in the World two years in a row at the World Whiskies Awards) is huge in flavor, with a compote of different fruits: Seville orange, quince paste, quite assertive wood, and walnuts, followed by aniseed and fennel, and a deep spiciness. The palate is sweet and velvety, with Old English Marmalade to the fore, along with sweet, dusty spices.

The secrets of ... Yamazaki

When Shinjiro Torii bought land near a small village on the old road between Kyoto and Osaka in 1921 he had a grand vision. There was no reason, he believed, that Japan couldn't make its own whiskey. And he would create it here, at Yamazaki.

The only thing missing in his great scheme was someone with whiskey-making knowledge. He found this in Masataka Taketsuru, a young scientist who had gone to Scotland to study chemistry, returning home with a Scots wife and a passion for whiskey making. Yamazaki began distilling in 1924. Five years later Japan's first whiskey, Shirofuda (White Label), was launched.

Yamazaki is one of the world's most remarkable distilleries, and experimentation has never ceased. This is in part due to the Japanese distillers' idiosyncrasy in using only their own whiskies for their blends. Thus, the more complex the blend,

the more whiskies are required, so constant innovation is essential. Yamazaki is also at the forefront of the new, export-driven Japanese whiskey industry. The domestic boom is long over, but distillers are courting a new generation. Though weaned on *shochu* (a traditional spirit), young Japanese, like their international contemporaries, are interested in single malt, individuality, and premium.

Who knows if Torii's vision ran to selling his whiskies in direct competition with Scotch, or if he dreamed that they would one day be seen as the equals of Scottish single malts. The fact is that they are.

▲ **PLACE OF POWER**
Yamazaki is the place where, in the 16th century, Sen no Rikyu, the creator of *cha-noyu* (tea ceremony), built his first tea house. The waters of three rivers merge here. Torii needed water and wanted humidity to help with maturation; this wooded site also simply felt right to him.

▲ **SUNTORY'S FLAGSHIP**
The original rustic wood and slate building is long gone, as are the first stills. Today the distillery is a rather grand, imposing red brick structure topped with two large pyramids

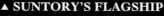

◄ WASHBACKS

Yamazaki processes unpeated, lightly peated, and heavily peated malt. The two mash tuns produce different types of wort, and various yeast strains are used. Wort and yeast come together in the washbacks, and fermentation begins, although the length varies.

▲ TASTING NEW MAKE

Suntory's most recent preference for direct firing and smaller stills adds weight to the new make spirit. This new make is a medium-bodied, fruity malt with a subtle depth in the middle of the palate. Future bottlings are likely to contain a whiff of smoke.

◄ STILLS

The stillhouse at Yamazaki contains a remarkable collection of stills, which are mostly run in tandem. They include steam-fired stills of differing shapes and sizes. This distillery is renowned for its willingness to experiment; the smaller, direct-fired stills were added in 2005.

▲ MATURATION

A broad range of woods is used for maturation, including new oak, ex-bourbon, and ex-sherry casks. There is even a whiskey that has been matured in casks formerly used to age plum liqueur. The official number of Yamazaki whiskey varieties has never been revealed

THE YAMAZAKI 12-YEAR-OLD

THE YAMAZAKI 10-YEAR-OLD

THE YAMAZAKI 25-YEAR-OLD

SUNTORY YAMAZAKI

Yamazaki 5–2–2, Honcho, Mishimagun, Osaka
www.suntory.co.jp

Yamazaki claims to be the first malt distillery built in Japan, and was home to the fathers of the nation's whiskey industry, Shinjiro Torii and Masataka Taketsuru. Like Hakushu, it produces a huge range of styles. The official single-malt bottlings concentrate on the sweet fruity expression. Single-cask bottlings have also been released. Most of the older expressions have been aged in ex-sherry casks, but there is the occasional Japanese-oak release for Japanese malt converts.

THE YAMAZAKI 12-YEAR-OLD

SINGLE MALT ABV 43%

The mainstay of the range, the 12-year-old is crisp, with a fresh nose of pineapple, citrus, flowers, dried herbs, and a little oak. The palate is sweet and filled with ripe soft fruits and a hint of smoke.

THE YAMAZAKI 10-YEAR-OLD

SINGLE MALT 40% ABV

The lightest of the range. The dominant aroma is one of sweet spices, light apple, and grape. There is some light oakiness on the palate.

THE YAMAZAKI 25-YEAR-OLD

SINGLE MALT 43% ABV

A huge, concentrated, almost balsamic sherried nose, with sweet raisin,

SUNTORY VINTAGE 1984

THE CASK OF YAMAZAKI 1990 SHERRY BUTT

THE YAMAZAKI 18-YEAR-OLD

pomegranate, molasses, fig jam, prune, rose petal, musk, leather, and burning leaves. The palate is bitter and quite tannic. It's very dry.

SUNTORY VINTAGE 1984

SINGLE MALT 56% ABV

An award-winning, heavily sherried expression. Very dark with a balsamic nose, wood bark, yew, plum pudding, and espresso coffee. The palate has black cherry, molasses toffee, and prune. Interesting mix of bitter and sweet, with strong tannins.

THE CASK OF YAMAZAKI 1990 SHERRY BUTT

SINGLE MALT 61% ABV

One of a regular series of single cask releases, this has an almost opaque

mahogany color and a nose filled with date, prune, and figgy sherried notes. Some peatiness adds complexity. The palate is grippy and autumnal with light woodsmoke, walnut, espresso (with sugar), and a long, firm finish that ends with a touch of molasses.

THE YAMAZAKI 18-YEAR-OLD

SINGLE MALT 43% ABV

With age, Yamazaki acquires more influence from oak. The estery notes of younger variants are replaced by ripe apple, violet, and a deep, sweet oakiness. This impression continues on the palate with a mossy, pine-like character and the classic Yamazaki richness in the middle of the mouth. This is an extremely classy whiskey.

REST OF
THE WORLD

European Whiskey

Outside the key whiskey nations of Scotland and Ireland, there is a smattering of whiskey distilleries across Western Europe. Northern countries such as Germany and Sweden have been distilling "aqua vitae" from grains for centuries, mainly in the form of vodka, gin, akvavit, korn, and schnapps. Southern countries such as France have long traditions of distilling fruits into eaux-de-vie.

In recent years, with global interest in whiskey increasing, some of these mostly small-scale, family-owned European distilleries have expanded into whiskey-making. In the north, such operations are often an extension of existing beer breweries, whereas in the south, the stills used for brandy may also be used for whiskey. For that reason, southern European whiskies often turn out fruitier than their northern counterparts. The use of a range of former wine casks for maturation also adds significantly to the sweet flavors of southern European whiskies.

The output of most European distilleries is small, but with a dedicated local following, so whiskey releases can sell out within a few days. Apart from the Swedish Mackmyra, few are available outside their own countries. Other tiny whiskey operations include Weutz (Austria), Fisselier (France), Brasch, Gruel, Höhler, Zaiser, and Rabel (Germany), Maison Les Vignettes and Bauernhof (Switzerland).

Further east, Turkey's state-owned brand Tekel cannot technically be called "whiskey" because it is made from a mash of malted barley and rice. Kizlyarskoye in Dagestan, Russia, was founded in 2003. There are plans to launch various expressions, including a malt and a grain whiskey.

PENDERYN PEATED

PENDERYN SHERRYWOOD

PENDERYN AUR CYMRU

PENDERYN

WALES

Penderyn, near Aberdare
www.welsh-whiskey.co.uk

Currently the only whiskey distillery in Wales, Penderyn was named "Microdistillery Whiskey of the Year" in 2008 by leading American whiskey magazine *Malt Advocate*. It is indeed micro, producing only one cask a day. After a slow start, the distillery is now acknowledged worldwide as making exquisite whiskies. In his *Whiskey Bible 2009*, Jim Murray describes Penderyn as "a prince of a Welsh whiskey truly fit for the Prince of Wales". And it was HRH Prince Charles who opened the distillery to the public in June 2008, eight years after the first distillate ran off the stills.

Whiskey-making in Wales started long before that: according to Penderyn, the Welsh may have been making whiskey (*"gwirod"*)

in the 4th century. It is also said that the American whiskey pioneers Evan Williams and Jack Daniel were from Welsh stock.

Penderyn whiskey is matured in ex-bourbon casks, mainly from Buffalo Trace *(see p222)* and Evan Williams *(see p228)*. The contents are then re-casked into ex-Madeira barrels—hence the sweet taste. The label does not state a specific age.

PENDERYN AUR CYMRU
SINGLE MALT 46% ABV
Zesty and fresh, this malt is prickly, fruity, and bitter-sweet.

PENDERYN PEATED
SINGLE MALT 46% ABV
Sweet, aromatic smoke followed by vanilla, green apples, and refreshing citrus notes.

PENDERYN SHERRYWOOD
SINGLE MALT 46% ABV
Rich dark fruits and caramel intermingle with green apples and hints of sugared almonds.

THE ENGLISH WHISKEY CO.

ENGLAND

St. George's Distillery, Harling Road, Roudham, Norfolk
www.englishwhiskey.co.uk

According to Alfred Barnard, in his 1887 tome *Distilleries of the United Kingdom and Ireland*, England had at least four distilleries in the 1800s. These had all gone by the turn of the 20th century and it was not until 2006 that pot stills produced malt spirit in England again, thanks to The English Whisky Co., which hired distilling legend Iain Henderson to set things up. The first bottling is expected to be released around Christmas 2009.

ENGLISH WHISKY CO. CHAPTER 3

NEW MAKE 40% ABV

It's not whiskey yet, as it has not been matured, but the new make is very fruity. Iain Henderson also made some peaty spirit in 2007.

FRYSK HYNDER

THE NETHERLANDS

Us Heit distillery, Snekerstraat 43, 8701 XC Bolsward, Friesland
www.usheitdistillery.nl

Us Heit (Frisian for "Our Father") was founded as a brewery in 1970. In 2002, owner Aart van der Linde, a whiskey enthusiast, decided to start distilling whiskey with barley from a local mill. It is the same barley from which Us Heit beer is made and it is malted at the distillery. A 3-year-old single malt, Frysk Hynder, has been released in limited quantities every year since 2005. Us Heit uses different types of cask for maturing, from ex-bourbon barrels to wine casks and sherry butts.

FRYSK HYNDER SHERRY MATURED

SINGLE MALT 43% ABV

Sweetish and remarkably soft for a young whiskey. Tasty, with a beautiful full body and distinctive sherry notes.

MILLSTONE

THE NETHERLANDS

Zuidam, Weverstraat 6, 5111 PW, Baarle Nassau
www.zuidam-distillers.com

What started as a gin distillery some 50 years ago is now a company with a second generation of the Zuidam family at the helm. It produces beautifully crafted single malts, alongside excellent young and old *jenevers*, as the Dutch call their gin. The Millstone 5-year-old single malt whiskey was introduced in 2007, to be followed by an 8-year-old sibling. Zuidam uses ex-bourbon as well as ex-sherry casks to mature its whiskey. A 10-year-old expression is in the making.

MILLSTONE 5-YEAR-OLD

SINGLE MALT 40% ABV

Delicate tones of fruit and honey combined with vanilla, wood, and a hint of coconut. Rich honey sweetness, delicate spicy notes, and a long vanilla oak finish.

VALLEY

THE NETHERLANDS

Asschatterweg 233, 3831 JP Leusden
www.valleibieren.nl/whiskey

In December 2007, the first 3-year-old single malt whiskey from this old-style farm distillery saw the light of day. It's a real cottage industry, having begun its life in 2002 when owner Bert Burger started to experiment with distilling on his kitchen table. It took him until 2004 to find an official brewery and distillery. Assisted by his son, Burger now makes Valley Whiskey, a whiskey liqueur, and several organic beers. The output is very small, and distribution is local.

VALLEY 3-YEAR-OLD

SINGLE MALT 40% ABV

Fruity, with hints of apricot, cloves, and dried fruit. Slightly metallic, with licorice in the finish.

This traditional Dutch windmill at Zuidam distillery in the Netherlands is put to good use in slowly grinding the malted barley for Millstone whiskey.

THE BELGIAN OWL

BELGIUM

The Owl Distillery, Rue Sainte Anne 94, B4460 Grâce-Hollogne
www.belgianwhiskey.com

Master Distiller Etienne Bouillon founded this distillery in the French-speaking part of Belgium in 2004. He uses home-grown barley and first-fill bourbon casks to produce a 3-year-old single malt whiskey. The first batch was bottled in the fall of 2007. The Belgian Owl Distillery was formerly known under the names Lambicool and PUR.E.

BELGIAN SINGLE MALT

SINGLE MALT 46% ABV
This non chill-filtered malt offers vanilla, coconut, banana, and ice cream, topped with fig, followed by a crescendo of other flavors such as lemon, apples, and ginger. A long finish, with ripe fruits and vanilla.

GOLDLYS

BELGIUM

Graanstokerij Filliers,
Leernsesteenweg 5, 9800 Deinze
www.filliers.be

The Flemish distiller Filliers has been making grain spirits since 1880. In 2008 it surprised the whiskey world by launching two whiskies it had been maturing for years. Their name comes from the Lys River, which is nicknamed the "Golden River" because of the flax retted (soaked) in it. Goldlys uses malt, rye, and corn, and is distilled twice, first in a column still, then in a pot still—a process that is quite similar to that used to make bourbon. The spirit is then matured in former bourbon casks.

GOLDLYS 10-YEAR-OLD

MIXED GRAIN WHISKEY 40% ABV
Spicy, sweet fruit, licorice, and a touch of wood. Some pepper in the short, dry finish.

GOUDEN CAROLUS

BELGIUM

Brouwerij Het Anker, Guido Gezellelaan 49, B-2800 Mechelen
www.hetanker.be

The Belgian beer brewery Het Anker—makers of the famous Gouden Carolus Tripel beer—first ventured into whiskey-making in 2003. The current owner, Charles Leclef, is the fifth generation of the de Van Breedam family to own the company. In 2008, 2,500 bottles of Gouden Carolus Single Malt were bottled and distributed.

GOUDEN CAROLUS

SINGLE MALT 40% ABV
Nicely balanced for a young whiskey, with fruity, woody notes.

ARMORIK

FRANCE

Distillerie Warenghem, Route de Guingamp, 22300 Lannion, Bretagne
www.distillerie-warenghem.com

The Warenghem Distillery was founded in 1900 to produce apple cider and fruit spirits. It was not until 99 years later that the owners decided to start making other types of spirits, including malted beers and whiskey. There are now two types of whiskey made here: Armorik, a single malt, and WB (Whiskey Breton), a blend. The type of casks used for maturation is not specified.

ARMORIK WHISKEY BRETON

SINGLE MALT 40% ABV
A young spirit, Armorik is fresh and very spicy, with a salty tang and a dry, oaky influence in the finish.

EDDU SILVER

EDDU GOLD

EDDU GREY ROCK

EDDU

FRANCE

*Des Menhirs, Pont Menhir, 29700
Plomelin, Bretagne
www.distillerie.fr*

This is from the land of *menhirs*
(standing stones) and Calvados
distilled from apples. The Des
Menhirs Distillery started life as
a manufacturer of apple cider in
1986, but in 1998 branched out
into whiskey. Most fruit distillers
that venture into whiskey-making
use their existing equipment to
distill whiskey on the side. Not so
this company: Des Menhirs built
a separate still for the exclusive
production of whiskey, which it
distills not from barley but from
buckwheat (*eddu* in Breton). The
distillery currently carries three
different expressions of its Eddu
whiskey—Silver, Gold, and Grey
Rock. The types of cask used are
not specified. In 2006 the distillery
was extended and now houses a
shop as well.

EDDU SILVER

BUCKWHEAT WHISKEY 40% ABV

Aromatic rose and heather on the
nose. Fruity, with a touch of honey,
marmalade, and some nutmeg. Velvety
body, with vanilla and oak in the finish.

EDDU GOLD

BUCKWHEAT WHISKEY 43% ABV

Almost identical to its Silver sibling—
with the same flowers and spices—but
higher in alcohol.

EDDU GREY ROCK

BLEND 40% ABV

A blended variety containing 30
percent buckwheat. Orange and
apricot flavors combine with broom
flower. A faint sea breeze is framed by
a hint of cinnamon. Balanced flavors
and a long, long finish.

GLANN AR MOR
FRANCE

Crec'h ar Fur, 22610 Pleubian,
Bretagne
www.glannarmor.com

Glann ar Mor means "by the sea" in Breton. The distillery opened in 2005 after eight years of planning. On November 17, 2008, the contents of one cask were emptied and bottled, rendering 305 bottles. The resulting unpeated whiskey is referred to as an Artisan Single Malt "inherited from the genuine Celtic tradition." It is not colored or chill-filtered. A second bottling, containing a peated expression, is due in November 2009.

GLANN AR MOR
SINGLE MALT 46% ABV
Fairly complex, with ginger, vanilla, and a whiff of the sea, then grassy and leafy. Big fruit, including ripe apples and pears, framed in fine oak.

GUILLON
FRANCE

Hameau de Vertuelle, 51150 Louvois,
Champagne
www.whiskey-guillon.com

The Guillon Distillery is located in the Champagne region of France, and was purpose-built in 1997 to produce whiskey. It started distilling in 1999, distinguishing itself by the use of a variety of ex-wine casks for maturation. For the first maturation period, ex-Burgundy casks are used. After that, the whiskey is finished for six months in casks that used to contain sweet wines like Banyuls, Loupiac, and Sauternes. Guillon bottles a premium blend at 40% ABV. The various single malts are bottled at 42, 43, and 46% ABV.

GUILLON NO. 1
SINGLE MALT 46% ABV
Highly aromatic, fruity, and elegant, thanks to the unusual finish in sweet-wine casks.

P&M
FRANCE

Domaine Mavela, Brasserie Pietra,
Route de La Marana, 20600
Furiani, Corsica
www.brasseriepietra.com

P&M is a fruitful cooperation between two companies on the Mediterranean island of Corsica. Founded as a brewery in 1996, Pietra produces the mash that is distilled at Mavela. The pure malt whiskey is aged in casks made of oak from the local forest. Other spirits produced at Mavela include P&M Blend and P&M Blend Supérieur. Cask type and age are not specified.

P&M PURE MALT
MALT 42% ABV
This complex, aromatic whiskey has a subtle aroma of honey, apricot, and citrus fruit, and a rich flavor.

UBERACH
FRANCE

Bertrand Distillery, 3 rue du
Maréchal Leclerc, BP 21,
67350 Uberach, Alsace
www.distillerie-bertrand.com

The Bertrand brandy and liqueur distillery in Alsace dates from 1874 and has been run by the same family ever since. The Alsace region is blessed with particularly fertile, alluvial soil and the area around the distillery produces a range of fruits that are used in some of Bertrand's spirits. The company has recently branched out to produce beer and two non-filtered whiskies, Uberach Single Malt and Uberach Single Cask.

UBERACH SINGLE MALT
SINGLE MALT 42.2% ABV
Floral, fruity, and spicy, with black tea and hints of plums, as well as wax, and tobacco notes. Aromatic with good balance and an oaky, fruity finish.

WAMBRECHIES

FRANCE

1 Rue de la Distillerie,
59118 Wambrechies,
Nord-Pas-de-Calais
www.wambrechies.com

Wambrechies was founded in 1817 as a *jenever* (gin) distillery and is one of only three stills left in the region. It continues to produce an impressive range of *jenevers*, as well as one malt whiskey and a *jenever* beer. Wambrechie whiskies are bottled at three and eight years old, with the younger whiskey consisting of a lighter, floral blend and the older having a deeper, spicy character.

WAMBRECHIES 8-YEAR-OLD

SINGLE MALT 40% ABV
Delicate nose, with aniseed, fresh paint, vanilla, and cereal notes. Smooth on the palate, with a fine malty profile. Spicy finish, with powdered ginger and milk chocolate.

HOLLE

SWITZERLAND

Hollen 52, 4426 Lauwil, Basel
www.single-malt.ch

Until July 1, 1999, it was strictly forbidden in Switzerland to distill spirit from grain, which was considered a food staple. After a change in the law, the Bader family, who had been making fruit spirits for a long time, started to distill from grains, and became the country's first whiskey producer.

HOLLE

SINGLE MALT 42% ABV
Delicate aromas of malt, wood, and vanilla, with a flavor of wine. There are two varieties: one is matured in a white-wine cask, the other in a red-wine cask. A cask strength version is bottled at 51.1% ABV.

SINGLE LAKELAND

SWITZERLAND

Zürcher Nägeligässli 7,
2562 Port

The Zürcher Brewery started distilling whiskey in 2003. The spirit matures in Oloroso sherry casks for three years. The first bottling was released in 2007 and is no longer available. There was another bottling in 2008, and more are planned.

SINGLE LAKELAND

SINGLE MALT 42% ABV
DISTILLED 2005 BOTTLED 2008
Perfectly balanced. Flavors of tannin and smoke from its three-year maturation in Oloroso sherry casks. Smooth vanilla and cinnamon aromas.

WHISKEY CASTLE

SWITZERLAND

Schlossstrasse 17, 5077 Elfingen
www.whiskey-castle.com

Käsers Schloss (the Swiss name of the distillery) is owned by Ruedi and Franziska Käser. The couple started producing whiskey in 2000 and expanded the business in 2006 to include themed events such as whiskey dinners and whiskey conferences at their premises. The brand name of their whiskey in English is Whiskey Castle, and there are a number of expressions, including Doublewood, which has a whiff of chestnut, and Edition Käser, which is matured in new Bordeaux casks.

WHISKEY CASTLE FULL MOON

SINGLE MALT 43% ABV
Made from smoked barley during the full moon, it is a young whiskey with a sweetish aroma and taste.

REISETBAUER 7-YEAR-OLD

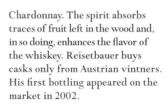

REISETBAUER 12-YEAR-OLD

WALDVIERTLER J. H. SPECIAL PURE RYE MALT "NOUGAT"

NOCK·LAND
AUSTRIA

*Wolfram Ortner, Untertscherner Weg 3,
9546 Bad Kleinkirchheim
www.wob.at*

Ortner specializes in luxury
products, especially cigars, glasses,
and fruit liqueurs. The company
started producing Nock-Land
whiskey in 1996, named after the
Nockberg Mountains nearby.
This blend is made from malted
barley and matured in new casks
made from a wide variety of
European oaks—Limousin, Allier,
Nevers, and Vosges among them—
as well as American oak.

NOCK·LAND WHISKEY
MALT 48% ABV
Sweet and malty with heavy notes of
spice and tobacco. Rounded off with
a faint whiff of honeycomb.

REISETBAUER
AUSTRIA

*Axberg 15, 4062 Kirchberg-Thening
www.reisetbauer.at*

Hans Reisetbauer initially made
a name for himself as a quality
distiller of fruits, carrying a fine
range of spirits. In 1995, he
decided to start distilling single
malt whiskey. In so doing he lays
claim to be the first Austrian
whiskey distiller—although
the same claim is made by the
Waldviertler Roggenhof
Distillery *(see next entry)*.

Keen to exploit his farmland
to its full potential, Reisetbauer
even grows his own barley; his
first crop of summer-brewing
barley was harvested in July 1995.

Malting and fermentation
both take place on Reisetbauer's
premises. The wash is distilled
twice in copper pot stills. For
maturation, Reisetbauer uses
casks that previously contained
Trockenbeerenauslese and

Chardonnay. The spirit absorbs
traces of fruit left in the wood and,
in so doing, enhances the flavor of
the whiskey. Reisetbauer buys
casks only from Austrian vintners.
His first bottling appeared on the
market in 2002.

REISETBAUER 7-YEAR-OLD
SINGLE MALT 43% ABV
Delicate and multi-layered on the
nose, with slightly roasted aromas
reminiscent of hazelnuts and dried
herbs. Pleasant notes of bread and
cereals on the palate. Slightly smoky,
with fine spice.

REISETBAUER 12-YEAR-OLD
MALT 48% ABV
Similar to the 7-year-old, with greater
emphasis on fruit notes from the wine
barrels used for maturation.

WALDVIERTLER
AUSTRIA

*Whiskeydestillerie J. Haider OG,
3664 Roggenreith 3
www.roggenhof.at*

The Waldviertler Roggenhof
Distillery was founded in 1995
and, like Reisetbauer *(see previous
entry)*, claims to be the first
whiskey distillery in Austria. It
produces five different whiskies.
Two are single malts—J. H. Single
Malt and J. H. Special Single Malt
"Karamell." The other three are
rye whiskies—J. H. Original Rye,
J. H. Pure Rye Malt, and J. H.
Special Pure Rye Malt "Nougat."

The company uses casks made
from Manharstberger oak trees
that grow in the local region. The
whiskies are matured for between
three and twelve years and offered
as single-cask bottlings. Alcohol
percentages vary from 41–54%
ABV, and the flavors range from
light vanilla to caramel, chocolate,
and nougat.

WALDVIERTLER J. H. SPECIAL SINGLE MALT "KARAMELL"

Johann Haider, the master distiller and joint owner of Waldviertler Roggenhof, has also created the "Whiskey Experience" on the premises, consisting of an audio-visual tour and a café in which to sample various whiskies in coffee. Seminars are given on Haider's book *Fascination Whiskey*. Other spirits made here include vodka, gin, and brandy, but—unusually for a Continental European distillery—whiskey is the main focus.

WALDVIERTLER J. H. SPECIAL PURE RYE MALT "NOUGAT"

RYE WHISKEY 41% ABV

A gentle, sweet taste of honey, harmonizing perfectly with the light vanilla taste.

WALDVIERTLER J. H. SPECIAL SINGLE MALT "KARAMELL"

SINGLE MALT 41% ABV

Smoky and dry, with an intense caramel flavor.

GOLD COCK
CZECH REPUBLIC

Jelinek Distillery,
Razov 472, 76312 Vizovice
www.rjelinek.cz

Jelinek Distillery was founded at the end of the 19th century, and acquired the Gold Cock brand from Tesetice, a Czech distillery that no longer exists. For its two expressions—Red Feathers and a 12-year-old—Jelinek uses Moravian barley and water is sourced from an underground well that is rich in minerals. The type of cask used is not specified.

GOLD COCK RED FEATHERS

BLEND 40% ABV

Light and grainy, slightly metallic, and sweetish.

PRINTER'S
CZECH REPUBLIC

Stock Plzen, Palirenska 2,
32600 Plzen
www.stock.cz

Stock Plzen was founded in the 1920s and is the best-known spirits producer in the Czech Republic, with a high-profile, high-volume ethos. The company makes 40 different spirits, including Printer's Whiskey, which it claims is made using traditional Scotch whisky production methods. Another offering is Whiskey Cream Stock, which is a cream liqueur made from Printer's Whiskey and bottled at 17% ABV.

PRINTER'S 6-YEAR-OLD

BLEND 40% ABV

A delicate peated whiskey aged in small oak barrels for a faster maturation.

AMMERTAL
GERMANY

Hotel Gasthof Lamm, Jesinger
Hauptstrasse 55/57, 72070 Tübingen
www.lamm-tuebingen.de

Volker Theurer, the owner of Hotel Gasthof Lamm, is also a distiller and makes a whiskey known as Black Horse Original Ammertal for a local market. The mash consists of 70 percent malted barley and 30 percent rye and wheat. It is aged in German oak ex-bourbon barrels and ex-sherry casks. A 5-year-old expression is due to be bottled under the label "Schwäbischer Single Malt."

ORIGINAL AMMERTAL

BLEND 40% ABV

Slightly nutty with some coffee notes and sweet grains.

FRÄNKISCHER
GERMANY

Reiner Mösslein, Untere Dorfstrasse 8, 97509 Zeilitzheim
www.weingeister.de

Reiner Mösslein Distillery produces just one malt whiskey—Fränkischer—and a variety of schnapps. The whiskey is distilled from a blend of home-grown barley and grain. The spirit then matures in charred-oak casks for five years, lending it a smoky aroma.

FRÄNKISCHER 5-YEAR-OLD
GRAIN WHISKEY 40% ABV
Chocolate and smoke on the nose, leading on to earthy flavors with oaky notes.

GLEN ELS
GERMANY

Hammerschmiede Spirituosen, Elsbach 11A, 37449 Zorge
www.hammerschmiede.de

The Hammerschmiede company was founded in 1984, and its first distillation of single malt whiskey took place in fall 2002.
The spirit is stored in a smithy dating from 1250, and matures in Bordeaux and German oak casks that previously contained sherry, port, Marsala, or Madeira. Glen Els is only available as a single cask expression bottled at cask strength.

GLEN ELS AMOROSO SHERRY CASK
SINGLE MALT 42.8% ABV
Immediately fruity, with a gentle smell of oak and a hint of vanilla and chocolate. The taste has some fruitcake, gentle vanilla, and toffee.

GRÜNER HUND
GERMANY

Fleischmann, Bamberger Strasse 2, 91330 Eggolsheim-Neuses
www.fleischmann-whiskey.de

The Fleischmann brandy distillery was founded in 1980 on the premises of the original family company—a grocery and tobacco shop. In 1996, after nearly 14 years of experimentation with whiskey-distilling, the company launched their first whiskey expression. There are now seven single cask malt whiskies available—Blaue Maus, Spinnaker, Krottentaler, Schwarzer Pirat, Grüner Hund, Austrasier, and Old Fahr—all bottled at 40% ABV.

GRÜNER HUND
SINGLE MALT 51% ABV
Roasted almonds and cocoa on the nose. Dark chocolate, chiles, and gingerbread on the tongue, with a dry and medium-long finish.

SLYRS
GERMANY

Bayrischzellerstrasse 13 , 83727 Schliersee, Ortsteil Neuhaus
www.slyrs.de

Slyrs was founded in 1999 and makes a credible whiskey, which is distributed by Lantenhammer, a schnapps distillery located in the same village. Slyrs is bottled after maturing for an unspecified time in new American white-oak barrels. In October 2008, Raritas Diaboli, a special cask-strength edition, was launched.

SLYRS
SINGLE MALT 43% ABV
Some flowery aromas and spicy notes deliver a nice and easy dram. The taste varies according to the vintage.

BRAUNSTEIN
DENMARK
Braunstein, Carlsensvej 5, 4600 Koge
www.braunstein.dk

A microbrewery located in an old warehouse in Koge harbor, Braunstein uses a small still to make spirit from malted barley. The resulting spirit is clean, fresh, and fruity. Maturation takes place in ex-Oloroso sherry casks. A new edition of the whiskey is added each year. The distillery also manufactures aquavit, herbal spirits, schnapps, and a beer called BB Amber Lager. Tastings are held each month.

BRAUNSTEIN
SINGLE MALT (VARIABLE ABV)
Fruits, raisins, and chocolate come to the fore in this single malt that varies in strength from batch to batch.

TEERENPELI
FINLAND
Teerenpeli, Hämeenkatu 19, Lahti
www.teerenpeli.com

The first Teerenpeli Brewery was founded in May 1995 in Restaurant Teerenpeli, and the beer won several medals. In 2002 the new brewery and distillery were opened in Restaurant Taivaanranta. The brew house is situated in the dining room, while the fermentation and distilling equipment are in the cellar, along with a visitor center. Casks of Teerenpeli new malt whiskey are available for sale to private individuals or corporate groups.

TEERENPELI 3-YEAR-OLD NO. 001
MALT 43% ABV
A lot of grain (barley), vanilla, and oak wood with a slightly thick body.

GOTLAND
SWEDEN
Gotland Whiskey AB, Sockerbruket, 62254 Romakloster
www.gotlandwhiskey.se

Many decades ago Sweden had a thriving whiskey industry. Along with Hven *(see next entry)* and Mackmyra *(see p318)*, the new Gotland Distillery—currently being built at the old Roma Sockerfabrik (sugar factory)—completes a trio that might revive the olden times. The distillery is the project of a company called Gotland Whiskey AB, and its first release is expected in 2012. The name Isle of Lime has been chosen for the forthcoming whiskey because a huge part of the island of Gotland is made up of limestone.

HVEN
SWEDEN
Backafallsbyn AB, Isle of Hven, 26013 S:t Ibb
www.hven.com

Whiskey is in the making at the Backafallsbyn AB micro-distillery on the island of Hven, in the Oresund Strait between Sweden and Denmark. Two different Spirits of Hven should be available from 2011. According to the makers' assessment of the new make spirit, one has fruit, raspberries, vanilla, and chocolate, followed by rhubarb and raisins. The other has sand, seaweed, and smoked fish, backed by honey sweetness mixed with apples and licorice. The owners of the micro-distillery are also planning to produce organic vodka and rum in the future.

MACKMYRA PRELUDIUM 05

MACKMYRA PRELUDIUM 06

MACKMYRA RESERVE ELEGANT SWEDISH OAK

MACKMYRA

SWEDEN

Mackmyra, Bruksgatan 4,
81832 Valbo
www.mackmyra.se

Mackmyra was founded in 1999
by the Swedish engineer Magnus
Dardanell and a group of friends.
The stills were made at Forsyth's
of Rothes in Speyside, Scotland.
The washbacks are Swedish, and
the mash tun is German.

   Mackmyra launched Preludium
01, the first bottling in a limited
series, in 2006. Preludiums 02,
03, 04, and 05 followed in rapid
succession. Preludium 06 was
released in December 2007,
followed by Special 01 in June
2008. The distillery also offers
single cask Reserve bottlings. These are
matured in small casks— 6.6-gallon
(30-liter)—which speeds up the
maturation process.

MACKMYRA PRELUDIUM 05

SINGLE MALT 48.4% ABV

Marzipan, custard, and a light citrus
note on the nose. Flavors of: crème
brûlée, bitter chocolate, and lemon
zest. A bit oily; slightly metallic and
grainy in the finish—creamier when
mixed with water.

MACKMYRA PRELUDIUM 06

SINGLE MALT 50.5% ABV

Fruity, with aromas of lemon, pear,
banana, and honey. Gentle hints of
caramel, roast oak, and pepper. A
distinctive smoky character, with
undertones of juniper. The finish
brings sweetness, roast oak cask,
smoke, and a touch of salt.

MACKMYRA RESERVE
ELEGANT SWEDISH OAK

SINGLE MALT 57% ABV

The Swedish oak Reserve is matured
for just three years, but is dark in color,
with a powerful nose and a spicy
character on the palate.

DYC PURE MALT

DYC FINE BLEND

DYC 8-YEAR-OLD

DYC

SPAIN

Beam Global España SA, Pasaje Molino del Arco, 40194 Palazuelos de Eresma, Segovia
www.dyc.es

The first whiskey distillery in Spain was founded in 1959 close to Segovia and started producing whiskey in 1963. It stands next to the Eresma River, famous for the excellent quality of its water. The distillery is currently owned by Fortune Brands, which distributes all its wines and spirits under its subsidiary Beam Global.

DYC (which stands for Destilerías y Crianza del Whiskey) comes in three versions. There is an unaged expression, called Fine Blend, and an 8-year-old, which are both blends of various grains. The Pure Malt, which has no age statement, is a blended malt.

The spirits mature in American oak barrels and are primarily sold on the home market. The Spanish tend to drink it in a mix with cola and ask at the bar for a "whiskey-dyc," pronouncing it "whiskey-dick."

DYC 8-YEAR-OLD

BLEND 40% ABV

Floral, spicy, smoky, grassy, with a hint of honey and heather. Smooth, creamy mouthfeel; malty with hints of vanilla, marzipan, apple, and citrus. A bittersweet, long, smooth finish.

DYC PURE MALT

BLENDED MALT 40% ABV

Sophisticated, fragrant bouquet with hints of citrus, sweetness, honey, and vanilla. Full-bodied, rich malt flavor. The finish is long, sophisticated, and subtle, with hints of heather, honey, and fruit.

DYC FINE BLEND

BLEND 40% ABV

Clean, with a hint of fruit, spice, and toasted wood. Malty, spicy, smooth, and creamy mouthfeel. The finish is smoky and spicy.

Asian Whiskey

India is the largest consumer of whiskey in the world. Along with other parts of Asia, its spirits industry was founded by European expatriates in the 18th century. Western spirits such as gin and whiskey were known throughout these countries as "Locally Made Foreign Liquor" (LMFL). In India, the British Raj named it "Indian Made Foreign Liquor" (IMFL).

To this day, the raw materials and processes for LMFL/IMFL are not defined by law. However, a brand of "Indian whiskey" made from molasses alcohol and whiskey essence is not allowed to bear the name "whiskey" within the EC and many other export markets. The Thai Mekhong brand used to be described as "whiskey," but is now marketed as "rum." Most LMFL and IMFL spirits are made in industrial ethanol plants. However, there are a few grain and pot still malt distilleries in India and Pakistan, and the Speyside-based Forsyth Group is currently helping to build new malt whiskey distilleries in Taiwan, South Korea, and China.

Categories of Asian whiskey:

Extra Neutral Alcohol (ENA) Made by fermentation and distillation in continuous stills, typically of molasses, rice, millet, buckwheat, or barley. Basic Asian whiskies are made from ENA mixed with whiskey essence and other artificial flavorings.

Blended Whiskey A mix of ENA whiskey and locally produced malt whiskey and/or bulk imported whiskey. Where an age statement is given, this is the age of the imported whiskey. The product does not pass the EC definition as "whiskey."

Malt Whiskey Blends of 100 percent malt whiskies, domestic or foreign, qualify as "whiskey" in the EC if matured for at least three years.

Single Malt Whiskey Made from malted barley in a single distillery. So long as this is matured for at least three years, it meets EC regulations.

MURREE

PAKISTAN

Murree Distillery, National Park Road, Rawalpindi
www.murreebrewery.com

Murree began life in 1860 as a brewery serving the needs of British troops stationed in the Punjab, and today it still makes the leading brand of beer in Pakistan. It was built in Ghora Gali, 6,000 ft (1,830 m) above sea level in the foothills of the Western Himalayas, and took its name from a nearby hill station. In 1889, the company built another brewery in Rawalpindi, and it was here, 10 years later, that the distillery was installed.

By this time, Rawalpindi was part of Pakistan, but a dispensation was granted to the non-Muslim owners to distill alcoholic drinks "for visitors and non-Muslims." This makes it the only distillery of alcoholic beverages in a Muslim country; the oldest continuing industrial enterprise in Pakistan;

and one of the oldest public companies on the subcontinent.

The barley comes from the UK and is malted in floor maltings and Saladin boxes. The four large open-air wash stills have stainless-steel pots and copper heads and condensers. Two spirit stills are under cover. Some of the spirit is filled into cask, most into large vats (some made from Australian oak), and matured in cellars equipped with a cooling system.

MURREE'S CLASSIC 8-YEAR-OLD

SINGLE MALT 43% ABV

A flowery nose and finish, somewhat green, with a hard-candy taste. Unlikely to be pure malt whiskey.

MURREE'S RAREST 21-YEAR-OLD

SINGLE MALT 43% ABV

This is the oldest whiskey to have been produced in Asia and has developed and deepened the Murree key notes with a big dose of wood-extractive flavors.

8PM

INDIA

Owner: Radico Khaitan
www.radicokhaitan.com

Launched as recently as 1999, 8PM had the singular distinction of selling a million cases in its first year (it now sells 3 million). The brand owner is Radico Khaitan, which describes itself as "one of India's oldest and largest liquor manufacturers." It is owned and managed by veteran distiller Dr. Lalit Khaitan and his son Abhishek. The company owns other whiskey brands, including Whytehall *(see p325)*, and it has recently formed a partnership with Diageo, the world's largest drinks conglomerate, to produce Masterstroke *(see p324)*.

The company's headquarters are at Rampur Distillery, Uttar Pradesh. Established in 1943, it is now a gigantic unit with a capacity of over 20 million gallons (90 million liters) of alcohol a year

in three distinct operations: a small malt distillery, a recently opened grain distillery, and a molasses distillery making ENA *(see p320)*, anhydrous alcohol, ethanol, and gasohol (which is mixed with gasoline and used as fuel). As well as whiskey, Radico Khaitan produces rum, brandy, gin, and vodka.

8PM CLASSIC

BLEND

Made from "a mix of quality grains," this has a core that promises *"thaath"* (boldness, opulence) and "the reach of a man to the dream world."

8PM ROYALE

BLEND

A blend of Indian spirits and mature Scotch malt whiskies.

AMRUT INDIAN SINGLE MALT CASK STRENGTH

AMRUT PEATED INDIAN SINGLE MALT

AMRUT SINGLE MALT

AMRUT

INDIA

Amrut Distilleries, 36 Sampangi Tank Road, Bangalore, Karnataka
www.amrutdistilleries.com

The family-owned company of Amrut Distilleries was founded in 1948 by Shri J. N. Radhakrishna Jagdale to supply bottled liquor to the Ministry of Defence. He was succeeded in 1976 by his son, Shri Neelakanta Rao Jagdale, the current chairman, who has focused on innovation, product quality, and transparency in the IMFL industry.

In 2002, Amrut experimented with the sale of miniatures in Indian restaurants in the UK. It was very successful in Glasgow, and the brand now features at European whiskey fairs.

In Hindu mythology, the *amrut* was a golden pot containing the elixir of life. The whiskey of the same name is made from barley grown in the Punjabi foothills of the Himalayas. This is malted in

Jaipur and distilled in small batches 3,000 ft (900 m) above sea level in Bangalore, where it is also matured in ex-bourbon and new oak casks and bottled without chill-filtration.

AMRUT INDIAN SINGLE MALT CASK STRENGTH

SINGLE MALT 61.9% ABV

Lightly fruity and cereal-like, with the bourbon cask introducing toffee. More woody, spicy, and malty with water. Similar in profile to a young Speyside malt.

AMRUT PEATED INDIAN SINGLE MALT

SINGLE MALT 62.78% ABV

Cereal and kippery smoke on the nose; oily, with salt and pepper. The taste is sweet and malty, with a whiff of smoke in the finish.

AMRUT SINGLE MALT

SINGLE MALT 40% ABV

A fresh and fruity nose, with a trace of spice, ginger, and anise. The taste is smooth and sweet, the finish is short.

ANTIQUITY
INDIA
Owner: United Spirits
www.unitedspirits.in

Antiquity is owned by the long-established Indian trading firm Shaw Wallace, now part of United Spirits. It is India's most expensive whiskey, and won a gold award at the World Beverage Competition in 2007 in the "Scotch Whisky" category. It is, in fact, a blend of Scotch whisky, Indian malt whiskey, and ENA.

United Spirits is the largest spirits company in India, and among the top three in the world. It is also the spirits division of the massive United Breweries Group.

ANTIQUITY
BLEND 42.8% ABV
A mild, biscuity nose, with some well-integrated fruit and floral notes. The taste is sweet overall, with some sulfur traces in the medium-length finish.

ARISTOCRAT
INDIA
Jagatjit Industries,
91 Nehru Place, New Delhi
www.jagatjit.com

Aristocrat comes from Jagatjit Industries—the third largest spirits producer in India, and a leading producer of IMFL from grains rather than molasses. The company was founded in 1944 by L. P. Jaiswal, under the patronage of the Maharaja of Kapurthala, Jagatjit Singh, with the guiding philosophy "Spirit of Excellence." Aristocrat is widely referred to as "AC" ("A" for "Aristo," "C" for "Crat") and a brand with this abbreviated name recently joined the portfolio.

ARISTOCRAT
BLEND 42.8% ABV
This is certainly not a pure malt whiskey. Indeed, some commentators believe it might be an IMFL with a dash of malt extract.

BAGPIPER
INDIA
Owner: United Spirits
www.unitedspirits.in

"The World's No.1 Non-Scotch Whiskey" sells nearly 14 million cases a year. An IMFL, probably made from molasses alcohol and concentrates, it was launched by the United Spirits subsidiary Herbertson's in 1987 and, in its first year, sold 100,000 cases. The brand has always been closely associated with Bollywood, India's huge film-production industry, and has successfully won accreditation from many movie stars. The company also broadcasts a weekly *Bagpiper* show on TV, and sponsors talent-spotting programs.

BAGPIPER GOLD
BLEND 42.8% ABV
Gold is the premium expression of Bagpiper, but it still has a somewhat artificial taste and is best drunk with a mixer like cola.

BLENDERS PRIDE
INDIA
Owner: Pernod Ricard
www.pernod-ricard.com

Since it fell under the ownership of Pernod Ricard, the brand has been neck and neck with Royal Challenge (see p325) as the bestseller in its sector. It is a premium IMFL (made from Scotch malts and Indian grains), whose name comes from a story about the master blenders who exposed a cask of whiskey to the warmth of the sun at regular intervals. The delicate sweetness and aromatic flavor of the blend are testimony to the success of their experiment.

BLENDERS PRIDE
BLEND 42.8% ABV
A smooth and rich mouthfeel, with a sweet taste that gives way to a disappointingly dull finish.

MCDOWELL'S NO. I RESERVE

MCDOWELL'S SINGLE MALT

IMPERIAL BLUE
INDIA

Owner: Pernod Ricard
www.pernod-ricard.com

Imperial Blue is Pernod Ricard's second bestselling brand in India, at over 3.8 million cases a year. Previously a Seagram's brand (and still labeled as such), it benefited hugely from Pernod Ricard's acquisition of Seagram in 2001, jumping from producing under half a million cases to over a million by 2002. Imperial Blue hit the headlines in 2008 when some bottles in Andhra Pradesh were found to be understrength. It later transpired that they had been sabotaged by disgruntled workers.

IMPERIAL BLUE
BLEND 42.8% ABV

In spite of the "grain" in its name, Imperial Blue is a blend of imported Scotch malt and locally made neutral spirit. It is light, sweet, and smooth.

MASTERSTROKE
INDIA

Owner: Diageo Radico
www.radicokhaitan.com
www.diageo.com

Masterstroke De Luxe Whiskey, an IMFL priced for the "prestige" category, was launched by Diageo Radico in February 2007. The company is a joint 50:50 venture between Radico Khaitan Ltd *(see p321),* "India's fastest-growing liquor manufacturer," and the world's largest drinks company, Diageo. It is their first joint venture. Within three months the brand was being endorsed by Bollywood superstar Shah Rukh Khan.

MASTERSTROKE
BLEND 42.8% ABV

A rich nose and mouthfeel, lent by a liberal amount of Blair Athol single malt. Well-balanced, with the light finish characteristic of IMFLs.

MCDOWELL'S
INDIA

Owner: United Spirits
www.unitedspirits.in

Scotsman Angus McDowell founded McDowell & Co. in Madras in 1826 as a trading company specializing in liquor and cigars. In 1951 it was acquired by Vitall Mallya, owner of United Breweries. McDowell's No.1 was launched in 1968, and currently sells over 9 million cases a year, making it the world's fourth largest-selling whiskey.

A malt whiskey distillery was commissioned by McDowell & Co. at Ponda, Goa, in 1971. It employs the distilling regime used for Scotch malt, with maturation in ex-bourbon casks for around three years. It is claimed that the heat and humidity of Goa leads to a more rapid maturation.

The product is described as "the first-ever indigenously developed single malt whiskey in Asia."

Three main expressions are available: two blends, called No. I Reserve and Signature Rare, and a single malt. McDowell also produces "the world's first diet whiskey," as it calls it. This is a blend of "reserve" whiskey and garcenia, an Indian herb reputed to control cholesterol levels and burn off fat.

MCDOWELL'S NO.I RESERVE
BLEND 42.8% ABV

"Blended with Scotch and Select Indian Malts," this has a nose of dried figs and sweet tobacco and, later, prunes and dates. A sweet taste initially, then burned sugar and a short finish.

MCDOWELL'S SINGLE MALT
SINGLE MALT 42.8% ABV

A true single malt, with a fresh cereal and fruity nose and a sweet, pleasantly citric taste, not unlike a young Speyside.

ROYAL CHALLENGE
INDIA
Owner: United Spirits
www.unitedspirits.in

This "blend of rare Scotch and matured Indian malt whiskies" is owned by Shaw Wallace, a part of United Spirits since 2005. It is described as "the iconic" premium Indian whiskey and, until 2008, it was also the bestselling premium Indian whiskey, but is now severely challenged by Blenders Pride.

ROYAL CHALLENGE
BLEND 42.8% ABV

A soft, rounded nose, with traces of malt, nuts, caramel, and a light rubber note. These aromas translate well in the taste at full strength. With water, it remains dense and full-bodied but the taste, diluted, is not as heavy. Very sweet, slightly nutty, and mouth-drying, but with a longish finish.

ROYAL STAG
INDIA
Owner: Pernod Ricard
www.pernod-ricard.com

Seagram's Royal Stag broke the million-cases-a-year barrier in 2000. Early the following year it was acquired by Pernod Ricard, when the Seagram empire was carved up between the French company and Diageo. The new owner continued the Seagram name, adopting the brand as its leader in the "prestige" sector of the vigorous Indian market. It also improved the blend, which is a combination of blended Scotch malts and Indian grain whiskies. Current sales are in excess of 5 million cases a year.

ROYAL STAG
BLEND 42.8% ABV

For a standard blend, this shapes up well: fresh and sweet to start, with spice and cereal notes, and a firm finish.

SIGNATURE
INDIA
Owner: United Spirits
www.unitedspirits.in

The recently introduced Signature Rare Aged Whiskey comes from the McDowell's stable, owned by United Spirits, and has the slogan "Success is Good Fun." It is a blend of Scotch and Indian malt whiskies and is the fastest-growing brand in the company's portfolio, selling over 600,000 cases in 2006–7. It has also won a clutch of international awards, including a gold in the Monde Selection 2006.

SIGNATURE
BLEND 42.8% ABV

A rich nose, with a distinct medicinal note. Straight, the taste is surprisingly sweet, with smoky and medicinal undertones, becoming less sweet with water. Relatively light in body, with a distinct peaty, smoky edge.

WHYTEHALL
INDIA
Owner: Radico Khaitan
www.radicokhaitan.com

Another Radico Khaitan brand *(see p 321)*, Whytehall became a part of the portfolio after Radico bought out the stake of its erstwhile joint venture partner, Bacardi, in Whytehall India Limited in July 2005.

Whytehall is made in the company's distillery at Hyderabad, and now sells half a million cases per annum. The brand won a silver medal at the International Wine and Spirit Competition 2007 and a gold medal at the Monde Selection in Belgium in 2008.

WHYTEHALL
BLEND 42.8% ABV

A superior IMFL blend of aged Scotch malts and Indian spirits.

Australasian Whiskey

Australia and New Zealand have a small number of whiskey distilleries producing malt. Some of these malts have been favorably compared with the best from Scotland. Tasmania, in particular, has ideal conditions for whiskey production. However, Australasian whiskies can be hard to track down outside the continent, as the markets are mainly domestic.

Until 1938, Australasia was the largest export market for Scotch whisky, and it is hardly surprising that enterprising settlers of Scots descent established distilleries in Australia and New Zealand during the 19th century. Most were illicit farm stills, but there were a couple of short-lived industrial ventures, like the New Zealand Distillery, Dunedin (1867–73), and the Crown Distillery, Auckland, New Zealand (1865–79), which both opened in response to the halving of duties on locally made spirits. They soon closed when duties rose again, following pressure on the government by Scottish banks, which were payrolling the construction of the country's railways.

The first attempt to revive the distilling tradition in New Zealand was Wilson's Willowbank Distillery at Dunedin (1964–95), whose Lammerlaw brand became reasonably well known in Europe and East Asia, as well as in its home market. During the 1990s, however, the focus for revival was in Australia, particularly in Tasmania, where five distilleries opened—though one (the Small Concern Distillery) has since closed. The reasons for this are a combination of climate—Tasmania has the purest air in the world, and copious clean water dumped on the island by the Roaring Forties—and plenty of fertile country for growing barley. A further three distilleries are now operating successfully in Southern Australia. These concerns are all "boutique" operations—small by choice and design—but they are now producing malt whiskies with a uniquely Australasian character.

BAKERY HILL PEATED MALT

BAKERY HILL CASK STRENGTH PEATED MALT

BAKERY HILL DOUBLE WOOD

BAKERY HILL

AUSTRALIA

28 Ventnor Street,
North Balwyn, Victoria
www.bakeryhilldistillery.com.au

"Single malt whiskey is more than a craft, it's our passion." So says David Baker, chemist and founder (together with his wife, Lynn) of Bakery Hill Distillery near Melbourne, Victoria. Their first spirit flowed in 2000.

The barley strains Australian Franklin and Australian Schooner are sourced locally and sometimes malted over locally cut peat. The wash is brewed in 1,000-liter (264-gallon) batches and distilled twice in a single copper pot still. Maturation is on-site in barrels from Jack Daniel Distillery *(see p238).* The ambient temperature at Bakery Hill is 10–30°C (50–86°F), so maturation is quicker than in Scotland.

Baker was determined to prove that top-quality malt whiskey could be made in Australia, and he has succeeded: his single cask, non chill-filtered malts are already winning awards. At the moment, however, they are only available from the distillery.

BAKERY HILL PEATED MALT

SINGLE MALT 46% ABV

A sweet and oaky balance of peat and malt on the nose. These aromas carry through in the taste.

BAKERY HILL CASK STRENGTH PEATED MALT

SINGLE MALT 59.88% ABV

Intense peatiness on the nose, with dark cherry. The taste is sweet (toffee, honeycomb), with some salt and smoke. It has a good texture.

BAKERY HILL DOUBLE WOOD

SINGLE MALT 46% ABV

Finished in French oak ex-wine casks after ex-bourbon-cask maturation. Apricot, coconut, and plum, then syrup, fruitcake, and cloves. Sweet taste, with orange marmalade and oak.

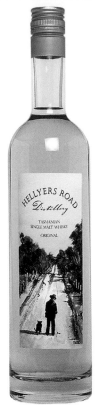

LARK'S SINGLE MALT

LARK'S PM

HELLYERS ROAD

AUSTRALIA

153 Old Surrey Road, Burnie, Tasmania
www.hellyersroaddistillery.com.au

Hellyers Road, opened in 1999, and owned by the Betta Milk Cooperative, now has about 3,000 ex-bourbon casks under maturation; it also produces a Tasmanian barley-based, pot-still vodka. The experience gained in running a milk processing plant has provided owner Laurie House with all the knowledge he needs to run this modern and highly automated plant.

The distillery is named after Henry Hellyer who, in the 1820s, created the first road into the interior of Tasmania, the same road that now leads to the distillery.

HELLYERS ROAD ORIGINAL

SINGLE MALT 46.2% ABV

A light-bodied, pale-colored malt, un-tinted and non chill-filtered. The nose is fresh and citric, with vanilla notes.

LARK

AUSTRALIA

14 Davey Street, Hobart, Tasmania
www.larkdistillery.com.au

The modern revival of whiskey-making in Australia began in Tasmania, with the opening of this small distillery in Hobart in 1992. It was the brainchild of Bill Lark, who, the story goes, was inspired by a bottle of single malt Scotch consumed during a fishing trip with his father-in-law, which prompted the question "why is nobody making malt whiskey in Tasmania today?" Lark realized that the island has all the right ingredients: plenty of rich barley fields, abundant pure soft water, peat bogs, and a perfect climate for maturation.

Lark located his distillery on the harborfront at Hobart, and is now assisted by his wife Lyn and daughter Kristy. They use locally grown Franklin barley, 50 percent of it re-dried over peat. The

Distilling Act 1901 required a minimum still capacity of 600 gallons (2,700 liters)—Lark's first task was to have this law amended so that they could use smaller stills. The distillery produces 10 to 12 22-gallon (100-liter) barrels of whiskey a month, as well as a range of other spirits, including liqueurs using the indigenous pepperberry spice. The malt is bottled from single casks at three to five years. Unusually, all Lark's products are Kosher Certified.

LARK'S SINGLE MALT

SINGLE MALT 58% ABV

Malty and lightly peated, with peppery notes. A smooth mouthfeel, with rich malt, apples and oak-wood, and some spice in the finish.

LARK'S PM

BLENDED MALT 45% ABV

Sweet and smoky on the nose and in the mouth; clean and lightly spicy. This can be regarded as a well-made "barley schnapps."

LIMEBURNERS

AUSTRALIA

Great Southern Distilling Company,
252 Frenchman Bay Road, Albany,
Western Australia
www.distillery.com.au

The Great Southern Distillery was built in 2007, the brainchild of lawyer and accountant Cameron Syme. Its location was chosen for Albany's cool, wet winters and enough breeze to provide 75 percent of its energy needs by wind power. It is close to the Margaret River wineries, which supply the ingredients for schnapps and liqueur-making. Limeburners whiskey is offered in single barrel bottlings: the first, (M2), launched in April 2008, won an award.

LIMEBURNERS BARREL M11

SINGLE MALT 43% ABV

The fourth bottling (M11), nicknamed "The Dark One," is from a French oak ex-brandy cask, re-racked into a second-fill ex-bourbon barrel.

SULLIVANS COVE PORT MATURATION

SULLIVANS COVE BOURBON MATURATION

NANT
AUSTRALIA

The Nant Estate, Bothwell, Tasmania
www.nantdistillery.com.au

The Nant estate in Tasmania, founded in 1821, was bought by Keith and Margaret Batt in 2004 with a view to building a distillery on the historic working farm. With the expert guidance of Bill Lark (*see Lark*), the distillery went into production in April 2008. The plan is to produce a limited number of casks each year. The barley and water for the distillery come from the estate, while a restored mill provides the grist. There is also an elegant new visitor center.

NANT DOUBLE MALT
BLENDED MALT 43% ABV

This is a vatting of two casks selected from other Tasmanian distilleries, and gives an idea of what Nant's own whiskey will taste like. Sweet and fruity, with plums and cream soda, it is medium-bodied and smooth.

SMITH'S
AUSTRALIA

Yalumba, Angaston, South Australia
www.yalumba.com

Samuel Smith arrived in Angaston in 1847, one of the first settlers. He was a brewer by trade and, within two years, had set up the Yalumba Winery, having made a small fortune in the goldfields of Victoria. In the early 1930s the company that bears his name installed a pot still at the winery to make brandy. This was used three times to distill a mash of locally grown barley malt (in 1997, 1998, and 2000). It was matured in a mix of sherry, French wine, bourbon, and new American oak casks and had a good reputation. Sadly, the still has been decommissioned.

SMITH'S ANGASTON
BLENDED MALT 40% ABV

Hay, vanilla, and toffee on the nose; sweet, light and delicate, with vanilla and nuts to taste; clean and sweet in the finish.

SULLIVANS COVE
AUSTRALIA

Tasmania Distillery, Lamb Place,
Cambridge, Tasmania
www.tasmaniadistillery.com.au

Sullivans Cove was the original British settlement at Hobart in Tasmania, and is now the brand name of the malt whiskies produced by the small Tasmania Distillery. This distillery was founded at Sullivans Cove in 1994, but changed hands in 2003, when the equipment was moved to Cambridge, on the outskirts of the city of Hobart.

Part-owner and Master Distiller Patrick Maguire admits that some of the early batches of spirit were not as good as they should be, but the whiskey is now winning awards (a gold and silver in blind tastings by the Whiskey Society of Australia in 2007). Locally grown, unpeated Franklin barley-malt is used. The spirit is brewed at

Cascade Brewery, distilled in a Charentais-style pot still, and bottled from single casks by hand. Like most other Australian distilleries, Tasmania also makes gin, vodka, and liqueurs.

SULLIVANS COVE PORT MATURATION
SINGLE MALT 60% ABV

Another 7-year-old, this time from a French oak ex-port cask. It has a floral nose, developing into rich malty stout; the taste is tannic and warming. This won the gold award at WSoA 2007.

SULLIVANS COVE BOURBON MATURATION
SINGLE MALT 60% ABV

This 7-year-old whiskey was matured in an American oak ex-bourbon cask. It is sweet and malty, with oaky and chocolate notes, and won the silver award at WSoA 2007.

Barley is grown in the foothills of the Stirling Ranges and in other pockets of Australia and New Zealand. Some distilleries, such as Lark, have experimented with new strains of barley that tolerate local conditions better than the strains grown in Europe.

LAMMERLAW

NEW ZEALAND

Bottled by Cadenhead
www.wmcadenhead.com

In 1974, the Wilson Brewery and
Malt Extract Company produced
New Zealand's first legal whiskey
for 100 years. Unfortunately, its
pot stills were made from stainless
steel, and the spirit was horrible. In
1981, the distillery was acquired
by Seagram, who vastly improved
quality and produced a 10-year-old
single malt—Lammerlaw—named
after the nearby mountain range.
The distillery was dismantled in
2002, and the casks passed to
Milford's owners *(see Milford)*.
Cadenhead has bottled Lammerlaw
in its World Whiskies series.

CADENHEAD'S LAMMERLAW
10-YEAR-OLD

SINGLE MALT 47.3% ABV
Light-bodied and somewhat "green"
and cereal-like, but pleasant to taste.

MACKENZIE

NEW ZEALAND

Southern Distilleries,
Stafford Street, Timaru
www.hokonuiwhiskey.com

The eponymous Mackenzie was a
shepherd and sheep-rustler during
the 1850s, and gave his name to
that part of the Southern Alps
between Canterbury and Otago
where he operated. He and his dog
are commemorated by monuments
in the district. Scotch was his
drink, and this recreation of his
favorite tipple is a blend of
Scotch and New Zealand malts
from Southern Distilleries, which
also makes Old Hokonui *(see
entry)*. The process and reduction
water used in Mackenzie's creation
flows from the Mackenzie Basin.

THE MACKENZIE

BLENDED MALT 40% ABV
A light and refreshing dram, with plain
caramel and oak notes.

MILFORD

NEW ZEALAND

The New Zealand Malt Whiskey
Company & Preston Associates,
14–16 Harbour St., Oamaru
www.milfordwhiskey.co.nz

Milford whiskey was originally
made at Willowbank Distillery in
Dunedin, South Island, which was
owned by the Wilson Brewery *(see
Lammerlaw)*. The New Zealand
Malt Whiskey Company now owns
the Milford label (and also the less
prestigious Prestons label) and is
building a new distillery at
Bannockburn, Central Otago. It
has also opened a retail warehouse
at Oamaru, where the new Milford
malt will be matured and bottled.

MILFORD 10-YEAR-OLD

SINGLE MALT 43% ABV
Often compared to a Scottish Lowland
malt, Milford's 10-year-old has a light,
dry, and fragrant nose; the taste is
sweet, then dry, with a slightly
woody, short finish.

OLD HOKONUI

NEW ZEALAND

Southern Distilleries,
Stafford Street, Timaru
www.hokonuiwhiskey.com

Southern Distilleries has two small
pot stills producing Old Hokonui
Moonshine, single malt, and
blended malts, using—as the
distillers put it—"Murdoch
McRae's original 1892 recipe."

McRae was the leading illicit
distiller in the district, having
learned the craft from his mother,
with whom he had arrived from
Kintail, Scotland, in 1872. Many
of his descendants also became
distillers and their story is told
with memorabilia in the Hokonui
Museum at Gore.

OLD HOKONUI

BLEND 40% ABV
Pale in color, and light-bodied, with a
smooth mouthfeel, and an oaky taste
with distinct smoky notes.

Your Tasting Notes...

You can use these pages to make your own notes about the appearance, aroma, taste, and finish of different whiskies that you have the opportunity to sample.

WHISKEY			
TYPE			
BOTTLER			
AGE			
APPEARANCE			
AROMA			
TASTE			
WITH WATER			
FINISH			
VERDICT	AGAIN & AGAIN SAME AGAIN NEVER AGAIN	AGAIN & AGAIN SAME AGAIN NEVER AGAIN	AGAIN & AGAIN SAME AGAIN NEVER AGAIN

WHISKEY			
TYPE			
BOTTLER			
AGE			
APPEARANCE			
AROMA			
TASTE			
WITH WATER			
FINISH			
VERDICT	AGAIN & AGAIN SAME AGAIN NEVER AGAIN	AGAIN & AGAIN SAME AGAIN NEVER AGAIN	AGAIN & AGAIN SAME AGAIN NEVER AGAIN

Your Tasting Notes...

You can use these pages to make your own notes about the appearance, aroma, taste, and finish of different whiskies that you have the opportunity to sample.

WHISKEY			
TYPE			
BOTTLER			
AGE			
APPEARANCE			
AROMA			
TASTE			
WITH WATER			
FINISH			
VERDICT	AGAIN & AGAIN SAME AGAIN NEVER AGAIN	AGAIN & AGAIN SAME AGAIN NEVER AGAIN	AGAIN & AGAIN SAME AGAIN NEVER AGAIN

WHISKEY			
TYPE			
BOTTLER			
AGE			
APPEARANCE			
AROMA			
TASTE			
WITH WATER			
FINISH			
VERDICT	AGAIN & AGAIN SAME AGAIN NEVER AGAIN	AGAIN & AGAIN SAME AGAIN NEVER AGAIN	AGAIN & AGAIN SAME AGAIN NEVER AGAIN

Your Tasting Notes...

You can use these pages to make your own notes about the appearance, aroma, taste, and finish of different whiskies that you have the opportunity to sample.

WHISKEY			
TYPE			
BOTTLER			
AGE			
APPEARANCE			
AROMA			
TASTE			
WITH WATER			
FINISH			
VERDICT	AGAIN & AGAIN SAME AGAIN NEVER AGAIN	AGAIN & AGAIN SAME AGAIN NEVER AGAIN	AGAIN & AGAIN SAME AGAIN NEVER AGAIN

WHISKEY			
TYPE			
BOTTLER			
AGE			
APPEARANCE			
AROMA			
TASTE			
WITH WATER			
FINISH			
VERDICT	AGAIN & AGAIN SAME AGAIN NEVER AGAIN	AGAIN & AGAIN SAME AGAIN NEVER AGAIN	AGAIN & AGAIN SAME AGAIN NEVER AGAIN

Your Tasting Notes...

You can use these pages to make your own notes about the appearance, aroma, taste, and finish of different whiskies that you have the opportunity to sample.

WHISKEY			
TYPE			
BOTTLER			
AGE			
APPEARANCE			
AROMA			
TASTE			
WITH WATER			
FINISH			
VERDICT	AGAIN & AGAIN SAME AGAIN NEVER AGAIN	AGAIN & AGAIN SAME AGAIN NEVER AGAIN	AGAIN & AGAIN SAME AGAIN NEVER AGAIN

WHISKEY			
TYPE			
BOTTLER			
AGE			
APPEARANCE			
AROMA			
TASTE			
WITH WATER			
FINISH			
VERDICT	AGAIN & AGAIN SAME AGAIN NEVER AGAIN	AGAIN & AGAIN SAME AGAIN NEVER AGAIN	AGAIN & AGAIN SAME AGAIN NEVER AGAIN

Glossary

ABV (alcohol by volume) This is the proportion of alcohol in a drink, expressed as a percentage. Whiskey is most commonly at 40% or 43% ABV.

Analyzer still *see* continuous distillation

Angels' share The expression given for the amount of liquid that evaporates from the cask during the period of *maturation*.

Batch distillation Distillation carried out in batches, as opposed to *continuous distillation*. Each batch may be marginally different, which gives the method an artisanal quality.

Barrel *see* cask

Blended malt A mix of single malt whiskies from more than one distillery.

Blended whiskey A mix of malt whiskies and grain whiskies.

Cask The oak container in which whiskey is matured. There are many different styles and sizes of cask as well as a principle distinction between the type of wood used: American or European oak. In the USA, whiskey is most commonly matured in barrels (180-200 liters). American barrels are re-used elsewhere; in Scotland they are often broken down and re-assembled as hogsheads (250 liters). Butts and puncheons (both 500 liters) are the largest casks used for maturing whiskey, having first been seasoned with, or used to age, sherry.

Cask finishing The practice of using a different cask (such as port, madeira, French wine, or rum casks) for the final period of the whiskey's maturation.

Cask strength Whiskey that is bottled straight from the cask

rather than first being diluted. It is typically around 57-63% ABV.

Column still Also known as a Coffey, Patent or continuous still, this is the type of still used for *continuous distillation*.

Condenser The vaporized spirit driven off the stills is turned into liquid in a condenser. The traditional type of condenser is a "worm tub"—a tapering coil of copper pipe set in a vat of cold water outside the still house. Worm tubs have largely been superseded by shell-and-tube condensers, usually situated inside the still house.

Continuous distillation The creation of spirit as an ongoing process, as opposed to *batch distillation*. Continuous distillation uses a column still (also known as a Patent or Coffey still) rather than a *pot still*. It has two connected columns: the Rectifier and the Analyzer. The cool wash travels down the Rectifier in a sealed coil, where it becomes heated. It then passes to the head of the Analyzer, down which it tricks over a series of perforated copper plates. Steam enters the foot of the Analyzer and bubbles through the wash, driving off alcoholic vapor, which rises up the Analyzer then passes to the foot of the Rectifier. Again it ascends, to be condensed by the cool wash (which is thus heated) as it rises in a zig-zag manner through another series of perforated copper plates. As the vapor rises it becomes purer and of higher strength, until it is drawn off at the "striking plate" at 94% ABV.

Cut points In the process of pot still distillation, the operator divides the run into three "cuts" to separate the usable spirit from rejected spirit, which must be re-distilled. The first cut contains the foreshots; the middle cut is the

section of usable spirit; the end cut contains the feints or aftershots.

Draff The Scottish name for the remains of the grain after mashing. It is a nutritious cattle fodder, used either wet or dried and pelletized.

Drum maltings Large cylinders in which grain is germinated during the industrial *malting* of barley. The drums are ventilated with temperature-controlled air and rotate so the grains do not stick together.

Dumping Emptying the contents of a cask into a vat, either prior to bottling or before putting into a different kind of cask.

Eau de vie Literally, "water of life," and usually used in reference to grape-based spirits. Compare with *uisge beatha*.

Expression The term given to a particular whiskey in relation to the overall output of a distillery or spirits company. It may refer to the age, as in 12-year-old expression, or to a particular characteristic, such as a cask strength expression.

Feints The final fraction of the spirit produced during a distillation run in batch distilling. Feints (also called tails or aftershots) are aromatically unpleasant, and are sent to a feints and foreshots receiver to be mixed with *low wines* and re-distilled.

Fermenter Another name for *mashtun*.

First fill The first time a cask has been used to hold whiskey other than bourbon, it is referred to as first-fill cask. A first-fill sherry cask will have held only sherry prior to its use for maturing whiskey; a first-fill bourbon cask will have been used once only to hold bourbon prior to its use in maturing whiskey.

Foreshots The first fraction of the distillation run in pot-still distillation. Foreshots (also known as heads) are not pure enough to be used and are returned to a feints and foreshots receiver to be re-distilled in the next run.

Grist Ground, malted grain. Water is added to grist to form the *mash*.

Heads *see* foreshots

High wines (US) A mix of spirit that has had its first distillation and the foreshots and feints from the second distillation. With a strength of around 28% ABV, high wines undergo a second distillation to create *new make*.

Independent bottler/bottling A company that releases bottles of whiskey independently of the official distillery bottlings. They buy small quantities of casks and bottle the whiskey as and when they choose.

Kilning In the process of *malting*, kilning involves gently heating the "green malt" to halt its germination and thereby retain its starch content for turning into sugars (in the mashing stage). Ultimately these sugars will be turned into alcohol. Peat may be added to the kiln to produce a smoky flavored malt.

Lomond still This pot still was designed so that a distillery could vary the character of spirit being produced. The level of *reflux* could be altered by way of an additional condenser on the still, so that a heavy or light style of spirit could be made, as required.

Low wines The spirit produced by the first distillation. It has a strength of about 21% ABV. Compare with *high wines*.

Lyne arm (or "lye pipe") The pipe running from the top of the still to the condenser. Its angle, height, and thickness all have a bearing on the characteristics of the spirit.

Malting The process of deliberately starting and stopping germination in grain to maximize its starch content. As the grain begins to germinate (through the influence of heat and moisture), it becomes "green malt" (grain that has just begun to sprout). The green malt undergoes kilning to produce malt.

Marrying The mixing of whiskies prior to bottling. It most often applies to blends, where whiskies of different types and from several distilleries are combined for a period in vats or casks to blend more fully before the whiskey is bottled.

Mash The mix of grist and water.

Mashbill The mix of grains used in the making of a particular whiskey. In the US, there are specific requirements about the percentage of certain grains for making bourbon, Tennessee whiskey, and rye, for example.

Mashtun The vessel in which the grist is mixed with hot water to convert starch in the grain into sugars, ready for fermentation. The fermentable liquid that results is known as *wort*; the solid residue (husks and spent grain) is *draff*.

Maturation For *new make* to become whiskey, it must go through a period of maturation in oak casks. The length of time varies: in Scotland and Ireland, the minimum period is three years; in the US, the minimum maturation is two years.

Middle cut *see* cut points

New make The clear, usable spirit that comes from the spirit still. It has a strength of about 70% ABV and is diluted to around 63–64% before being put into casks for maturation. In the US, new make is called white dog.

Peating Adding peat to the kiln ovens when *malting* barley to impart a smoky, phenolic aroma and taste to the whiskey. Barley that has undergone this process is known as peated malt.

Phenols A group of aromatic chemical compounds. In whiskey-making, the term is used in respect of the chemicals that impart smoky and medicinal flavors to malt and the whiskey made from it, which may be described as phenolic. Phenols are measured in parts per million (ppm). Highly phenolic whiskies, such as Laphroaig and Ardbeg, will use malt peated to a level of between 35 and 50 ppm.

Poteen *see* uisce poitin

Pot still The large onion-shaped vessels, nearly always made of copper, used for batch distillation. Pot stills vary in size and shape, and these variations affect the style of spirit produced.

ppm *see* phenols

Proof The old term for the alcoholic proportion of a spirit, now superseded by ABV. The American proof figure, which is different to Imperial proof, is twice that of the ABV percentage.

Rectifier *see* continuous distillation

Reflux The process by which heavier alcoholic vapors fall back into the still rather than passing along the *lyne arm* to the *condenser*. By falling back, these vapors are re-distilled, becoming purer and lighter. The size, height, and shape of the still, and how it is operated, contribute to the degree of reflux, and therefore to the lightness and character of the spirit. Long-necked stills have a greater degree of reflux and produce a more delicate style of spirit than squatter stills, which tend to make heavier, "oilier" whiskies.

Run In batch distillation—as carried out using pot stills—the extent of distillation is referred to as a run. The spirit produced during the run is variable in quality, and is divided by *cut points*.

Saladin box Used in the industrial *malting* of barley, these are large rectangular troughs in which the grains are germinated. Air is blown through the barley in the trough and the grain turned by mechanical screws to prevent the grains from sticking together.

Silent distillery A distillery in which whiskey production has stopped—possibly only temporarily.

Single cask A bottling that comes from just one cask (often bottled at *cask strength*).

Single malt A malt whiskey that is the product of just one distillery.

Spirit safe A glass-fronted cabinet through which the distilled spirit passes and which is used to monitor the purity of the spirit. The stillman operates the spirits safe during a run to assess its quality and make *cut points*.

Spirit still In *batch distillation*, the spirit still is used for the second distillation, in which the spirit from the *wash still* is distilled again to produce *new make*.

Still The vessel in which distillation takes place. There are two basic types: a *pot still* for *batch distillation* and a *column still* for *continuous distillation*.

Tails *see* feints

Triple distillation Most batch distillation involves two distillations: in a *wash still* and in a *spirits still*. Triple distillation—the traditional method in Ireland—involves a third distillation, which is said to produce a smoother spirit.

Uisge beatha / uisce beatha The Scottish Gaelic and Irish Gaelic terms, respectively, from which the word whiskey derives. The term means "water of life," and so is synonymous with *eau de vie* and *aqua vita*.

Uisce poitin Historically, the Irish Gaelic term for non-licensed whiskey, usually known as poteen.

Vatting The mixing of whiskey from several casks. This is usually done to achieve a consistency of flavor over time. (*see also* marrying).

Viscimetric whorls The eddies and vortices observable when water is added to whiskey. The capacity of an individual whiskey to sustain viscimation is termed its viscimetric potential.

Wash The resultant liquid when yeast is added to the *wort*, fermenting into a kind of ale. Wash has an alcoholic strength of about 7% ABV. It passes into a *wash still* for the first distillation.

Wash still In *batch distillation*, the wash still is used for the first distillation, in which the *wash* is distilled.

Washbacks The fermenting vessels in which yeast is added to the *wort* to make *wash*. Called "fermenters" in the US.

Wood finish *see* cask finish

Worm / worm tubs *see* condensers

Wort The liquid made by mixing hot water with grist in a *mashtun*.

Reference

WHISKEY OWNERSHIP

It can, at times, be difficult to work out exactly which company owns a specific whiskey brand or distillery. As firms have merged or been bought out by larger business groups, the trail is sometimes rather elusive and confusing. Here is a brief summary of the major conglomerations, which elucidates how they have emerged and transformed over time into the key big players in the world of whiskey today: Diageo, Chivas Brothers/Pernod Ricard, United Spirits (the UB group), and Beam Global (itself part of Fortune Brands).

THE RISE OF DIAGEO

The Distillers Company Limited (**DCL**) was founded in 1877 as an amalgamation of six leading grain whisky distilleries. In 1894 it opened its first malt whisky distillery (Knockdhu), and, in the early 20th century, began to acquire blending companies and their brands. Following "The Big Amalgamation" in 1925, when the big blending firms Walkers, Dewars, and Buchanans joined DCL, it became the largest distiller in the world at the time.

In 1987 DCL was acquired by Guinness, and the whisky side of the business was renamed United Distillers. Then in 1998 Guinness merged with Grand Metropolitan, who had a drinks subsidiary called Independent Distillers & Vintners. The combined operating name for this subsidiary and United Distillers became United Distillers & Vintners (**UDV**).

In the same year (1998) that Guinness merged with Grand Metropolitan, **Diageo** was formed as the holding company. Two years later the corporate structure was simplified and UDV was replaced as the trading entity by Diageo.

Diageo owns a plethora of whiskey brands, including venerable old blends such as Buchanan's, Haig, and Johnnie Walker. It also owns many Scotch whisky distilleries—its flagships are the 12 that produce the Classic Malts range: Caol Ila, Cardhu, Clynelish, Cragganmore, Dalwhinnie, Glen Elgin, Glenkinchie, Knockando, Lagavulin, Oban, Talisker, and Royal Lochnagar.

CHIVAS & PERNOD RICARD

Founded in Aberdeen in 1801, **Chivas Brothers** was a wine & spirits merchant. It was acquired by the Canadian distiller Seagram in 1949. Seagram went on to acquire or build nine distilleries and a number of leading blends.

In 2001, Seagram decided to divest itself of its alcoholic beverages divisions, which was divided between Diageo and Pernod Ricard. Chivas remains the whiskey arm of Pernod Ricard.

The French distiller **Pernod Ricard** entered the Scotch whisky industry with the purchase of Aberlour Distillery in 1974, but moved into the "First Division" when it acquired part of the Seagram's drinks empire in 2001. This included The Glenlivet Distillery, together with the Chivas Regal brand, and six of Allied-Domecq's distilleries in 2005, together with Ballantine's. Pernod Ricard owns brands such as Ballantine's, Chivas Regal, Jameson, Paddy, and Powers, and prestigious distilleries such as Glenlivet, Aberlour, Scapa, and Longmorn. In the States, it owns the Wild Turkey brand and, in Canada, Wiser's.

IRISH DISTILLERS

The story of Irish Distillers goes back to 1867, when five small distillers in County Cork amalgamated to form The Cork Distillers Company (**CDC**), which consolidated its production at Midleton Distillery.

That was the status quo until almost 100 years later, when, in 1966, The Irish Distillers Group (**IDG**) was formed by the merger of Power's, Jameson's, and CDC. Power's and Jameson's historic distilleries in Dublin were closed by the early 1970s, and a large new distillery was built at Midleton in 1975 to accommodate production of all the whiskeys in the IDG stable. IDG was taken over by Pernod Ricard in 1988.

UNITED SPIRITS

Part of the UB Group, **United Spirits** is the third biggest spirits producer, after Diageo and Pernod Ricard. It has only recently stepped into this position, through its acquisition of **Whyte & Mackay** in 2007. With this purchase came several Scottish distilleries, including Dalmore and Jura. Whyte & Mackay continues to represent United Spirits in the Scotch whisky sector.

BEAM GLOBAL

This subsidiary of Fortune Brands in the US owns the Jim Beam brand, as well as Maker's Mark and Canadian Club. Its Scotch whisky ownership includes Laphroaig and the Teacher's blend.

BACARDI

The famous rum maker **Bacardi** joined the Scotch whisky industry in 1992 with the acquisition of William Lawson Ltd., owner of Macduff Distillery (*see* Glen Deveron). In 1998 Bacardi acquired John Dewar & Sons, together with four distilleries, from Diageo and became a major player in Scotch whisky.

ALLIED-DOMECQ

Though now broken up, Allied-Domecq in its 1990s heyday was one of the world's biggest whiskey companies. It began as **Allied Breweries**, which acquired Teacher's in 1976, and changed the name of its spirits division to **Allied Distillers** when it bought Hiram Walker, owner of Ballantine's brands and distilleries, in 1987. Three years later the company acquired Whitbread's whisky interests and moved into the big league.

In 1993, with the acquisition of the Spanish distiller and sherry-maker Pedro Domecq, the name was changed to **Allied-Domecq**, which became the third largest drinks company in the world. Allied-Domecq was broken up in 2005, with Teacher's going to Beam Global and Ballantine's to French drinks giant Pernod Ricard.

WHISKEY RANGES

Throughout this book, and when studying or buying whiskey, three key whiskey ranges are regularly mentioned: Flora & Fauna, Classic Malts, and Rare Malts. Here is a little background information about each of them.

Classic Malts A range of six malts was introduced by United Distillers in 1987/88. The malts came from UD's Cragganmore, Dalwhinnie, Glenkinchie, Lagavulin, Oban, and Talisker distilleries. Under the ownership of Diageo, the range has been expanded to 12 of its flagship malts: the six original members of the range, plus Caol Ila, Cardhu, Clynelish, Glen Elgin, Knockando, and Royal Lochnagar.

Flora & Fauna In the early 1990s, UDV introduced the Flora & Fauna range of single malt bottlings from all of its distilleries. Diageo continued to produce the range but recently decided that it will be discontinued.

Rare Malts A selection of small batch bottlings from UDV at natural strength and color, without chill-filtration. They were released between 1995 and 2006, and 36 distilleries were represented in the range.

WHISKEY SHOPS

AUSTRALIA

**Scotch Malt Whisky
Society in Australia**
mail order to members only
www.smws.com.au

Single Malt Whisky Club
119 Johnston St., Annandale,
NSW, 2038
+ 61 (2) 9660 1947
www.singlemalt.com.au

AUSTRIA

Potstill
Strozzigasse 37, 1080 Wien
+43 (0)676 965 89 36
www.potstill.org

BELGIUM

Whiskycorner
Kraaistraat 18, 3530 Houthalen
+32 (0)89 386233
www.whiskycorner.be

Jurgen's Whiskyhuis
Gaverland 70, 9620 Zottegem
+32 (0) 9 336 51 06
www.whiskyhuis.be

FRANCE

La Maison du Whisky
20 rue d'Anjou, 75008 Paris
+33 (0)1 42 65 03 16
www.whisky.fr

also at 47 rue Jean Chatel
97400 Saint-Denis
+33 (0)2 62 21 31 19

GERMANY

Cadenhead's Whisky Market
Luxemburger Strasse 257
50939 Köln
+49 (0)221 283 1834
www.cadenhead.de

Celtic Whisk(e)y & Versand
Otto Steudel, Bulmannstrasse 26
90459 Nürnberg
+49 (0)911 450974-30
www.whisky.de/celtic

Weinquelle Lühmann
Lubeckerstrasse 145
22087 Hamburg
+49 (0)40 256 391
www.weinquelle.com

Whisky & Cigars
Sophienstrasse 8-9
10178 Berlin-Mitte
+49 (0)30 282 03 76
www.whisky-cigars.de

Whisky Corner
Reichertsfeld 2
92278 Illschwang
+49 (0)96 6695 1213
www.whisky-corner.de

IRELAND

Celtic Whisky Shop
27–28 Dawson Street, Dublin 2
+353 (0)1 675 9744

Mitchell & Son
The CHQ building
IFSC Docklands, Dublin 1
+353 (01) 612 5540
www.mitchellandson.com

also at Glasthule
54 Glasthule Road
Sandycove, County Dublin
+353 (01) 230 2301

JAPAN

Shinanoya
Kabukicho 1-12-9, Shinjuku
Kabukicho, Tokyo
+81 (0)3 3204 2365
(more branches throughout Tokyo)

Kawachiya
Udagawacho 30, Shibuya, Tokyo
+81 (0)3 3462 6604
(more branches throughout Tokyo)

Tanakaya
3-4-14 Mejiro, Toshima-ku, Tokyo
+81 (0)3 3953 8888

NEW ZEALAND

The Whisky Shop
Shop 11 Elliott Stables
41 Elliott Street, CBD
Auckland
0800 4 944759
www.whiskyshop.co.nz

RUSSIA

Whisky World Shop
9 Tverskoy Boulevard
123104 Moscow
+7 495 787 9150
www.whiskyworld.ru

UNITED KINGDOM

Berry Brothers & Rudd
3 St. James's Street
London SW1A 1EG
+44 (0)20 7396 9600
www.bbr.com

Cadenheads Whisky Shop
172 Canongate, Royal Mile
Edinburgh EH8 8BN
+44 (0)131 556 5864
www.wmcadenhead.com

Gordon & MacPhail
58–60 South Street, Elgin
Moray IV30 1JY
+44 (0)1343 545110
www.gordonandmacphail.com

Loch Fyne Whiskies
Inverary, Argyll PA32 8UD
+44 (0)1499 302 219
www.lfw.co.uk

Milroys of Soho
3 Greek Street, London W1D 4NX
+44 (0) 20 7437 2385
www.milroys.co.uk

Royal Mile Whiskies
279 High Street, Royal Mile
Edinburgh EH1 1PW
+44 (0)131 5249380
www.royalmilewhiskies.com

also at 3 Bloomsbury Street
London WC1B 3QE

Scotch Malt Whisky Society
mail order to members only
www.smws.com

The Vintage House
42 Old Compton Street
London W1D 4LR
+44 (0)20 7437 5112
www.sohowhisky.com

Whisky Castle
Main Street, Tomintoul
Aberdeenshire AB37 9EX
+44 (0)1807 580 213
www.whiskycastle.co.uk

The Whisky Exchange
Vinopolis, 1 Bank End
London SE1 9BU
mail order +44 (0)208 838 9388
www.thewhiskyexchange.com

The Whiskey Shop
12 branches in England and Scotland
mail order +44 (0)1463 710525
www.whiskyshop.com

The Whisky Shop Dufftown
1 Fife Street, Dufftown, Keith,
Moray AB55 4AL
+44 (0)1340 821097
www.whiskyshopdufftown.co.uk

USA

D&M
2200 Fillmore Street
San Francisco, CA 94115
(415) 346 1325
(800) 637 0292
www.dandm.com

Park Avenue Liquor Shop
292 Madison Avenue, New York
NY 10017
(212) 685 2442
www.parkaveliquor.com

Sam's Wine & Spirits
1720 North Marcey Street, Chicago
IL 60614
(866) 726 7946
www.samswine.com

The Whisky Shop
360 Sutter Street, San Francisco
CA, 94108
+001 (415) 989 1030
www.whiskyshopusa.com

WHISKEY WEBSITES

blog.maltadvocate.com
www.maltmadness.com
www.maltmaniacs.org
www.nonjatta.blogspot.com
www.peatfreak.com
www.singlemalt.tv
www.spiritofislay.net
www.thewhiskychannel.com
www.whiskycast.com
www.whiskyforum.se
www.whiskymag.com
www.whisky-pages.com

Index

5 of Spades 283
8PM 321
10 of Clubs 283
100 Pipers 20
1185 Special Reserve 271

A

A. & A. Crawford 70
A. Smith Bowman
   Distillery 263
Aberfeldy 20
Aberlour **20**, 65, 94, 95, 156
a'bunadh 21
Ace of Diamonds 283
Ace of Spades 283
Adam Millars & Co 205
Adelphi 88
Ailsa Bay Distillery 82, 111
Akuto, Ichiro 282
Albert B. Blanton
   Distillery 227
Alberta Distillery 271, 279
Alberta Premium 271
Alberta Springs 271
Aldour Distillery 51
Allied Distillers 27, 83, 130,
   144, 272, **342**
Allied Domecq 60, 116, 157,
   164, **342**
Allied Lyons 50, 279
Allt-a-Bhainne 21
Alltech 259
American Brands 250
American Spirit 220, 264
Ammertal 315
Amrut 322
Anchor Distilling Company
   250, 259
Ancient Age 220, 222
Ancient Age Distillery 227
AnCnoc **22**, 117, 150
Anderson, James 262
Andrew A. Watt & Co 215
Andrews, Mark 199
Angostura Distillery 257
Angus Dundee **23**, 83, 175
Antiquary, The 23
Antiquity 323
Ardbeg **24–5**, 60, 104
Ardmore **29**, 41, 83, 171
Aristocrat 323
Armorik 310
Arran 29
Arran Distillers 136

Arthur Bell & Sons **42**, 51,
   78, 117, 147
Asahi Breweries 288
Asyla 66
Auchentoshan **30–31**
Auchroisk 32
Aultmore 32, 76
Aultmore-Glenlivet
   Distillery 32
Austin Nicholls & Co 220,
   256, 264
Australia 326–30
Austria 306, 314–15

B

Bacardi 22, 32, 70, 76, 83,
   154, 180, **342**
Bader family 313
Bagpiper 323
Baileys 176
Bailie Nicol Jarvie 32, 104
Baker, David 327
Baker, Lynn 327
Baker's 220
Baker's Kentucky 242
Bakery Hill 327
Balblair **33**, 102, 116,
   117, 150
Ballantine's **34–5**, 83, 108,
   272, 136, 144, 157
Ballast Point 259
Balmenach **36**, 116, 117
Balvenie, The **36–7**, 65, 94,
   111, 144
barley 8, 12–13, 40–41
Barnard, Alfred 27, 102,
   132, 202, 308
Barrel Select 277
Barrell House 259
Barton **220**, 244, 254, 258
Barton Brands Ltd 134, 135,
   220, 244, 254, 258, 271
Basil Hayden's **221**, 242, 245
Batt, Keith 329
Batt, Margaret 329
Beam Global 319, 171, **342**
Beam, Baker 220
Beam, Craig 221, 228
Beam, David 242
Beam, Jim
   (James Beauregard) 220
Beam, John 240
Beam, Parker 221, 228, 251
Beam's Small Batch Bourbon
   Collection 220
Begg, John 155
Belgian Owl, The 310

Belgium 310
Bell, Arthur 42
Bell's 42, 51, 78, 146
Ben Nevis 43
BenRiach **44–5**, 136, 142
Benrinnes 32, **50**, 70
Benromach 48–9
Bernheim 221
Bernheim Distillery **221**,
   233, 236, 254
Bernheim Original 236
Bernheim, Isaac Wolfe 233
Berry Brothers & Rudd
   71, 106
Bertrand Distillery 312
Betta Milk Cooperative 328
Black & White **51**, 76, 108
Black Bottle 50
Black Bush 186
Black Dog 50
Black Grouse, The 80–81
Black Label 271
Black Velvet 271
Bladnoch 51
Blair Athol 42, **51**, 78
Blanton, Colonel Albert Bacon
   221, 222
Blanton, Colonel Benjamin
   255
Blanton's 221
blended malt 12, 174
blended whisky *see* blends
Blenders Pride 323
blends 11, 12, **79**
Blum, Harry 242
Boehm, Jacob 242
Bombay Sapphire 22
Booker's 221
Booker's Kentucky 242
Boston Distillery 249, 250
Bottled-in-Bond Act 1897
   251
bottlers 88–9
bottles 146–7
Bouillon, Etienne 310
Boulevard Distillery 264
bourbon 13, **223**
Bowman, Abram Smith 263
Bowmore 31, **52–3**, 56, 128
Braemar 150
Braes of Glenlivet 58
Braeval 22, **58**, 76
Braunstein 317
Bronfman Distillers 278
Bronfman, Edgar 58
Bronfman, Sam 276, 278
Brooks, Alfred 118

Brora Distillery 66
Brown, George Garvin
   222, 250
Brown, John Thompson
   Street 222
Brown, Peter 134
Brown, William 134
Brown-Forman **222**, 227,
   235, 240, 250, 254, 266
Bruichladdich 45, 47,
   56–7, 89
Buchanan, James 51, 58, 108
Buchanan, Norman 60
Buchanan's 27, 51, 58, 108
Buffalo Trace 220, 221,
   222, 224, 227, 230,
   255, 258, 261
Buffalo Trace Antique
   Collection 225, 233, 257
Buffalo Trace Experimental
   Collection 222
Bulleit Bourbon 225, 228
Bulleit, Augustus 225
Bulleit, Tom 225
Bulloch, Alexander 135
Bunnahabhain 12, 58–9
Bunnahabhain Distillery 50
Burger, Bert 308
Burn Stewart Distillers 45,
   50, 58, 76, 157, 172
Burnfoot Distillery 96
Bush, Scott 258
Bushmills **186–7**, 193,
   198, 199, 202
   Secrets of 188–9
Busuttil, Jim 251

C

C.D. & G. Grahams 50
C.L. WorldBrands Ltd 50
Cadenhead 22, 66, 89, 331
Call, Dan 238
Cameron Brig 12, **60**, 165
Cameronbridge Distillery
   60, 78
Campari Group (Gruppo
   Campari) 98, 150
Campbell, Archibald 122
Campbell Distillers 23
Campbeltown 19, 296
Canada 268–79
Canadian Club 272, 273
Canadian Industrial
   Alcohol 109
Canadian Mist 271
Canny Man's pub 62–63
Caol Ila 42, **60–61**, 151

PICTURE CREDITS

Deepak Aggarwal © DK Images: 323 Antiquity, Bagpiper, Blenders Pride, 324 Imperial Blue, Masterstroke, McDowell's, 325 Royal Challenge

Alamy Images: 196–7 © FAN Travelstock/Alamy, 206–7 © David Sanger Photography/Alamy, 252–3 © Peter Horree/Alamy, 274–5 © Design Pics Inc./Alamy

Paul Bock © Beam Global: 132–3 Laphroaig Distillery

Dave Broom: 290 Chichibu Distillery

Chris Bunting: 282 Golden Horse, 286 The Crane bar, Tokyo

Corbis: 330 © Doug Pearson/JAI/Corbis

Peter Mulryan: 11 bottling line, 210–11 Midleton's water source, local barley, the mashtun, Jameson bottling line, 212 a field of barley near Midleton

Thameside Media/Michael ellis © DK Images: 2, 4, 6, 8–11, 14–15, 21 Allt-A-Bhainne, 26–7, 28, 36 Balmenach, 38–9, 40–1, 46–7, 42 Bell's, 43 Ben Nevis, 51 Bladnoch, Blair Athol, 58 Braeval, 60 Caol Ila Distillers Edition, 61 Caperdonich, 62–3, 70 Crawford's, 71 Cutty Sark, Dailuaine, Dallas Dhu, 76 Deanston, 78 Dimple, Dufftown, Edradour, 79, 82 Fettercairn, 82 Glenallachie, 83 Glenburgie, Glen Deveron, 84–5, 94–5, 98 Glen Grant, Glen Keith, 102 Glenlossie, 108 Glen Ord, Glen Scotia, Glen Spey, Glentauchers, 109 Glenturret, 111 Haig, 112–113, 117 Inchgower, 117 Invergordon, 120–1, 122 Kilchoman, 123, 124–5, 127, 128 Lagavulin 16-year-old, 21-year-old, 129 Lagavulin 30-year-old, Distillers Edition, 131, 134 Lauder's, 135 Linkwood, Loch Fyne Living Cask, Loch Lomond, 136 Long John, Longmorn, 138, 142 Mannochmore, 144 Millburn, Miltonduff, 145 Mortlach, Oban Distillers Edition, 148, 151 Poit Dubh, Port Ellen, Prime Blue, 152–3, 158–9, 160 Sheep Dip, 164 Stewarts Cream of the Barley, 165, 166–7, 170 Tamdhu, 171 Teaninich G&M, Te Bheag, 174, 176–7, 179 White Horse, 181, 190 Coleraine, 193, 194 Craoi Na Mona, 194 Feckin' Irish, 195 Green Spot, 223, 225 Bulleit, 226, 229, 233 I.W. Harper, 237 Henry McKenna, 245 Knob Creek, 257 Seagram's 7 Crown, 259, 260–1, 262, 263, 264 Kentucky Spirit, 265 Rare Breed, 270, 276

Crown Royal, 277 Glen Breton, 277 Hirsch, 278 Seagram's, 285, 288, 289, 292, 293, 296, 302, 303, 306, 310 Goldlys, Gouden Carolus, Armorik, 315 Gold Cock, 316 Slyrs, 320, 322, 326, 331 Lammerlaw; cartography by Rosalyn Ellis, Nora Zimerman, Steve Crozier

The Whisky Couple: 230 Wild Turkey sign, 231 Maker's Mark, 239 tasting glasses, 241, 246–7 copper pot stills, 247 rick houses

The Whisky Exchange: 237 Hirsch Reserve

The publishers would like to thank the following producers for their assistance with the project and kind permission to reproduce their photographs:

Aberfeldy Distillery; Aberlour Distillery; Alberta Distillery: Alberta, Tangle Ridge, Windsor Canadian; Allied Distillers; Anchor Distilling Company: Old Potrero; Angus Dundee; Ardbeg Distillery; Ardmore Distillery; Arran Distillers: Arran, Lochranza; Auchroisk Distillery; Aultmore Distillery; Bacardi & Company: Dewar's, Royal Brackla, William Lawson's; Backafallsbyn AB: Hven; Bakery Hill Distillery; Balblair Distillery; The Balvenie Distillery Company; Beam Global España: DYC; Beam Global Distribution (UK): Ardmore, Laphroaig, Teacher's; Beam Global Spirits & Wine, Inc. (USA): Baker's® Kentucky Straight Bourbon Whiskey (53.5% Alc./Vol. ©CST), James B. Beam Distilling Co., Clermont, KY; Basil Hayden's® Kentucky Straight Bourbon Whiskey (40% Alc./Vol. ©CST), Kentucky Springs Distilling Co., Clermont, KY; Booker's® Kentucky Straight Bourbon Whiskey (60.5% - 63.5% Alc./Vol. ©CST), James B. Beam Distilling Co., Clermont, KY; Clermont Distillery; Canadian Club® Blended Canadian Whisky (40% alc./vol. ©CST) Canadian Club Import Company, Deerfield, IL; Jim Beam Black® Kentucky Straight Bourbon Whiskey (43% Alc./Vol. ©CST), James B. Beam Distilling Co., Clermont, KY; Jim Beam® Kentucky Straight Bourbon Whiskey (40% Alc./Vol. ©2009), James B. Beam Distilling Co., Clermont, KY; Jim Beam's Choice® Kentucky Straight Bourbon Whiskey (40% Alc./Vol. ©2009), James B. Beam Distilling Co., Clermont, KY; Jim Beam® Straight Rye Whiskey (40% Alc./Vol. ©CST), James B. Beam Distilling Co.,

Clermont, KY; Kessler® American Blended Whiskey Lightweight Traveler® (40% Alc./Vol. 72.5% Grain Neutral Spirits, ©2009), Julius Kessler Company, Deerfield, IL; Knob Creek® Kentucky Straight Bourbon Whiskey (50% Alc./Vol. ©2009), Knob Creek Distillery, Clermont, KY; Maker's Mark® Bourbon Whisky (45% Alc./Vol. ©CST), Maker's Mark Distillery, Inc., Loretto, KY; Old Crow® Kentucky Straight Bourbon Whiskey (40% Alc./Vol. ©2009), W.A. Gaines, Div. of The Old Crow Distillery Company, Frankfort, KY; Old Grand-Dad® Kentucky Straight Bourbon Whiskey (43%, 50% and 57% Alc./Vol. ©2009), The Old Grand-Dad Distillery Company, Frankfort, KY; Old Taylor® Kentucky Straight Bourbon Whiskey (40% Alc./Vol. ©CST), The Old Taylor Distillery Company, Frankfort, KY; Belmont Farms of Virginia: Virginia Lightning; Benriach Distillery; Benrinnes Distillery; Benromach Distillery; Berry Brothers & Rudd: Cutty Sark; Bertrand Distillery: Uberach; Betta Milk Cooperative: Hellyers Road; Bowmore Distillery; Braunstein; Brown-Forman Corporation: Canadian Mist, Early Times, Old Forester, Woodford Reserve, Jack Daniel's, Bruichladdich Distillery; Buffalo Trace Distillery: Ancient Age, Blanton's, Buffalo Trace, Eagle Rare, Elmer T. Lee, Experimental Collection, George T. Stagg, Hancock's Reserve, Old Charter, Rock Hill Farms, Sazerac Rye, Thomas H. Handy, W.L. Weller; Bunnahabhain Distillery; Burn Stewart Distillers: Black Bottle, Deanston, Scottish Leader; The Old Bushmills Distillery Co: Bushmills, The Irishman, Knappogue Castle; Campari Drinks Group: Glen Grant, Old Smuggler; Cardhu Distillery; Castle Brands Inc.: Jefferson's, Sam Houston; Chivas Brothers: 100 Pipers, Ballantine's, Chivas Regal, Clan Campbell, Imperial, Long John, Passport, Queen Anne, Royal Salute, Something Special, Stewarts Cream of the Barley, Strathclyde, Strathisla, Tormore; Clear Creek Distillery: McCarthy's; Clontarf Distillery; Clynelish Distillery; Compass Box Delicious Whisky; Constellation Spirits Inc.: Very Old Barton®, Kentucky Gentleman®, Kentucky Tavern®, Ridgemont®, Ten High®, Tom Moore®, Black Velvet®; Cooley Distillery: Connemara, Cooley, Greenore, Inishowen, Kilbeggan, Locke's, Magilligan, Tyrconnel, Wild Geese; Copper Fox Distillery: Wasmund's; Corby Distilleries:

Wiser's; Craigellachie Distillery; Cragganmore Distillery; Des Menhirs: Eddu; Diageo plc: Bell's, Black & White, Buchanan's, Bulleit Bourbon, Bushmills, Cameron Brig, Caol Ila, Cardhu, Crown Royal, Dalwhinnie, Dimple, Glen Elgin, Haig, J&B, Johnnie Walker, Lagavulin, Linkwood, Oban, Old Parr, Royal Lochnagar, Teaninich, Usher's Green Stripe, VAT 69, White Horse, Windsor; Diageo Canada: Seagram's; Domaine Charbay: Charbay; Domaine Mavela: P&M; Edrington Group: The Famous Grouse, Tamdhu; The English Whisky Co.; Fleischmann: Grüner Hund; Four Roses Distillery; The Gaelic Whisky Co.: Mac Na Mara, Poit Dhubh; George A. Dickel & Co.: George Dickel; Girvan Distillery; Glann Ar Mor; Glencadam Distillery; Glendronach Distillery; Glendullan Distillery; Glenfarclas Distillery; Glenfiddich Distillery; Glenglassaugh Distillery; Glengoyne Distillery; Glenkinchie Distillery; Glenlivet Distillery; The Glenmorangie Company: Bailie Nicol Jarvie, Glenmorangie, James Martin's; Glen Moray Distillery; Glenora Distillery: Glen Breton; Glenrothes Distillery; Glenturret Distillery; Gotland Whisky AB; Graanstokerij Filliers: Goldlys; Great Southern Distilling Company: Limeburners; Guillon Distillery; Hammerschmiede Spirituosen: Glen Els; Heaven Hill Distilleries, Inc.: Bernheim, Elijah Craig, Evan Williams, Heaven Hill, Georgia Moon, Heaven Hill, Parker's, Mellow Corn, Old Fitzgerald, Parker's, Pikesville, Rittenhouse Rye; Highland Park Distillery; Highwood Distillers; Holle; Hotel Gasthof Lamm:Ammertal; Ian MacLeod: Langs; International Beverage Holdings; Inver House Distillers: Catto's, Hankey Bannister, Inver House, MacArthur's, Pinwinnie Royale, Speyburn; Isle of Arran: Robert Burns; Jagatjit Industries: Aristocrat; Jura Distillery; Käsers Schloss: Whisky Castle; Kentucky Bourbon Distillers, Ltd.: Johnny Drum, Noah's Mill; Kilchoman Distillery; Kirin Holdings Company; Kittling Ridge Distillery: Forty Creek; Knockdhu Distillery: AnCnoc; Knockeen Hills; La Maison du Whisky: Nikka; La Marttiniquaise: Label 5; Lark Distillery; Last Drop Distillers; Leopold Bros; Lotte Chilsung: Scotch Blue; Luxco Spirited Brands: Rebel Yell; Macallan; Macduff International: Grand Macnish, Islay Mist, Lauder's; Mackmyra; McMenamin's Group: Edgefield; Midleton Distillery: Clontarf, Crested Ten,

Dungourney, Green Spot, The Irishman, Jameson, Midleton, Paddy, Powers, Redbreast, Tullamore Dew; Morrison Bowmore Distillers: Auchentoshan, Bowmore, Glen Garioch, McClelland's, Yamazaki; Murree Distillery; The Nant Estate; The New Zealand Malt Whisky Company: Milford; The Nikka Whisky Distilling Co.; Number One Drinks Company: Chichibu, Hanyu, Ichiro's Malt; Old Pulteney Distillery; The Owl Distillery: The Belgian Owl; Pernod Ricard USA: American Spirit, Russell's Reserve, Wild Turkey; Piedmont Distillers: Catdaddy; Preiss Imports; Radico Khaitan: 8PM, Whytehall; Reiner Mösslein: Fränkischer; Reisetbauer; Richard Joynson: Loch Fyne; Rogue Spirits; Rosebank Distillery; Saint James Spirits: Peregrine Rock; Scapa Distillery; Southern Distilleries: MacKenzie, Old Hokonui; Spencerfield Spirits: Pig's Nose; Speyside Distillery; Springbank Distillers: Hazelburn, Longrow, Springbank; St George Spirits; Stock Plzen: Printer's; Stranahan's Colorado Whiskey; Suntory Group; Tasmania Distillery: Sullivan's Cove; Teerenpeli; Templeton Rye; Talisker Distillery; Tobermory Distillery: Ledaig, Tobermory; Tomatin Distillery: The Antiquary, The Talisman, Tomatin; Tomintoul Distillery; Triple Eight Distillery: The Notch; Tullibardine Distillery; Tuthilltown Distillery: Hudson; United Spirits; Us Heit Distillery: Frysk Hynder; Vallei Distillery: Valley; Waldviertler Whiskydestillerie; Wambrechies Distillery; Welsh Whisky Company: Penderyn; Whyte & Mackay: Black Dog, The Claymore, Cluny, The Dalmore, Findlater's, John Barr, Tamnavulin, Whyte & Mackay; William Grant & Sons: Clan MacGregor, Glenfiddich, Grant's, Ladyburn, Monkey Shoulder; Wolfram Ortner: Nock-Land; Yalumba: Smith's; Zuidam Distillery: Millstone; Zürcher Brewery: Single Lakeland

ACKNOWLEDGMENTS

Thameside Media would like to thank the following people and companies for their help and kind permission to photograph at their premises:

Jane Grimley at Aberfeldy Distillery, Ann Miller at Aberlour Distillery, Michael Heads at Ardbeg Distillery, Rob, Robbie, and Brian at Balvenie and Glenfiddich distilleries, Adam Holden at Berry Brothers & Rudd, Dave and Heather at Bowmore Distillery, Mark and Duncan at Bruichladdich Distillery, John MacLellan at Bunnhabhain Distillery, Ewan Mackintosh at Caol Ila Distillery, the staff and owners of The Canny Man's in Edinburgh, Stephanie Macleod at Dewar's, Ian and Claire at Gordon & MacPhail, Cathy and Ruth at Kilchoman Distillery, Ruth and Ian (Pinky) at Lagavulin Distillery, Vicky Stevens, Graham Holyoake, and David McLean at Laphroaig Distillery, Margaret and Morag at Macallan Distillery, staff at The Mash Tun in Aberlour, Philip Shorten at Milroy's of Soho, Graham Logie at Port Ellen Maltings, Gary at Speyside Cooperage, The Whisky Shop Dufftown.

Thameside Media would also like to thank the following individuals for their kind assistance with the project: Sukhinder Singh and staff at The Whisky Exchange, London (www.thewhiskyexchange.com), Marisa Renzullo, Casper Morris, Becky Offringa of The Whisky Couple, Aparna Sharma at DK India office.

And a big thank you to Stuart Bale and Luca Saladini at The Albannach bar in London for guidance with, and mixing of, the cocktails featured on pp112–13.

WRITERS

DAVE BROOM
Dave is editor of *Whisky Magazine Japan*, contributing editor to *Whisky Magazine*, a regular columnist on many periodicals, has written a dozen books, and won three Glenfiddich Awards for his writing. He is a respected taster, and in demand as a teacher and lecturer. For this book, Dave wrote the section on Japanese whisky.

TOM BRUCE-GARDYNE
Tom is an expert on Scotch malt and has written several books on the subject, including *Scotch Whisky* and *The Scotch Whisky Book*. He is a regular contributor to *Whisky Magazine*, *Wine and Spirit*, and the *The Herald*. Tom wrote the entries on Scotland's malt whiskies.

IAN BUXTON
Elected Keeper of the Quaich (1991)—the Scotch Whisky industry's highest accolade—and a Liveryman of the Worshipful Company of Distillers, Ian is a member of *Whisky Magazine's* "World Whiskies Awards" tasting panel and also Director of the World Whiskies Conference. He writes for *Whisky Magazine*, *Scottish Field*, and *The Times* among other titles. He recently edited and contributed to the *Gedenkshrift* for *Michael Jackson Beer Hunter*, *Whisky Chaser* and is currently working on a history of Glenglassaugh Distillery. Ian wrote the entries on Scotland's blended whiskies for this book.

CHARLES MACLEAN
Charlie has been writing about whisky since 1981, and has published 10 books on the subject, including *Scotch Whisky: A Liquid History*, which won the 2005 James Beard Award "Best Book on Wine & Spirits". He was Founding Editor of *Whisky Magazine* and is the presenter of the world's only TV channel dedicated to whisky, www.singlemalt.tv. He is Editor-in-Chief of this book, and also wrote the sections on Canadian, Asian, and Australasian whiskies.

PETER MULRYAN
Peter is the author of four books on spirits: *The Whiskeys of Ireland*, *Poteen—Irish Moonshine*, *Bushmills—400 years* and *Irish Whiskey Guide*. He has contributed to numerous publications, including *Whisky Magazine*, and, as a television producer, specializes in food and drink programmes. Peter wrote the section on Irish whiskey.

HANS OFFRINGA
With his wife, Becky, Hans conducts presentations in Europe and the USA as The Whisky Couple (www.thewhiskycouple.com). He has written and translated more than 15 books on whisky, and contributes to *Whisky Passion*, *Whiskyetc*, *The Malt Advocate*, and various whisky websites. He wrote the section on European whisky in this book.

GAVIN D. SMITH
Gavin is the author of 10 whisky-related books, a contributing editor to www.whisky-pages.com, and was the founding editor of drinks magazine *Fine Expressions*. He is also a regular contributor to *Whisky Magazine* and *The Malt Advocate*, and undertakes speaking engagements and tutored whisky tastings. He wrote the USA chapter in this book.